LYNCHBURG COLLEGE
SYMPOSIUM READINGS

CLASSICAL SELECTIONS ON GREAT ISSUES

SERIES TWO
VOLUME III

MAN AND THE IMAGINATION

Aristotle
Tolstoy
Dante
Milton
Sophocles
Shakespeare
Cervantes
Marlow
Keats
Tennyson
Yeats
Browning
Voltaire

UNIVERSITY
PRESS OF
AMERICA

SERIES TWO
SYMPOSIUM READINGS
Lynchburg College in Virginia

Compiled and Edited by the
following faculty members of Lynchburg College:

Kenneth E. Alrutz, Ph.D., University of Pennsylvania; Assistant
Professor of English

Virginia B. Berger, M.A., Harvard University; Associate Professor
of Music

Anne Marshall Bippus, Ed.D., University of Virginia; Associate
Professor of Education

James L. Campbell, Ph.D., University of Virginia; Associate Professor of English

Robert L. Frey, Ph.D., University of Minnesota; Professor of
History

James A. Huston, Ph.D., New York University; Dean of the College,
Professor of History and International Relations

Shannon McIntyre Jordan, Ph.D., University of Georgia; Instructor
in Philosophy

Jan G. Linn, D.Min., Christian Theological Seminary; Assistant
Professor, College Chaplain

Peggy S. Pittas, M.A., Dalhousie University; Associate Professor
of Psychology

Clifton W. Potter, Jr., Ph.D., University of Virginia; Professor
of History

Julius A. Sigler, Ph.D., University of Virginia; Professor of
Physics

Phillip H. Stump, Ph.D., University of California at Los Angeles;
Assistant Professor of History

Thomas C. Tiller, Ph.D., Florida State University; Dean of Student
Affairs, Professor of Education

Library of Congress Catalog Card Number: 81-43905

INTRODUCTION TO VOLUME III

Man uses his imagination to recreate and interpret the past, to order, enlarge, and attempt to come to terms with his experience in the present, and to project possibilities for the future. While the precise operation of this mental faculty is somewhat mysterious, man's creations provide ample proof of its powers. The use of the imagination is commonly associated with artistic efforts, but man uses his imagination in practically all activities and fields of endeavor.

The readings in this volume - and all the others - are the products of the human imagination. Whether they are the speeches of Athenian and Spartan politicians as recreated by Thycydides, Plato's description of the ideal state, Freud's analyzing personality, or Einstein's explaining how the universe operates, these selections are illustrations of the joy of creativity.

CONTENTS

Aristotle, POETICS   (Trans. by Ingram Bywater)

Leo Tolstoy,   WHAT IS ART?

1. By harmony Aristotle refers to the appropriate
   choice of musical sounds. What does he mean by
   imitation?

2. What is Aristotle's definition of tragedy?

3. Name the six elements which every tragedy must have.
   Which is the most important?

4. Define the following terms: a complete action, an
   action of a certain magnitude, a unified plot, an
   episodic plot, the rule of probability or necessity,
   reversal of fortune, and recognition.

5. What kind of personality in the chief character is
   best suited to tragedy's required change of fortune
   from good to bad?

6. According to Aristotle, what is the most effective
   way of handling fear and pity in a plot?

7. Name the four points needed for a well-drawn character.

8. Distinguish between a tragedy and an epic.

9. Why have countless dramatists since Aristotle found
   this essay useful to them?

10. What qualities do the first and second definitions
    lack which Tolstoy regards as essential? What qual-
    ities do the first and third definitions contain
    which Tolstoy regards as incorrect?

11. In Tolstoy's opinion, why did Plato want certain
    kinds of art banished from the Republic?

12. In Tolstoy's opinion, what is the social value of art?

13. Is Tolstoy's definition of art exact and complete? If so, how? If not, why not?

14. Is it possible to have a single, complete definition of art? If so, give it. If not, state the reason.

Aristotle (384-322 B.C.), whom medieval scholars called "the philosopher", made the classical statement on Greek tragedy in his *Poetics*, a work which has had a profound influence on succeeding generations of poets, dramatists, critics, and philosophers. The word *poetico* has its ultimate derivation from the Greek word *poesis* which means to create or produce.

DE POETICA

(*Poetics*)

1 Our subject being Poetry, I propose to speak not only of the 1447ª
art in general but also of its species and their respective capac-
ities; of the structure of plot required for a good poem; of the number and nature of the constituent parts of a poem; and likewise of 10
any other matters in the same line of inquiry. Let us follow the natural
order and begin with the primary facts.

Epic poetry and Tragedy, as also Comedy, Dithyrambic poetry,
and most flute-playing and lyre-playing, are all, viewed as a whole, 15
modes of imitation. But at the same time they differ from one another in three ways, either by a difference of kind in their means, or
by differences in the objects, or in the manner of their imitations.

I. Just as colour and form are used as means by some, who
(whether by art or constant practice) imitate and portray many
things by their aid, and the voice is used by others; so also in the 20
above-mentioned group of arts, the means with them as a whole are
rhythm, language, and harmony—used, however, either singly or in
certain combinations. A combination of harmony and rhythm alone is
the means in flute-playing and lyre-playing, and any other arts
there may be of the same description, e. g. imitative piping. Rhythm 25
alone, without harmony, is the means in the dancer's imitations;
for even he, by the rhythms of his attitudes, may represent men's
characters, as well as what they do and suffer. There is further an
art which imitates by language alone, without harmony, in prose or
in verse, and if in verse, either in some one or in a plurality of metres. 1447ᵇ
This form of imitation is to this day without a name. We have no
common name for a mime of Sophron or Xenarchus and a Socratic 10
Conversation; and we should still be without one even if the imitation
in the two instances were in trimeters or elegiacs or some other kind
of verse—though it is the way with people to tack on 'poet' to the
name of a metre, and talk of elegiac-poets and epic-poets, thinking
that they call them poets not by reason of the imitative nature of their 15
work, but indiscriminately by reason of the metre they write in. Even
if a theory of medicine or physical philosophy be put forth in a
metrical form, it is usual to describe the writer in this way; Homer

and Empedocles, however, have really nothing in common apart
from their metre; so that, if the one is to be called a poet, the other
20 should be termed a physicist rather than a poet. We should be in the
same position also, if the imitation in these instances were in all the
metres, like the *Centaur* (a rhapsody in a medley of all metres) of
Chaeremon; and Chaeremon one has to recognize as a poet. So much,
then, as to these arts. There are, lastly, certain other arts, which com-
25 bine all the means enumerated, rhythm, melody, and verse, e. g.
Dithyrambic and Nomic poetry, Tragedy and Comedy: with this
difference, however, that the three kinds of means are in some of them
all employed together, and in others brought in separately, one after
the other. These elements of difference in the above arts I term the
means of their imitation.

1448ⁿ 2 II. The objects the imitator represents are actions, with agents
who are necessarily either good men or bad—the diversities of
human character being nearly always derivative from this primary
distinction, since the line between virtue and vice is one dividing the
whole of mankind. It follows, therefore, that the agents represented
must be either above our own level of goodness, or beneath it, or just
such as we are; in the same way as, with the painters, the personages
of Polygnotus are better than we are, those of Pauson worse, and
those of Dionysius just like ourselves. It is clear that each of the
above-mentioned arts will admit of these differences, and that it will
become a separate art by representing objects with this point of
difference. Even in dancing, flute-playing, and lyre-playing such
10 diversities are possible; and they are also possible in the nameless
art that uses language, prose or verse without harmony, as its means;
Homer's personages, for instance, are better than we are; Cleophon's
are on our own level; and those of Hegemon of Thasos, the first
writer of parodies, and Nicochares, the author of the *Diliad*, are be-
15 neath it. The same is true of the Dithyramb and the Nome: the personages may be presented in them with the difference exemplified in
the . . . of . . . and Argas, and in the Cyclopses of Timotheus and
Philoxenus. This difference it is that distinguishes Tragedy and
Comedy also; the one would make its personages worse, and the other
better, than the men of the present day.

3 III. A third difference in these arts is in the manner in which
20 each kind of object is represented. Given both the same means and
the same kind of object for imitation, one may either (1) speak
at one moment in narrative and at another in an assumed character,

as Homer does; or (2) one may remain the same throughout, without any such change; or (3) the imitators may represent the whole story dramatically, as though they were actually doing the things described.

As we said at the beginning, therefore, the differences in the imitation of these arts come under three heads, their means, their objects, and their manner.

So that as an imitator Sophocles will be on one side akin to 25 Homer, both portraying good men; and on another to Aristophanes, since both present their personages as acting and doing. This in fact, according to some, is the reason for plays being termed dramas, because in a play the personages act the story. Hence too both Tragedy and Comedy are claimed by the Dorians as their discover- 30 ies; Comedy by the Megarians—by those in Greece as having arisen when Megara became a democracy, and by the Sicilian Megarians on the ground that the poet Epicharmus was of their country, and a good deal earlier than Chionides and Magnes; even Tragedy also is claimed by certain of the Peloponnesian Dorians. In support of this claim they point to the words 'comedy' and 'drama'. Their word 35 for the outlying hamlets, they say, is *comae,* whereas Athenians call them *demes*—thus assuming that comedians got the name not from their *comoe* or revels, but from their strolling from hamlet to hamlet, lack of appreciation keeping them out of the city. Their word also 1448ᵇ for 'to act', they say, is *dran,* whereas Athenians use *prattein.*

So much, then, as to the number and nature of the points of difference in the imitation of these arts.

4 It is clear that the general origin of poetry was due to two causes, each of them part of human nature. Imitation is natural to man from 5 childhood, one of his advantages over the lower animals being this, that he is the most imitative creature in the world, and learns at first by imitation. And it is also natural for all to delight in works of imitation. The truth of this second point is shown by experience: 10 though the objects themselves may be painful to see, we delight to view the most realistic representations of them in art, the forms for example of the lowest animals and of dead bodies. The explanation is to be found in a further fact: to be learning something is the greatest of pleasures not only to the philosopher but also to the rest of mankind, however small their capacity for it; the reason 15 of the delight in seeing the picture is that one is at the same time learning—gathering the meaning of things, e. g. that the man there is so-and-so; for if one has not seen the thing before, one's pleasure will

not be in the picture as an imitation of it, but will be due to the execu-
20 tion or colouring or some similar cause. Imitation, then, being
natural to us—as also the sense of harmony and rhythm, the metres
being obviously species of rhythms—it was through their original
aptitude, and by a series of improvements for the most part gradual
on their first efforts, that they created poetry out of their improvisations.

Poetry, however, soon broke up into two kinds according to the
25 differences of character in the individual poets; for the graver among
them would represent noble actions, and those of noble personages;
and the meaner sort the actions of the ignoble. The latter class produced invectives at first, just as others did hymns and panegyrics.
We know of no such poem by any of the pre-Homeric poets, though
there were probably many such writers among them; instances, however, may be found from Homer downwards, e. g. his *Margites,* and
30 the similar poems of others. In this poetry of invective its natural
fitness brought an iambic metre into use; hence our present term
'iambic', because it was the metre of their 'iambs' or invectives
against one another. The result was that the old poets became some
of them writers of heroic and others of iambic verse. Homer's position, however, is peculiar: just as he was in the serious style the
35 poet of poets, standing alone not only through the literary excellence,
but also through the dramatic character of his imitations, so too he
was the first to outline for us the general forms of Comedy by producing not a dramatic invective, but a dramatic picture of the Ridiculous; his *Margites* in fact stands in the same relation to our come-
1449ᵃ dies as the *Iliad* and *Odyssey* to our tragedies. As soon, however, as
Tragedy and Comedy appeared in the field, those naturally drawn
to the one line of poetry became writers of comedies instead of iambs,
5 and those naturally drawn to the other, writers of tragedies instead of
epics, because these new modes of art were grander and of more
esteem than the old.

If it be asked whether Tragedy is now all that it need be in its
formative elements, to consider that, and decide it theoretically and
in relation to the theatres, is a matter for another inquiry.
10 It certainly began in improvisations—as did also Comedy; the
one originating with the authors of the Dithyramb, the other with
those of the phallic songs, which still survive as institutions in many
of our cities. And its advance after that was little by little, through
their improving on whatever they had before them at each stage.
It was in fact only after a long series of changes that the movement
15 of Tragedy stopped on its attaining to its natural form. (1) The

6

number of actors was first increased to two by Aeschylus, who cur-
tailed the business of the Chorus, and made the dialogue, or spoken
portion, take the leading part in the play. (2) A third actor and
scenery were due to Sophocles. (3) Tragedy acquired also its magnitude. Discarding short stories and a ludicrous diction, through its ²⁰
passing out of its satyric stage, it assumed, though only at a late
point in its progress, a tone of dignity; and its metre changed then
from trochaic to iambic. The reason for their original use of the
trochaic tetrameter was that their poetry was satyric and more connected with dancing than it now is. As soon, however, as a spoken
part came in, nature herself found the appropriate metre. The iambic,
we know, is the most speakable of metres, as is shown by the fact ²⁵
that we very often fall into it in conversation, whereas we rarely talk
hexameters, and only when we depart from the speaking tone of
voice. (4) Another change was a plurality of episodes or acts. As for
the remaining matters, the superadded embellishments and the account of their introduction, these must be taken as said, as it
would probably be a long piece of work to go through the details.   ³⁰

5 As for Comedy, it is (as has been observed˙) an imitation of
men worse than the average; worse, however, not as regards any and
every sort of fault, but only as regards one particular kind, the
Ridiculous, which is a species of the Ugly. The Ridiculous may be
defined as a mistake or deformity not productive of pain or harm to ³⁵
others; the mask, for instance, that excites laughter, is something
ugly and distorted without causing pain.
   Though the successive changes in Tragedy and their authors are
not unknown, we cannot say the same of Comedy; its early stages
passed unnoticed, because it was not as yet taken up in a serious 1449ᵇ
way. It was only at a late point in its progress that a chorus of
comedians was officially granted by the archon; they used to be mere
volunteers. It had also already certain definite forms at the time when
the record of those termed comic poets begins. Who it was who supplied it with masks, or prologues, or a plurality of actors and the like,
has remained unknown. The invented Fable, or Plot, however, origi- ⁵
nated in Sicily with Epicharmus and Phormis; of Athenian poets
Crates was the first to drop the Comedy of invective and frame
stories of a general and non-personal nature, in other words, Fables
or Plots.
   Epic poetry, then, has been seen to agree with Tragedy to this
extent, that of being an imitation of serious subjects in a grand kind of ¹⁰

7

verse. It differs from it, however, (1) in that it is in one kind of verse
and in narrative form; and (2) in its length—which is due to its
action having no fixed limit of time, whereas Tragedy endeavours
to keep as far as possible within a single circuit of the sun, or something near that. This, I say, is another point of difference between
15 them, though at first the practice in this respect was just the same
in tragedies as in epic poems. They differ also (3) in their constituents, some being common to both and others peculiar to Tragedy—
hence a judge of good and bad in Tragedy is a judge of that in epic
poetry also. All the parts of an epic are included in Tragedy; but
those of Tragedy are not all of them to be found in the Epic.

20 6   Reserving hexameter poetry and Comedy for consideration hereafter, let us proceed now to the discussion of Tragedy; before doing
so, however, we must gather up the definition resulting from what
has been said. A tragedy, then, is the imitation of an action that is
25 serious and also, as having magnitude, complete in itself; in language
with pleasurable accessories, each kind brought in separately in the
parts of the work; in a dramatic, not in a narrative form; with incidents arousing pity and fear, wherewith to accomplish its catharsis of
such emotions. Here by 'language with pleasurable accessories' I
mean that with rhythm and harmony or song superadded; and by
30 'the kinds separately' I mean that some portions are worked out with
verse only, and others in turn with song.
     I. As they act the stories, it follows that in the first place the Spec-
tacle (or stage-appearance of the actors) must be some part of the
whole; and in the second Melody and Diction, these two being the
means of their imitation. Here by 'Diction' I mean merely this,
35 the composition of the verses; and by 'Melody', what is too completely understood to require explanation. But further: the subject
represented also is an action; and the action involves agents, who
must necessarily have their distinctive qualities both of character and
1450ᵃ thought, since it is from these that we ascribe certain qualities to
their actions. There are in the natural order of things, therefore,
two causes, Thought and Character, of their actions, and consequently of their success or failure in their lives. Now the action (that
which was done) is represented in the play by the Fable or Plot. The
Fable, in our present sense of the term, is simply this, the combination of the incidents, or things done in the story; whereas Character
5 is what makes us ascribe certain moral qualities to the agents; and

8

Thought is shown in all they say when proving a particular point or, it may be, enunciating a general truth. There are six parts consequently of every tragedy, as a whole (that is) of such or such quality, viz. a Fable or Plot, Characters, Diction, Thought, Spectacle, and Melody; two of them arising from the means, one from the manner, 10 and three from the objects of the dramatic imitation; and there is nothing else besides these six. Of these, its formative elements, then, not a few of the dramatists have made due use, as every play, one may say, admits of Spectacle, Character, Fable, Diction, Melody, and Thought.

II. The most important of the six is the combination of the 15 incidents of the story. Tragedy is essentially an imitation not of persons but of action and life, of happiness and misery. All human happiness or misery takes the form of action; the end for which we live is a certain kind of activity, not a quality. Character gives us qualities, but it is in our actions—what we do—that we are happy or the reverse. In a play accordingly they do not act in order to portray the 20 Characters; they include the Characters for the sake of the action. So that it is the action in it, i. e. its Fable or Plot, that is the end and purpose of the tragedy; and the end is everywhere the chief thing. Besides this, a tragedy is impossible without action, but there may be one without Character. The tragedies of most of the moderns are 25 characterless—a defect common among poets of all kinds, and with its counterpart in painting in Zeuxis as compared with Polygnotus; for whereas the latter is strong in character, the work of Zeuxis is devoid of it. And again: one may string together a series of characteristic speeches of the utmost finish as regards Diction and Thought, and yet fail to produce the true tragic effect; but one will 30 have much better success with a tragedy which, however inferior in these respects, has a Plot, a combination of incidents, in it. And again: the most powerful elements of attraction in Tragedy, the Peripeties and Discoveries, are parts of the Plot. A further proof is in 35 the fact that beginners succeed earlier with the Diction and Characters than with the construction of a story; and the same may be said of nearly all the early dramatists. We maintain, therefore, that the first essential, the life and soul, so to speak, of Tragedy is the Plot; and that the Characters come second—compare the parallel in paint- 1450ᵇ ing, where the most beautiful colours laid on without order will not give one the same pleasure as a simple black-and-white sketch of a portrait. We maintain that Tragedy is primarily an imitation of action, and that it is mainly for the sake of the action that it imitates the personal agents. Third comes the element of Thought, i. e. the power 5

9

of saying whatever can be said, or what is appropriate to the occasion. This is what, in the speeches in Tragedy, falls under the arts of Politics and Rhetoric; for the older poets make their personages discourse like statesmen, and the modern like rhetoricians. One must not confuse it with Character. Character in a play is that which reveals the moral purpose of the agents, i. e. the sort of thing they seek or avoid, where that is not obvious—hence there is no room for Character in a speech on a purely indifferent subject. Thought, on the
10 other hand, is shown in all they say when proving or disproving some particular point, or enunciating some universal proposition. Fourth among the literary elements is the Diction of the personages, i. e., as before explained, the expression of their thoughts in words, which
15 is practically the same thing with verse as with prose. As for the two remaining parts, the Melody is the greatest of the pleasurable accessories of Tragedy. The Spectacle, though an attraction, is the least artistic of all the parts, and has least to do with the art of poetry. The tragic effect is quite possible without a public performance and actors; and besides, the getting-up of the Spectacle is more a matter
20 for the costumier than the poet.

7   Having thus distinguished the parts, let us now consider the proper construction of the Fable or Plot, as that is at once the first and the most important thing in Tragedy. We have laid it down that a tragedy is an imitation of an action that is complete in itself, as a whole of
25 some magnitude; for a whole may be of no magnitude to speak of. Now a whole is that which has beginning, middle, and end. A beginning is that which is not itself necessarily after anything else, and which has naturally something else after it; an end is that which
30 is naturally after something itself, either as its necessary or usual consequent, and with nothing else after it; and a middle, that which is by nature after one thing and has also another after it. A well-constructed Plot, therefore, cannot either begin or end at any point one likes; beginning and end in it must be of the forms just described. Again: to be beautiful, a living creature, and every whole made up of
35 parts, must not only present a certain order in its arrangement of parts, but also be of a certain definite magnitude. Beauty is a matter of size and order, and therefore impossible either (1) in a very minute creature, since our perception becomes indistinct as it approaches instantaneity; or (2) in a creature of vast size—one, say, 1.000 miles long—as in that case, instead of the object being seen
1451 all at once, the unity and wholeness of it is lost to the beholder.

10

Just in the same way, then, as a beautiful whole made up of parts, or a beautiful living creature, must be of some size, but a size to be taken in by the eye, so a story or Plot must be of some length, but of a ⁵ length to be taken in by the memory. As for the limit of its length, so far as that is relative to public performances and spectators, it does not fall within the theory of poetry. If they had to perform a hundred tragedies, they would be timed by water-clocks, as they are said to have been at one period. The limit, however, set by the actual nature of the thing is this: the longer the story, consistently 10 with its being comprehensible as a whole, the finer it is by reason of its magnitude. As a rough general formula, 'a length which allows of the hero passing by a series of probable or necessary stages from misfortune to happiness, or from happiness to misfortune', may suffice as a limit for the magnitude of the story.   15

8   The Unity of a Plot does not consist, as some suppose, in its having one man as its subject. An infinity of things befall that one man, some of which it is impossible to reduce to unity; and in like manner there are many actions of one man which cannot be made to form one action. One sees, therefore, the mistake of all the poets who have 20 written a *Heracleid*, a *Theseid*, or similar poems; they suppose that, because Heracles was one man, the story also of Heracles must be one story. Homer, however, evidently understood this point quite well, whether by art or instinct, just in the same way as he excels the rest in every other respect. In writing an *Odyssey*, he did not make the poem cover all that ever befell his hero—it befell him, for instance, 25 to get wounded on Parnassus and also to feign madness at the time of the call to arms, but the two incidents had no necessary or probable connexion with one another—instead of doing that, he took as the subject of the *Odyssey*, as also of the *Iliad*, an action with a Unity of the kind we are describing. The truth is that, just as in the other 30 imitative arts one imitation is always of one thing, so in poetry the story, as an imitation of action, must represent one action, a complete whole, with its several incidents so closely connected that the transposal or withdrawal of any one of them will disjoin and dislocate the whole. For that which makes no perceptible difference by its presence or absence is no real part of the whole.   35

9   From what we have said it will be seen that the poet's function is to describe, not the thing that has happened, but a kind of thing that might happen. i. e. what is possible as being probable or necessary. The distinction between historian and poet is not in the one 1451

11

writing prose and the other verse—you might put the work of
Herodotus into verse, and it would still be a species of history; it
consists really in this, that the one describes the thing that has been,
5 and the other a kind of thing that might be. Hence poetry is something more philosophic and of graver import than history, since its
statements are of the nature rather of universals, whereas those of
history are singulars. By a universal statement I mean one as to
what such or such a kind of man will probably or necessarily say or
do—which is the aim of poetry, though it affixes proper names to the
10 characters; by a singular statement, one as to what, say, Alcibiades
did or had done to him. In Comedy this has become clear by this
time; it is only when their plot is already made up of probable incidents that they give it a basis of proper names, choosing for the purpose any names that may occur to them, instead of writing like the old
15 iambic poets about particular persons. In Tragedy, however, they still
adhere to the historic names; and for this reason: what convinces is
the possible; now whereas we are not yet sure as to the possibility
of that which has not happened, that which has happened is manifestly possible, else it would not have come to pass. Nevertheless even
in Tragedy there are some plays with but one or two known names in
20 them, the rest being inventions; and there are some without a single
known name, e. g. Agathon's *Antheus*, in which both incidents and
names are of the poet's invention; and it is no less delightful on that
account. So that one must not aim at a rigid adherence to the tradi-
25 tional stories on which tragedies are based. It would be absurd, in
fact, to do so, as even the known stories are only known to a few,
though they are a delight none the less to all.

It is evident from the above that the poet must be more the poet of
his stories or Plots than of his verses, inasmuch as he is a poet by
virtue of the imitative element in his work, and it is actions that he
imitates. And if he should come to take a subject from actual history,
30 he is none the less a poet for that; since some historic occurrences
may very well be in the probable and possible order of things; and it
is in that aspect of them that he is their poet.

Of simple Plots and actions the episodic are the worst. I call a Plot
episodic when there is neither probability nor necessity in the
35 sequence of its episodes. Actions of this sort bad poets construct
through their own fault, and good ones on account of the players.
His work being for public performance, a good poet often stretches
out a Plot beyond its capabilities, and is thus obliged to twist the
sequence of incident.

1452ᵃ Tragedy, however, is an imitation not only of a complete action,

but also of incidents arousing pity and fear. Such incidents have the
very greatest effect on the mind when they occur unexpectedly and
at the same time in consequence of one another; there is more of
the marvellous in them then than if they happened of themselves or 5
by mere chance. Even matters of chance seem most marvellous if
there is an appearance of design as it were in them; as for instance
the statue of Mitys at Argos killed the author of Mitys' death by
falling down on him when a looker-on at a public spectacle; for incidents like that we think to be not without a meaning. A Plot, there- 1c
fore, of this sort is necessarily finer than others.

10   Plots are either simple or complex, since the actions they represent are naturally of this twofold description. The action, proceeding
in the way defined, as one continuous whole, I call simple, when the 15
change in the hero's fortunes takes place without Peripety or Discovery; and complex, when it involves one or the other, or both. These
should each of them arise out of the structure of the Plot itself, so as
to be the consequence, necessary or probable, of the antecedents.
There is a great difference between a thing happening *propter hoc* and 20
post hoc.

11   A Peripety is the change of the kind described from one state
of things within the play to its opposite, and that too in the way we
are saying, in the probable or necessary sequence of events; as it is
for instance in *Oedipus*: here the opposite state of things is produced 25
by the Messenger, who, coming to gladden Oedipus and to remove his
fears as to his mother, reveals the secret of his birth. And in
Lynceus: just as he is being led off for execution, with Danaus at
his side to put him to death, the incidents preceding this bring it about
that he is saved and Danaus put to death. A Discovery is, as the 30
very word implies, a change from ignorance to knowledge, and thus to
either love or hate, in the personages marked for good or evil fortune.
The finest form of Discovery is one attended by Peripeties, like that
which goes with the Discovery in *Oedipus*. There are no doubt other
forms of it; what we have said may happen in a way in reference to
inanimate things, even things of a very casual kind; and it is also pos- 35
sible to discover whether some one has done or not done something.
But the form most directly connected with the Plot and the action of
the piece is the first-mentioned. This, with a Peripety, will arouse 1452ᵇ
either pity or fear—actions of that nature being what Tragedy is as-

sumed to represent; and it will also serve to bring about the happy or
unhappy ending. The Discovery, then, being of persons, it may be that
of one party only to the other, the latter being already known; or
5 both the parties may have to discover themselves. Iphigenia, for
instance, was discovered to Orestes by sending the letter; and another Discovery was required to reveal him to Iphigenia.

Two parts of the Plot, then, Peripety and Discovery, are on mat-
10 ters of this sort. A third part is Suffering; which we may define as an
action of a destructive or painful nature, such as murders on the stage,
tortures, woundings, and the like. The other two have been already
explained.

12 The parts of Tragedy to be treated as formative elements in the
15 whole were mentioned in a previous Chapter. From the point of view,
however, of its quantity, i.e. the separate sections into which it is
divided, a tragedy has the following parts: Prologue, Episode,
Exode, and a choral portion, distinguished into Parode and Stasimon;
these two are common to all tragedies, whereas songs from the stage
20 and *Commoe* are only found in some. The Prologue is all that precedes
the Parode of the chorus; an Episode all that comes in between two
whole choral songs; the Exode all that follows after the last choral
song. In the choral portion the Parode is the whole first statement of
the chorus; a Stasimon, a song of the chorus without anapaests or
trochees; a *Commos*, a lamentation sung by chorus and actor in con-
25 cert. The parts of Tragedy to be used as formative elements in the
whole we have already mentioned; the above are its parts from the
point of view of its quantity, or the separate sections into which
it is divided.

13 The next points after what we have said above will be these:
(1) What is the poet to aim at, and what is he to avoid, in constructing his Plots? and (2) What are the conditions on which the
tragic effect depends?
30 We assume that, for the finest form of Tragedy, the Plot must
be not simple but complex; and further, that it must imitate actions
arousing fear and pity, since that is the distinctive function of this
kind of imitation. It follows, therefore, that there are three forms of
Plot to be avoided. (1) A good man must not be seen passing from
happiness to misery, or (2) a bad man from misery to happiness.
35 The first situation is not fear-inspiring or piteous, but simply odious
to us. The second is the most untragic that can be; it has no one of the

14

requisites of Tragedy; it does not appeal either to the human feeling in us, or to our pity, or to our fears. Nor, on the other hand, should 1453ᵃ (3) an extremely bad man be seen falling from happiness into misery. Such a story may arouse the human feeling in us, but it will not move us to either pity or fear; pity is occasioned by undeserved ⁵ misfortune, and fear by that of one like ourselves; so that there will be nothing either piteous or fear-inspiring in the situation. There remains, then, the intermediate kind of personage, a man not pre-eminently virtuous and just, whose misfortune, however, is brought upon him not by vice and depravity but by some error of judgement, of the number of those in the enjoyment of great reputation and pros- 10 perity; e. g. Oedipus, Thyestes, and the men of note of similar families. The perfect Plot, accordingly, must have a single, and not (as some tell us) a double issue; the change in the hero's fortunes must be not from misery to happiness, but on the contrary from happiness to misery; and the cause of it must lie not in any depravity, but in some 15 great error on his part; the man himself being either such as we have described, or better, not worse, than that. Fact also confirms our theory. Though the poets began by accepting any tragic story that came to hand, in these days the finest tragedies are always on the story of some few houses, on that of Alcmeon, Oedipus, Orestes, 20 Meleager, Thyestes, Telephus, or any others that may have been in-volved, as either agents or sufferers, in some deed of horror. The theoretically best tragedy, then, has a Plot of this description. The critics, therefore, are wrong who blame Euripides for taking this line in his tragedies, and giving many of them an unhappy ending. It is, 25 as we have said, the right line to take. The best proof is this: on the stage, and in the public performances, such plays, properly worked out, are seen to be the most truly tragic; and Euripides, even if his execution be faulty in every other point, is seen to be nevertheless the most tragic certainly of the dramatists. After this comes the construc- 30 tion of Plot which some rank first, one with a double story (like the *Odyssey*) and an opposite issue for the good and the bad per-sonages. It is ranked as first only through the weakness of the audi-ences; the poets merely follow their public, writing as its wishes 35 dictate. But the pleasure here is not that of Tragedy. It belongs rather to Comedy, where the bitterest enemies in the piece (e. g. Orestes and Aegisthus) walk off good friends at the end, with no slaying of any one by any one.

14 The tragic fear and pity may be aroused by the Spectacle; but 1453ᵇ they may also be aroused by the very structure and incidents of the

play—which is the better way and shows the better poet. The Plot in fact should be so framed that, even without seeing the things take place, he who simply hears the account of them shall be filled with horror and pity at the incidents; which is just the effect that the mere recital of the story in *Oedipus* would have on one. To produce this same effect by means of the Spectacle is less artistic, and requires extraneous aid. Those, however, who make use of the Spectacle to put before us that which is merely monstrous and not productive of fear, are wholly out of touch with Tragedy; not every kind of pleasure should be required of a tragedy, but only its own proper pleasure.

The tragic pleasure is that of pity and fear, and the poet has to produce it by a work of imitation; it is clear, therefore, that the causes should be included in the incidents of his story. Let us see, then, what kinds of incident strike one as horrible, or rather as piteous. In a deed of this description the parties must necessarily be either friends, or enemies, or indifferent to one another. Now when enemy does it on enemy, there is nothing to move us to pity either in his doing or in his meditating the deed, except so far as the actual pain of the sufferer is concerned; and the same is true when the parties are indifferent to one another. Whenever the tragic deed, however, is done within the family—when murder or the like is done or meditated by brother on brother, by son on father, by mother on son, or son on mother—these are the situations the poet should seek after. The traditional stories, accordingly, must be kept as they are, e.g. the murder of Clytaemnestra by Orestes and of Eriphyle by Alcmeon. At the same time even with these there is something left to the poet himself; it is for him to devise the right way of treating them. Let us explain more clearly what we mean by 'the right way'. The deed of horror may be done by the doer knowingly and consciously, as in the old poets, and in Medea's murder of her children in Euripides. Or he may do it, but in ignorance of his relationship, and discover that afterwards, as does the Oedipus in Sophocles. Here the deed is outside the play; but it may be within it, like the act of the Alcmeon in Astydamas, or that of the Telegonus in *Ulysses Wounded*. A third possibility is for one meditating some deadly injury to another, in ignorance of his relationship, to make the discovery in time to draw back. These exhaust the possibilities, since the deed must necessarily be either done or not done, and either knowingly or unknowingly.

The worst situation is when the personage is with full knowledge on the point of doing the deed, and leaves it undone. It is odious and also (through the absence of suffering) untragic; hence it is that no one is made to act thus except in some few instances, e. g. Haemon 1454ᵃ and Creon in *Antigone*. Next after this comes the actual perpetration of the deed meditated. A better situation than that, however, is for the deed to be done in ignorance, and the relationship discovered afterwards, since there is nothing odious in it, and the Discovery will serve to astound us. But the best of all is the last; what 5 we have in *Cresphontes,* for example, where Merope, on the point of slaying her son, recognizes him in time; in *Iphigenia*, where sister and brother are in a like position; and in *Helle,* where the son recognizes his mother, when on the point of giving her up to her enemy.

This will explain why our tragedies are restricted (as we said just now) to such a small number of families. It was accident rather than 10 art that led the poets in quest of subjects to embody this kind of incident in their Plots. They are still obliged, accordingly, to have recourse to the families in which such horrors have occurred.

On the construction of the Plot, and the kind of Plot required for Tragedy, enough has now been said. 15

15 In the Characters there are four points to aim at. First and foremost, that they shall be good. There will be an element of character in the play, if (as has been observed) what a personage says or does reveals a certain moral purpose; and a good element of character, if the purpose so revealed is good. Such goodness is possible in every type of personage, even in a woman or a slave, though the one is 20 perhaps an inferior, and the other a wholly worthless being. The second point is to make them appropriate. The Character before us may be, say, manly; but it is not appropriate in a female Character to be manly, or clever. The third is to make them like the reality, which is not the same as their being good and appropriate, in our sense of 25 the term. The fourth is to make them consistent and the same throughout; even if inconsistency be part of the man before one for imitation as presenting that form of character, he should still be consistently inconsistent. We have an instance of baseness of character, not required for the story, in the Menelaus in *Orestes*; of the incongruous and unbefitting in the lamentation of Ulysses in *Scylla,* 30 and in the (clever) speech of Melanippe; and of inconsistency in *Iphigenia at Aulis,* where Iphigenia the suppliant is utterly unlike the later Iphigenia. The right thing, however, is in the Characters

17

just as in the incidents of the play to endeavour always after the
35 necessary or the probable; so that whenever such-and-such a personage says or does such-and-such a thing, it shall be the necessary
or probable outcome of his character; and whenever this incident follows on that, it shall be either the necessary or the probable consequence of it. From this one sees (to digress for a moment) that the
1454ᵇ Dénouement also should arise out of the plot itself, and not depend
on a stage-artifice, as in *Medea,* or in the story of the (arrested)
departure of the Greeks in the *Iliad.* The artifice must be reserved
for matters outside the play—for past events beyond human knowl-
5 edge, or events yet to come, which require to be foretold or announced; since it is the privilege of the Gods to know everything.
There should be nothing improbable among the actual incidents. If
it be unavoidable, however, it should be outside the tragedy, like the
improbability in the *Oedipus* of Sophocles. But to return to the Characters. As Tragedy is an imitation of personages better than the
ordinary man, we in our way should follow the example of good
10 portrait-painters, who reproduce the distinctive features of a man,
and at the same time, without losing the likeness, make him hand-
somer than he is. The poet in like manner, in portraying men quick or
slow to anger, or with similar infirmities of character, must know
how to represent them as such, and at the same time as good men,
as Agathon and Homer have represented Achilles.
15 All these rules one must keep in mind throughout, and, further,
those also for such points of stage-effect as directly depend on the art
of the poet, since in these too one may often make mistakes. Enough,
however, has been said on the subject in one of our published writ-
ings.

16 Discovery in general has been explained already. As for the
20 species of Discovery, the first to be noted is (1) the least artistic form
of it, of which the poets make most use through mere lack of invention. Discovery by signs or marks. Of these signs some are congenital,
like the 'lance-head which the Earth-born have on them', or 'stars',
such as Carcinus brings in his *Thyestes*; others acquired after birth—
these latter being either marks on the body, e. g. scars, or external
tokens, like necklaces, or (to take another sort of instance) the ark
25 in the Discovery in *Tyro.* Even these, however, admit of two uses,
a better and a worse; the scar of Ulysses is an instance; the Discovery of him through it is made in one way by the nurse and in

another by the swineherds. A Discovery using signs as a means of assurance is less artistic, as indeed are all such as imply reflection: whereas one bringing them in all of a sudden, as in the *Bath-story,* ³⁰ is of a better order. Next after these are (2) Discoveries made directly by the poet; which are inartistic for that very reason; e. g. Orestes' Discovery of himself in *Iphigenia*: whereas his sister reveals who she is by the letter, Orestes is made to say himself what the poet rather ³⁵ than the story demands. This, therefore, is not far removed from the first-mentioned fault, since he might have presented certain tokens as well. Another instance is the 'shuttle's voice' in the *Tereus* of Sophocles. (3) A third species is Discovery through memory, from a man's consciousness being awakened by something seen. Thus 14⁵⁵ in *The Cyprioe* of Dicaeogenes, the sight of the picture makes the man burst into tears; and in the *Tale of Alcinous,* hearing the harper Ulysses is reminded of the past and weeps; the Discovery of them being the result. (4) A fourth kind is Discovery through reasoning; e. g. in *The Choephoroe*; 'One like me is here; there is no one ⁵ like me but Orestes; he, therefore, must be here.' Or that which Polyidus the Sophist suggested for *Iphigenia*; since it was natural for Orestes to reflect: 'My sister was sacrificed, and I am to be sacrificed like her.' Or that in the *Tydeus* of Theodectes: 'I came to find a son, and am to die myself.' Or that in *The Phinidae*: ³¹ on seeing ¹⁰ the place the women inferred their fate, that they were to die there, since they had also been exposed there. (5) There is, too, a composite Discovery arising from bad reasoning on the side of the other party. An instance of it is in *Ulysses the False Messenger*: he said he should know the bow—which he had not seen; but to suppose from ¹⁵ that that he would know it again (as though he had once seen it) was bad reasoning. (6) The best of all Discoveries, however, is that arising from the incidents themselves, when the great surprise comes about through a probable incident, like that in the *Oedipus* of Sophocles; and also in *Iphigenia*:³² for it was not improbable that she should wish to have a letter taken home. These last are the only Discoveries independent of the artifice of signs and necklaces. Next ²⁰ after them come Discoveries through reasoning.

17 At the time when he is constructing his Plots, and engaged on the Diction in which they are worked out, the poet should remember (1) to put the actual scenes as far as possible before his eyes. In this

²⁵ way, seeing everything with the vividness of an eye-witness as it were, he will devise what is appropriate, and be least likely to overlook incongruities. This is shown by what was censured in Carcinus, the return of Amphiaraus from the sanctuary; it would have passed unnoticed, if it had not been actually seen by the audience; but on the stage his play failed, the incongruity of the incident offending the spectators.

(2) As far as may be, too, the poet should even act his story with ³⁰ the very gestures of his personages. Given the same natural qualifications, he who feels the emotions to be described will be the most convincing; distress and anger, for instance, are portrayed most truthfully by one who is feeling them at the moment. Hence it is that poetry demands a man with a special gift for it, or else one with a touch of madness in him; the former can easily assume the required mood, and the latter may be actually beside himself with emotion.

(3) His story, again, whether already made or of his own making, ^{1455b} he should first simplify and reduce to a universal form, before proceeding to lengthen it out by the insertion of episodes. The following will show how the universal element in *Iphigenia*, for instance, may be viewed: A certain maiden having been offered in sacrifice, and spirited away from her sacrificers into another land, where the cus- ⁵ tom was to sacrifice all strangers to the Goddess, she was made there the priestess of this rite. Long after that the brother of the priestess happened to come; the fact, however, of the oracle having for a certain reason bidden him go thither, and his object in going, are outside the Plot of the play. On his coming he was arrested, and about to be sacrificed, when he revealed who he was—either as ¹⁰ Euripides puts it, or (as suggested by Polyidus) by the not improbable exclamation, 'So I too am doomed to be sacrificed, as my sister was'; and the disclosure led to his salvation. This done, the next thing, after the proper names have been fixed as a basis for the story, is to work in episodes or accessory incidents. One must mind, however, that the episodes are appropriate, like the fit of madness in ¹⁵ Orestes, which led to his arrest, and the purifying, which brought about his salvation. In plays, then, the episodes are short; in epic poetry they serve to lengthen out the poem. The argument of the *Odyssey* is not a long one. A certain man has been abroad many years; Poseidon is ever on the watch for him, and he is all alone. Matters at ²⁰ home too have come to this, that his substance is being wasted and his son's death plotted by suitors to his wife. Then he arrives there himself after his grievous sufferings; reveals himself, and falls on his enemies; and the end is his salvation and their death. This being

all that is proper to the *Odyssey*, everything else in it is episode.

18 (4) There is a further point to be borne in mind. Every tragedy is in part Complication and in part Dénouement; the incidents before the opening scene, and often certain also of those within the play, forming the Complication; and the rest the Dénouement. By 25 Complication I mean all from the beginning of the story to the point just before the change in the hero's fortunes; by Dénouement, all from the beginning of the change to the end. In the *Lynceus* of Theodectes, for instance, the Complication includes, together with the 30 presupposed incidents, the seizure of the child and that in turn of the parents; and the Dénouement all from the indictment for the 1456ᵃ7 murder to the end. Now it is right, when one speaks of a tragedy as the same or not the same as another, to do so on the ground before all else of their Plot, i. e. as having the same or not the same Complication and Dénouement. Yet there are many dramatists who, after a good Complication, fail in the Dénouement. But it is necessary for both points of construction to be always duly mastered. (5) There are four 1455ᵇ32 distinct species of Tragedy—that being the number of the constituents also that have been mentioned: first, the complex Tragedy, which is all Peripety and Discovery; second, the Tragedy of suffering, e. g. the *Ajaxes* and *Ixions*; third, the Tragedy of character, e. g. 1456ᵃ *The Phthiotides* and *Peleus*. The fourth constituent is that of 'Spectacle', exemplified in *The Phorcides,* in *Prometheus,* and in all plays with the scene laid in the nether world. The poet's aim, then, should be to combine every element of interest, if possible, or else the more important and the major part of them. This is now especially necessary owing to the unfair criticism to which the poet is subjected in these days. Just because there have been poets before 5 him strong in the several species of tragedy, the critics now expect the one man to surpass that which was the strong point of each one of his predecessors. (6) One should also remember what has been said more 10 than once, and not write a tragedy on an epic body of incident (i. e. one with a plurality of stories in it), by attempting to dramatize, for instance, the entire story of the *Iliad*. In the epic owing to its scale every part is treated at proper length; with a drama, however, on the same story the result is very disappointing. This is shown by the fact 15 that all who have dramatized the fall of Ilium in its entirety, and

21

not part by part, like Euripides, of the whole of the Niobe story, instead of a portion, like Aeschylus, either fail utterly or have but ill success on the stage; for that and that alone was enough to ruin even a play by Agathon. Yet in their Peripeties, as also in their simple
20 plots, the poets I mean show wonderful skill in aiming at the kind of effect they desire—a tragic situation that arouses the human feeling in one, like the clever villain (e. g. Sisyphus) deceived, or the brave wrongdoer worsted. This is probable, however, only in Agathon's sense, when he speaks of the probability of even improbabilities com-
25 ing to pass. (7) The Chorus too should be regarded as one of the actors; it should be an integral part of the whole, and take a share in the action—that which it has in Sophocles, rather than in Euripides. With the later poets, however, the songs in a play of theirs have no more to do with the Plot of that than of any other tragedy. Hence it is that they are now singing intercalary pieces, a practice first intro-
30 duced by Agathon. And yet what real difference is there between singing such intercalary pieces, and attempting to fit in a speech, or even a whole act, from one play into another?

19 The Plot and Characters having been discussed, it remains to consider the Diction and Thought. As for the Thought, we may
35 assume what is said of it in our Art of Rhetoric, as it belongs more properly to that department of inquiry. The Thought of the person- ages is shown in everything to be effected by their language—in every effort to prove or disprove, to arouse emotion (pity, fear, anger, and
1456ᵇ the like), or to maximize or minimize things. It is clear, also, that their mental procedure must be on the same lines in their actions likewise, whenever they wish them to arouse pity or horror, or to
5 have a look of importance or probability. The only difference is that with the act the impression has to be made without explanation; whereas with the spoken word it has to be produced by the speaker, and result from his language. What, indeed, would be the good of the speaker, if things appeared in the required light even apart from any- thing he says?

As regards the Diction, one subject for inquiry under this head is the turns given to the language when spoken; e. g. the difference
1C between command and prayer, simple statement and threat, ques- tion and answer, and so forth. The theory of such matters, however, belongs to Elocution and the professors of that art. Whether the poet knows these things or not, his art as a poet is never seriously criti-
15 cized on that account. What fault can one see in Homer's 'Sing of the

22

wrath, Goddess'?—which Protagoras has criticizea as being a command where a prayer was meant, since to bid one do or not do,
he tells us, is a command. Let us pass over this, then, as appertaining
to another art, and not to that of poetry.

20 The Diction viewed as a whole is made up of the following parts: 20
the Letter (or ultimate element), the Syllable, the Conjunction, the
Article, the Noun, the Verb, the Case, and the Speech. (1) The Letter is an indivisible sound of a particular kind, one that may become
a factor in an intelligible sound. Indivisible sounds are uttered by the
brutes also, but no one of these is a Letter in our sense of the term.
These elementary sounds are either vowels, semi-vowels, or mutes. A 25
vowel is a Letter having an audible sound without the addition of
another Letter. A semi-vowel, one having an audible sound by the
addition of another Letter; e. g. S and R. A mute, one having no
sound at all by itself, but becoming audible by an addition, that of one
of the Letters which have a sound of some sort of their own; e.g. 30
G and D. The Letters differ in various ways: as produced by different
conformations or in different regions of the mouth; as aspirated,
not aspirated, or sometimes one and sometimes the other; as long,
short, or of variable quantity; and further as having an acute, grave,
or intermediate accent. The details of these matters we must leave
to the metricians. (2) A Syllable is a non-significant composite sound, 35
made up of a mute and a Letter having a sound (a vowel or semi-
vowel); for GR, without an A, is just as much a Syllable as GRA.
with an A. The various forms of the Syllable also belong to the
theory of metre. (3) A Conjunction is (a) a non-significant sound
which, when one significant sound is formable out of several, neither 1457ᵃ
hinders nor aids the union, and which, if the Speech thus formed
stands by itself (apart from other Speeches), must not be inserted
at the beginning of it; e. g. μέν, δή, τοι, δέ. Or (b) a non-significant
sound capable of combining two or more significant sounds into one; 5
e. g. ἀμφί, περί, &c. (4) An Article is a non-significant sound
marking the beginning, end, or dividing-point of a Speech, its natural
place being either at the extremities or in the middle. (5) A Noun 10
or name is a composite significant sound not involving the idea of
time, with parts which have no significance by themselves in it. It is
to be remembered that in a compound we do not think of the parts
as having a significance also by themselves: in the name 'Theodorus',
for instance, the δῶρον means nothing to us. (6) A Verb is a
composite significant sound involving the idea of time, with parts
which (just as in the Noun) have no significance by themselves in it. 15

Already famous for his novels, plays, short stories, and essays, Leo Tolstoy (1828-1910) published
What is Art? in 1896 in an edition which he found ac-
ceptable. This work, from which the following excerpt
is taken, had been previously censored by the Russian
government which changed its meaning and emphasis. Tolstoy's concern with the importance of communication in
What is Art? arose from his strong desire that literature should promote the growth of Christian brotherhood.

CHAPTER FIVE

WHAT is art—if we put aside the conception of beauty, which confuses the whole matter? The latest and most comprehensible definitions of art, apart from the conception of beauty, are the following: (1) Art is an activity arising even in the animal kingdom, *a*, springing from sexual desire and the propensity to play (Schiller, Darwin, Spencer), and *b*, accompanied by a pleasurable excitement of the nervous system (Grant Allen). This is the physiological-evolutionary definition. (2) Art is the external manifestation by means of lines, colors, movements, sounds, or words, of emotions felt by man (Véron). This is the experimental definition. According to the very latest definition, (3) Art is "the production of some permanent object or passing action, which is fitted, not only to supply an active enjoyment to the producer, but to convey a pleasurable impression to a number of spectators or listeners, quite apart from any personal advantage to be derived from it" (Sully).

Notwithstanding the superiority of these definitions to the metaphysical definitions which depended on the conception of beauty, they are yet far from exact. The first, the physiological-evolutionary definition (1*a*), is inexact because, instead of speaking about the artistic activity itself, which is the real matter in hand, it treats of the derivation of art. The modification of it (1*b*), based on the physiological effects on the human organism, is inexact because within the limits of such definition many other human activities can be included, as has occurred in the neo-aesthetic theories, which reckon as art the preparation of handsome clothes, pleasant scents, and even victuals.

The experimental definition (2), which makes art consist in the expression of emotions, is inexact because a man may express his emotions by means of lines, colors, sounds, or words, and yet may not act on others by such expression, and then the manifestation of his emotions is not art.

The third definition (that of Sully) is inexact because in the production of objects or actions affording pleasure to the producer and a pleasant emotion to the spectators or hearers, apart from personal advantage, may be included the showing of conjuring tricks or gymnastic exercises and other activities which are not art. And further, many things, the production of which does not afford pleasure to the producer and the sensation received from which is unpleasant, such as gloomy, heartrending scenes in a poetic description or a play, may nevertheless be undoubted works of art.

The inaccuracy of all these definitions arises from the fact that in them all (as also in the metaphysical definitions) the object considered is the pleasure art may give, and not the purpose it may serve in the life of man and of humanity.

In order correctly to define art, it is necessary, first of all, to cease to consider it as a means to pleasure and to consider it as one of the conditions of human life. Viewing it in this way we cannot fail to observe that art is one of the means of intercourse between man and man.

Every work of art causes the receiver to enter into a certain kind of relationship both with him who produced, or is producing, the art, and with all those who, simultaneously, previously, or subsequently, receive the same artistic impression.

Speech, transmitting the thoughts and experiences of men, serves as a means of union among them, and art acts in a similar manner. The peculiarity of this latter means of intercourse, distinguishing it from intercourse by means of words, consists in this, that whereas by words a man transmits his thoughts to another, by means of art he transmits his feelings.

The activity of art is based on the fact that a man, receiving through his sense of hearing or sight another man's expression of feeling, is capable of experiencing the emotion which moved the man who expressed it. To take the simplest example: one man laughs, and another who hears becomes merry; or a man weeps, and another who hears feels sorrow. A man is excited or irritated, and another man seeing him comes to a similar state of mind. By his movements or by the sounds of his voice, a man expresses courage and determination or sadness and calmness, and this state of mind passes on to others. A man suffers, expressing his sufferings by groans and spasms, and this suffering transmits itself to other people; a man expresses his feeling of admiration, devotion, fear, respect, or love to certain objects, persons, or phenomena, and others are infected by the same feelings of admiration, devotion, fear, respect, or love to the same objects, persons, and phenomena.

And it is upon this capacity of man to receive another man's expression of feeling and experience those feelings himself, that the activity of art is based.

If a man infects another or others directly, immediately, by his appearance or by the sounds he gives vent to at the very time he experiences the feeling; if he causes another man to yawn when he himself cannot help yawning, or to laugh or cry when he himself is obliged to laugh or cry, or to suffer when he himself is suffering—that does not amount to art.

Art begins when one person, with the object of joining another or others to himself in one and the same feeling, expresses that feeling by certain external indications. To take the simplest example: a boy, having experienced, let us say, fear on encountering a wolf, relates that encounter; and, in order to evoke in others the feeling he has experienced, describes himself, his condition before the encounter, the surroundings, the wood, his own lightheartedness, and then the wolf's appearance, its movements, the distance between himself and the wolf, etc. All this, if only the boy, when telling the story, again experiences the feelings he had lived through and infects the hearers and compels them to feel what the narrator had experienced, is art. If even the boy had not seen a wolf but had frequently been afraid of one, and if, wishing to evoke in others the fear he had felt, he invented an encounter with a wolf and recounted it so as to make his hearers share the feelings he experienced when he feared the wolf, that also would be art. And just in the same way it is art if a man, having experienced either the fear of suffering or the attraction of enjoyment (whether in reality or in imagination), expresses these feelings on canvas or in marble so that others are infected by them. And it is also art if a man feels or imagines to himself feelings of delight, gladness, sorrow, despair, courage, or despondency and the transition from one to another of these feelings, and expresses these feelings by sounds so that the hearers are infected by them and experience them as they were experienced by the composer.

The feelings with which the artist infects others may be most various—very strong or very weak, very important or very insignificant, very bad or very good: feelings of love for one's own country, self-devotion and submission to fate or to God expressed in a drama, raptures of lovers described in a novel, feelings of voluptuousness expressed in a picture, courage expressed in a triumphal march, merriment evoked by a dance, humor evoked by a funny story, the feeling of quietness transmitted by an evening landscape or by a lullably, or the feeling of admiration evoked by a beautiful arabesque—it is all art.

If only the spectators or auditors are infected by the feelings which the author has felt, it is art.

To evoke in oneself a feeling one has once experienced, and having evoked it in oneself, then, by means of movements, lines, colors, sounds, or forms expressed in words, so to transmit that feeling that others may experience the same feeling— this is the activity of art.

Art is a human activity consisting in this, that one man consciously, by means of certain external signs, hands on to others feelings he has lived through, and that other people are infected by these feelings and also experience them.

Art is not, as the metaphysicians say, the manifestation of some mysterious Idea of beauty or God; it is not, as the aesthetical physiologists say, a game in which man lets off his excess of stored-up energy; it is not the expression of man's emotions by external signs; it is not the production of pleasing objects; and, above all, it is not pleasure; but it is a means of union among men, joining them together in the

WHAT IS ART?

same feelings, and indispensable for the life and progress toward well-being of individuals and of humanity.

As, thanks to man's capacity to express thoughts by words, every man may know all that has been done for him in the realms of thought by all humanity before his day, and can in the present, thanks to this capacity to understand the thoughts of others, become a sharer in their activity and can himself hand on to his contemporaries and descendants the thoughts he has assimilated from others, as well as those which have arisen within himself; so, thanks to man's capacity to be infected with the feelings of others by means of art, all that is being lived through by his contemporaries is accessible to him, as well as the feelings experienced by men thousands of years ago, and he has also the possibility of transmitting his own feelings to others.

If people lacked this capacity to receive the thoughts conceived by the men who preceded them and to pass on to others their own thoughts, men would be like wild beasts, or like Kaspar Hauser.

And if men lacked this other capacity of being infected by art, people might be almost more savage still, and, above all, more separated from, and more hostile to, one another.

And therefore the activity of art is a most important one, as important as the activity of speech itself and as generally diffused.

We are accustomed to understand art to be only what we hear and see in theaters, concerts, and exhibitions, together with buildings, statues, poems, novels. . . . But all this is but the smallest part of the art by which we communicate with each other in life. All human life is filled with works of art of every kind—from cradlesong, jest, mimicry, the ornamentation of houses, dress, and utensils, up to church services, buildings, monuments, and triumphal processions. It is all artistic activity. So that by art, in the limited sense of the word, we do not mean all human activity transmitting feelings, but only that part which we for some reason select from it and to which we attach special importance.

This special importance has always been given by all men to that part of this activity which transmits feelings flowing from their religious perception, and this small part of art they have specifically called art, attaching to it the full meaning of the word.

That was how men of old—Socrates, Plato, and Aristotle—looked on art. Thus did the Hebrew prophets and the ancient Christians regard art; thus it was, and still is, understood by the Mohammedans, and thus it still is understood by religious folk among our own peasantry.

Some teachers of mankind—as Plato in his *Republic* and people such as the primitive Christians, the strict Mohammedans, and the Buddhists—have gone so far as to repudiate all art.

People viewing art in this way (in contradiction to the prevalent view of today which regards any art as good if only it affords pleasure) considered, and consider, that art (as contrasted with speech, which need not be listened to) is so highly dangerous in its power to infect people against their wills that mankind will lose far less by banishing all art than by tolerating each and every art.

Evidently such people were wrong in repudiating all art, for they denied that which cannot be denied—one of the indispensable means of communication, without which mankind could not exist. But not less wrong are the people of civilized European society of our class and day in favoring any art if it but serves beauty, i.e., gives people pleasure.

Formerly people feared lest among the works of art there might chance to be some causing corruption, and they prohibited art altogether. Now they only fear lest they should be deprived of any enjoyment art can afford, and patronize any art. And I think the last error is much grosser than the first and that its consequences are far more harmful.

Dante Alighieri, THE INFERNO (Trans. by Henry F. Cary)

John Milton, PARADISE LOST

1. Why did Dante choose Vergil to lead him through Hell and Beatrice to lead him into Paradise?

2. If you were to sentence and punish the sins mentioned, would you agree or disagree with Dante's arrangement? Explain.

3. If these are historical figures whom you would place on the various rings in Hell, where would you station them, and why?

4. What is the theme of this selection from Dante?

5. What kind of theology does Dante portray? How does this compare with Milton's?

6. What are Eve's motives for suggesting to Adam that they divide their labors?

7. What objections does Adam use against Eve's proposal? Who wins the argument and why?

8. What techniques does Satan use in his seduction of Eve? Why does she succumb to this temptation, and what are the results of her choice?

9. Why has the fall of man been called the central myth of western civilization?

Falsely charged with corruption, Dante Alighieri (1265-1321) died in exile far from his beloved Florence. Little is known about his life save a few details about his public career which ended so tragically. During his forced absence from Florence he wrote the *Divine Comedy*, a three-part epic in the Tuscan dialect. The popularity of "Inferno," "Purgatory," and "Paradiso" set the fashion for the use of vernacular Italian as a literary language.

31

THE DIVINE COMEDY

INFERNO [HELL]

CANTO I

ARGUMENT.—The writer, having lost his way in a gloomy forest, and being hindered by certain wild beasts from ascending a mountain, is met by Virgil, who promises to show him the punishments of Hell, and afterward of Purgatory; and that he shall then be conducted by Beatrice into Paradise. He follows the Roman poet.

IN the midway[1] of this our mortal life,
   I found me in a gloomy wood, astray
   Gone from the path direct: and e'en to tell,
It were no easy task, how savage wild
That forest, how robust and rough its growth,
Which to remember only, my dismay
Renews, in bitterness not far from death.
Yet, to discourse of what there good befel,
All else will I relate discover'd there.

   How first I enter'd it I scarce can say,
Such sleepy dulness in that instant weigh'd
My senses down, when the true path I left;
But when a mountain's foot I reach'd, where closed
The valley that had pierced my heart with dread,
I look'd aloft, and saw his shoulders broad
Already vested with that planet's beam,[2]
Who leads all wanderers safe through every way.

   Then was a little respite to the fear,
That in my heart's recesses deep had lain
All of that night, so pitifully past:
And as a man, with difficult short breath,
Forespent with toiling, 'scaped from sea to shore,
Turns to the perilous wide waste, and stands

---

[1] "In the midway." The era of the poem is intended by these words to be fixed to the thirty-fifth year of the poet's age, A.D. 1300. In his Convito, human life is compared to an arch or bow, the highest point of which is, in those well framed by nature, at their thirty-fifth year.

[2] "That planet's beam." The sun.

At gaze; e'en so my spirit, that yet fail'd,
Struggling with terror, turn'd to view the straits
That none hath passed and lived. My weary frame
After short pause recomforted, again
I journey'd on over that lonely steep,
The hinder foot[3] still firmer. Scarce the ascent
Began, when, lo! a panther,[4] nimble, light,
And cover'd with a speckled skin, appear'd;
Nor, when it saw me, vanish'd; rather strove
To check my onward going; that oft-times,
With purpose to retrace my steps, I turn'd.

    The hour was morning's prime, and on his way
Aloft the sun ascended with those stars,[5]
That with him rose when Love Divine first moved
Those its fair works: so that with joyous hope
All things conspired to fill me, the gay skin
Of that swift animal, the matin dawn,
And the sweet season. Soon that joy was chased.
And by new dread succeeded, when in view
A lion came, 'gainst me as it appear'd,
With his head held aloft and hunger-mad,
That e'en the air was fear-struck. A she-wolf
Was at his heels, who in her leanness seem'd
Full of all wants, and many a land hath made
Disconsolate ere now. She with such fear
O'erwhelm'd me, at the sight of her appall'd,
That of the height all hope I lost. As one,
Who, with his gain elated, sees the time
When all unawares is gone, he inwardly
Mourns with heart-griping anguish; such was I,
Haunted by that fell beast, never at peace,
Who coming o'er against me, by degrees
Impell'd me where the sun in silence rests.

    While to the lower space with backward step
I fell, my ken discern'd the form of one
Whose voice seem'd faint through long disuse of speech.
When him in that great desert I espied,

[3] "The hinder foot." In ascending a hill the weight of the body rests on the hinder foot.
[4] "A panther." Pleasure or luxury.

[5] "With those stars." The sun was in Aries, in which sign he supposes it to have begun its course at the creation.

"Have mercy on me," cried I out aloud,
"Spirit! or living man! whate'er thou be."
   He answered: "Now not man, man once I was,
And born of Lombard parents, Mantuans both
By country, when the power of Julius yet
Was scarcely firm. At Rome my life was past,
Beneath the mild Augustus, in the time
Of fabled deities and false. A bard
Was I, and made Anchises' upright son
The subject of my song, who came from Troy,
When the flames prey'd on Ilium's haughty towers.
But thou, say wherefore to such perils past
Return'st thou? wherefore not this pleasant mount
Ascendest, cause and source of all delight?"
"And art thou then that Virgil, that well-spring,
From which such copious floods of eloquence
Have issued?" I with front abash'd replied.
"Glory and light of all the tuneful train!
May it avail me, that I long with zeal
Have sought thy volume, and with love immense
Have conn'd it o'er. My master thou, and guide!
Thou he from whom alone I have derived
That style, which for its beauty into fame
Exalts me. See the beast, from whom I fled.
O save me from her, thou illustrious sage!
For every vein and pulse throughout my frame
She hath made tremble." He, soon as he saw
That I was weeping, answer'd, "Thou must needs
Another way pursue, if thou wouldst 'scape
From out that savage wilderness. This beast,
At whom thou criest, her way will suffer none
To pass, and no less hinderance makes than death:
So bad and so accursed in her kind,
That never sated is her ravenous will,
Still after food more craving than before.
To many an animal in wedlock vile
She fastens, and shall yet to many more,
Until that greyhound[6] come, who shall destroy

---

[6] This passage has been commonly understood as a eulogium on the liberal
spirit of his Veronese patron, Can Grande
della Scala.

Her with sharp pain. He will not life support
By earth nor its base metals, but by love,
Wisdom, and virtue; and his land shall be
The land 'twixt either Feltro.[7] In his might
Shall safety to Italia's plains arise,
For whose fair realm, Camilla, virgin pure,
Nisus, Euryalus, and Turnus fell.
He, with incessant chase, through every town
Shall worry, until he to hell at length
Restore her, thence by envy first let loose.
I, for thy profit pondering, now devise
That thou mayst follow me; and I, thy guide,
Will lead thee hence through an eternal space,
Where thou shalt hear despairing shrieks, and see
Spirits of old tormented, who invoke
A second death;[8] and those next view, who dwell
Content in fire,[9] for that they hope to come,
Whene'er the time may be, among the blest,
Into whose regions if thou then desire
To ascend, a spirit worthier[10] than I
Must lead thee, in whose charge, when I depart,
Thou shalt be left: for that Almighty King,
Who reigns above, a rebel to His law
Adjudges me; and therefore hath decreed
That, to His city, none through me should come.
He in all parts hath sway; there rules, there holds
His citadel and throne. O happy those,
Whom there He chuses!" I to him in few:
"Bard! by that God, whom thou didst not adore,
I do beseech thee (that this ill and worse
I may escape) to lead me where thou said'st,
That I Saint Peter's gate[11] may view, and those
Who, as thou tell'st, are in such dismal plight."
Onward he moved, I close his steps pursued.

[7] Verona, the country of Can della Scala, is situated between Feltro, a city in the Marca Trivigiana, and Monte Feltro, a city in the territory of Urbino.

[8] "A second death." "And in these days men shall seek death, and shall not find it; and shall desire to die, and death shall flee from them." Rev. ix. 6.

[9] The spirits in Purgatory.

[10] "A spirit worthier." Beatrice, who conducts the Poet through Paradise.

[11] The gate of Purgatory, which the Poet feigns to be guarded by an angel placed there by St. Peter.

CANTO II

ARGUMENT.—After the invocation, which poets are used to prefix to their works, he shows that, on a consideration of his own strength, he doubted whether it sufficed for the journey proposed to him, but that, being comforted by Virgil, he at last took courage, and followed him as his guide and master.

NOW was the day departing, and the air,
    Imbrown'd with shadows, from their toils released
    All animals on earth; and I alone
Prepared myself the conflict to sustain,
Both of sad pity, and that perilous road,
Which my unerring memory shall retrace.
    O Muses! O high genius! now vouchsafe
Your aid. O mind! that all I saw hast kept
Safe in a written record, here thy worth
And eminent endowments come to proof.
    I thus began: "Bard! thou who art my guide,
Consider well, if virtue be in me
Sufficient, ere to this high enterprise
Thou trust me. Thou hast told that Silvius' sire,[1]
Yet clothed in corruptible flesh, among
The immortal tribes had entrance, and was there
Sensibly present. Yet if Heaven's great Lord,
Almighty foe to ill, such favor show'd
In contemplation of the high effect,
Both what and who from him should issue forth,
It seems in reason's judgment well deserved;
Sith he of Rome and of Rome's empire wide,
In Heaven's empyreal height was chosen sire:
Both which, if truth be spoken, were ordain'd
And stablish'd for the holy place, where sits
Who to great Peter's sacred chair succeeds.
He from this journey, in thy song renown'd,
Learn'd things, that to his victory gave rise
And to the papal robe. In after-times
The Chosen Vessel[2] also travel'd there,
To bring us back assurance in that faith
Which is the entrance to salvation's way.
But I, why should I there presume? or who
Permits it? not Æneas I, nor Paul.

---

[1] "Silvius' sire." Æneas.   [2] "The Chosen Vessel." St. Paul.

Myself I deem not worthy, and none else
Will deem me. I, if on this voyage then
I venture, fear it will in folly end.
Thou, who art wise, better my meaning know'st,
Than I can speak." As one, who unresolves
What he hath late resolved, and with new thoughts
Changes his purpose, from his first intent
Removed; e'en such was I on that dun coast,
Wasting in thought my enterprise, at first
So eagerly embraced. "If right thy words
I scan," replied that shade magnanimous,
"Thy soul is by vile fear assail'd, which oft
So overcasts a man, that he recoils
From noblest resolution, like a beast
At some false semblance in the twilight gloom.
That from this terror thou mayst free thyself,
I will instruct thee why I came, and what
I heard in that same instant, when for thee
Grief touch'd me first. I was among the tribe,
Who rest suspended,[3] when a dame, so blest
And lovely I besought her to command,
Call'd me; her eyes were brighter than the star
Of day; and she, with gentle voice and soft,
Angelically tuned, her speech address'd:
'O courteous shade of Mantua! thou whose fame
Yet lives, and shall live long as nature lasts!
A friend, not of my fortune but myself,
On the wide desert in his road has met
Hindrance so great, that he through fear has turn'd.
Now much I dread lest he past help have stray'd,
And I be risen too late for his relief,
From what in heaven of him I heard. Speed now,
And by thy eloquent persuasive tongue,
And by all means for his deliverance meet,
Assist him. So to me will comfort spring.
I, who now bid thee on this errand forth,
Am Beatrice;[4] from a place I come

---

[3] The spirits in Limbo, neither admitted to a state of glory nor doomed to punishment.

[4] "Beatrice." The daughter of Folco Portinari, who is here invested with the character of celestial wisdom or theology.

Revisited with joy. Love brought me thence,
Who prompts my speech. When in my Master's sight
I stand, thy praise to him I oft will tell.'
    "She then was silent, and I thus began:
'O Lady! by whose influence alone
Mankind excels whatever is contain'd
Within that heaven which hath the smallest orb,
So thy command delights me, that to obey,
If it were done already, would seem late.
No need hast thou further to speak thy will:
Yet tell the reason, why thou art not loth
To leave that ample space, where to return
Thou burnest, for this centre here beneath.'
    "She then: 'Since thou so deeply wouldst inquire,
I will instruct thee briefly why no dread
Hinders my entrance here. Those things alone
Are to be fear'd whence evil may proceed;
None else, for none are terrible beside.
I am so framed by God, thanks to His grace!
That any sufferance of your misery
Touches me not, nor flame of that fierce fire
Assails me. In high Heaven a blessed Dame[5]
Resides, who mourns with such effectual grief
That hindrance, which I send thee to remove,
That God's stern judgment to her will inclines.'
To Lucia,[6] calling, her she thus bespake:
'Now doth thy faithful servant need thy aid,
And I commend him to thee.' At her word
Sped Lucia, of all cruelty the foe,
And coming to the place, where I abode
Seated with Rachel, her of ancient days,
She thus address'd me: "Thou true praise of God!
Beatrice! why is not thy succour lent
To him, who so much loved thee, as to leave
For thy sake all the multitude admires?
Dost thou not hear how pitiful his wail,
Nor mark the death, which in the torrent flood,
Swoln mightier than a sea, him struggling holds?"

[5] "A blessed Dame." The Divine
Mercy.

[6] "Lucia." The enlightening Grace of
Heaven; as it is commonly explained.

Ne'er among men did any with such speed
Haste to their profit, flee from their annoy,
As, when these words were spoken, I came here,
Down from my blessed seat, trusting the force
Of thy pure eloquence, which thee, and all
Who well have mark'd it, into honor brings.'

    "When she had ended, her bright beaming eyes
Tearful she turn'd aside; whereat I felt
Redoubled zeal to serve thee. As she will'd,
Thus am I come: I saved thee from the beast,
Who thy near way across the goodly mount
Prevented. What is this comes o'er thee then?
Why, why dost thou hang back? why in thy breast
Harbour vile fear? why hast not courage there,
And noble daring; since three maids,[7] so blest,
Thy safety plan, e'en in the court of Heaven;
And so much certain good my words forebode?"

    As florets, by the frosty air of night
Bent down and closed, when day has blanch'd their leaves,
Rise all unfolded on their spiry stems;
So was my fainting vigor new restored,
And to my heart such kindly courage ran,
That I as one undaunted soon replied:
"O full of pity she, who undertook
My succour! and thou kind, who didst perform
So soon her true behest! With such desire
Thou hast disposed me to renew my voyage,
That my first purpose fully is resumed.
Lead on: one only will is in us both.
Thou art my guide, my master thou, and lord."
    So spake I; and when he had onward moved,
I enter'd on the deep and woody way.

[7] "Three maids." The Divine Mercy, Lucia and Beatrice.

CANTO VII

ARGUMENT.—In the present Canto, Dante describes his descent into the fourth
circle, at the beginning of which he sees Plutus stationed. Here one like doom awaits
the prodigal and the avaricious; which is, to meet in direful conflict, rolling great
weights against each other with mutual upbraidings. From hence Virgil takes occasion
to show how vain the goods that are committed into the charge of Fortune; and this
moves our author to inquire what being that Fortune is, of whom he speaks: which
question being resolved, they go down into the fifth circle, where they find the
wrathful and gloomy tormented in the Stygian lake. Having made a compass round
great part of this lake, they come at last to the base of a lofty tower.

"AH me! O Satan! Satan!"[1] loud exclaim'd
    Plutus, in accent hoarse of wild alarm:
    And the kind sage, whom no event surprised,
To comfort me thus spake: "Let not thy fear
Harm thee, for power in him, be sure, is none

[1] "Pape Satan, Pape Satan, aleppe;" words without meaning.

To hinder down this rock thy safe descent."
Then to that swoln lip turning, "Peace!" he cried,
"Curst wolf! thy fury inward on thyself
Prey, and consume thee! Through the dark profound,
Not without cause, he passes. So 'tis will'd
On high, there where the great Archangel pour'd
Heaven's vengeance on the first adulterer proud."

As sails, full spread and bellying with the wind,
Drop suddenly collapsed, if the mast split;
So to the ground down dropp'd the cruel fiend.

Thus we, descending to the fourth steep ledge,
Gain'd on the dismal shore, that all the woe
Hems in of all the universe. Ah me!
Almighty Justice! in what store thou heap'st
New pains, new troubles, as I here beheld.
Wherefore doth fault of ours bring us to this?

E'en as a billow, on Charybdis rising,
Against encounter'd billow dashing breaks;
Such is the dance this wretched race must lead,
Whom more than elsewhere numerous here I found.
From one side and the other, with loud voice,
Both roll'd on weights, by main force of their breasts,
Then smote together, and each one forthwith
Roll'd them back voluble, turning again;
Exclaiming these, "Why holdest thou so fast?"
Those answering, "And why castest thou away?"
So, still repeating their despiteful song,
They to the opposite point, on either hand,
Traversed the horrid circle; then arrived,
Both turn'd them round, and through the middle space,
Conflicting met again. At sight whereof
I, stung with grief, thus spake: "O say, my guide!
What race is this. Were these, whose heads are shorn,
On our left hand, all separate to the Church?"

He straight replied: "In their first life, these all
In mind were so distorted, that they made,
According to due measure, of their wealth
No use. This clearly from their words collect,
Which they howl forth, at each extremity
Arriving of the circle, where their crime

Contrary in kind disparts them. To the Church
Were separate those, that with no hairy cowls
Are crowned, both Popes and Cardinals, o'er whom
Avarice dominion absolute maintains."
   I then: " 'Mid such as these some needs must be,
Whom I shall recognize, that with the blot
Of these foul sins were stain'd." He answering thus:
"Vain thought conceivest thou. That ignoble life,
Which made them vile before, now makes them dark,
And to all knowledge indiscernible.
For ever they shall meet in this rude shock:
These from the tomb with clenched grasp shall rise,
Those with close-shaven locks. That ill they gave,
And ill they kept, hath of the beauteous world
Deprived, and set them at this strife, which needs
No labor'd phrase of mine to set it off.
Now mayst thou see, my son! how brief, how vain,
The goods committed into Fortune's hands,
For which the human race keep such a coil!
Not all the gold that is beneath the moon,
Or ever hath been, of these toil-worn souls
Might purchase rest for one." I thus rejoin'd:
"My guide! of these this also would I learn;
This Fortune, that thou speak'st of, what it is,
Whose talons grasp the blessings of the world."
   He thus: "O beings blind! what ignorance
Besets you! Now my judgment hear and mark.
He, whose transcendent wisdom passes all,
The heavens creating, gave them ruling powers
To guide them; so that each part shines to each,
Their light in equal distribution pour'd.
By similar appointment he ordain'd,
Over the world's bright images to rule,
Superintendence of a guiding hand
And general minister, which, at due time,
May change the empty vantages of life
From race to race, from one to other's blood,
Beyond prevention of man's wisest care:
Wherefore one nation rises into sway,
Another languishes, e'en as her will

41

Decrees, from us conceal'd, as in the grass
The serpent train. Against her nought avails
Your utmost wisdom. She with foresight plans,
Judges, and carries on her reign, as theirs
The other powers divine. Her changes know
None intermission: by necessity
She is made swift, so frequent come who claim
Succession in her favors. This is she,
So execrated e'en by those whose debt
To her is rather praise: they wrongfully
With blame requite her, and with evil word;
But she is blessed, and for that recks not:
Amidst the other primal beings glad
Rolls on her sphere, and in her bliss exults.
Now on our way pass we, to heavier woe
Descending: for each star is falling now,
That mounted at our entrance, and forbids
Too long our tarrying." We the circle cross'd
To the next steep, arriving at a well,
That boiling pours itself down to a foss
Sluiced from its source. Far murkier was the wave
Than sablest grain: and we in company
Of the inky waters, journeying by their side,
Enter'd, though by a different track, beneath.
Into a lake, the Stygian named, expands
The dismal stream, when it hath reach'd the foot
Of the gray wither'd cliffs. Intent I stood
To gaze, and in the marish sunk descried
A miry tribe, all naked, and with looks
Betokening rage. They with their hands alone
Struck not, but with the head, the breast, the feet,
Cutting each other piecemeal with their fangs.

  The good instructor spake: "Now seest thou, son!
The souls of those, whom anger overcame.
This too for certain know, that underneath
The water dwells a multitude, whose sighs
Into these bubbles make the surface heave,
As thine eye tells thee wheresoe'er it turn.
Fix'd in the slime, they say: 'Sad once were we,
In the sweet air made gladsome by the sun,

42

Carrying a foul and lazy mist within:
Now in these murky settlings are we sad.'
Such dolorous strain they gurgle in their throats,
But word distinct can utter none." Our route
Thus compass'd we, a segment widely stretch'd
Between the dry embankment, and the core
Of the loath'd pool, turning meanwhile our eyes
Downward on those who gulp'd its muddy lees;
Nor stopp'd, till to a tower's low base we came.

CANTO VIII

ARGUMENT.—A signal having been made from the tower, Phlegyas, the ferryman of the lake, speedily crosses it, and conveys Virgil and Dante to the other side. On their passage, they meet with Filippo Argenti, whose fury and torment are described. They then arrive at the city of Dis, the entrance whereto is denied, and the portals closed against them by many Demons.

MY theme pursuing, I relate, that ere
We reach'd the lofty turret's base, our eyes
Its height ascended, where we mark'd uphung
Two cressets, and another saw from far
Return the signal, so remote, that scarce
The eye could catch its beam. I, turning round
To the deep source of knowledge, thus inquired:
"Say what this means; and what, that other light
In answer set: what agency doth this?"
    "There on the filthy waters," he replied,
"E'en now what next awaits us mayst thou see,
If the marsh-gendered fog conceal it not."
    Never was arrow from the cord dismiss'd,
That ran its way so nimbly through the air,
As a small bark, that through the waves I spied
Toward us coming, under the sole sway
Of one that ferried it, who cried aloud:
"Art thou arrived, fell spirit?"—"Phlegyas, Phlegyas,[1]
This time thou criest in vain," my lord replied;
"No longer shalt thou have us, but while o'er
The slimy pool we pass." As one who hears
Of some great wrong he hath sustain'd, whereat

[1] Phlegyas, so incensed against Apollo for having violated his daughter Coronis, that he set fire to the temple of that deity, by whose vengeance he was cast into Tartarus. See Virgil, Æneas, l. vi. 618.

43

Inly he pines: so Phlegyas inly pined
In his fierce ire. My guide, descending, stepp'd
Into the skiff, and bade me enter next,
Close at his side; nor, till my entrance, seem'd
The vessel freighted. Soon as both embark'd,
Cutting the waves, goes on the ancient prow,
More deeply than with others it is wont.

While we our course o'er the dead channel held,
One drench'd in mire before me came, and said:
"Who art thou, that thus comest ere thine hour?"

I answer'd: "Though I come, I tarry not:
But who art thou, that art become so foul?"

"One, as thou seest, who mourn:" he straight
    replied.

To which I thus: "In mourning and in woe,
Curst spirit! tarry thou. I know thee well,
E'en thus in filth disguised." Then stretch'd he forth
Hands to the bark; whereof my teacher sage
Aware, thrusting him back: "Away! down there
To the other dogs!" then, with his arms my neck
Encircling, kiss'd my cheek, and spake: "O soul,
Justly disdainful! blest was she in whom
Thou wast conceived. He in the world was one
For arrogance noted: to his memory
No virtue lends its lustre; even so
Here is his shadow furious. There above,
How many now hold themselves mighty kings,
Who here like swine shall wallow in the mire,
Leaving behind them horrible dispraise."

I then: "Master! him fain would I behold
Whelm'd in these dregs, before we quit the lake."

He thus: "Or ever to thy view the shore
Be offer'd, satisfied shall be that wish,
Which well deserves completion." Scarce his words
Were ended, when I saw the miry tribes
Set on him with such violence, that yet
For that render I thanks to God, and praise.
"To Filippo Argenti!"[2] cried they all:

---

[2] Boccaccio tells us, "he was a man remarkable for the large proportions and extraordinary vigor of his bodily frame, and the extreme waywardness and irascibility of his temper."—"Decameron." G. ix. N. 8.

And on himself the moody Florentine
Turn'd his avenging fangs. Him here we left,
Nor speak I of him more. But on mine ear
Sudden a sound of lamentation smote,
Whereat mine eye unbarr'd I sent abroad.

   And thus the good instructor: "Now, my son
Draws near the city, that of Dis is named,
With its grave denizens, a mighty throng."
   I thus: "The minarets already, Sir!
There, certes, in the valley I descry,
Gleaming vermilion, as if they from fire
Had issued." He replied: "Eternal fire,
That inward burns, shows them with ruddy flame
Illumed; as in this nether Hell thou seest."
   We came within the fosses deep, that moat
This region comfortless. The walls appear'd
As they were framed of iron. We had made
Wide circuit, ere a place we reach'd, where loud
The mariner cried vehement: "Go forth:
The entrance is here." Upon the gates I spied
More than a thousand, who of old from Heaven
Were shower'd. With ireful gestures, "Who is this,"
They cried, "that, without death first felt, goes through
The regions of the dead?" My sapient guide
Made sign that he for secret parley wish'd;
Whereat their angry scorn abating, thus
They spake: "Come thou alone; and let him go,
Who hath so hardily enter'd this realm.
Alone return he by his witless way;
If well he knew it, let him prove. For thee,
Here shalt thou tarry, who through clime so dark
Hast been his escort." Now bethink thee, reader!
What cheer was mine at sound of those curst words.
I did believe I never should return.
   "O my loved guide! who more than seven times[3]

---

[3] "Seven times." The commentators, says Venturi, perplex themselves with the inquiry what seven perils these were from which Dante had been delivered by Virgil. Reckoning the beasts in the first Canto as one of them, and adding Charon, Minos, Cerberus, Plutus, Phlegyas, and Filippo Argenti, as so many others, we shall have the number; and if this be not satisfactory, we may suppose a determinate to have been put for an indeterminate number.

Security hast render'd me, and drawn
From peril deep, whereto I stood exposed,
Desert me not," I cried, "in this extreme.
And, if our onward going be denied,
Together trace we back our steps with speed."
   My liege, who thither had conducted me,
Replied: "Fear not: for of our passage none
Hath power to disappoint us, by such high
Authority permitted. But do thou
Expect me here; meanwhile, thy wearied spirit
Comfort, and feed with kindly hope, assured
I will not leave thee in this lower world."
This said, departs the sire benevolent,
And quits me. Hesitating I remain
At war, 'twixt will and will not, in my thoughts.
   I could not hear what terms he offer'd them,
But they conferr'd not long, for all at once
Pellmell rush'd back within. Closed were the gates,
By those our adversaries, on the breast
Of my liege lord: excluded, he return'd
To me with tardy steps. Upon the ground
His eyes were bent, and from his brow erased
All confidence, while thus in sighs he spake:
"Who hath denied me these abodes of woe?"
Then thus to me: "That I am anger'd, think
No ground of terror: in this trial I
Shall vanquish, use what arts they may within
For hindrance. This their insolence, not new,[4]
Erewhile at gate less secret they display'd,
Which still is without bolt; upon its arch
Thou saw'st the deadly scroll: and even now,
On this side of its entrance, down the steep,
Passing the circles, unescorted, comes
One whose strong might can open us this land."

[4] Virgil assures our poet that these evil spirits had formerly shown the same insolence when our Saviour descended into hell. They attempted to prevent him from entering at the gate, over which Dante had read the fatal inscription. "That gate which," says the Roman poet, "an angel had just passed, by whose aid we shall overcome this opposition, and gain admittance into the city."

CANTO IX

ARGUMENT.—After some hindrances, and having seen the hellish furies and other monsters, the Poet, by the help of an angel, enters the city of Dis, wherein he discovers that the heretics are punished in tombs burning with intense fire; and he, together with Virgil, passes onward between the sepulchres and the walls of the city.

THE hue,[1] which coward dread on my pale cheeks
Imprinted when I saw my guide turn back,
Chased that from his which newly they had worn,
And inwardly restrain'd it. He, as one
Who listens, stood attentive: for his eye
Not far could lead him through the sable air,
And the thick-gathering cloud. "It yet behoves
We win this fight;" thus he began: "if not,
Such aid to us is offer'd—Oh! how long
Me seems it, ere the promised help arrive."
 I noted, how the sequel of his words
Cloked their beginning; for the last he spake
Agreed not with the first. But not the less
My fear was at his saying; sith I drew
To import worse, perchance, than that he held,
His mutilated speech. "Doth ever any
Into this rueful concave's extreme depth
Descend, out of the first degree, whose pain
Is deprivation merely of sweet hope?"
 Thus I inquiring. "Rarely," he replied,
"It chances, that among us any makes
This journey, which I wend. Erewhile, 'tis true,
Once came I here beneath, conjured by fell
Erichtho,[2] sorceress, who compell'd the shades
Back to their bodies. No long space my flesh
Was naked of me, when within these walls
She made me enter, to draw forth a spirit
From out of Judas' circle. Lowest place
Is that of all, obscurest, and removed

[1] "The hue." Virgil, perceiving that Dante was pale with fear, restrained those outward tokens of displeasure which his own countenance had betrayed.

[2] Erichtho, a Thessalian sorceress (Lucan, "Pharsal." l. vi.), was employed by Sextus, son of Pompey the Great, to conjure up a spirit, who should inform him of the issue of the civil wars between his father and Cæsar.

47

Farthest from Heaven's all-circling orb. The road
Full well I know: thou therefore rest secure.
That lake, the noisome stench exhaling, round
The city of grief encompasses, which now
We may not enter without rage." Yet more
He added: but I hold it not in mind,
For that mine eye toward the lofty tower
Had drawn me wholly, to its burning top;
Where, in an instant, I beheld uprisen
At once three hellish furies stain'd with blood.
In limb and motion feminine they seem'd;
Around them greenest hydras twisting roll'd
Their volumes; adders and cerastes crept
Instead of hair, and their fierce temples bound.
    He, knowing well the miserable hags
Who tend the queen of endless woe, thus spake:
"Mark thou each dire Erynnis. To the left,
This is Megæra; on the right hand, she
Who wails, Alecto; and Tisiphone
I' th' midst." This said, in silence he remain'd.
Their breast they each one clawing tore; themselves
Smote with their palms, and such thrill clamour raised,
That to the bard I clung, suspicion-bound.
"Hasten Medusa: so to adamant
Him shall we change;" all looking down exclaim'd:
"E'en when by Theseus' might assail'd, we took
No ill revenge." "Turn thyself round and keep
Thy countenance hid; for if the Gorgon dire
Be shown, and thou shouldst view it, thy return
Upwards would be forever lost." This said,
Himself, my gentle master, turn'd me round;
Nor trusted he my hands, but with his own
He also hid me. Ye of intellect
Sound and entire, mark well the lore[3] conceal'd

[3] The Poet probably intends to call the reader's attention to the allegorical and mystic sense of the present Canto, and not, as Venturi supposes, to that of the whole work. Landino supposes this hidden meaning to be that in the case of those vices which proceed from intemperance, reason, figured under the person of Virgil, with the ordinary grace of God, may be a sufficient safeguard; but that in the instance of more heinous crimes, such as those we shall hereafter see punished, a special grace, represented by the angel, is requisite for our defence.

Under close texture of the mystic strain.
  And now there came o'er the perturbed waves
Loud-crashing, terrible, a sound that made
Either shore tremble, as if of a wind
Impetuous, from conflicting vapors sprung,
That 'gainst some forest driving all his might,
Plucks off the branches, beats them down, and hurls
Afar; then, onward passing, proudly sweeps
His whirlwind rage, while beasts and shepherds fly.
  Mine eyes he loosed, and spake: "And now direct
Thy visual nerve along that ancient foam,
There, thickest where the smoke ascends." As frogs
Before their foe the serpent, through the wave
Ply swiftly all, till at the ground each one
Lies on a heap; more than a thousand spirits
Destroy'd, so saw I fleeing before one
Who pass'd with unwet feet the Stygian sound.
He, from his face removing the gross air,
Oft his left hand forth stretch'd, and seem'd alone
By that annoyance wearied. I perceived
That he was sent from Heaven; and to my guide
Turn'd me, who signal made, that I should stand
Quiet, and bend to him. Ah me! how full
Of noble anger seem'd he. To the gate
He came, and with his wand touch'd it, whereat
Open without impediment it flew.
  "Outcasts of heaven! O abject race, scorn'd!"
Began he, on the horrid grunsel standing,
"Whence doth this wild excess of insolence
Lodge in you? wherefore kick you 'gainst that will
Ne'er frustrate of its end, and which so oft
Hath laid on you enforcement of your pangs?
What profits at the Fates to butt the horn?
Your Cerberus,[4] if ye remember, hence
Bears still, peel'd of their hair, his throat and maw."

[4] "Your Cerberus." Cerberus is feigned to have been dragged by Hercules, bound with a threefold chain, of which, says the angel, he still bears the marks. Lombardi blames the other interpreters for having supposed that the angel attributes this exploit to Hercules, a fabulous hero, rather than to our Saviour. It would seem as if the good father had forgotten that Cerberus is himself no less a creature of the imagination than the hero who encountered him.

This said, he turn'd back o'er the filthy way,
And syllable to us spake none; but wore
The semblance of a man by other care
Beset, and keenly prest, than thought of him
Who in his presence stands. Then we our steps
Toward that territory moved, secure
After the hallow'd words. We, unopposed,
There enter'd; and, my mind eager to learn
What state a fortress like to that might hold,
I, soon as enter'd, throw mine eye around,
And see, on every part, wide-stretching space,
Replete with bitter pain and torment ill.
  As where Rhone stagnates on the plains of Arles,[5]
Or as at Pola,[6] near Quarnaro's gulf,
That closes Italy and laves her bounds,
The place is all thick spread with sepulchres;
So was it here, save what in horror here
Excell'd: for 'midst the graves were scattered flames,
Wherewith intensely all throughout they burn'd,
That iron for no craft there hotter needs.
  Their lids all hung suspended; and beneath,
From them forth issued lamentable moans,
Such as the sad and tortured well might raise.
  I thus: "Master! say who are these, interr'd
Within these vaults, of whom distinct we hear
The dolorous sighs." He answer thus return'd:
"The arch-heretics are here, accompanied
By every sect their followers; and much more
Than thou believest, the tombs are freighted: like
With like is buried; and the monuments
Are different in degrees of heat." This said,
He to the right hand turning, on we pass'd
Betwixt the afflicted and the ramparts high.

[5] "The plains of Arles." In Provençe. These sepulchres are mentioned in the Life of Charlemagne, which has been attributed to Archbishop Turpin, cap. 28, and 30, and by Fazio degli Uberti, Dittamondo, L. iv. cap. xxi.

[6] "At Pola." A city of Istria, situated near the gulf of Quarnaro, in the Adriatic Sea.

CANTO X

ARGUMENT.—Dante, having obtained permission from his guide, holds discourse with Farinata degli Uberti and Cavalcante Cavalcanti, who lie in their fiery tombs that are yet open, and not to be closed up till after the last judgment. Farinata predicts the Poet's exile from Florence; and shows him that the condemned have knowledge of future things, but are ignorant of what is at present passing, unless it be revealed by some newcomer from earth.

NOW by a secret pathway we proceed,
    Between the walls, that hem the region round,
    And the tormented souls: my master first,
I close behind his steps. "Virtue supreme!"
I thus began: "Who through these ample orbs
In circuit lead'st me, even as thou will'st;
Speak thou, and satisfy my wish. May those,
Who lie within these sepulchres, be seen?
Already all the lids are raised, and none
O'er them keeps watch." He thus in answer spake:
"They shall be closed all, what-time they here
From Josaphat[1] return'd shall come, and bring
Their bodies, which above they now have left.
The cemetery on this part obtain,
With Epicurus, all his followers,
Who with the body make the spirit die.
Here therefore satisfaction shall be soon,
Both to the question ask'd, and to the wish[2]
Which thou conceal'st in silence." I replied:
"I keep not, guide beloved! from thee my heart
Secreted, but to shun vain length of words;
A lesson erewhile taught me by thyself."

    "O Tuscan! thou, who through the city of fire
Alive art passing, so discreet of speech:
Here, please thee, stay awhile. Thy utterance
Declares the place of thy nativity
To be that noble land, with which perchance

[1] "Josaphat." It seems to have been a common opinion among the Jews, as well as among many Christians, that the general judgment will be held in the valley of Josaphat, or Jehoshaphat. "I will also gather all nations, and will bring them down into the valley of Jehoshaphat, and will plead with them there for my people, and for my heritage Israel, whom they have scattered among the nations, and parted my land."—Joel, iii. 2.

[2] "The wish." The wish that Dante had not expressed was to see and converse with the followers of Epicurus; among whom, we shall see, were Farinata degli Uberti and Cavalcante Cavalcanti.

I too severely dealt." Sudden that sound
Forth issued from a vault, whereat, in fear,
I somewhat closer to my leader's side
Approaching, he thus spake: "What dost thou? Turn:
Lo! Farinata[3] there, who hath himself
Uplifted: from his girdle upwards, all
Exposed, behold him." On his face was mine
Already fix'd: his breast and forehead there
Erecting, seem'd as in high scorn he held
E'en Hell. Between the sepulchres, to him
My guide thrust me, with fearless hands and prompt;
This warning added: "See thy words be clear."

He, soon as there I stood at the tomb's foot,
Eyed me a space; then in disdainful mood
Address'd me: "Say what ancestors were thine."

I, willing to obey him, straight reveal'd
The whole, nor kept back aught: whence he, his brow
Somewhat uplifting, cried: "Fiercely were they
Adverse to me, my. party, and the blood
From whence I sprang: twice,[4] therefore, I abroad
Scatter'd them." "Though driven out, yet they each
    time
From all parts," answer'd I, "return'd: an art
Which yours have shown they are not skill'd to learn."

Then, peering forth from the unclosed jaw,
Rose from his side a shade,[5] high as the chin,
Leaning, methought, upon its knees upraised.
It look'd around, as eager to explore
If there were other with me; but perceiving
That fond imagination quench'd, with tears
Thus spake: "If thou through this blind prison go'st,
Led by thy lofty genius and profound,

---

[3] "Farinata." Farinata degli Uberti, a noble Florentine, was the leader of the Ghibelline faction, when they obtained a signal victory over the Guelfi at Montaperto, near the river Arbia. Macchiavelli calls him "a man of exalted soul, and great military talents."—"Hist. of Flor." b. ii. His grandson. Bonifacio, commonly called Fazio degli Uberti, wrote a poem, entitled the "Dittamonodo," in imitation of Dante.

[4] "Twice." The first time in 1248, when they were driven out by Frederick the Second. See G. Villani, lib. vi. c. xxxiv.; and the second time in 1260. See note to v. 83.

[5] "A shade." The spirit of Cavalcante Cavalcanti, a noble Florentine, of the Guelf party.

Where is my son?[6] and wherefore not with thee?"
I straight replied: "Not of myself I come;
By him, who there expects me, through this clime
Conducted, whom perchance Guido thy son
Had in contempt."[7] Already had his words
And mode of punishment read me his name,
Whence I so fully answer'd. He at once
Exclaim'd, up starting, "How! said'st thou, he *had*?
No longer lives he? Strikes not on his eye
The blessed daylight?" Then, of some delay
I made ere my reply, aware, down fell
Supine, nor after forth appear'd he more.

Meanwhile the other, great of soul, near whom
I yet was station'd, changed not countenance stern,
Nor moved the neck, nor bent his ribbed side.
"And if," continuing the first discourse,
"They in this art," he cried, "small skill have shown;
That doth torment me more e'en than this bed.
But not yet fifty times[8] shall be relumed
Her aspect, who reigns here queen of this realm,[9]
Ere thou shalt know the full weight of that art.
So to the pleasant world mayst thou return,
As thou shalt tell me why, in all their laws,
Against my kin this people is so fell."

"The slaughter[10] and great havoc," I replied,
"That color'd Arbia's flood with crimson stain—

---

[6] "My son." Guido, the son of Cavalcante Cavalcanti: "he whom I call the
first of my friends," says Dante in his
"Vita Nuova" where the commencement
of their friendship is related. From the
character given of him by contemporary
writers, his temper was well formed to
assimilate with that of our Poet. "He
was," according to G. Villani, lib. viii.
c. xli., "of a philosophical and elegant
mind, if he had not been too delicate and
fastidious."

[7]   "———— Guido they soon
      Had in contempt."
Guido Cavalcanti, being more given to
philosophy than poetry, was perhaps no
great admirer of Virgil.

[8] "Not yet fifty times." "Not fifty

months shall be passed, before thou shalt
learn, by woeful experience, the difficulty
of returning from banishment to thy
native city."

[9] "Queen of this realm." The moon,
one of whose titles in heathen mythology
was Proserpine, queen of the shades below.

[10] "The slaughter." "By means of
Farinata degli Uberti, the Guelfi were
conquered by the army of King Man-
fredi, near the river Arbia, with so great
a slaughter, that those who escaped from
that defeat took refuge, not in Florence,
which city they considered as lost to them,
but in Lucca."—Macchiavelli, "Hist. of
Flor." b. ii. and G. Villani, lib. vi. c.
lxxx. and lxxxi.

To these impute, that in our hallow'd dome
Such orisons[11] ascend." Sighing he shook
The head, then thus resumed: "In that affray
I stood not singly, nor, without just cause,
Assuredly, should with the rest have stirr'd;
But singly there I stood,[12] when, by consent
Of all, Florence had to the ground been razed,
The one who openly forbade the deed."

"So may thy lineage find at last repose,"
I thus adjured him, "as thou solve this knot,
Which now involves my mind. If right I hear,
Ye seem to view beforehand that which time
Leads with him, of the present uninform'd."

"We view, as one who hath an evil sight,"
He answer'd, "plainly, objects far remote;
So much of his large splendor yet imparts
The Almighty Ruler: but when they approach,
Or actually exist, our intellect
Then wholly fails; nor of your human state,
Except what others bring us, know we aught.
Hence therefore mayst thou understand, that all
Our knowledge in that instant shall expire,
When on futurity the portals close."

Then conscious of my fault,[13] and by remorse
Smitten, I added thus: "Now shalt thou say
To him there fallen, that his offspring still
Is to the living join'd; and bid him know,
That if from answer, silent, I abstain'd,

---

[11] "Such orisons." This appears to allude to certain prayers which were offered up in the churches of Florence, for deliverance from the hostile attempts of the Uberti; or, it may be that the public councils being held in churches, the speeches delivered in them against the Uberti are termed "orisons," or prayers.

[12] "Singly there I stood." Guido Novello assembled a council of the Ghibellini at Empoli; where it was agreed by all, that, in order to maintain the ascendancy of the Ghibelline party in Tuscany, it was necessary to destroy Florence, which could serve only (the people of that city being Guelfi) to enable the party attached to

the church to recover its strength. This cruel sentence, passed upon so noble a city, met with no opposition from any of its citizens or friends, except Farinata degli Uberti, who openly and without reserve forbade the measure; affirming, that he had endured so many hardships, with no other view than that of being able to pass his days in his own country. Macchiavelli, Hist. of Flor. b. ii.

[13] "My fault." Dante felt remorse for not having returned an immediate answer to the inquiry of Cavalcante, from which delay he was led to believe that his son Guido was no longer living.

'Twas that my thought was occupied, intent
Upon that error, which thy help hath solved."
  But now my master summoning me back
I heard, and with more eager haste besought
The spirit to inform me, who with him
Partook his lot. He answer thus return'd:
"More than a thousand with me here are laid.
Within is Frederick,[14] second of that name,
And the Lord Cardinal,[15] and of the rest
I speak not." He, this said, from sight withdrew.
But I my steps toward the ancient bard
Reverting, ruminated on the words
Betokening me such ill. Onward he moved,
And thus, in going, question'd: "Whence the amaze
That holds thy senses wrapt?" I satisfied
The inquiry, and the sage enjoin'd me straight:
"Let thy safe memory store what thou hast heard,
To thee importing harm; and note thou this,"
With his raised finger bidding me take heed,
"When thou shalt stand before her gracious beam,[16]
Whose bright eye all surveys, she of thy life
The future tenor will to thee unfold."
  Forthwith he to the left hand turn'd his feet:
We left the wall, and toward the middle space
Went by a path that to a valley strikes,
Which e'en thus high exhaled its noisome steam.

---

[14] "Frederick." The Emperor Frederick II., who died in 1250. See notes to Canto xiii.

[15] "The Lord Cardinal." Ottaviano Ubaldini, a Florentine, made cardinal in 1245, and deceased about 1273. On account of his great influence, he was generally known by the appellation of "the Cardinal." It is reported of him that he declared if there were any such thing as a human soul he had lost his for the Ghibellini.

[16] "Her gracious beam." Beatrice.

CANTO XI

ARGUMENT.—Dante arrives at the verge of a rocky precipice which encloses the seventh circle, where he sees the sepulchre of Anastasius the Heretic; behind the lid of which pausing a little, to make himself capable by degrees of enduring the fetid smell that steamed upward from the abyss, he is instructed by Virgil concerning the manner in which the three following circles are disposed, and what description of sinners is punished in each. He then inquires the reason why the carnal, the gluttonous, the avaricious and prodigal, the wrathful and gloomy, suffer not their punishments within the city of Dis. He next asks how the crime of usury is an offence against God; and at length the two Poets go toward the place from whence a passage leads down to the seventh circle.

UPON the utmost verge of a high bank,
    By craggy rocks environ'd round, we came.
    Where woes beneath, more cruel yet, were
        stow'd:
And here, to shun the horrible excess
Of fetid exhalation upward cast
From the profound abyss, behind the lid
Of a great monument we stood retired,
Whereon this scroll I-mark'd: "I have in charge
Pope Anastasius,[1] whom Photinus drew
From the right path." "Ere our descent, behoves
We make delay, that somewhat first the sense,
To the dire breath accustom'd, afterward
Regard it not." My master thus; to whom
Answering I spake: "Some compensation find,
That the time pass not wholly lost." He then:
"Lo! how my thoughts e'en to thy wishes tend.
My son! within these rocks," he thus began,
"Are three close circles in gradation placed,
As these which now thou leavest. Each one is full
Of spirits accurst; but that the sight alone
Hereafter may suffice thee, listen how
And for what cause in durance they abide.
    "Of all malicious act abhorr'd in Heaven,
The end is injury; and all such end
Either by force or fraud works other's woe.
But fraud, because of man's peculiar evil,

---

[1] By some supposed to have been Anastasius II.; by others, the fourth of that name; while a third set, jealous of the integrity of the papal faith, contend that our poet has confounded him with Anastasius I., Emperor of the East.

To God is more displeasing; and beneath,
The fraudulent are therefore doom'd to endure
Severer pang. The violent occupy
All the first circle; and because, to force,
Three persons are obnoxious, in three rounds,
Each within other separate, is it framed.
To God, his neighbor, and himself, by man
Force may be offer'd; to himself I say,
And his possessions, as thou soon shalt hear
At full. Death, violent death, and painful wounds
Upon his neighbor he inflicts; and wastes,
By devastation, pillage, and the flames,
His substance. Slayers, and each one that smites
In malice, plunderers, and all robbers, hence
The torment undergo of the first round,
In different herds. Man can do violence
To himself and his own blessings: and for this,
He, in the second round must aye deplore
With unavailing penitence his crime,
Whoe'er deprives himself of life and light,
In reckless lavishment his talent wastes,
And sorrows there where he should dwell in joy.
To God may force be offer'd, in the heart
Denying and blaspheming His high power,
And Nature with her kindly law contemning.
And thence the inmost round marks with its seal
Sodom, and Cahors, and all such as speak
Contemptuously of the Godhead in their hearts.
   "Fraud, that in every conscience leaves a sting,
May be by man employ'd on one, whose trust
He wins, or on another, who withholds
Strict confidence. Seems as the latter way
Broke but the bond of love which Nature makes.
Whence in the second circle have their nest,
Dissimulation, witchcraft, flatteries,
Theft, falsehood, simony, all who seduce
To lust, or set their honesty at pawn,
With such vile scum as these. The other way
Forgets both Nature's general love, and that
Which thereto added afterward gives birth
To special faith. Whence in the lesser circle,

Point of the universe, dread seat of Dis,
The traitor is eternally consumed."
 I thus: "Instructor, clearly thy discourse
Proceeds, distinguishing the hideous chasm
And its inhabitants with skill exact.
But tell me this: they of the dull, fat pool,
Whom the rain beats, or whom the tempest drives,
Or who with tongues so fierce conflicting meet,
Wherefore within the city fire-illumed
Are not these punish'd, if God's wrath be on them?
And if it be not, wherefore in such guise
Are they condemn'd?" He answer thus return'd:
"Wherefore in dotage wanders thus thy mind,
Not so accustom'd? or what other thoughts
Possess it? Dwell not in thy memory
The words, wherein thy ethic page[2] describes
Three dispositions adverse to Heaven's will,
Incontinence, malice, and mad brutishness,
And how incontinence the least offends
God, and least guilt incurs? If well thou note
This judgment, and remember who they are,
Without these walls to vain repentance doom'd,
Thou shalt discern why they apart are placed
From these fell spirits, and less wreakful pours
Justice divine on them its vengeance down."
 "O sun! who healest all imperfect sight,
Thou so content'st me, when thou solvest my doubt,
That ignorance not less than knowledge charms.
Yet somewhat turn thee back," I in these words
Continued, "where thou said'st, that usury
Offends celestial Goodness; and this knot
Perplex'd unravel." He thus made reply:
"Philosophy, to an attentive ear,
Clearly points out, not in one part alone,
How imitative Nature takes her course
From the celestial mind, and from its art:
And where her laws[3] the Stagirite unfolds,

---

[2] "Thy ethic page." He refers to Aristotle's Ethics, lib. vii. c. 1: "——let it be defined that respecting morals there are three sorts of things to be avoided, malice, incontinence, and brutishness."
[3] "Her laws." Aristotle's Physics, lib. ii. c. 2: "Art imitates nature."

Not many leaves scann'd o'er, observing well
Thou shalt discover, that your art on her
Obsequious follows, as the learner treads
In his instructor's step; so that your art
Deserves the name of second in descent
From God. These two, if thou recall to mind
Creation's holy book,⁴ from the beginning
Were the right source of life and excellence
To human-kind. But in another path
The usurer walks; and Nature in herself
And in her follower thus he sets at nought,
Placing elsewhere his hope.⁵ But follow now
My steps on forward journey bent; for now
The Pisces play with undulating glance
Along the horizon, and the Wain⁶ lies all
O'er the northwest; and onward there a space
Is our steep passage down the rocky height."

CANTO XXXIV

ARGUMENT.—In the fourth and last round of the ninth circle, those who have
betrayed their benefactors are wholly covered with ice. And in the midst is Lucifer,
at whose back Dante and Virgil ascend, till by a secret path they reach the surface of
the other hemisphere of the earth, and once more obtain sight of the stars.

"THE banners of Hell's Monarch do come forth
Toward us; therefore look," so spake my guide,
"If thou discern him." As, when breathes a cloud
Heavy and dense, or when the shades of night
Fall on our hemisphere, seems view'd from far
A windmill, which the blast stirs briskly round;
Such was the fabric then methought I saw.

To shield me from the wind, forthwith I drew
Behind my guide: no covert else was there.

Now came I (and with fear I bid my strain
Record the marvel) where the souls were all
Whelm'd underneath, transparent, as through glass
Pellucid the frail stem. Some prone were laid;
Others stood upright, this upon the soles,
That on his head, a third with face to feet
Arch'd like a bow. When to the point we came,
Whereat my guide was pleased that I should see

⁷ The friar Alberigo.

59

The creature eminent in beauty once,
He from before me stepp'd and made me pause.
"Lo!" he exclaim'd, "lo! Dis; and lo! the place,
Where thou hast need to arm thy heart with strength."
How frozen and how faint I then became,
Ask me not, reader! for I write it not;
Since words would fail to tell thee of my state.
I was not dead nor living. Think thyself,
If quick conception work in thee at all,
How I did feel. That emperor, who sways
The realm of sorrow, at mid breast from the ice
Stood forth; and I in stature am more like
A giant, than the giants are his arms.
Mark now how great that whole must be, which suits
With such a part. If he were beautiful
As he is hideous now, and yet did dare
To scowl upon his Maker, well from him
May all our misery flow. Oh what a sight!
How passing strange it seem'd, when I did spy
Upon his head three faces: one in front
Of hue vermilion, the other two with this
Midway each shoulder join'd and at the crest;
The right 'twixt wan and yellow seem'd; the left
To look on, such as come from whence old Nile
Stoops to the lowlands. Under each shot forth
Two mighty wings, enormous as became
A bird so vast. Sails never such I saw
Outstretch'd on the wide sea. No plumes had they,
But were in texture like a bat; and these
He flapp'd i' th' air, that from him issued still
Three winds, wherewith Cocytus to its depth
Was frozen. At six eyes he wept: the tears
Adown three chins distill'd with bloody foam.
At every mouth his teeth a sinner champ'd,
Bruised as with ponderous engine; so that three
Were in this guise tormented. But far more
Than from that gnawing, was the foremost pang'd
By the fierce rending, whence oft-times the back
Was stript of all its skin. "That upper spirit,
Who hath worst punishment," so spake my guide,

60

"Is Judas, he that hath his head within
And plies the feet without. Of th' other two,
Whose heads are under, from the murky jaw
Who hangs, is Brutus:[1] lo! how he doth writhe
And speaks not. The other, Cassius, that appears
So large of limb. But night now reascends;
And it is time for parting. All is seen."
I clipp'd him round the neck; for so he bade:
And noting time and place, he, when the wings
Enough were oped, caught fast the shaggy sides,
And down from pile to pile descending stepp'd
Between the thick fell and the jagged ice.
Soon as he reach'd the point, whereat the thigh
Upon the swelling of the haunches turns,
My leader there, with pain and struggling hard,
Turn'd round his head where his feet stood before,
And grappled at the fell as one who mounts;
That into Hell methought we turn'd again.
"Expect that by such stairs as these," thus spake
The teacher, panting like a man forespent,
"We must depart from evil so extreme:"
Then at a rocky opening issued forth,
And placed me on the brink to sit, next join'd
With wary step my side. I raised mine eyes,
Believing that I Lucifer should see
Where he was lately left, but saw him now
With legs held upward. Let the grosser sort,
Who see not what the point was I had past,
Bethink them if sore toil oppress'd me then.
"Arise," my master cried, "upon thy feet.
The way is long, and much uncouth the road;
And now within one hour and a half of noon[2]
The sun returns." It was no palace-hall

[1] "Brutus." Landino struggles to extricate Brutus from the unworthy lot which is here assigned him. He maintains that by Brutus and Cassius are not meant the individuals known by those names, but any who put a lawful monarch to death. Yet if Cæsar was such, the conspirators might be regarded as deserving of their doom. If Dante, however, believed Brutus to have been actuated by evil motives in putting Cæsar to death, the excellence of the patriot's character in other respects would only have aggravated his guilt in that particular.

[2] The Poet uses the Hebrew manner of computing the day, according to which the third hour answers to our twelve o'clock at noon.

Lofty and luminous wherein we stood,
But natural dungeon where ill-footing was
And scant supply of light. "Ere from the abyss
I separate," thus when risen I began:
"My guide! vouchsafe few words to set me free
From error's thraldom. Where is now the ice?
How standeth he in posture thus reversed?
And how from eve to morn in space so brief
Hath the sun made his transit?" He in few
Thus answering spake: "Thou deemest thou art still
On the other side the centre, where I grasp'd
The abhorred worm that boreth through the world.
Thou wast on the other side, so long as I
Descended; when I turn'd, thou didst o'erpass
That point, to which from every part is dragg'd
All heavy substance. Thou art now arrived
Under the hemisphere opposed to that,
Which the great continent doth overspread,
And underneath whose canopy expired
The Man, that was born sinless and so lived.
Thy feet are planted on the smallest sphere,
Whose other aspect is Judecca. Morn
Here rises, when there evening sets: and he,
Whose shaggy pile we scaled, yet standeth fix'd,
As at the first. On this part he fell down
From Heaven; and th' earth here prominent before,
Through fear of him did veil her with the sea,
And to our hemisphere retired. Perchance,
To shun him, was the vacant space left here,
By what of firm land on this side appears,[3]
That sprang aloof." There is a place beneath,
From Belzebub as distant, as extends
The vaulted tomb;[4] discover'd not by sight,
But by the sound of brooklet, that descends
This way along the hollow of a rock,
Which, as it winds with no precipitous course,
The wave hath eaten. By that hidden way
My guide and I did enter, to return

[3] The mountain of Purgatory.
[4] "The vaulted tomb" ("La tomba"). This word is used to express the whole depth of the infernal region.

To the fair world: and heedless of repose
We climb'd, he first, I following his steps,
Till on our view the beautiful lights of Heaven
Dawn'd through a circular opening in the cave:
Thence issuing we again beheld the stars.

Scholar, poet, and civil servant, John Milton (1608-1674) did not merely observe the events of his turbulent era; he was part of them. After the death of Oliver Cromwell in 1658, whom he served as Latin secretary, Milton devoted himself to his poetry, and in particular to *Paradise Lost* which was published in 1667. An imaginative retelling of the story of Adam and Eve as recorded in the book of Genesis, *Paradise Lost* comprises twelve books. The following selection, book nine, is a dramatization of the climactic fall of man and its aftermath.

PARADISE LOST

BOOK IX.

THE ARGUMENT.

Satan, having compassed the earth, with meditated guile returns, as a mist, by night into Paradise; enters into the serpent sleeping. Adam and Eve in the morning go forth to their labours, which Eve proposes to divide in several places, each labouring apart : Adam consents not, alleging the danger, lest that enemy of whom they were forewarned should attempt her, found alone : Eve, loath to be thought not circumspect or firm enough, urges her going apart, the rather desirous to make trial of her strength ; Adam at last yields : the serpent finds her alone : his subtle approach, first gazing, then speaking ; with much flattery extolling Eve above all other creatures. Eve, wondering to hear the serpent speak, asks how he attained to human speech, and such understanding, not till now ; the serpent answers, that by tasting of a certain tree in the garden he attained both to speech and reason, till then void of both : Eve requires him to bring her to that tree, and finds it to be the tree of knowledge forbidden : the serpent, now grown bolder, with many wiles and arguments, induces her at length to eat : she, pleased with the taste, deliberates a while whether to impart thereof to Adam or not ; at last brings him of the fruit ; relates what persuaded her to eat thereof : Adam, at first amazed, but perceiving her lost, resolves, through vehemence of love, to perish with her ; and, extenuating the trespass, eats also of the fruit : the effects thereof in them both ; they seek to cover their nakedness ; then fall to variance and accusation of one another.

No more of talk where God or Angel guest
With Man, as with his friend, familiar us'd
'To sit indulgent, and with him partake
Rural repast; permitting him the while
Venial discourse unblam'd.   I now must change
Those notes to tragick; foul distrust and breach
Disloyal on the part of Man, revolt,
And disobedience: on the part of Heaven
Now alienated, distance and distaste,
Anger and just rebuke, and judgement given,
That brought into this world a world of woe,

Sin and her shadow Death, and Misery,
Death's harbinger: Sad task! yet argument
Not less but more heroick than the wrath
Of stern Achilles on his foe pursued
Thrice fugitive about Troy wall; or rage
Of Turnus for Lavinia disespoused;
Or Neptune's ire, or Juno's, that so long
Perplex'd the Greek, and Cytherea's son;
If answerable style I can obtain
Of my celestial patroness, who deigns
Her nightly visitation unimplor'd,
And dictates to me slumbering; or inspires
Easy my unpremeditated verse:
Since first this subject for heroick song
Pleas'd me long choosing, and beginning late;
Not sedulous by nature to indite
Wars, hitherto the only argument
Heroick deem'd; chief mastery to dissect
With long and tedious havoc, fabled knights
In battles feign'd: the better fortitude
Of patience and heroick martyrdom
Unsung; or to describe races and games,
Or tilting furniture, imblazon'd shields,
Impresses quaint, caparisons and steeds,
Bases and tinsel trappings, gorgeous knights
At joust and tournament; then marshall'd feast
Served up in hall with sewers and seneschals;
The skill of artifice or office mean,
Not that which justly gives heroick name
To person or to poem. Me, of these
Nor skill'd nor studious, higher argument
Remains; sufficient of itself to raise

That name, unless an age too late, or cold
Climate, or years, damp my intended wing
Depress'd; and much they may, if all be mine,
Not hers, who brings it nightly to my ear.
　　The sun was sunk, and after him the star
Of Hesperus, whose office is to bring
Twilight upon the earth, short arbiter
'Twixt day and night, and now from end to end
Night's hemisphere had veil'd the horizon round:
When Satan, who late fled before the threats
Of Gabriel out of Eden, now improv'd
In meditated fraud and malice, bent
On Man's destruction, maugre what might hap
Of heavier on himself, fearless return'd.
By night he fled, and at midnight return'd
From compassing the earth; cautious of day,
Since Uriel, regent of the sun, descried
His entrance, and forewarn'd the Cherubim
That kept their watch; thence full of anguish driven,
The space of seven continued nights he rode
With darkness; thrice the equinoctial line
He circled; four times cross'd the car of night
From pole to pole, traversing each colure;
On the eighth return'd; and on the coast averse
From entrance or Cherubic watch, by stealth
Found unsuspected way.　There was a place,
Now not, though sin, not time, first wrought the change,
Where Tigris, at the foot of Paradise,
Into a gulf shot under ground, till part
Rose up a fountain by the tree of life:
In with the river sunk and with it rose
Satan, involved in rising mist; then sought
Where to lie hid: sea he had search'd, and land,

From Eden over Pontus and the pool
Mæotis, up beyond the river Ob ;
Downward as far antarctick : and in length,
West from Orontes to the ocean barr'd
At Darien;[3] thence to the land where flows
Ganges and Indus : Thus the orb he roam'd
With narrow search; and with inspection deep
Consider'd every creature, which of all
Most opportune might serve his wiles; and found
The Serpent subtlest beast of all the field.
Him after long debate, irresolute
Of thoughts revolv'd, his final sentence chose
Fit vessel, fittest imp of fraud, in whom
To enter, and his dark suggestions hide
From sharpest sight; for, in the wily snake
Whatever sleights, none would suspicious mark,
As from his wit and native subtlety
Proceeding; which, in other beasts observ'd,
Doubt might beget of diabolick power
Active within, beyond the sense of brute.
Thus he resolved, but first from inward grief
His bursting passion into plaints thus pour'd.

O Earth, how like to Heaven, if not preferr'd
More justly, seat worthier of gods, as built
With second thoughts, reforming what was old !
For what god, after better, worse would build ?
Terrestrial Heaven, danced round by other Heavens
That shine, yet bear their bright officious lamps,
Light above light, for thee alone, as seems,
In thee concentering all their precious beams
Of sacred influence ! As God in heaven
Is center, yet extends to all ; so thou,

Centering, receiv'st from all those orbs: in thee,
Not in themselves, all their known virtue appears
Productive in herb, plant, and nobler birth
Of creatures animate with gradual life
Of growth, sense, reason, all summ'd up in Man.
With what delight could I have walk'd thee round,
If I could joy in aught, sweet interchange
Of hill, and valley, rivers, woods, and plains,
Now land, now sea, and shores with forest crown'd,
Rocks, dens, and caves! But I in none of these
Find place or refuge; and the more I see
Pleasures about me, so much more I feel
Torment within me, as from the hateful siege
Of contraries; all good to me becomes
Bane, and in Heaven much worse would be my state.
But neither here seek I, no, nor in Heaven
To dwell, unless by mastering Heaven's Supreme;
Nor hope to be myself less miserable
By what I seek, but others to make such
As I, though thereby worse to me redound:
For only in destroying I find ease
To my relentless thoughts; and, him destroyed,
Or won to what may work his utter loss,
For whom all this was made, all this will soon
Follow, as to him link'd in weal or woe;
In woe then; that destruction wide may range:
To me shall be the glory sole among
The infernal Powers, in one day to have marr'd
What he, Almighty styled, six nights and days
Continued making; and who knows how long
Before had been contriving? though perhaps
Not longer than since I, in one night, freed
From servitude inglorious well nigh half
The Angelick name, and thinner left the throng

Of his adorers: He, to be avenged,
And to repair his numbers thus impair'd,
Whether such virtue spent of old now fail'd
More Angels to create, if they at least
Are his created, or, to spite us more,
Determin'd to advance into our room
A creature form'd of earth, and him endow,
Exalted from so base original,
With heavenly spoils, our spoils: What he decreed,
He effected; Man he made, and for him built
Magnificent this world, and earth his seat,
Him lord pronounc'd; and, O indignity!
Subjected to his service angel-wings,
And flaming ministers to watch and tend
Their earthly charge: Of these the vigilance
I dread; and, to elude, thus wrapt in mist
Of midnight vapour glide obscure, and pry
In every bush and brake, where hap may find
The serpent sleeping; in whose mazy folds
To hide me, and the dark intent I bring.
O foul descent! that I, who erst contended
With gods to sit the highest, am now constrain'd
Into a beast; and, mix'd with bestial slime,
This essence to incarnate and imbrute,
That to the highth of Deity aspir'd!
But what will not ambition and revenge
Descend to?   Who aspires, must down as low
As high he soar'd; obnoxious, first or last,
To basest things.   Revenge, at first though sweet,
Bitter ere long, back on itself recoils:
Let it; I reck not, so it light well aim'd,
Since higher I fall short, on him who next
Provokes my envy, this new favourite
Of Heaven, this man of clay, son of despite,

Whom, us the more to spite, his Maker rais'd
From dust: Spite then with spite is best repaid.
   So saying, through each thicket dank or dry,
Like a black mist low-creeping, he held on
His midnight-search, where soonest he might find
The serpent: him fast sleeping soon he found
In labyrinth of many a round self-roll'd,
His head the midst, well stored with subtile wiles:
Not yet in horrid shade or dismal den,
Nor nocent yet; but, on the grassy herb,
Fearless unfear'd he slept: in at his mouth
The Devil enter'd; and his brutal sense,
In heart or head, possessing, soon inspir'd
With act intelligential; but his sleep
Disturb'd not, waiting close the approach of morn.
Now, when as sacred light began to dawn
In Eden on the humid flowers, that breath'd
Their morning incense, when all things that breathe,
From the Earth's great altar send up silent praise
To the Creator, and his nostrils fill
With grateful smell, forth came the human pair,
And join'd their vocal worship to the quire
Of creatures wanting voice; that done, partake
The season, prime for sweetest scents and airs:
Then commune how that day they best may ply
Their growing work: for much their work outgrew
The hands' despatch of two gardening so wide;
And Eve first to her husband thus began:
   Adam, well may we labour still to dress
This garden, still to tend plant, herb, and flower,
Our pleasant task enjoin'd; but, till more hands
Aid us, the work under our labour grows,
Luxurious by restraint; what we by day
Lop overgrown, or prune, or prop, or bind,

One night or two with wanton growth derides
Tending to wild.   Thou therefore now advise,
Or bear what to my mind first thoughts present:
Let us divide our labours; thou where choice
Leads thee, or where most needs, whether to wind
The woodbine round this arbour, or direct
The clasping ivy where to climb; while I,
In yonder spring of roses intermix'd
With myrtle, find what to redress till noon:
For, while so near each other thus all day
Our task we choose, what wonder if so near
Looks intervene and smiles, or objects new
Casual discourse draw on; which intermits
Our day's work, brought to little, though begun
Early, and the hour of supper comes unearn'd:
    To whom mild answer Adam thus return'd.
Sole Eve, associate sole, to me beyond
Compare above all living creatures dear!
Well hast thou motion'd, well thy thoughts employ'd
How we might best fulfil the work which here
God hath assign'd us; nor of me shalt pass
Unprais'd; for nothing lovelier can be found
In woman, than to study household good,
And good works in her husband to promote.
Yet not so strictly hath our Lord impos'd
Labour, as to debar us when we need
Refreshment, whether food or talk between,
Food of the mind, or this sweet intercourse
Of looks and smiles; for smiles from reason flow,
To brute denied, and are of love the food;
Love, not the lowest end of human life.
For not to irksome toil, but to delight,
He made us, and delight to reason join'd.
These paths and bowers doubt not but our joint hands

Will keep from wilderness with ease, as wide
As we need walk, till younger hands ere long
Assist us: But, if much converse perhaps
Thee satiate, to short absence I could yield;
For solitude sometimes is best society,
And short retirement urges sweet return.
But other doubt possesses me, lest harm
Befall thee sever'd from me; for thou know'st
What hath been warn'd us, what malicious foe
Envying our happiness, and of his own
Despairing, seeks to work us woe and shame
By sly assault; and somewhere nigh at hand
Watches, no doubt, with greedy hope to find,
His wish and best advantage, us asunder ;
Hopeless to circumvent us join'd, where each
To other speedy aid might lend at need:
Whether his first design be to withdraw
Our feälty from God, or to disturb
Conjugal love, than which perhaps no bliss
Enjoy'd by us excites his envy more;
Or this, or worse, leave not the faithful side
That gave thee being, still shades thee, and protects.
The wife, where danger or dishonour lurks,
Safest and seemliest by her husband stays,
Who guards her, or with her the worst endures.
  To whom the virgin majesty of Eve,
As one who loves, and some unkindness meets,
With sweet austere composure thus replied.
  Offspring of Heaven and Earth, and all Earth's lord!
That such an enemy we have, who seeks
Our ruin, both by thee inform'd I learn,
And from the parting Angel overheard,
As in a shady nook I stood behind,
Just then return'd at shut of evening flowers.

But that thou shouldst my firmness therefore doubt
To God or thee, because we have a foe
May tempt it, I expected not to hear.
His violence thou fear'st not, being such
As we, not capable of death or pain,
Can either not receive, or can repel.
His fraud is then thy fear; which plain infers
Thy equal fear, that my firm faith and love
Can by his fraud be shaken or seduc'd;
Thoughts, which how found they harbour in thy breast,
Adam, misthought of her to thee so dear?
   To whom with healing words Adam replied.
Daughter of God and Man, immortal Eve!
For such thou art; from sin and blame entire:
Not diffident of thee do I dissuade
Thy absence from my sight, but to avoid
The attempt itself, intended by our foe.
For he who tempts, though in vain, at least asperses
The tempted with dishonour foul; suppos'd
Not incorruptible of faith, not proof
Against temptation: Thou thyself with scorn
And anger wouldst resent the offer'd wrong,
Though ineffectual found: misdeem not then,
If such affront I labour to avert
From thee alone, which on us both at once
The enemy, though bold, will hardly dare;
Or daring, first on me the assault shall light.
Nor thou his malice and false guile contemn;
Subtle he needs must be who could seduce
Angels; nor think superfluous others' aid.
I from the influence of thy looks receive
Access in every virtue; in thy sight
More wise, more watchful, stronger if need were
Of outward strength; while shame, thou looking on,

Shame to be overcome or overreach'd,
Would utmost vigour raise, and rais'd unite.
Why shouldst not thou like sense within thee feel
When I am present, and thy trial choose
With me, best witness of thy virtue tried?

    So spake domestick Adam in his care
And matrimonial love; but Eve, who thought
Less áttributed to her faith sincere,
Thus her reply with accent sweet renew'd.

    If this be our condition, thus to dwell
In narrow circuit, straiten'd by a foe,
Subtle or violent, we not endued
Single with like defence, wherever met;
How are we happy, still in fear of harm?
But harm precedes not sin: only our foe,
Tempting, affronts us with his foul esteem
Of our integrity: his foul esteem
Sticks no dishonour on our front, but turns
Foul on himself; then wherefore shunn'd or fear'd
By us? who rather double honour gain
From his surmise prov'd false; find peace within,
Favour from Heaven, our witness, from the event.
And what is faith, love, virtue, unassay'd
Alone, without exteriour help sustain'd?
Let us not then suspect our happy state
Left so imperfect by the Maker wise,
As not secure to single or combin'd.
Frail is our happiness, if this be so,
And Eden were no Eden, thus expos'd.

    To whom thus Adam fervently replied.
O Woman, best are all'things as the will
Of God ordain'd them: His creating hand
Nothing imperfect or deficient left
Of all that he created, much less Man,

Or aught that might his happy state secure,
Secure from outward force: within himself
The danger lies, yet lies within his power:
Against his will he can receive no harm.
But God left free the will; for what obeys
Reason, is free; and Reason he made right,
But bid her well beware, and still erect;
Lest, by some fair-appearing good surpris'd,
She dictate false; and misinform the will
To do what God expressly hath forbid.
Not then mistrust, but tender love, enjoins
That I should mind thee oft; and mind thou me.
Firm we subsist, yet possible to swerve;
Since Reason not impossibly may meet
Some specious object by the foe suborn'd,
And fall into deception unaware,
Not keeping strictest watch, as she was warn'd.
Seek not temptation then, which to avoid
Were better, and most likely if from me
Thou sever not :   Trial will come unsought.
Wouldst thou approve thy constancy, approve
First thy obedience; the other who can know,
Not seeing thee attempted, who attest ?
But if thou think, trial unsought may find
Us both securer than thus warn'd thou seem'st,
Go, for thy stay, not free, absents thee more;
Go in thy native innocence; rely
On what thou hast of virtue; summon all!
For God towards thee hath done his part, do thine.
    So spake the patriarch of mankind; but Eve
Persisted; yet submiss, though last, replied:
    With thy permission, then, and thus forewarn'd,
Chiefly by what thy own last reasoning words
Touch'd only; that our trial, when least sought,

May find us both perhaps far less prepar'd,
The willinger I go, nor much expect
A foe so proud will first the weaker seek;
So bent, the more shall shame him his repulse.
    Thus saying, from her husband's hand her hand
Soft she withdrew; and, like a Wood-Nymph light,
Oread or Dryad, or of Delia's train,
Betook her to the groves; but Delia's self
In gait surpass'd, and goddess-like deport,
Though not as she with bow and quiver arm'd,
But with such gardening tools as Art yet rude,
Guiltless of fire, had form'd, or Angels brought.
To Pales, or Pomona, thus adorn'd,
Likest she seem'd Pomona when she fled
Vertumnus, or to Ceres in her prime,
Yet virgin of Proserpina from Jove.
Her long with ardent look his eye pursued
Delighted, but desiring more her stay.
Oft he to her his charge of quick return
Repeated; she to him as oft engag'd
To be return'd by noon amid the bower,
And all things in best order to invite
Noontide repast, or afternoon's repose.
O much deceiv'd, much failing, hapless Eve,
Of thy presumed return! event perverse!
Thou never from that hour in Paradise
Found'st either sweet repast or sound repose;
Such ambush, hid among sweet flowers and shades,
Waited with hellish rancour imminent
To intercept thy way, or send thee back,
Despoil'd of innocence, of faith, of bliss.
For now, and since first break of dawn, the Fiend,

Mere serpent in appearance, forth was come;
And on his quest, where likeliest he might find
The only two of mankind, but in them
The whole included race, his purpos'd prey,
In bower and field he sought, where any tuft
Of grove or garden plot more pleasant lay,
Their tendance, or plantation for delight;
By fountain or by shady rivulet
He sought them both, but wish'd his hap might find
Eve separate; he wish'd, but not with hope
Of what so seldom chanc'd; when to his wish,
Beyond his hope, Eve separate he spies,
Veil'd in a cloud of fragrance, where she stood,
Half spied, so thick the roses bushing round
About her glow'd, oft stooping to support
Each flower of slender stalk, whose head, though gay
Carnation, purple, azure, or speck'd with gold,
Hung drooping unsustain'd; them she upstays
Gently with myrtle band, mindless the while
Herself, though fairest unsupported flower,
From her best prop so far, and storm so nigh.
Nearer he drew, and many a walk travérs'd
Of stateliest covert, cedar, pine, or palm;
Then voluble and bold, now hid, now seen,
Among thick-woven arborets, and flowers
Imborder'd on each bank, the hand of Eve:
Spot more delicious than those gardens feign'd,
Or of revived Adonis, or renown'd
Alcinous host of old Laertes' son;
Or that, not mystic, where the sapient king
Held dalliance with his fair Egyptian spouse.

Much he the place admir'd, the person more.
As one who long in populous city pent,
Where houses thick and sewers annoy the air,
Forth issuing on a summer's morn, to breathe
Among the pleasant villages and farms
Adjoin'd, from each thing met conceives delight;
The smell of grain, or tedded grass, or kine,
Or dairy, each rural sight, each rural sound;
If chance, with nymph-like step, fair virgin pass,
What pleasing seem'd, for her now pleases more;
She most, and in her look sums all delight:
Such pleasure took the Serpent to behold
This flowery plat, the sweet recess of Eve
Thus early, thus alone: Her heavenly form
Angelick, but more soft and feminine,
Her graceful innocence, her every air
Of gesture or least action, overaw'd
His malice, and with rapine sweet bereav'd
His fierceness of the fierce intent it brought:
That space the Evil one abstracted stood
From his own evil, and for the time remain'd
Stupidly good; of enmity disarm'd,
Of guile, of hate, of envy, of revenge:
But the hot Hell that always in him burns,
Though in mid Heaven, soon ended his delight,
And tortures him now more, the more he sees
Of pleasure not for him ordain'd; then soon
Fierce hate he recollects, and all his thoughts
Of mischief, gratulating, thus excites.

 Thoughts, whither have ye led me! with what sweet
Compulsion thus transported, to forget
What hither brought us! hate, not love; nor hope
Of Paradise for Hell, hope here to taste
Of pleasure; but all pleasure to destroy,

Save what is in destroying; other joy
To me is lost.   Then, let me not let pass
Occasion which now smiles; behold alone
The woman, opportune to all attempts,
Her husband, for I view far round, not nigh,
Whose higher intellectual more I shun,
And strength, of courage haughty, and of limb
Heroick built, though of terrestrial mould;
Foe not informidable! exempt from wound,
I not; so much hath Hell debas'd, and pain
Enfeebled me, to what I was in Heaven.
She fair, divinely fair, fit love for gods!
Not terrible, though terrour be in love
And beauty, not approach'd by stronger hate,
Hate stronger under show of love well feign'd;
The way which to her ruin now I tend.

So spake the enemy of mankind enclosed
In serpent, inmate bad! and toward Eve
Address'd his way: not with indented wave,
Prone on the ground, as since; but on his rear,
Circular base of rising folds that tower'd
Fold above fold, a surging maze! his head
Crested aloft, and carbuncle his eyes;
With burnish'd neck of verdant gold, erect
Amidst his circling spires, that on the grass
Floated redundant: pleasing was his shape
And lovely; never since of serpent-kind
Lovelier; not those that in Illyria changed
Hermione and Cadmus, or the god
In Epidaurus;   nor to which transform'd

Ammonian Jove, or Capitoline, was seen;
He with Olympias; this with her who bore
Scipio, the highth of Rome.   With tract oblique
At first, as one who sought access, but fear'd
To interrupt, sidelong he works his way.
As when a ship, by skilful steersman wrought
Nigh river's mouth, or foreland, where the wind
Veers oft, as oft so steers, and shifts her sail:
So varied he, and of his tortuous train
Curl'd many a wanton wreath in sight of Eve,
To lure her eye; she, busied, heard the sound
Of rustling leaves, but minded not, as us'd
To such disport before her through the field,
From every beast; more duteous at her call
Than at Circean call the herd disguis'd.
He, bolder now, uncall'd before her stood,
But as in gaze admiring: oft he bow'd
His turret crest, and sleek enamell'd neck,
Fawning ; and lick'd the ground whereon she trod.
His gentle dumb expression turn'd at length
The eye of Eve to mark his play; he, glad
Of her attention gain'd, with serpent-tongue
Organic, or impulse of vocal air,
His fraudulent temptation thus began:
    Wonder not, sovran Mistress, if perhaps
Thou canst, who art sole wonder! much less arm
Thy looks, the Heaven of mildness, with disdain,
Displeas'd that I approach thee thus, and gaze
Insatiate; I thus single; nor have fear'd
Thy awful brow, more awful thus retir'd.
Fairest resemblance of thy Maker fair,
Thee all things living gaze on, all things thine

By gift, and thy celestial beauty adore
With ravishment beheld! there best beheld,
Where universally admir'd; but here
In this enclosure wild, these beasts among,
Beholders rude, and shallow to discern
Half what in thee is fair, one man except,
Who sees thee? (and what is one?) who should be seen
A goddess among gods, ador'd and serv'd
By Angels numberless, thy daily train.

So gloz'd the Tempter, and his proem tun'd:
Into the heart of Eve his words made way,
Though at the voice much marvelling; at length,
Not unamaz'd, she thus in answer spake.

What may this mean? language of man pronounc'd
By tongue of brute, and human sense express'd?
The first, at least, of these I thought denied
To beasts; whom God, on their creation-day,
Created mute to all articulate sound:
The latter I demur; for in their looks
Much reason, and in their actions, oft appears.
Thee, Serpent, subtlest beast of all the field
I knew, but not with human voice endued;
Redouble then this miracle, and say
How cam'st thou speakable of mute, and how
To me so friendly grown above the rest
Of brutal kind, that daily are in sight?
Say, for such wonder claims attention due.

To whom the guileful Tempter thus replied.
Empress of this fair world, resplendent Eve!
Easy to me it is to tell thee all
What thou command'st; and right thou should'st be obey'd:
I was at first as other beasts that graze
The trodden herb, of abject thoughts and low,
As was my food; nor aught but food discern'd

82

Or sex, and apprehended nothing high:
Till, on a day roving the field, I chanc'd
A goodly tree far distant to behold,
Loaden with fruit of fairest colours mix'd,
Ruddy and gold: I nearer drew to gaze;
When from the boughs a savoury odour blown,
Grateful to appetite, more pleas'd my sense
Than smell of sweetest fennel, or the teats
Of ewe or goat dropping with milk at even,
Unsuck'd of lamb or kid, that tend their play.
To satisfy the sharp desire I had
Of tasting those fair apples, I resolv'd
Not to defer; hunger and thirst at once,
Powerful persuaders, quicken'd at the scent
Of that alluring fruit, urg'd me so keen.
About the mossy trunk I wound me soon;
For, high from ground, the branches would require
Thy utmost reach or Adam's: Round the tree
All other beasts that saw, with like desire
Longing and envying stood, but could not reach.
Amid the tree now got, where plenty hung
Tempting so nigh, to pluck and eat my fill
I spar'd not; for, such pleasure till that hour,
At feed or fountain, never had I found.
Sated at length, ere long I might perceive
Strange alteration in me, to degree
Of reason in my inward power; and speech
Wanted not long; though to this shape retain'd.
Thenceforth to speculations high or deep
I turn'd my thoughts, and with capacious mind
Consider'd all things visible in Heaven,
Or Earth, or Middle; all things fair and good:
But all that fair and good in thy divine
Semblance, and in thy beauty's heavenly ray,

United I beheld; no fair to thine
Equivalent or second; which compell'd
Me thus, though importune perhaps, to come
And gaze, and worship thee of right declar'd
Sovran of creatures, universal Dame!
 So talk'd the spirited sly Snake; and Eve,
Yet more amaz'd, unwary thus replied.
 Serpent, thy overpraising leaves in doubt
The virtue of that fruit, in thee first prov'd:
But say, where grows the tree? from hence how far?
For many are the trees of God that grow
In Paradise, and various, yet unknown
To us; in such abundance lies our choice,
As leaves a greater store of fruit untouch'd,
Still hanging incorruptible, till men
Grow up to their provision, and more hands
Help to disburden Nature of her birth.
 To whom the wily Adder, blithe and glad.
Empress, the way is ready, and not long;
Beyond a row of myrtles, on a flat,
Fast by a fountain, one small thicket past
Of blowing myrrh and balm: if thou accept
My conduct, I can bring thee thither soon.
 Lead then, said Eve. He, leading, swiftly roll'd
In tangles, and made intricate seem straight,
To mischief swift. Hope elevates, and joy
Brightens his crest; as when a wandering fire,
Compact of unctuous vapour, which the night
Condenses, and the cold environs round,
Kindled through agitation to a flame,
Which oft, they say, some evil Spirit attends,
Hovering and blazing with delusive light,
Misleads the amaz'd night wanderer from his way
To bogs and mires, and oft through pond or pool,

There swallow'd up and lost, from succour far.
So glister'd the dire Snake, and into fraud
Led Eve, our credulous mother, to the tree
Of prohibition, root of all our woe;
Which, when she saw, thus to her guide she spake.
    Serpent, we might have spared our coming hither,
Fruitless to me, though fruit be here to excess,
The credit of whose virtue rest with thee;
Wonderous indeed, if cause of such effects.
But of this tree we may not taste nor touch;
God so commanded, and left that command
Sole daughter of his voice; the rest, we live
Law to ourselves; our reason is our law.
    To whom the Tempter guilefully replied.
Indeed? hath God then said that of the fruit
Of all these garden trees ye shall not eat,
Yet lords declared of all in earth or air?
To whom thus Eve, yet sinless. Of the fruit
Of each tree in the garden we may eat;
But of the fruit of this fair tree amidst
The garden, God hath said, Ye shall not eat
Thereof, nor shall ye touch it, lest ye die.
    She scarce had said, though brief, when now more bold
The Tempter, but with show of zeal and love
To man, and indignation at his wrong,
New part puts on; and, as to passion mov'd,
Fluctuates disturb'd, yet comely and in act
Rais'd, as of some great matter to begin.
As when of old some orator renown'd,
In Athens or free Rome, where eloquence
Flourish'd, since mute! to some great cause address'd,
Stood in himself collected; while each part,
Motion, each act, won audience ere the tongue;
Sometimes in highth began, as no delay

Of preface brooking, through his zeal of right:
So standing, moving, or to highth upgrown,
The Tempter, all impassion'd, thus began.

   O sacred, wise, and wisdom-giving Plant,
Mother of science! now I feel thy power
Within me clear; not only to discern
Things in their causes, but to trace the ways
Of highest agents, deem'd however wise.
Queen of this universe! do not believe
Those rigid threats of death: ye shall not die:
How should you? By the fruit? it gives you life
To knowledge; by the threatener? look on me,
Me, who have touch'd and tasted; yet both live,
And life more perfect have attain'd than Fate
Meant me, by venturing higher than my lot.
Shall that be shut to Man, which to the Beast
Is open? or will God incense his ire
For such a petty trespass? and not praise
Rather your dauntless virtue, whom the pain
Of death denounc'd, whatever thing death be,
Deterr'd not from achieving what might lead
To happier life, knowledge of good and evil;
Of good, how just? of evil, if what is evil
Be real, why not known, since easier shunn'd?
God therefore cannot hurt ye, and be just;
Not just, not God; not fear'd then, nor obey'd:
Your fear itself of death removes the fear.
Why then was this forbid? Why, but to awe?
Why, but to keep ye low and ignorant,
His worshippers? He knows that in the day
Ye eat thereof, your eyes, that seem so clear,
Yet are but dim, shall perfectly be then
Open'd and clear'd, and ye shall be as gods,
Knowing both good and evil, as they know.

That ye shall be as gods, since I as man,
Internal man, is but proportion meet;
I, of brute, human; ye, of human, gods.
So ye shall die, perhaps, by putting off
Human, to put on gods; death to be wish'd,
Though threaten'd, which no worse than this can bring.
And what are gods, that man may not become
As they, participating God-like food?
The gods are first, and that advantage use
On our belief, that all from them proceeds:
I question it; for this fair earth I see,
Warm'd by the sun, producing every kind,
Them, nothing: if they all things, who enclos'd
Knowledge of good and evil in this tree,
That whoso eats thereof forthwith attains
Wisdom without their leave? and wherein lies
The offence, that man should thus attain to know?
What can your knowledge hurt him, or this tree
Impart against his will, if all be his?
Or is it envy? and can envy dwell
In heavenly breasts? These, these, and many more
Causes, import your need of this fair fruit.
Goddess humane, reach then, and freely taste.
　　He ended; and his words, replete with guile,
Into her heart too easy entrance won:
Fix'd on the fruit she gaz'd, which to behold
Might tempt alone; and in her ears the sound
Yet rung of his persuasive words, impregn'd
With reason, to her seeming, and with truth:
Meanwhile the hour of noon drew on, and wak'd
An eager appetite, raised by the smell
So savoury of that fruit, which with desire,
Inclinable now grown to touch or taste,

Solicited her longing eye; yet first
Pausing awhile, thus to herself she mus'd.
    Great are thy virtues, doubtless, best of fruits,
Though kept from man, and worthy to be admir'd;
Whose taste, too long forborne, at first assay
Gave elocution to the mute, and taught
The tongue not made for speech to speak thy praise:
Thy praise he also, who forbids thy use
Conceals not from us, naming thee the tree
Of knowledge, knowledge both of good and evil;
Forbids us then to taste! but his forbidding
Commends thee more, while it infers the good
By thee communicated, and our want:
For good unknown, sure is not had; or, had
And yet unknown, is as not had at all.
In plain then, what forbids he but to know,
Forbids us good, forbids us to be wise?
Such prohibitions bind not. But, if death
Bind us with after-bands, what profits then
Our inward freedom? In the day we eat
Of this fair fruit, our doom is, we shall die!
How dies the Serpent? he hath eat'n and lives,
And knows, and speaks, and reasons, and discerns,
Irrational till then. For us alone
Was death invented? or to us denied
This intellectual food, for beasts reserv'd?
For beasts it seems: yet that one beast which first
Hath tasted envies not, but brings with joy
The good befallen him, author unsuspect,
Friendly to man, far from deceit or guile.
What fear I then? rather, what know to fear
Under this ignorance of good and evil,
Of God or death, of law or penalty?
Here grows the cure of all, this fruit divine,

Fair to the eye, inviting to the taste,
Of virtue to make wise: What hinders, then,
To reach, and feed at once both body and mind ?
  So saying, her rash hand in evil hour
Forth reaching to the fruit, she pluck'd, she eat!
Earth felt the wound; and Nature from her seat,
Sighing through all her works, gave signs of woe
That all was lost.   Back to the thicket slunk
The guilty Serpent; and well might; for Eve,
Intent now wholly on her taste, nought else
Regarded; such delight till then, as seem'd,
In fruit she never tasted, whether true
Or fancied so, through expectation high
Of knowledge; nor was Godhead from her thought.
Greedily she ingorg'd without restraint,
And knew not eating death: Satiate at length,
And highten'd as with wine, jocund and boon,
Thus to herself she pleasingly began.
  O sovran, virtuous, precious of all trees
In Paradise ! of operation blest
To sapience, hitherto obscur'd, infam'd,
And thy fair fruit let hang, as to no end
Created; but henceforth my early care,
Not without song, each morning, and due praise,
Shall tend thee, and the fertile burden ease
Of thy full branches offer'd free to all;
Till, dieted by thee, I grow mature
In knowledge, as the gods, who all things know;
Though others envy what they cannot give:
For had the gift been theirs, it had not here
Thus grown.   Experience, next, to thee I owe,
Best guide; not following thee, I had remain'd
In ignorance; thou open'st Wisdom's way,
And giv'st access, though secret she retire.

And I perhaps am secret: Heaven is high,
High, and remote to see from thence distinct
Each thing on Earth; and other care perhaps
May have diverted from continual watch
Our Great Forbidder, safe with all his spies
About him. But to Adam in what sort
Shall I appear? shall I to him make known
As yet my change, and give him to partake
Full happiness with me? or rather not,
But keep the odds of knowledge in my power
Without copartner? so to add what wants
In female sex, the more to draw his love,
And render me more equal; and perhaps,
A thing not undesirable, sometime
Superiour; for, inferiour, who is free?
This may be well: But what if God have seen,
And death ensue? then I shall be no more!
And Adam, wedded to another Eve,
Shall live with her enjoying, I extinct;
A death to think! Confirm'd then I resolve,
Adam shall share with me in bliss or woe:
So dear I love him, that with him all deaths
I could endure, without him live no life.
    So saying, from the tree her step she turn'd;
But first low reverence done, as to the Power
That dwelt within, whose presence had infus'd
Into the plant sciential sap, deriv'd
From nectar, drink of gods. Adam the while,
Waiting desirous her return, had wove
Of choicest flowers a garland, to adorn
Her tresses, and her rural labours crown;
As reapers oft are wont their harvest queen.
Great joy he promis'd to his thoughts, and new
Solace in her return, so long delay'd;

Yet oft his heart, divine of something ill,
Misgave him; he the faltering measure felt;
And forth to meet her went, the way she took
That morn when first they parted; by the tree
Of knowledge he must pass; there he her met,
Scarce from the tree returning; in her hand
A bough of fairest fruit, that downy smil'd,
New gather'd, and ambrosial smell diffus'd.
To him she hasted; in her face excuse
Came prologue, and apology too prompt;
Which, with bland words at will, she thus address'd.

   Hast thou not wonder'd, Adam, at my stay?
Thee I have miss'd, and thought it long, depriv'd
Thy presence; agony of love till now
Not felt, nor shall be twice; for never more
Mean I to try, what rash untried I sought,
The pain of absence from thy sight.   But strange
Hath been the cause, and wonderful to hear:
This tree is not, as we are told, a tree
Of danger tasted, nor to evil unknown
Opening the way, but of divine effect
To open eyes, and make them gods who taste;
And hath been tasted such: The serpent wise,
Or not restrain'd as we, or not obeying,
Hath eaten of the fruit; and is become,
Not dead, as we are threaten'd, but thenceforth
Endued with human voice and human sense,
Reasoning to admiration; and with me
Persuasively hath so prevail'd, that I
Have also tasted, and have also found
The effects to correspond; opener mine eyes,
Dim erst, dilated spirits, ampler heart,

And growing up to Godhead; which for thee
Chiefly I sought, without thee can despise.
For bliss, as thou hast part, to me is bliss;
Tedious, unshar'd with thee, and odious soon.
Thou therefore also taste, that equal lot
May join us, equal joy, as equal love;
Lest, thou not tasting, different degree
Disjoin us, and I then too late renounce
Deity for thee, when Fate will not permit.

    Thus Eve with countenance blithe her story told;
But in her cheek distemper flushing glow'd.
On the other side Adam, soon as he heard
The fatal trespass done by Eve, amaz'd,
Astonied stood, and blank, while horrour chill
Ran through his veins, and all his joints relax'd;
From his slack hand the garland wreath'd for Eve
Down dropt, and all the faded roses shed:
Speechless he stood and pale, till thus at length
First to himself he inward silence broke.

    O fairest of Creation, last and best
Of all God's works, Creature in whom excell'd
Whatever can to sight or thought be form'd,
Holy, divine, good, amiable, or sweet!
How art thou lost! how on a sudden lost,
Defac'd, deflower'd, and now to death devote!
Rather, how hast thou yielded to transgress
The strict forbiddence, how to violate
The sacred fruit forbidd'n! Some cursed fraud
Of enemy hath beguil'd thee, yet unknown,
And me with thee hath ruin'd; for with thee
Certain my resolution is to die:
How can I live without thee! how forego
Thy sweet convérse, and love so dearly join'd,
To live again in these wild woods forlorn!

Should God create another Eve, and I
Another rib afford, yet loss of thee
Would never from my heart: no, no! I feel
The link of Nature draw me: flesh of flesh,
Bone of my bone thou art, and from thy state
Mine never shall be parted, bliss or woe.

   So having said, as one from sad dismay
Recomforted, and after thoughts disturb'd
Submitting to what seem'd remediless,
Thus in calm mood his words to Eve he turn'd.

   Bold deed thou hast presumed, adventurous Eve,
And peril great provoked, who thus hast dar'd,
Had it been only coveting to eye
That sacred fruit, sacred to abstinence,
Much more to taste it under ban to touch.
But past who can recall, or done undo?
Not God omnipotent, nor Fate; yet so
Perhaps thou shalt not die, perhaps the fact
Is not so heinous now, foretasted fruit,
Profan'd first by the serpent, by him first
Made common, and unhallow'd, ere our taste;
Nor yet on him found deadly; he yet lives,
Lives, as thou saidst, and gains to live, as Man,
Higher degree of life; inducement strong
To us, as likely tasting to attain
Proportional ascent; which cannot be
But to be gods, or angels, demigods.
Nor can I think that God, Creator wise,
Though threatening, will in earnest so destroy
Us his prime creatures, dignified so high,
Set over all his works; which in our fall,
For us created, needs with us must fail,
Dependent made: so God shall uncreate,
Be frustrate, do, undo, and labour lose;

Not well conceiv'd of God, who, though his power
Creation could repeat, yet would be loath
Us to abolish, lest the Adversary
Triumph, and say, " Fickle their state whom God
Most favours; who can please him long?   Me first
He ruin'd, now Mankind; whom will he next?"
Matter of scorn, not to be given the Foe.
However, I with thee have fix'd my lot,
Certain to undergo like doom: If death
Consort with thee, death is to me as life;
So forcible within my heart I feel
The bond of Nature draw me to my own;
My own in thee, for what thou art is mine;
Our state cannot be sever'd; we are one,
One flesh; to lose thee were to lose myself.
    So Adam; and thus Eve to him replied.
O glorious trial of exceeding love,
Illustrious evidence, example high!
Engaging me to emulate; but, short
Of thy perfection, how shall I attain,
Adam, from whose dear side I boast me sprung,
And gladly of our union hear thee speak,
One heart, one soul in both; whereof good proof
This day affords, declaring thee resolv'd
Rather than death, or aught than death more dread,
Shall separate us, link'd in love so dear,
To undergo with me one guilt, one crime,
If any be, of tasting this fair fruit;
Whose virtue (for of good still good proceeds,
Direct, or by occasion) hath presented
This happy trial of thy love, which else
So eminently never had been known?
Were it I thought death menac'd would ensue
This my attempt, I would sustain alone

The worst, and not persuade thee, rather die
Deserted, than oblige thee with a fact
Pernicious to thy peace; chiefly assur'd
Remarkably so late of thy so true,
So faithful, love unequall'd: but I feel
Far otherwise the event; not death, but life
Augmented, open'd eyes, new hopes, new joys,
Taste so divine, that what of sweet before
Hath touch'd my sense, flat seems to this, and harsh.
On my experience, Adam, freely taste,
And fear of death deliver to the winds.

   So saying, she embrac'd him, and for joy
Tenderly wept; much won, that he his love
Had so ennobled, as of choice to incur
Divine displeasure for her sake, or death.
In recompence (for such compliance bad
Such recompence best merits), from the bough
She gave him of that fair enticing fruit
With liberal hand: he scrupled not to eat,
Against his better knowledge; not deceiv'd,
But fondly overcome with female charm.

   Earth trembled from her entrails, as again
In pangs; and Nature gave a second groan;
Sky lower'd; and, muttering thunder, some sad drops
Wept at completing of the mortal sin
Original: while Adam took no thought,
Eating his fill; nor Eve to iterate
Her former trespass fear'd, the more to soothe
Him with her lov'd society; that now,
As with new wine intoxicated both,
They swim in mirth, and fancy that they feel
Divinity within them breeding wings,
Wherewith to scorn the earth: But that false fruit

Far other operation first display'd,
Carnal desire inflaming; he on Eve
Began to cast lascivious eyes; she him
As wantonly repaid: in lust they burn:
Till Adam thus 'gan Eve to dalliance move.
    Eve, now I see thou art exact of taste,
And elegant, of sapience no small part;
Since to each meaning savour we apply,
And palate call judicious: I the praise
Yield thee, so well this day thou hast purvey'd.
Much pleasure we have lost, while we abstain'd
From this delightful fruit, nor known till now
True relish, tasting; if such pleasure be
In things to us forbidd'n, it might be wish'd
For this one tree had been forbidden ten.
But come, so well refresh'd, now let us play,
As meet is, after such delicious fare;
For never did thy beauty, since the day
I saw thee first and wedded thee, adorn'd
With all perfections, so inflame my sense
With ardour to enjoy thee, fairer now
Than ever; bounty of this virtuous tree!
    So said he, and forbore not glance or toy
Of amorous intent; well understood
Of Eve, whose eye darted contagious fire.
Her hand he seiz'd; and to a shady bank,
Thick overhead with verdant roof imbower'd,
He led her nothing loth; flowers were the couch,
Pansies, and violets, and asphodel,
And hyacinth; Earth's freshest, softest lap.
There they their fill of love and love's disport
Took largely, of their mutual guilt the seal,
The solace of their sin; till dewy sleep
Oppress'd them, wearied with their amorous play.

Soon as the force of that fallacious fruit,
That with exhilarating vapour bland
About their spirits had play'd, and inmost powers
Made err, was now exhal'd; and grosser sleep,
Bred of unkindly fumes, with conscious dreams
Incumber'd, now had left them; up they rose
As from unrest; and, each the other viewing,
Soon found their eyes how open'd, and their minds
How darken'd; innocence, that as a veil
Had shadow'd them from knowing ill, was gone;
Just confidence, and native righteousness,
And honour, from about them, naked left
To guilty Shame: he covered, but his robe
Uncover'd more. So rose the Danite strong,
Herculean Samson, from the harlot-lap
Of Philistéan Delilah, and wak'd
Shorn of his strength. They destitute and bare
Of all their virtue: Silent, and in face
Confounded, long they sat, as stricken mute;
Till Adam, though not less than Eve abash'd,
At length gave utterance to these words constrain'd.
    O Eve, in evil hour thou didst give ear
To that false worm, of whomsoever taught
To counterfeit Man's voice; true in our fall,
False in our promised rising; since our eyes
Open'd we find indeed, and find we know
Both good and evil; good lost, and evil got;
Bad fruit of knowledge, if this be to know;
Which leaves us naked thus, of honour void,
Of innocence, of faith, of purity,
Our wonted ornaments now soil'd and stain'd,
And in our faces evident the signs
Of foul concupiscence; whence evil store;
Even shame, the last of evils; of the first

97

Be sure then.—How shall I behold the face
Henceforth of God or angel, erst with joy
And rapture so oft beheld? Those heavenly shapes
Will dazzle now this earthly with their blaze,
Insufferably bright. O might I here
In solitude live savage, in some glade
Obscur'd, where highest woods, impenetrable
To star or sunlight, spread their umbrage broad
And brown as evening: Cover me, ye Pines!
Ye Cedars, with innumerable boughs
Hide me, where I may never see them more!—
But let us now, as in bad plight, devise
What best may for the present serve to hide
The parts of each from other that seem most
To shame obnoxious, and unseemliest seen;
Some tree, whose broad smooth leaves together sew'd,
And girded on our loins, may cover round
Those middle parts; that this new-comer, Shame,
There sit not, and reproach us as unclean.
  So counsell'd he, and both together went
Into the thickest wood; there soon they chose
The fig-tree; not that kind for fruit renown'd,
But such as at this day, to Indians known
In Malabar or Decan spreads her arms,
Branching so broad and long, that in the ground
The bended twigs take root, and daughters grow
About the mother tree, a pillar'd shade
High over-arch'd, and echoing walks between:
There oft the Indian herdsman, shunning heat,
Shelters in cool, and tends his pasturing herds
At loopholes cut through thickest shade: Those leaves
They gather'd, broad as Amazonian targe;
And, with what skill they had, together sew'd,

To gird their waist; vain covering, if to hide
Their guilt and dreaded shame!   O how unlike
To that first naked glory!   Such of late
Columbus found the American, so girt
With feather'd cincture; naked else, and wild
Among the trees, on isles and woody shores.
Thus fenc'd, and, as they thought, their shame in part
Cover'd, but not at rest or ease of mind,
They sat them down to weep; nor only tears
Rain'd at their eyes, but high winds worse within
Began to rise, high passions, anger, hate,
Mistrust, suspicion, discord; and shook sore
Their inward state of mind, calm region once
And full of peace, now tost and turbulent:
For Understanding rul'd not, and the Will
Heard not her lore; both in subjection now
To sensual Appetite, who, from beneath,
Usurping, over sovran Reason claim'd
Superiour sway: From thus distemper'd breast,
Adam, estrang'd in look, and alter'd style,
Speech intermitted thus to Eve renew'd.
    Would thou hadst hearken'd to my words, and stay'd
With me, as I besought thee, when that strange
Desire of wandering this unhappy morn,
I know not whence possess'd thee; we had then
Remain'd still happy; not, as now, despoil'd
Of all our good, sham'd, naked, miserable!
Let none henceforth seek needless cause to approve
The faith they owe: when earnestly they seek
Such proof, conclude they then begin to fail.
    To whom, soon mov'd with touch of blame, thus Eve.
What words have pass'd thy lips, Adam severe!
Imputest thou that to my default, or will
Of wandering, as thou call'st it, which who knows

But might as ill have happened, thou being by,
Or to thyself perhaps? Hadst thou been there,
Or here the attempt, thou couldst not have discern'd
Fraud in the serpent, speaking as he spake;
No ground of enmity between us known,
Why he should mean me ill, or seek to harm.
Was I to have never parted from thy side?
As good have grown there still a lifeless rib.
Being as I am, why didst not thou, the head,
Command me absolutely not to go,
Going into such danger, as thou saidst?
Too facile then, thou didst not much gainsay;
Nay, didst permit, approve, and fair dismiss.
Hadst thou been firm and fix'd in thy dissent,
Neither had I transgress'd, nor thou with me.
　　To whom, then first incens'd, Adam replied.
Is this the love, is this the recompence
Of mine to thee, ingrateful Eve! express'd
Immutable, when thou wert lost, not I;
Who might have lived, and 'joyed immortal bliss,
Yet willingly chose rather death with thee?
And am I now upbraided as the cause
Of thy transgressing? Not enough severe,
It seems, in thy restraint: What could I more?
I warn'd thee, I admonish'd thee, foretold
The danger, and the lurking enemy
That lay in wait; beyond this had been force;
And force upon free will hath here no place.
But confidence then bore thee on, secure
Either to meet no danger, or to find
Matter of glorious trial; and perhaps
I also err'd, in overmuch admiring
What seem'd in thee so perfect, that I thought
No evil durst attempt thee; but I rue

That errour now, which is become my crime,
And thou the accuser.   Thus it shall befall
Him who, to worth in women overtrusting,
Lets her will rule; restraint she will not brook;
And left to herself, if evil thence ensue,
She first his weak indulgence will accuse.
   Thus they in mutual accusation spent
The fruitless hours, but neither self-condemning;
And of their vain contést appeared no end.

Sophocles, OEDIPUS THE KING (Trans. by R. C. Jebb)

1. To Aristotle, *Oedipus Rex* was the perfect tragedy. Why?

2. What is the theme of *Oedipus Rex?*

3. What is Oedipus' tragic flaw?

4. When does the climax of the play occur?

5. Define dramatic irony and cite two or three examples from *Oedipus Rex.*

6. Is there a religious message in this play? Explain.

7. What aspects of the story of Oedipus led Freud to formulate his theory of the Oedipus complex?

     Sophocles (496?-406 B.C.) lived during the golden age of Greece, and is regarded as one of the world's greatest dramatists. *Oedipus Rex* is the first play in a trilogy which depicts the downfall of Oedipus, King of Thebes, his exile, his death, and the life of his daughter, Antigone. Because he considered *Oedipus Rex* the finest example of tragic drama, Aristotle used it as his example of a model tragedy in *The Poetics.*

OEDIPUS THE KING

by

SOPHOCLES

CHARACTERS IN THE PLAY

OEDIPUS, *King of Thebes*
PRIEST OF ZEUS
CREON, *brother of* JOCASTA
TEIRESIAS, *the blind prophet*
JOCASTA
FIRST MESSENGER, *a shepherd from Corinth*
A SHEPHERD, *formerly in the service of Laius*
SECOND MESSENGER, *from the house*
CHORUS OF THEBAN ELDERS

Mute Persons
A train of Suppliants (old men, youths, and children).
The children ANTIGONE *and* ISMENE, *daughters of*
OEDIPUS *and* JOCASTA

OEDIPUS THE KING

(SCENE:—*Before the royal palace of Oedipus at Thebes. In front of the large central doors there is an altar; a smaller altar stands also near each of the two side-doors. Suppliants —old men, youths, and young children—are seated on the steps of the altars. They are dressed in white tunics and cloaks,—their hair bound with white fillets. On the altars they have laid down olive-branches wreathed with fillets of wool. The* PRIEST OF ZEUS, *a venerable man, is alone standing, facing the central doors of the palace. These are now thrown open. Followed by two attendants, who place themselves on either side of the doors,* OEDIPUS *enters, in the robes of a king. For a moment he gazes silently on the groups at the altars, and then speaks.*)

OEDIPUS

MY CHILDREN, latest-born to Cadmus who was of old, why are ye set before me thus with wreathed branches of suppliants, while the city reeks with incense, rings with prayers for health and cries of woe? I deemed it unmeet, my children, to hear these things at the mouth of others, and have come hither myself, I, Oedipus renowned of all.

Tell me, then, thou venerable man—since it is thy natural part to speak for these—in what mood are ye placed here, with what dread or what desire? Be sure that I would gladly give all aid; hard of heart were I, did I not pity such suppliants as these.

PRIEST OF ZEUS

Nay, Oedipus, ruler of my land, thou seest of what years we are who beset thy altars,—some, nestlings still too tender

for far flights,—some, bowed with age, priests, as I of Zeus,
—and these, the chosen youth; while the rest of the folk sit
with wreathed branches in the market-places, and before the
two shrines of Pallas, and where Ismenus gives answer by
fire.

For the city, as thou thyself seest, is now too sorely vexed,
and can no more lift her head from beneath the angry waves
of death; a blight is on her in the fruitful blossoms of the
land, in the herds among the pastures, in the barren pangs
of women; and withal the flaming god, the malign plague,
hath swooped on us, and ravages the town; by whom the
house of Cadmus is made waste, but dark Hades rich in
groans and tears.

It is not as deeming thee ranked with gods that I and
these children are suppliants at thy hearth, but as deeming
thee first of men, both in life's common chances, and when
mortals have to do with more than man: seeing that thou
camest to the town of Cadmus, and didst quit us of the tax
that we rendered to the hard songstress; and this, though
thou knewest nothing from us that could avail thee, nor
hadst been schooled; no, by a god's aid, 'tis said and believed, didst thou uplift our life.

And now, Oedipus, king glorious in all eyes, we beseech
thee, all we suppliants, to find for us some succour, whether
by the whisper of a god thou knowest it, or haply as in the
power of man; for I see that, when men have been proved
in deeds past, the issues of their counsels, too, most often
have effect.

On, best of mortals, again uplift our State! On, guard thy
fame,—since now this land calls thee saviour for thy former
zeal; and never be it our memory of thy reign that we were
first restored and afterward cast down: nay, lift up this
State in such wise that it fall no more!

With good omen didst thou give us that past happiness;
now also show thyself the same. For if thou art to rule this
land, even as thou art now its lord, 'tis better to be lord of

men than of a waste: since neither walled town nor ship is anything, if it is void and no men dwell with thee therein.

OEDIPUS

Oh my piteous children, known, well known to me are the desires wherewith ye have come: well wot I that ye suffer all; yet, sufferers as ye are, there is not one of you whose suffering is as mine. Your pain comes on each one of you for himself alone, and for no other; but my soul mourns at once for the city, and for myself, and for thee.

So that ye rouse me not, truly, as one sunk in sleep: no, be sure that I have wept full many tears, gone many ways in wanderings of thought. And the sole remedy which, well pondering, I could find, this I have put into act. I have sent the son of Menoeceus, Creon, mine own wife's brother, to the Pythian house of Phoebus, to learn by what deed or word I might deliver this town. And already, when the lapse of days is reckoned, it troubles me what he doth; for he tarries strangely, beyond the fitting space. But when he comes, then shall I be no true man if I do not all that the god shows.

PRIEST

Nay, in season hast thou spoken; at this moment these sign to me that Creon draws near.

OEDIPUS

O king Apollo, may he come to us in the brightness of saving fortune, even as his face is bright!

PRIEST

Nay, to all seeming, he brings comfort; else would he not be coming crowned thus thickly with berry-laden bay.

OEDIPUS

We shall know soon: he is at range to hear.—(*Enter* CREON) Prince, my kinsman, son of Menoeceus, what news hast thou brought us from the god?

CREON

Good news: I tell thee that even troubles hard to bear,—
if haply they find the right issue,—will end in perfect peace.

OEDIPUS

But what is the oracle? So far, thy words make me neither
bold nor yet afraid.

CREON

If thou wouldest hear while these are nigh, I am ready to
speak; or else to go within.

OEDIPUS

Speak before all: the sorrow which I bear is for these more
than for mine own life.

CREON

With thy leave, I will tell what I heard from the god.
Phoebus our lord bids us plainly to drive out a defiling
thing, which (he saith) hath been harboured in this land, and
not to harbour it, so that it cannot be healed.

OEDIPUS

By what rite shall we cleanse us? What is the manner of
the misfortune?

CREON

By banishing a man, or by bloodshed in quittance of
bloodshed, since it is that blood which brings the tempest
on our city.

OEDIPUS

And who is the man whose fate he thus reveals?

CREON

Laius, king, was lord of our land before thou wast pilot of
this State.

OEDIPUS

I know it well—by hearsay, for I saw him never.

CREON

He was slain; and the god now bids us plainly to wreak vengeance on his murderers—whosoever they be.

OEDIPUS

And where are they upon the earth? Where shall the dim track of this old crime be found?

CREON

In this land,—said the god. What is sought for can be caught; only that which is not watched escapes.

OEDIPUS

And was it in the house, or in the field, or on strange soil that Laius met this bloody end?

CREON

'Twas on a visit to Delphi, as he said, that he had left our land; and he came home no more, after he had once set forth.

OEDIPUS

And was there none to tell? Was there no comrade of his journey who saw the deed, from whom tidings might have been gained, and used?

CREON

All perished, save one who fled in fear, and could tell for certain but one thing of all that he saw.

OEDIPUS

And what was that? One thing might show the clue to many, could we get but a small beginning for hope.

CREON

He said that robbers met and fell on them, not in one man's might, but with full many hands.

OEDIPUS

How, then, unless there was some trafficking in bribes from here, should the robber have dared thus far?

CREON

Such things were surmised; but, Laius once slain, amid our troubles no avenger arose.

OEDIPUS

But, when royalty had fallen thus, what trouble in your path can have hindered a full search?

CREON

The riddling Sphinx had made us let dark things go, and was inviting us to think of what lay at our doors.

OEDIPUS

Nay, I will start afresh, and once more make dark things plain. Right worthily hath Phoebus, and worthily hast thou, bestowed this care on the cause of the dead; and so, as is meet, ye shall find me too leagued with you in seeking vengeance for this land, and for the god besides. On behalf of no far-off friend, no, but in mine own cause, shall I dispel this taint. For whoever was the slayer of Laius might wish to take vengeance on me also with a hand as fierce. Therefore, in doing right to Laius, I serve myself.

Come, haste ye, my children, rise from the altar-steps, and lift these suppliant boughs; and let some other summon hither the folk of Cadmus, warned that I mean to leave nought untried; for our health (with the god's help) shall be made certain—or our ruin.

PRIEST

My children, let us rise; we came at first to seek what this man promises of himself. And may Phoebus, who sent these oracles, come to us therewith, our saviour and deliverer from the pest.

(*Exeunt* OEDIPUS *and* PRIEST. *Enter* CHORUS OF THEBAN ELDERS.)

CHORUS (*singing*)

strophe 1

O sweetly-speaking message of Zeus, in what spirit hast thou come from golden Pytho unto glorious Thebes? I am on the rack, terror shakes my soul, O thou Delian healer to whom wild cries rise, in holy fear of thee, what thing thou wilt work for me, perchance unknown before, perchance renewed with the revolving years: tell me, thou immortal Voice, born of Golden Hope!

antistrophe 1

First call I on thee, daughter of Zeus, divine Athena, and on thy sister, guardian of our land, Artemis, who sits on her throne of fame, above the circle of our Agora, and on Phoebus the far-darter: O shine forth on me, my three-fold help against death! If ever aforetime, in arrest of ruin hurrying on the city, ye drove a fiery pest beyond our borders, come now also!

strophe 2

Woe is me, countless are the sorrows that I bear; a plague is on all our host, and thought can find no weapon for defence. The fruits of the glorious earth grow not; by no birth of children do women surmount the pangs in which they shriek; and life on life mayest thou see sped like bird on nimble wing, aye, swifter than resistless fire, to the shore of the western god.

antistrophe 2

By such deaths, past numbering, the city perishes: unpitied, her children lie on the ground, spreading pestilence, with none to mourn: and meanwhile young wives, and grey-haired mothers with them, uplift a wail at the steps of the altars, some here, some there, entreating for their weary woes. The prayer to the Healer rings clear, and blent therewith, the voice of lamentation: for these things, golden daughter of Zeus, send us the bright face of comfort.

strophe 3

And grant that the fierce god of death, who now with no brazen shields, yet amid cries as of battle, wraps me in the flame of his onset, may turn his back in speedy flight from our land, borne by a fair wind to the great deep of Amphitrite, or to those waters in which none find haven, even to the Thracian wave; for if night leave aught undone, day follows to accomplish this. O thou who wieldest the powers of the fire-fraught lightning, O Zeus our father, slay him beneath thy thunderbolt!

antistrophe 3

Lycean King, fain were I that thy shafts also, from thy bent bow's string of woven gold, should go abroad in their might, our champions in the face of the foe; yea, and the flashing fires of Artemis wherewith she glances through the Lycian hills. And I call him whose locks are bound with gold, who is named with the name of this land, ruddy Bacchus to whom Bacchants cry, the comrade of the Maenads, to draw near with the blaze of his blithe torch, our ally against the god unhonoured among gods.

(OEDIPUS *enters during the closing strains of the choral song.*)

OEDIPUS

Thou prayest: and in answer to thy prayer,—if thou wilt give a loyal welcome to my words and minister to thine own disease,—thou mayest hope to find succour and relief from woes. These words will I speak publicly, as one who has been a stranger to this report, a stranger to the deed; for I should not be far on the track, if I were tracing it alone, without a clue. But as it is,—since it was only after the time of the deed that I was numbered a Theban among Thebans,—to you, the Cadmeans all, I do thus proclaim.

Whosoever of you knows by whom Laius son of Labdacus was slain, I bid him to declare all to me. And if he is afraid, I tell him to remove the danger of the charge from his path by denouncing himself; for he shall suffer nothing else unlovely, but only leave the land, unhurt. Or if any one knows an alien, from another land, as the assassin, let him not keep silence; for I will pay his guerdon, and my thanks shall rest with him besides.

But if ye keep silence—if any one, through fear, shall seek to screen friend or self from my behest—hear ye what I then shall do. I charge you that no one of this land, whereof I hold the empire and the throne, give shelter or speak word unto that murderer, whosoever he be,—make him partner of his prayer or sacrifice, or serve him with the lustral rite; but that all ban him their homes, knowing that *this* is our defiling thing, as the oracle of the Pythian god hath newly shown me. I then am on this wise the ally of the god and of the slain. And I pray solemnly that the slayer, whoso he be, whether his hidden guilt is lonely or hath partners, evilly, as he is evil, may wear out his unblest life. And for myself I pray that if, with my privity, he should become an inmate of my house, I may suffer the same things which even now I called down upon others. And on you I lay it to make all these words good, for my sake, and for the sake of the god, and for our land's, thus blasted with barrenness by angry heaven.

For even if the matter had not been urged on us by a god, it was not meet that ye should leave the guilt thus unpurged, when one so noble, and he your king, had perished; rather were ye bound to search it out. And now, since 'tis I who hold the powers which once he held, who possess his bed and the wife who bare seed to him; and since, had his hope of issue not been frustrate, children born of one mother would have made ties betwixt him and me—but, as it was, fate swooped upon his head; by reason of these things will I uphold this cause, even as the cause of mine own sire, and will leave nought untried in seeking to find him whose hand shed that blood, for the honour of the son of Labdacus and of Polydorus and elder Cadmus and Agenor who was of old.

And for those who obey me not, I pray that the gods send them neither harvest of the earth nor fruit of the womb, but that they be wasted by their lot that now is, or by one yet more dire. But for all you, the loyal folk of Cadmus to whom these things seem good, may Justice, our ally, and all the gods be with you graciously for ever.

LEADER OF THE CHORUS

As thou hast put me on my oath, on my oath, O king, I will speak. I am not the slayer, nor can I point to him who slew. As for the question, it was for Phoebus, who sent it, to tell us this thing—who can have wrought the deed.

OEDIPUS

Justly said; but no man on the earth can force the gods to what they will not.

LEADER

I would fain say what seems to me next best after this.

OEDIPUS

If there is yet a third course, spare not to show it.

LEADER

I know that our lord Teiresias is the seer most like to our lord Phoebus; from whom, O king, a searcher of these things might learn them most clearly.

OEDIPUS

Not even this have I left out of my cares. On the hint of Creon, I have twice sent a man to bring him; and this long while I marvel why he is not here.

LEADER

Indeed (his skill apart) the rumours are but faint and old.

OEDIPUS

What rumours are they? I look to every story.

LEADER

Certain wayfarers were said to have killed him.

OEDIPUS

I, too, have heard it, but none sees him who saw it.

LEADER

Nay, if he knows what fear is, he will not stay when he hears thy curses, so dire as they are.

OEDIPUS

When a man shrinks not from a deed, neither is he scared by a word.

LEADER

But there is one to convict him. For here they bring at last the godlike prophet, in whom alone of men doth live the truth.

(*Enter* TEIRESIAS, *led by a boy.*)

OEDIPUS

Teiresias, whose soul grasps all things, the lore that may be told and the unspeakable, the secrets of heaven and the low things of earth,—thou feelest, though thou canst not see, what a plague doth haunt our State,—from which, great prophet, we find in thee our protector and only saviour. Now, Phoebus—if indeed thou knowest it not from the messengers—sent answer to our question that the only riddance from this pest which could come was if we should learn aright the slayers of Laius, and slay them, or send them into exile from our land. Do thou, then, grudge neither voice of birds nor any other way of seer-lore that thou hast, but rescue thyself and the State, rescue me, rescue all that is defiled by the dead. For we are in thy hand; and man's noblest task is to help others by his best means and powers.

TEIRESIAS

Alas, how dreadful to have wisdom where it profits not the wise! Aye, I knew this well, but let it slip out of mind; else would I never have come here.

OEDIPUS

What now? How sad thou hast come in!

TEIRESIAS

Let me go home; most easily wilt thou bear thine own burden to the end, and I mine, if thou wilt consent.

OEDIPUS

Thy words are strange, nor kindly to this State which nurtured thee, when thou withholdest this response.

TEIRESIAS

Nay, I see that thou, on thy part, openest not thy lips in season: therefore I speak not, that neither may I have thy mishap.

OEDIPUS

For the love of the gods, turn not away, if thou hast knowledge: all we suppliants implore thee on our knees.

TEIRESIAS

Aye, for ye are all without knowledge; but never will I reveal my griefs—that I say not thine.

OEDIPUS

How sayest thou? Thou knowest the secret, and wilt not tell it, but art minded to betray us and to destroy the State?

TEIRESIAS

I will pain neither myself nor thee. Why vainly ask these things? Thou wilt not learn them from me.

OEDIPUS

What, basest of the base,—for thou wouldest anger a very stone,—wilt thou never speak out? Can nothing touch thee? Wilt thou never make an end?

TEIRESIAS

Thou blamest my temper, but seest not that to which thou
thyself art wedded: no, thou findest fault with me.

OEDIPUS

And who would not be angry to hear the words with which
thou now dost slight this city?

TEIRESIAS

The future will come of itself, though I shroud it in silence.

OEDIPUS

Then, seeing that it must come, thou on thy part shouldst
tell me thereof.

TEIRESIAS

I will speak no further; rage, then, if thou wilt, with the
fiercest wrath thy heart doth know.

OEDIPUS

Aye, verily, I will not spare—so wroth I am—to speak all
my thought. Know that thou seemest to me e'en to have
helped in plotting the deed, and to have done it, short of
slaying with thy hands. Hadst thou eyesight, I would have
said that the doing, also, of this thing was thine alone.

TEIRESIAS

In sooth?—I charge thee that thou abide by the decree of
thine own mouth, and from this day speak neither to these
nor to me: *thou* art the accursed defiler of this land.

OEDIPUS

So brazen with thy blustering taunt? And wherein dost
thou trust to escape thy due?

TEIRESIAS

I have escaped: in my truth is my strength.

OEDIPUS

Who taught thee this? It was not, at least, thine art.

TEIRESIAS

Thou: for thou didst spur me into speech against my will.

OEDIPUS

What speech? Speak again that I may learn it better.

TEIRESIAS

Didst thou not take my sense before? Or art thou tempting me to talk?

OEDIPUS

No, I took it not so that I can call it known:—speak again.

TEIRESIAS

I say that thou art the slayer of the man whose slayer thou seekest.

OEDIPUS

Now thou shalt rue that thou hast twice said words so dire.

TEIRESIAS

Wouldst thou have me say more, that thou mayest be more wroth?

OEDIPUS

What thou wilt; it will be said in vain.

TEIRESIAS

I say that thou hast been living in unguessed shame with thy nearest kin, and seest not to what woe thou hast come.

OEDIPUS

Dost thou indeed think that thou shalt always speak thus without smarting?

TEIRESIAS

Yes, if there is any strength in truth.

OEDIPUS

Nay, there is,—for all save thee; for thee that strength is not, since thou art maimed in ear, and in wit, and in eye.

117

TEIRESIAS

Aye, and thou art a poor wretch to utter taunts which every man here will soon hurl at thee.

OEDIPUS

Night, endless night hath thee in her keeping, so that thou canst never hurt me, or any man who sees the sun.

TEIRESIAS

No, thy doom is not to fall by *me:* Apollo is enough, whose care it is to work that out.

OEDIPUS

Are these Creon's devices, or thine?

TEIRESIAS

Nay, Creon is no plague to thee; thou art thine own.

OEDIPUS

O wealth, and empire, and skill surpassing skill in life's keen rivalries, how great is the envy that cleaves to you, if for the sake, yea, of this power which the city hath put into my hands, a gift unsought, Creon the trusty, Creon mine old friend, hath crept on me by stealth, yearning to thrust me out of it, and hath suborned such a scheming juggler as this, a tricky quack, who hath eyes only for his gains, but in his art is blind!

Come, now, tell me, where hast thou proved thyself a seer? Why, when the Watcher was here who wove dark song, didst thou say nothing that could free this folk? Yet the riddle, at least, was not for the first comer to read; there was need of a seer's skill; and none such thou wast found to have either by help of birds, or as known from any god: no, I came, I, Oedipus, the ignorant, and made her mute, when I had seized the answer by my wit, untaught of birds. And it is I whom thou art trying to oust, thinking to stand close to Creon's throne. Methinks thou and the plotter of these things will rue your zeal to purge the land. Nay, didst thou not seem to be an old man, thou shouldst have learned to thy cost how bold thou art.

LEADER

To our thinking, both this man's words and thine, Oedipus, have been said in anger. Not for such words is our need, but to seek how we shall best discharge the mandates of the god.

TEIRESIAS

King though thou art, the right of reply, at least, must be deemed the same for both; of that I too am lord. Not to thee do I live servant, but to Loxias; and so I shall not stand enrolled under Creon for my patron. And I tell thee—since thou hast taunted me even with blindness—that thou hast sight, yet seest not in what misery thou art, nor where thou dwellest, nor with whom. Dost thou know of what stock thou art? And thou hast been an unwitting foe to thy own kin, in the shades, and on the earth above; and the double lash of thy mother's and thy father's curse shall one day drive thee from this land in dreadful haste, with darkness then on the eyes that now see true.

And what place shall not be harbour to thy shriek, what of all Cithaeron shall not ring with it soon, when thou hast learnt the meaning of the nuptials in which, within that house, thou didst find a fatal haven, after a voyage so fair? And a throng of other ills thou guessest not, which shall make thee level with thy true self and with thine own brood.

Therefore heap thy scorns on Creon and on my message: for no one among men shall ever be crushed more miserably than thou.

OEDIPUS

Are these taunts to be indeed borne from *him?*—Hence, ruin take thee! Hence, this instant! Back!—away!—avaunt thee from these doors!

TEIRESIAS

I had never come, not I, hadst thou not called me.

119

OEDIPUS

I knew not that thou wast about to speak folly, or it had been long ere I had sent for thee to my house.

TEIRESIAS

Such am I,—as thou thinkest, a fool; but for the parents who begat thee, sane.

OEDIPUS

What parents? Stay . . . and who of men is my sire?

TEIRESIAS

This day shall show thy birth and shall bring thy ruin.

OEDIPUS

What riddles, what dark words thou always speakest!

TEIRESIAS

Nay, art not thou most skilled to unravel dark speech?

OEDIPUS

Make that my reproach in which thou shalt find me great.

TEIRESIAS

Yet 'twas just that fortune that undid thee.

OEDIPUS

Nay, if I delivered this town, I care not.

TEIRESIAS

Then I will go: so do thou, boy, take me hence.

OEDIPUS

Aye, let him take thee: while here, thou art a hindrance, thou, a trouble: when thou hast vanished, thou wilt not vex me more.

TEIRESIAS

I will go when I have done mine errand, fearless of thy frown: for thou canst never destroy me. And I tell thee—the man of whom thou hast this long while been in quest, utter-

ing threats, and proclaiming a search into the murder of
Laius—that man is here,—in seeming, an alien sojourner,
but anon he shall be found a native Theban, and shall not
be glad of his fortune. A blind man, he who now hath sight,
a beggar, who now is rich, he shall make his way to a strange
land, feeling the ground before him with his staff. And he
shall be found at once brother and father of the children
with whom he consorts; son and husband of the woman who
bore him; heir to his father's bed, shedder of his father's
blood.

So go thou in and think on that; and if thou find that I
have been at fault, say thenceforth that I have no wit in
prophecy.

(TEIRESIAS *is led out by the boy.* OEDIPUS *enters the palace.*)

CHORUS (*singing*)

strophe 1

Who is he of whom the divine voice from the Delphian rock hath spoken, as having wrought with red
hands horrors that no tongue can tell?

It is time that he ply in flight a foot stronger than
the feet of storm-swift steeds: for the son of Zeus is
springing on him, all armed with fiery lightnings, and
with him come the dread, unerring Fates.

antistrophe 1

Yea, newly given from snowy Parnassus, the message hath flashed forth to make all search for the unknown man. Into the wild wood's covert, among caves
and rocks he is roaming, fierce as a bull, wretched and
forlorn on his joyless path, still seeking to put from him
the doom spoken at Earth's central shrine: but that
doom ever lives, ever flits around him.

strophe 2

Dreadly, in sooth, dreadly doth the wise augur move
me, who approve not, nor am able to deny. How to
speak, I know not; I am fluttered with forebodings;

121

neither in the present have I clear vision, nor of the future. Never in past days, nor in these, have I heard how the house of Labdacus or the son of Polybus had, either against other, any grief that I could bring as proof in assailing the public fame of Oedipus, and seeking to avenge the line of Labdacus for the undiscovered murder.

antistrophe 2

Nay, Zeus indeed and Apollo are keen of thought, and know the things of earth; but that mortal seer wins knowledge above mine, of this there can be no sure test; though man may surpass man in lore. Yet, until I see the word made good, never will I assent when men blame Oedipus. Before all eyes, the winged maiden came against him of old, and he was seen to be wise; he bore the test, in welcome service to our State; never, therefore, by the verdict of my heart shall he be adjudged guilty of crime.

(Enter CREON*)*

CREON

Fellow-citizens, having learned that Oedipus the king lays dire charges against me, I am here, indignant. If, in the present troubles, he thinks that he has suffered from *me,* by word or deed, aught that tends to harm, in truth I crave not my full term of years, when I must bear such blame as this. The wrong of this rumour touches me not in one point alone, but has the largest scope, if I am to be called a traitor in the city, a traitor too by thee and by my friends.

LEADER OF THE CHORUS

Nay, but this taunt came under stress, perchance, of anger, rather than from the purpose of the heart.

CREON

And the saying was uttered, that *my* counsels won the seer to utter his falsehoods?

Oedipus the King

Such things were said—I know not with what meaning.

CREON

And was this charge laid against me with steady eyes and
steady mind?

LEADER

I know not; I see not what my masters do: but here comes
our lord forth from the house.

(Enter OEDIPUS)

OEDIPUS

Sirrah, how camest thou here? Hast thou a front so bold
that thou hast come to my house, who art the proved assassin of its master,—the palpable robber of my crown? Come,
tell me, in the name of the gods, was it cowardice or folly
that thou sawest in me, that thou didst plot to do this thing?
Didst thou think that I would not note this deed of thine
creeping on me by stealth, or, aware, would not ward it off?
Now is not thine attempt foolish,—to seek, without followers or friends, a throne,—a prize which followers and wealth
must win?

CREON

Mark me now,—in answer to thy words, hear a fair reply,
and then judge for thyself on knowledge.

OEDIPUS

Thou art apt in speech, but I have a poor wit for thy lessons, since I have found thee my malignant foe.

CREON

Now first hear how I will explain this very thing—

OEDIPUS

Explain me not one thing—that thou art not false.

CREON

If thou deemest that stubbornness without sense is a good
gift, thou art not wise.

OEDIPUS

If thou deemest that thou canst wrong a kinsman and
escape the penalty, thou art not sane.

CREON

Justly said, I grant thee: but tell me what is the wrong
that thou sayest thou hast suffered from me.

OEDIPUS

Didst thou advise, or didst thou not, that I should send
for that reverend seer?

CREON

And now I am still of the same mind.

OEDIPUS

How long is it, then, since Laius—

CREON

Since Laius . . . ? I take not thy drift . . .

OEDIPUS

—was swept from men's sight by a deadly violence?

CREON

The count of years would run far into the past.

OEDIPUS

Was this seer, then, of the craft in those days?

CREON

Yea, skilled as now, and in equal honour.

OEDIPUS

Made he, then, any mention of me at that time?

CREON

Never, certainly, when I was within hearing.

OEDIPUS

But held ye not a search touching the murder?

CREON

Due search we held, of course—and learned nothing.

OEDIPUS

And how was it that this sage did not tell his story *then?*

CREON

I know not; where I lack light, 'tis my wont to be silent.

OEDIPUS

Thus much, at least, thou knowest, and couldst declare with light enough.

CREON

What is that? If I know it, I will not deny.

OEDIPUS

That, if he had not conferred with thee, he would never have named *my* slaying of Laius.

CREON

If so he speaks, thou best knowest; but I claim to learn from thee as much as thou hast now from me.

OEDIPUS

Learn thy fill: I shall never be found guilty of the blood.

CREON

Say, then—thou hast married my sister?

OEDIPUS

The question allows not of denial.

CREON

And thou rulest the land as she doth, with like sway?

OEDIPUS

She obtains from me all her desire.

CREON
And rank not I as a third peer of you twain?

OEDIPUS
Aye, 'tis just therein that thou art seen a false friend.

CREON
Not so, if thou wouldst reason with thine own heart as I with mine. And first weigh this,—whether thou thinkest that any one would choose to rule amid terrors rather than in unruffled peace,—granting that he is to have the same powers. Now I, for one, have no yearning in my nature to be a king rather than to do kingly deeds, no, nor hath any man who knows how to keep a sober mind. For now I win all boons from thee without fear; but, were I ruler myself, I should be doing much e'en against mine own pleasure.

How, then, could royalty be sweeter for me to have than painless rule and influence? Not yet am I so misguided as to desire other honours than those which profit. Now, all wish me joy; now, every man has a greeting for me; now, those who have a suit to thee crave speech with me, since therein is all their hope of success. Then why should I resign these things, and take those? No mind will become false, while it is wise. Nay, I am no lover of such policy, and, if another put it into deed, never could I bear to act with him.

And, in proof of this, first, go to Pytho, and ask if I brought thee true word of the oracle; then next, if thou find that I have planned aught in concert with the soothsayer, take and slay me, by the sentence not of one mouth, but of twain—by mine own, no less than thine. But make me not guilty in a corner, on unproved surmise. It is not right to adjudge bad men good at random, or good men bad. I count it a like thing for a man to cast off a true friend as to cast away the life in his own bosom, which most he loves. Nay, thou wilt learn these things with sureness in time, for time alone shows a just man; but thou couldst discern a knave even in one day.

126

LEADER

Well hath he spoken, O king, for one who giveth heed not
to fall: the quick in counsel are not sure.

OEDIPUS

When the stealthy plotter is moving on me in quick sort,
I, too, must be quick with my counterplot. If I await him in
repose, his ends will have been gained, and mine missed.

CREON

What wouldst thou, then? Cast me out of the land?

OEDIPUS

Not so: I desire thy death—not thy banishment—that
thou mayest show forth what manner of thing is envy.

CREON

Thou speakest as resolved not to yield or to believe?

OEDIPUS

No; for thou persuadest me not that thou art worthy of
belief.

CREON

No, for I find thee not sane.

OEDIPUS

Sane, at least, in mine own interest.

CREON

Nay, thou shouldst be so in mine also.

OEDIPUS

Nay, thou art false.

CREON

But if thou understandest nought?

OEDIPUS

Yet must I rule.

CREON

Not if thou rule ill.

OEDIPUS

Hear him, O Thebes!

CREON

Thebes is for me also—not for thee alone.

(JOCASTA *enters from the palace.*)

LEADER

Cease, princes; and in good time for you I see Jocasta coming yonder from the house, with whose help ye should compose your present feud.

JOCASTA

Misguided men, why have ye raised such foolish strife of tongues? Are ye not ashamed, while the land is thus sick, to stir up troubles of your own? Come, go thou into the house, —and thou, Creon, to thy home,—and forbear to make much of a petty grief.

CREON

Kinswoman, Oedipus thy lord claims to do dread things unto me, even one or other of two ills,—to thrust me from the land of my fathers, or to slay me amain.

OEDIPUS

Yea; for I have caught him, lady, working evil, by ill arts, against my person.

CREON

Now may I see no good, but perish accursed, if I have done aught to thee of that wherewith thou chargest me!

JOCASTA

O, for the gods' love, believe it, Oedipus—first, for the awful sake of this oath unto the gods,—then for my sake and for theirs who stand before thee!

(The following lines between the Chorus *and* Oedipus *and between the* Chorus, Jocasta, *and* Oedipus *are chanted responsively.)*

Chorus

strophe 1

Consent, reflect, hearken, O my king, I pray thee!

Oedipus

What grace, then, wouldest thou have me grant thee?

Chorus

Respect him who aforetime was not foolish, and who now is strong in his oath.

Oedipus

Now dost thou know what thou cravest?

Chorus

Yea.

Oedipus

Declare, then, what thou meanest.

Chorus

That thou shouldest never use an unproved rumour to cast a dishonouring charge on the friend who has bound himself with a curse.

Oedipus

Then be very sure that, when thou seekest this, for me thou art seeking destruction, or exile from this land.

Chorus

strophe 2

No, by him who stands in the front of all the heavenly host, no, by the Sun! Unblest, unfriended, may I die by the uttermost doom, if I have that thought! But my unhappy soul is worn by the withering of the land, and again by the thought that our old sorrows should be crowned by sorrows springing from you twain.

129

Oedipus the King

OEDIPUS

Then let him go, though I am surely doomed to death, or
to be thrust dishonoured from the land. Thy lips, not his,
move my compassion by their plaint; but he, where'er he be,
shall be hated.

CREON

Sullen in yielding art thou seen, even as vehement in the
excesses of thy wrath; but such natures are justly sorest for
themselves to bear.

OEDIPUS

Then wilt thou not leave me in peace, and get thee gone?

CREON

I will go my way; I have found thee undiscerning, but in
the sight of these I am just.

(*Exit* CREON)

CHORUS

antistrophe 1

Lady, why dost thou delay to take yon man into the
house?

JOCASTA

I will do so, when I have learned what hath chanced.

CHORUS

Blind suspicion, bred of talk, arose; and, on the other
part, injustice wounds.

JOCASTA

It was on both sides?

CHORUS

Aye.

JOCASTA

And what was the story?

130

CHORUS

Enough, methinks, enough—when our land is already
vexed—that the matter should rest where it ceased.

OEDIPUS

Seest thou to what thou hast come, for all thy honest
purpose, in seeking to slack and blunt my zeal?

CHORUS

antistrophe 2

King, I have said it not once alone—be sure that I
should have been shown a madman, bankrupt in sane
counsel, if I put thee away—thee, who gavest a true
course to my beloved country when distraught by
troubles—thee, who now also art like to prove our pros-
pering guide.

JOCASTA

In the name of the gods, tell me also, O king, on what account thou hast conceived this steadfast wrath.

OEDIPUS

That will I; for I honour thee, lady, above yonder men:—
the cause is Creon, and the plots that he hath laid against
me.

JOCASTA

Speak on—if thou canst tell clearly how the feud began.

OEDIPUS

He says that I stand guilty of the blood of Laius.

JOCASTA

As on his own knowledge? Or on hearsay from another?

OEDIPUS

Nay, he hath made a rascal seer his mouthpiece; as for
himself, he keeps his lips wholly pure.

131

JOCASTA

Then absolve thyself of the things whereof thou speakest; hearken to me, and learn for thy comfort that nought of mortal birth is a sharer in the science of the seer. I will give thee pithy proof of that.

An oracle came to Laius once—I will not say from Phoebus himself, but from his ministers—that the doom should overtake him to die by the hand of his child, who should spring from him and me.

Now Laius,—as, at least, the rumour saith,—was murdered one day by foreign robbers at a place where three highways meet. And the child's birth was not three days past, when Laius pinned its ankles together, and had it thrown, by others' hands, on a trackless mountain.

So, in that case, Apollo brought it not to pass that the babe should become the slayer of his sire, or that Laius should die—the dread thing which he feared—by his child's hand. Thus did the messages of seer-craft map out the future. Regard them, thou, not at all. Whatsoever needful things the god seeks, he himself will easily bring to light.

OEDIPUS

What restlessness of soul, lady, what tumult of the mind hath just come upon me since I heard thee speak!

JOCASTA

What anxiety hath startled thee, that thou sayest this?

OEDIPUS

Methought I heard this from thee,—that Laius was slain where three highways meet.

JOCASTA

Yea, that was the story; nor hath it ceased yet.

OEDIPUS

And where is the place where this befell?

Oedipus the King

JOCASTA

The land is called Phocis; and branching roads lead to the same spot from Delphi and from Daulia.

OEDIPUS

And what is the time that hath passed since these things were?

JOCASTA

The news was published to the town shortly before thou wast first seen in power over this land.

OEDIPUS

O Zeus, what hast thou decreed to do unto me?

JOCASTA

And wherefore, Oedipus, doth this thing weigh upon thy soul?

OEDIPUS

Ask me not yet; but say what was the stature of Laius, and how ripe his manhood.

JOCASTA

He was tall,—the silver just lightly strewn among his hair; and his form was not greatly unlike to thine.

OEDIPUS

Unhappy that I am! Methinks I have been laying myself even now under a dread curse, and knew it not.

JOCASTA

How sayest thou? I tremble when I look on thee, my king.

OEDIPUS

Dread misgivings have I that the seer can see. But thou wilt show better if thou wilt tell me one thing more.

JOCASTA

Indeed—though I tremble—I will answer all thou askest, when I hear it.

OEDIPUS

Went he in small force, or with many armed followers, like a chieftain?

JOCASTA

Five they were in all,—a herald one of them; and there was one carriage, which bore Laius.

OEDIPUS

Alas! 'Tis now clear indeed.—Who was he who gave you these tidings lady?

JOCASTA

A servant—the sole survivor who came home.

OEDIPUS

Is he haply at hand in the house now?

JOCASTA

No, truly; so soon as he came thence, and found thee reigning in the stead of Laius, he supplicated me, with hand laid on mine, that I would send him to the fields, to the pastures of the flocks, that he might be far from the sight of this town. And I sent him; he was worthy, for a slave, to win e'en a larger boon than that.

OEDIPUS

Would, then, that he could return to us without delay!

JOCASTA

It is easy: but wherefore dost thou enjoin this?

OEDIPUS

I fear, lady, that mine own lips have been unguarded; and therefore am I fain to behold him.

JOCASTA

Nay, he shall come. But I too, methinks, have a claim to
learn what lies heavy on thy heart, my king.

OEDIPUS

Yea, and it shall not be kept from thee, now that my forebodings have advanced so far. Who, indeed, is more to me
than thou, to whom I should speak in passing through such
a fortune as this?

My father was Polybus of Corinth,—my mother, the
Dorian Merope; and I was held the first of all the folk in
that town, until a chance befell me, worthy, indeed, of wonder, though not worthy of mine own heat concerning it. At
a banquet, a man full of wine cast it at me in his cups that
I was not the true son of my sire. And I, vexed, restrained
myself for that day as best I might; but on the next I went
to my mother and father, and questioned them; and they
were wroth for the taunt with him who had let that word fly.
So on their part I had comfort; yet was this thing ever rank-
ling in my heart; for it still crept abroad with strong rumour.
And, unknown to mother or father, I went to Delphi; and
Phoebus sent me forth disappointed of that knowledge for
which I came, but in his response set forth other things, full
of sorrow and terror and woe; even that I was fated to defile
my mother's bed; and that I should show unto men a brood
which they could not endure to behold; and that I should be
the slayer of the sire who begat me.

And I, when I had listened to this, turned to flight from
the land of Corinth, thenceforth wotting of its region by the
stars alone, to some spot where I should never see fulfilment
of the infamies foretold in mine evil doom. And on my way
I came to the regions in which thou sayest that this prince
perished. Now, lady, I will tell thee the truth. When in my
journey I was near to those three roads, there met me a
herald, and a man seated in a carriage drawn by colts, as
thou hast described; and he who was in front, and the old

135

man himself, were for thrusting me rudely from the path. Then, in anger, I struck him who pushed me aside—the driver; and the old man, seeing it, watched the moment when I was passing, and, from the carriage, brought his goad with two teeth down full upon my head. Yet was he paid with interest; by one swift blow from the staff in this hand he was rolled right out of the carriage, on his back; and I slew every man of them.

But if this stranger had any tie of kinship with Laius, who is now more wretched than the man before thee? What mortal could prove more hated of heaven? Whom no stranger, no citizen, is allowed to receive in his house; whom it is unlawful that any one accost; whom all must repel from their homes! And this—this curse—was laid on me by no mouth but mine own! And I pollute the bed of the slain man with the hands by which he perished. Say, am I vile? Oh, am I not utterly unclean?—seeing that I must be banished, and in banishment see not mine own people, nor set foot in mine own land, or else be joined in wedlock to my mother, and slay my sire, even Polybus, who begat and reared me.

Then would not he speak aright of Oedipus, who judged these things sent by some cruel power above man? Forbid, forbid, ye pure and awful gods, that I should see that day! No, may I be swept from among men, ere I behold myself visited with the brand of such a doom!

LEADER OF THE CHORUS
To us, indeed, these things, O king, are fraught with fear; yet have hope, until at last thou hast gained full knowledge from him who saw the deed.

OEDIPUS
Hope, in truth, rests with me thus far alone; I can await the man summoned from the pastures.

JOCASTA
And when he has appeared—what wouldst thou have of him?

Oedipus the King

OEDIPUS

I will tell thee. If his story be found to tally with thine, I, at least, shall stand clear of disaster.

JOCASTA

And what of special note didst thou hear from me?

OEDIPUS

Thou wast saying that he spoke of Laius as slain by robbers. If, then, he still speaks, as before, of several, I was not the slayer: a solitary man could not be held the same with that band. But if he names one lonely wayfarer, then beyond doubt this guilt leans to me.

JOCASTA

Nay, be assured that thus, at least, the tale was first told; he cannot revoke that, for the city heard it, not I alone. But even if he should diverge somewhat from his former story, never, king, can he show that the murder of Laius, at least, is truly square to prophecy; of whom Loxias plainly said that he must die by the hand of my child. Howbeit that poor innocent never slew him, but perished first itself. So henceforth, for what touches divination, I would not look to my right hand or my left.

OEDIPUS

Thou judgest well. But nevertheless send some one to fetch the peasant, and neglect not this matter.

JOCASTA

I will send without delay. But let us come into the house: nothing will I do save at thy good pleasure.

(OEDIPUS *and* JOCASTA *go into the palace.*)

CHORUS (*singing*)

strophe 1

May destiny still find me winning the praise of reverent purity in all words and deeds sanctioned by those laws of range sublime, called into life throughout the high clear heaven, whose father is Olympus alone; their parent was no race of mortal men, no, nor shall oblivion ever lay them to sleep; the god is mighty in them, and he grows not old.

antistrophe 1

Insolence breeds the tyrant; Insolence, once vainly surfeited on wealth that is not meet nor good for it, when it hath scaled the top-most ramparts, is hurled to a dire doom, wherein no service of the feet can serve. But I pray that the god never quell such rivalry as benefits the State; the god will I ever hold for our protector.

strophe 2

But if any man walks haughtily in deed or word, with no fear of Justice, no reverence for the images of gods, may an evil doom seize him for his ill-starred pride, if he will not win his vantage fairly, nor keep him from unholy deeds, but must lay profaning hands on sanctities.

Where such things are, what mortal shall boast any more that he can ward the arrows of the gods from his life? Nay, if such deeds are in honour, wherefore should we join in the sacred dance?

antistrophe 2

No more will I go reverently to earth's central and inviolate shrine, no more to Abae's temple or Olympia, if these oracles fit not the issue, so that all men shall point at them with the finger. Nay, king,—if thou art rightly called,—Zeus all-ruling, may it not escape thee and thine ever-deathless power!

The old prophecies concerning Laius are fading; already men are setting them at nought, and nowhere is Apollo glorified with honours; the worship of the gods is perishing.

(JOCASTA *comes forth, bearing a branch, wreathed with festoons of wool, which, as a suppliant, she is about to lay on the altar of the household god, Lycean Apollo, in front of the palace.*)

JOCASTA

Princes of the land, the thought has come to me to visit the shrines of the gods, with this wreathed branch in my hands, and these gifts of incense. For Oedipus excites his soul overmuch with all manner of alarms, nor, like a man of sense, judges the new things by the old, but is at the will of the speaker, if he speak terrors.

Since, then, by counsel I can do no good, to thee, Lycean Apollo, for thou art nearest, I have come, a suppliant with these symbols of prayer, that thou mayest find us some riddance from uncleanness. For now we are all afraid, seeing *him* affrighted, even as they who see fear in the helmsman of their ship.

(*While* JOCASTA *is offering her prayers to the god, a* MESSENGER, *evidently a stranger, enters and addresses the Elders of the* CHORUS.)

MESSENGER

Might I learn from you, strangers, where is the house of the king Oedipus? Or, better still, tell me where he himself is—if ye know.

LEADER OF THE CHORUS

This is his dwelling, and he himself, stranger, is within; and this lady is the mother of his children.

MESSENGER

Then may she be ever happy in a happy home, since she is his heaven-blest queen.

JOCASTA

Happiness to thee also, stranger! 'tis the due of thy fair greeting.—But say what thou hast come to seek or to tell.

Oedipus the King

MESSENGER

Good tidings, lady, for thy house and for thy husband.

JOCASTA

What are they? And from whom hast thou come?

MESSENGER

From Corinth: and at the message which I will speak anon
thou wilt rejoice—doubtless; yet haply grieve.

JOCASTA

And what is it? How hath it thus a double potency?

MESSENGER

The people will make him king of the Isthmian land, as
'twas said there.

JOCASTA

How then? Is the aged Polybus no more in power?

MESSENGER

No, verily: for death holds him in the tomb.

JOCASTA

How sayest thou? Is Polybus dead, old man?

MESSENGER

If I speak not the truth, I am content to die.

JOCASTA

O handmaid, away with all speed, and tell this to thy
master! O ye oracles of the gods, where stand ye now! This
is the man whom Oedipus long feared and shunned, lest he
should slay him; and now this man hath died in the course
of destiny, not by his hand.

(OEDIPUS *enters from the palace.*)

OEDIPUS

Jocasta, dearest wife, why hast thou summoned me forth
from these doors?

140

JOCASTA

Hear this man, and judge, as thou listenest, to what the
awful oracles of the gods have come.

OEDIPUS

And he—who may he be, and what news hath he for me?

JOCASTA

He is from Corinth, to tell that thy father Polybus lives
no longer, but hath perished.

OEDIPUS

How, stranger? Let me have it from thine own mouth.

MESSENGER

If I must first make these tidings plain, know indeed that
he is dead and gone.

OEDIPUS

By treachery, or by visit of disease?

MESSENGER

A light thing in the scale brings the aged to their rest.

OEDIPUS

Ah, he died, it seems, of sickness?

MESSENGER

Yea, and of the long years that he had told.

OEDIPUS

Alas, alas! Why, indeed, my wife, should one look to the
hearth of the Pythian seer, or to the birds that scream above
our heads, on whose showing I was doomed to slay my sire?
But he is dead, and hid already beneath the earth; and here
am I, who have not put hand to spear.—Unless, perchance,
he was killed by longing for me: thus, indeed, I should be
the cause of his death. But the oracles as they stand, at least,
Polybus hath swept with him to his rest in Hades: they are
worth nought.

JOCASTA
Nay, did I not so foretell to thee long since?

OEDIPUS
Thou didst: but I was misled by my fear.

JOCASTA
Now no more lay aught of those things to heart.

OEDIPUS
But surely I must needs fear my mother's bed?

JOCASTA
Nay, what should mortal fear, for whom the decrees of Fortune are supreme, and who hath clear foresight of nothing? 'Tis best to live at random, as one may. But fear not thou touching wedlock with thy mother. Many men ere now have so fared in dreams also: but he to whom these things are as nought bears his life most easily.

OEDIPUS
All these bold words of thine would have been well, were not my mother living; but as it is, since she lives, I must needs fear—though thou sayest well.

JOCASTA
Howbeit thy father's death is a great sign to cheer us.

OEDIPUS
Great, I know; but my fear is of her who lives.

MESSENGER
And who is the woman about whom ye fear?

OEDIPUS
Merope, old man, the consort of Polybus.

MESSENGER
And what is it in her that moves your fear?

OEDIPUS

A heaven-sent oracle of dread import, stranger.

MESSENGER

Lawful, or unlawful, for another to know?

OEDIPUS

Lawful, surely. Loxias once said that I was doomed to espouse mine own mother, and to shed with mine own hands my father's blood. Wherefore my home in Corinth was long kept by me afar; with happy event, indeed,—yet still 'tis sweet to see the face of parents.

MESSENGER

Was it indeed for fear of this that thou wast an exile from that city?

OEDIPUS

And because I wished not, old man, to be the slayer of my sire.

MESSENGER

Then why have I not freed thee, king, from this fear, seeing that I came with friendly purpose?

OEDIPUS

Indeed thou shouldst have guerdon due from me.

MESSENGER

Indeed 'twas chiefly for this that I came—that, on thy return home, I might reap some good.

OEDIPUS

Nay, I will never go near my parents.

MESSENGER

Ah my son, 'tis plain enough that thou knowest not what thou doest.

OEDIPUS

How, old man? For the gods' love, tell me.

MESSENGER
If for these reasons thou shrinkest from going home.

OEDIPUS
Aye, I dread lest Phoebus prove himself true for me.

MESSENGER
Thou dreadest to be stained with guilt through thy parents?

OEDIPUS
Even so, old man—this it is that ever affrights me.

MESSENGER
Dost thou know, then, that thy fears are wholly vain?

OEDIPUS
How so, if I was born of those parents?

MESSENGER
Because Polybus was nothing to thee in blood.

OEDIPUS
What sayest thou? Was Polybus not my sire?

MESSENGER
No more than he who speaks to thee, but just so much.

OEDIPUS
And how can my sire be level with him who is as nought to me?

MESSENGER
Nay, he begat thee not, any more than I.

OEDIPUS
Nay, wherefore, then, called he me his son?

MESSENGER
Know that he had received thee as a gift from my hands of yore.

OEDIPUS

And yet he loved me so dearly, who came from another's hand?

MESSENGER

Yea, his former childlessness won him thereto.

OEDIPUS

And thou—hadst thou bought me or found me by chance, when thou gavest me to him?

MESSENGER

Found thee in Cithaeron's winding glens.

OEDIPUS

And wherefore wast thou roaming in those regions?

MESSENGER

I was there in charge of mountain flocks.

OEDIPUS

What, thou wast a shepherd—a vagrant hireling?

MESSENGER

But thy preserver, my son, in that hour.

OEDIPUS

And what pain was mine when thou didst take me in thine arms?

MESSENGER

The ankles of thy feet might witness.

OEDIPUS

Ah me, why dost thou speak of that old trouble?

MESSENGER

I freed thee when thou hadst thine ankles pinned together.

OEDIPUS

Aye, 'twas a dread brand of shame that I took from my cradle.

MESSENGER

Such, that from that fortune thou wast called by the name which still is thine.

OEDIPUS

Oh, for the gods' love—was the deed my mother's or father's? Speak!

MESSENGER

I know not; he who gave thee to me wots better of that than I.

OEDIPUS

What, thou hadst me from another? Thou didst not light on me thyself?

MESSENGER

No: another shepherd gave thee up to me.

OEDIPUS

Who was he? Art thou in case to tell clearly?

MESSENGER

I think he was called one of the household of Laius.

OEDIPUS

The king who ruled this country long ago?

MESSENGER

The same: 'twas in his service that the man was a herd.

OEDIPUS

Is he still alive, that I might see him?

MESSENGER

Nay, ye folk of the country should know best.

OEDIPUS

Is there any of you here present that knows the herd of whom he speaks—that hath seen him in the pastures or the

town? Answer! The hour hath come that these things should
be finally revealed.

LEADER OF THE CHORUS

Methinks he speaks of no other than the peasant whom
thou wast already fain to see; but our lady Jocasta might
best tell that.

OEDIPUS

Lady, wottest thou of him whom we lately summoned? Is
it of him that this man speaks?

JOCASTA

Why ask of whom he spoke? Regard it not . . . waste
not a thought on what he said . . . 'twere idle.

OEDIPUS

It must not be that, with such clues in my grasp, I should
fail to bring my birth to light.

JOCASTA

For the gods' sake, if thou hast any care for thine own
life, forbear this search! My anguish is enough.

OEDIPUS

Be of good courage; though I be found the son of servile
mother,—aye, a slave by three descents,—*thou* wilt not be
proved base-born.

JOCASTA

Yet hear me, I implore thee: do not thus.

OEDIPUS

I must not hear of not discovering the whole truth.

JOCASTA

Yet I wish thee well—I counsel thee for the best.

OEDIPUS

These best counsels, then, vex my patience.

JOCASTA

Ill-fated one! Mayst thou never come to know who thou art!

OEDIPUS

Go, some one, fetch me the herdsman hither,—and leave yon woman to glory in her princely stock.

JOCASTA

Alas, alas, miserable!—that word alone can I say unto thee, and no other word henceforth for ever.

(She rushes into the palace.)

LEADER

Why hath the lady gone, Oedipus, in a transport of wild grief? I misdoubt, a storm of sorrow will break forth from this silence.

OEDIPUS

Break forth what will! Be my race never so lowly, I must crave to learn it. Yon woman, perchance,—for she is proud with more than a woman's pride—thinks shame of my base source. But I, who hold myself son of Fortune that gives good, will not be dishonoured. She is the mother from whom I spring; and the months, my kinsmen, have marked me sometimes lowly, sometimes great. Such being my lineage, never more can I prove false to it, or spare to search out the secret of my birth.

CHORUS *(singing)*

strophe

If I am a seer or wise of heart, O Cithaeron, thou shalt not fail—by yon heaven, thou shalt not!—to know at tomorrow's full moon that Oedipus honours thee as native to him, as his nurse, and his mother, and that thou art celebrated in our dance and song, because thou art well-pleasing to our prince. O Phoebus to whom we cry, may these things find favour in thy sight!

148

antistrophe

Who was it, my son, who of the race whose years are many that bore thee in wedlock with Pan, the mountain-roaming father? Or was it a bride of Loxias that bore thee? For dear to him are all the upland pastures. Or perchance 'twas Cyllene's lord, or the Bacchants' god, dweller on the hill-tops, that received thee, a new-born joy, from one of the Nymphs of Helicon, with whom he most doth sport.

OEDIPUS

Elders, if 'tis for me to guess, who have never met with him, I think I see the herdsman of whom we have long been in quest; for in his venerable age he tallies with yon stranger's years, and withal I know those who bring him, methinks, as servants of mine own. But perchance thou mayest have the advantage of me in knowledge, if thou hast seen the herdsman before.

LEADER

Aye, I know him, be sure; he was in the service of Laius—trusty as any man, in his shepherd's place.

(*The* HERDSMAN *is brought in.*)

OEDIPUS

I ask thee first, Corinthian stranger, is this he whom thou meanest?

MESSENGER

This man whom thou beholdest.

OEDIPUS

Ho thou, old man—I would have thee look this way, and answer all that I ask thee. Thou wast once in the service of Laius?

HERDSMAN

I was—a slave not bought, but reared in his house.

Oedipus the King

OEDIPUS

Employed in what labour, or what way of life?

HERDSMAN

For the best part of my life I tended flocks.

OEDIPUS

And what the regions that thou didst chiefly haunt?

HERDSMAN

Sometimes it was Cithaeron, sometimes the neighbouring ground.

OEDIPUS

Then wottest thou of having noted yon man in these parts—

HERDSMAN

Doing what? . . . What man dost thou mean? . . .

OEDIPUS

This man here—or of having ever met him before?

HERDSMAN

Not so that I could speak at once from memory.

MESSENGER

And no wonder, master. But I will bring clear recollection to his ignorance. I am sure that he well wots of the time when we abode in the region of Cithaeron,—he with two flocks, I, his comrade, with one,—three full half-years, from spring to Arcturus; and then for the winter I used to drive my flock to mine own fold, and he took his to the fold of Laius. Did aught of this happen as I tell, or did it not?

HERDSMAN

Thou speakest the truth—though 'tis long ago.

MESSENGER

Come, tell me now—wottest thou of having given me a boy in those days, to be reared as mine own foster-son?

150

HERDSMAN

What now? Why dost thou ask the question?

MESSENGER

Yonder man, my friend, is he who then was young.

HERDSMAN

Plague seize thee—be silent once for all!

OEDIPUS

Ha! chide him not, old man—thy words need chiding more than his.

HERDSMAN

And wherein, most noble master, do I offend?

OEDIPUS

In not telling of the boy concerning whom he asks.

HERDSMAN

He speaks without knowledge—he is busy to no purpose.

OEDIPUS

Thou wilt not speak with a good grace, but thou shalt on pain.

HERDSMAN

Nay, for the gods' love, misuse not an old man!

OEDIPUS

Ho, some one—pinion him this instant!

HERDSMAN

Alas, wherefore? what more wouldst thou learn?

OEDIPUS

Didst thou give this man the child of whom he asks?

HERDSMAN

I did,—and would I had perished that day!

OEDIPUS

Well, thou wilt come to that, unless thou tell the honest truth.

HERDSMAN

Nay, much more am I lost, if I speak.

OEDIPUS

The fellow is bent, methinks, on more delays . . .

HERDSMAN

No, no!—I said before that I gave it to him.

OEDIPUS

Whence hadst thou got it? In thine own house, or from another?

HERDSMAN

Mine own it was not—I had received it from a man.

OEDIPUS

From whom of the citizens here? from what home?

HERDSMAN

Forbear, for the gods' love, master, forbear to ask more!

OEDIPUS

Thou art lost if I have to question thee again.

HERDSMAN

It was a child, then, of the house of Laius.

OEDIPUS

A slave? or one born of his own race?

HERDSMAN

Ah me—I am on the dreaded brink of speech.

OEDIPUS

And I of hearing; yet must I hear.

HERDSMAN

Thou must know, then, that 'twas said to be his own child
but thy lady within could best say how these things are.

OEDIPUS

How? She gave it to thee?

HERDSMAN

Yea, O king.

OEDIPUS

For what end?

HERDSMAN

That I should make away with it.

OEDIPUS

Her own child, the wretch?

HERDSMAN

Aye, from fear of evil prophecies.

OEDIPUS

What were they?

HERDSMAN

The tale ran that he must slay his sire.

OEDIPUS

Why, then, didst thou give him up to this old man?

HERDSMAN

Through pity, master, as deeming that he would bear him
away to another land, whence he himself came; but he saved
him for the direst woe. For if thou art what this man saith,
know that thou wast born to misery.

OEDIPUS

Oh, oh! All brought to pass—all true! Thou light, may I
now look my last on thee—I who have been found accursed
in birth, accursed in wedlock, accursed in the shedding of
blood!

(*He rushes into the palace.*)

Oedipus the King

CHORUS (*singing*)

strophe 1

Alas, ye generations of men, how mere a shadow do I count your life! Where, where is the mortal who wins more of happiness than just the seeming, and, after the semblance, a falling away? Thine is a fate that warns me,—thine, thine, unhappy Oedipus—to call no earthly creature blest.

antistrophe 1

For he, O Zeus, sped his shaft with peerless skill, and won the prize of an all-prosperous fortune; he slew the maiden with crooked talons who sang darkly; he arose for our land as a tower against death. And from that time, Oedipus, thou hast been called our king, and hast been honoured supremely, bearing sway in great Thebes.

strophe 2

But now whose story is more grievous in men's ears? Who is a more wretched captive to fierce plagues and troubles, with all his life reversed?

Alas, renowned Oedipus! The same bounteous place of rest sufficed thee, as child and as sire also, that thou shouldst make thereon thy nuptial couch. Oh, how can the soil wherein thy father sowed, unhappy one, have suffered thee in silence so long?

antistrophe 2

Time the all-seeing hath found thee out in thy despite: he judgeth the monstrous marriage wherein begetter and begotten have long been one.

Alas, thou child of Laius, would, would that I had never seen thee! I wail as one who pours a dirge from his lips; sooth to speak, 'twas thou that gavest me new life, and through thee darkness hath fallen upon mine eyes.

(*Enter* SECOND MESSENGER *from the palace.*)

154

SECOND MESSENGER

Ye who are ever most honoured in this land, what deeds shall ye hear, what deeds behold, what burden of sorrow shall be yours, if, true to your race, ye still care for the house of Labdacus! For I ween that not Ister nor Phasis could wash this house clean, so many are the ills that it shrouds, or will soon bring to light,—ills wrought not unwittingly, but of purpose. And those griefs smart most which are seen to be of our own choice.

LEADER

Indeed those which we knew before fall not short of claiming sore lamentation: besides them, what dost thou announce?

SECOND MESSENGER

This is the shortest tale to tell and to hear: our royal lady Jocasta is dead.

LEADER

Alas, hapless one! From what cause?

SECOND MESSENGER

By her own hand. The worst pain in what hath chanced is not for you, for yours it is not to behold. Nevertheless, so far as mine own memory serves, ye shall learn that unhappy woman's fate.

When, frantic, she had passed within the vestibule, she rushed straight towards her nuptial couch, clutching her hair with the fingers of both hands; once within the chamber, she dashed the doors together at her back; then called on the name of Laius, long since a corpse, mindful of that son, begotten long ago, by whom the sire was slain, leaving the mother to breed accursed offspring with his own.

And she bewailed the wedlock wherein, wretched, she had borne a two-fold brood, husband by husband, children by her child. And how thereafter she perished, is more than I know. For with a shriek Oedipus burst in, and suffered us not to watch her woe unto the end; on him, as he rushed around, our eyes were set. To and fro he went, asking us to give him a sword,—asking where he should find the wife who was no wife, but a mother whose womb had borne alike himself and his children. And, in his frenzy, a power above man was his guide; for 'twas none of us mortals who were nigh. And with a dread shriek, as though some one beckoned him on, he sprang at the double doors, and from their sockets forced the bending bolts, and rushed into the room.

There beheld we the woman hanging by the neck in a twisted noose of swinging cords. But he, when he saw her, with a dread, deep cry of misery, loosed the halter whereby she hung. And when the hapless woman was stretched upon the ground, then was the sequel dread to see. For he tore from her raiment the golden brooches wherewith she was decked, and lifted them, and smote full on his own eye-balls, uttering words like these: 'No more shall ye behold such horrors as I was suffering and working! long enough have ye looked on those whom ye ought never to have seen, failed in knowledge of those whom I yearned to know—henceforth ye shall be dark!'

To such dire refrain, not once alone but oft struck he his eyes with lifted hand; and at each blow the ensanguined eye-balls bedewed his beard, nor sent forth sluggish drops of gore, but all at once a dark shower of blood came down like hail.

From the deeds of twain such ills have broken forth, not on one alone, but with mingled woe for man and wife. The old happiness of their ancestral fortune was aforetime happiness indeed; but to-day—lamentation, ruin, death, shame, all earthly ills that can be named—all, all are theirs.

LEADER

And hath the sufferer now any respite from pain?

SECOND MESSENGER

He cries for some one to unbar the gates and show to all the Cadmeans his father's slayer, his mother's—the unholy word must not pass my lips,—as purposing to cast himself out of the land, and abide no more, to make the house accursed under his own curse. Howbeit he lacks strength, and one to guide his steps; for the anguish is more than man may bear. And he will show this to thee also; for lo, the bars of the gates are withdrawn, and soon thou shalt behold a sight which even he who abhors it must pity.

(*The central door of the palace is now opened.* OEDIPUS *comes forth, leaning on attendants; the bloody stains are still upon his face. The following lines between* OEDIPUS *and the* CHORUS *are chanted responsively.*)

CHORUS

O dread fate for men to see, O most dreadful of all that have met mine eyes! Unhappy one, what madness hath come on thee? Who is the unearthly foe that, with a bound of more than mortal range, hath made thine ill-starred life his prey?

Alas, alas, thou hapless one! Nay, I cannot e'en look on thee, though there is much that I would fain ask, fain learn, much that draws my wistful gaze,—with such a shuddering dost thou fill me!

OEDIPUS

Woe is me! Alas, alas, wretched that I am! Whither, whither am I borne in my misery? How is my voice swept abroad on the wings of the air? Oh my Fate, how far hast thou sprung!

CHORUS

To a dread place, dire in men's ears, dire in their sight.

OEDIPUS

strophe I

O thou horror of darkness that enfoldest me, visitant unspeakable, resistless, sped by a wind too fair!

Ay me! and once again, ay me!

How is my soul pierced by the stab of these goads, and withal by the memory of sorrows!

CHORUS

Yea, amid woes so many a twofold pain may well be thine to mourn and to bear.

OEDIPUS

antistrophe 1

Ah, friend, thou still art steadfast in thy tendance of me,—thou still hast patience to care for the blind man! Ah me! Thy presence is not hid from me—no, dark though I am, yet know I thy voice full well.

CHORUS

Man of dread deeds, how couldst thou in such wise quench thy vision? What more than human power urged thee?

OEDIPUS

strophe 2

Apollo, friends, Apollo was he that brought these my woes to pass, these my sore, sore woes: but the hand that struck the eyes was none save mine, wretched that I am! Why was I to see, when sight could show me nothing sweet?

CHORUS

These things were even as thou sayest.

OEDIPUS

Say, friends, what can I more behold, what can I love, what greeting can touch mine ear with joy? Haste, lead me from the land, friends, lead me hence, the utterly lost, the thrice accursed, yea, the mortal most abhorred of heaven!

CHORUS

Wretched alike for thy fortune and for thy sense thereof, would that I had never so much as known thee!

OEDIPUS

antistrophe 2

Perish the man, whoe'er he was, that freed me in the pastures from the cruel shackle on my feet, and saved me from death, and gave me back to life,—a thankless deed! Had I died then, to my friends and to thine own soul I had not been so sore a grief.

CHORUS

I also would have had it thus.

OEDIPUS

So had I not come to shed my father's blood, nor been called among men the spouse of her from whom I sprang: but now am I forsaken of the gods, son of a defiled mother, successor to his bed who gave me mine own wretched being: and if there be yet a woe surpassing woes, it hath become the portion of Oedipus.

CHORUS

I know not how I can say that thou hast counselled well: for thou wert better dead than living and blind.

OEDIPUS

Show me not at large that these things are not best done thus: give me counsel no more. For, had I sight, I know not with what eyes I could e'en have looked on my father, when I came to the place of the dead, aye, or on my miserable mother, since against both I have sinned such sins as strangling could not punish. But deem ye that the sight of children, born as mine were born, was lovely for me to look upon? No, no, not lovely to mine eyes for ever! No, nor was this town with its towered walls, nor the sacred statues of the gods, since I, thrice wretched that I am,—I, noblest of the sons of Thebes,—have doomed myself to know these no more, by mine own command that all should thrust away the impious one,—even him whom gods have shown to be unholy—and of the race of Laius!

After bearing such a stain upon me, was I to look with steady eyes on this folk? No, verily: no, were there yet a way to choke the fount of hearing, I had not spared to make a fast prison of this wretched frame, that so I should have known nor sight nor sound; for 'tis sweet that our thought should dwell beyond the sphere of griefs.

Alas, Cithaeron, why hadst thou a shelter for me? When I was given to thee, why didst thou not slay me straightway, that so I might never have revealed my source to men? Ah, Polybus,—ah, Corinth, and thou that wast called the ancient house of my fathers, how seeming-fair was I your nurseling, and what ills were festering beneath! For now I am found evil, and of evil birth. O ye three roads, and thou secret glen,—thou coppice, and narrow way where three paths met —ye who drank from my hands that father's blood which was mine own,—remember ye, perchance, what deeds I wrought for you to see,—and then, when I came hither, what fresh deeds I went on to do?

O marriage-rites, ye gave me birth, and when ye had brought me forth, again ye bore children to your child, ye created an incestuous kinship of fathers, brothers, sons,— brides, wives, mothers,—yea, all the foulest shame that is wrought among men! Nay, but 'tis unmeet to name what 'tis unmeet to do:—haste ye, for the gods' love, hide me somewhere beyond the land, or slay me, or cast me into the sea, where ye shall never behold me more! Approach,—deign to lay your hands on a wretched man;—hearken, fear not,— my plague can rest on no mortal beside.

(*Enter* CREON)

LEADER

Nay, here is Creon, in meet season for thy requests, crave they act or counsel; for he alone is left to guard the land in thy stead.

160

OEDIPUS

Ah me! how indeed shall I accost him? What claim to credence can be shown on my part? For in the past I have been found wholly false to him.

CREON

I have not come in mockery, Oedipus, nor to reproach thee with any bygone fault. (*To the attendants.*) But ye, if ye respect the children of men no more, revere at least the all-nurturing flame of our lord the Sun,—spare to show thus nakedly a pollution such as this,—one which neither earth can welcome, nor the holy rain, nor the light. Nay, take him into the house as quickly as ye may; for it best accords with piety that kinsfolk alone should see and hear a kinsman's woes.

OEDIPUS

For the gods' love—since thou hast done a gentle violence to my presage, who hast come in a spirit so noble to me, a man most vile—grant me a boon:—for thy good I will speak, not for mine own.

CREON

And what wish art thou so fain to have of me?

OEDIPUS

Cast me out of this land with all speed, to a place where no mortal shall be found to greet me more.

CREON

This would I have done, be thou sure, but that I craved first to learn all my duty from the god.

OEDIPUS

Nay, his behest hath been set forth in full,—to let me perish, the parricide, the unholy one, that I am.

CREON

Such was the purport; yet, seeing to what a pass we have come, 'tis better to learn clearly what should be done.

161

OEDIPUS

Will ye, then, seek a response on behalf of such a wretch as I am?

CREON

Aye, for thou thyself wilt now surely put faith in the god.

OEDIPUS

Yea; and on thee lay I this charge, to thee will I make this entreaty:—give to her who is within such burial as thou thyself wouldest; for thou wilt meetly render the last rites to thine own. But for me—never let this city of my sire be condemned to have me dwelling therein, while I live: no, suffer me to abide on the hills, where yonder is Cithaeron, famed as mine,—which my mother and sire, while they lived, set for my appointed tomb,—that so I may die by their decree who sought to slay me. Howbeit of thus much am I sure,—that neither sickness nor aught else can destroy me; for never had I been snatched from death, but in reserve for some strange doom.

Nay, let *my* fate go whither it will: but as touching my children,—I pray thee, Creon, take no care on thee for my sons; they are men, so that, be they where they may, they can never lack the means to live. But my two girls, poor hapless ones,—who never knew my table spread apart, or lacked their father's presence, but ever in all things shared my daily bread,—I pray thee, care for *them;* and—if thou canst—suffer me to touch them with my hands, and to indulge my grief. Grant it, prince, grant it, thou noble heart! Ah, could I but once touch them with my hands, I should think that they were with me, even as when I had sight. . .

(CREON's *attendants lead in the children* ANTIGONE *and* ISMENE.)

Ha? O ye gods, can it be my loved ones that I hear sobbing,—can Creon have taken pity on me and sent me my children—my darlings? Am I right?

Oedipus the King

CREON

Yea: 'tis of my contriving, for I knew thy joy in them of old,—the joy that now is thine.

OEDIPUS

Then blessed be thou, and, for guerdon of this errand, may heaven prove to thee a kinder guardian than it hath to me! My children, where are ye? Come hither,—hither to the hands of him whose mother was your own, the hands whose offices have wrought that your sire's once bright eyes should be such orbs as these,—his, who seeing nought, knowing nought, became your father by her from whom he sprang! For you also do I weep—behold you I cannot—when I think of the bitter life in days to come which men will make you live. To what company of the citizens will ye go, to what festival, from which ye shall not return home in tears, instead of sharing in the holiday? But when ye are now come to years ripe for marriage, who shall he be, who shall be the man, my daughters, that will hazard taking unto him such reproaches as must be baneful alike to my offspring and to yours? For what misery is wanting? Your sire slew his sire, he had seed of her who bare him, and begat you at the sources of his own being! Such are the taunts that will be cast at you; and who then will wed? The man lives not, no, it cannot be, my children, but ye must wither in barren maidenhood.

Ah, son of Menoeceus, hear me—since thou art the only father left to them, for we, their parents, are lost, both of us,—allow them not to wander poor and unwed, who are thy kinswomen, nor abase them to the level of my woes. Nay, pity them, when thou seest them at this tender age so utterly forlorn, save for thee. Signify thy promise, generous man, by the touch of thy hand! To you, my children, I would have given much counsel, were your minds mature; but now I would have this to be your prayer—that ye live where occasion suffers, and that the life which is your portion may be happier than your sire's.

CREON

Thy grief hath had large scope enough: nay, pass into the house.

OEDIPUS

I must obey, though 'tis in no wise sweet.

CREON

Yea: for it is in season that all things are good.

OEDIPUS

Knowest thou, then, on what conditions I will go?

CREON

Thou shalt name them; so shall I know them when I hear.

OEDIPUS

See that thou send me to dwell beyond this land.

CREON

Thou askest me for what the god must give.

OEDIPUS

Nay, to the gods I have become most hateful.

CREON

Then shalt thou have thy wish anon.

OEDIPUS

So thou consentest?

CREON

'Tis not my wont to speak idly what I do not mean.

OEDIPUS

Then 'tis time to lead me hence.

CREON

Come, then,—but let thy children go.

OEDIPUS

Nay, take not these from me!

Oedipus the King

CREON

Crave not to be master in all things: for the mastery which thou didst win hath not followed thee through life.

CHORUS (*singing*)

Dwellers in our native Thebes, behold, this is Oedipus, who knew the famed riddle, and was a man most mighty; on whose fortunes what citizen did not gaze with envy? Behold into what a stormy sea of dread trouble he hath come!

Therefore, while our eyes wait to see the destined final day, we must call no one happy who is of mortal race, until he hath crossed life's border, free from pain.

William Shakespeare,   KING LEAR

1. Analyze and evaluate *King Lear* according to the
    standards suggested by Aristotle in *The Poetics*.

2. What two major mistakes, one political and the
    other philosophical, does Lear make in the open-
    ing scene of the play?

3. Discuss the overwhelming irony of Lear's remark to
    Cordelia: "Nothing can come of nothing." Note the
    numerous "nothings" throughout the play.

4. What is the subplot of *King Lear?* Who are the prin-
    cipal characters? Summarize the action and relate
    the subplot to the main plot.

5. What happens to King Lear on the heath and what
    does he learn as a result of the experience?

6. Discuss the character of the Fool in *King Lear*.
    Describe his function in the play; pay particular
    attention to some of his remarks to Lear.

7. In Act I, scene ii, Gloucester and Edmund comment
    on the causes of the various disorders that they
    have observed. Examine their positions and decide
    whose explanation is supported by the action of the
    play.

8. Do you agree or disagree with the world view re-
    flected in *King Lear?*

     William Shakespeare (1564-1616) is almost univer-
sally regarded as the greatest writer of the English
language. His poetry and plays have been enjoyed and
admired for the past three hundred and fifty years. Of
his works, the greatest are generally considered to be
the four major tragedies: *Hamlet, Macbeth, Othello,* and
King Lear.

THE TRAGEDY OF KING LEAR

[DRAMATIS PERSONÆ

LEAR, King of Britain.	Doctor.
KING OF FRANCE.	Fool.
DUKE OF BURGUNDY.	OSWALD, steward to Goneril.
DUKE OF CORNWALL.	A Captain employed by Edmund.
DUKE OF ALBANY.	Gentleman attendant on Cordelia.
EARL OF KENT.	A Herald.
EARL OF GLOUCESTER.	Servants to Cornwall
EDGAR, son to Gloucester.	
EDMUND, bastard son to Gloucester.	GONERIL,
CURAN, a courtier.	REGAN, } daughters to Lear.
Old Man, tenant to Gloucester.	CORDELIA,

Knights of Lear's train, Captains, Messengers, Soldiers, and Attendants

SCENE: BRITAIN]

ACT I

SCENE I. [*King Lear's palace*]

Enter KENT, GLOUCESTER, *and* EDMUND

Kent

I THOUGHT the King had more affected the Duke of Albany
than Cornwall.

Glou. It did always seem so to us; but now, in the division
of the kingdom, it appears not which of the Dukes he values most;
for qualities are so weigh'd, that curiosity in neither can make
choice of either's moiety.

Kent. Is not this your son, my lord?

Glou. His breeding, sir, hath been at my charge. I have so often
blush'd to acknowledge him, that now I am braz'd' to 't.

Kent. I cannot conceive you.

Glou. Sir, this young fellow's mother could; whereupon she grew
round-womb'd, and had, indeed, sir, a son for her cradle ere she
had a husband for her bed. Do you smell a fault?

167

Kent. I cannot wish the fault undone, the issue of it being so proper.

Glou. But I have a son, sir, by order of law, some year elder than this, who yet is no dearer in my account. Though this knave came something saucily into the world before he was sent for, yet was his mother fair; there was good sport at his making, and the whoreson must be acknowledged. Do you know this noble gentleman, Edmund?

Edm. No, my lord.

Glou. My Lord of Kent. Remember him hereafter as my honourable friend.

Edm. My services to your lordship.

Kent. I must love you, and sue to know you better.

Edm. Sir, I shall study deserving.

Glou. He hath been out nine years, and away he shall again. The King is coming.

Sennet. Enter one bearing a coronet, then KING LEAR, *then the* DUKES OF ALBANY *and* CORNWALL, *next* GONERIL, REGAN, COR-DELIA, *with followers*

Lear. Attend the lords of France and Burgundy, Gloucester.

Glou. I shall, my lord.   *Exeunt* [GLOUCESTER *and* EDMUND].

Lear. Meantime we shall express our darker purpose.
Give me the map there. Know that we have divided
In three our kingdom; and 'tis our fast intent
To shake all cares and business from our age,
Conferring them on younger strengths, while we
Unburden'd crawl toward death. Our son of Cornwall,
And you, our no less loving son of Albany,
We have this hour a constant will to publish
Our daughters' several dowers, that future strife
May be prevented now. The Princes, France and Burgundy,
Great rivals in our youngest daughter's love,
Long in our court have made their amorous sojourn,
And here are to be answer'd. Tell me, my daughters,—

Since now we will divest us both of rule,
Interest of territory, cares of state,—
Which of you shall we say doth love us most,
That we our largest bounty may extend
Where nature doth with merit challenge? Goneril,
Our eldest-born, speak first.

 Gon. Sir, I love you more than word can wield the matter;
Dearer than eye-sight, space, and liberty;
Beyond what can be valued, rich or rare;
No less than life, with grace, health, beauty, honour;
As much as child e'er lov'd, or father found;
A love that makes breath poor, and speech unable:
Beyond all manner of so much I love you.

 Cor. [*Aside.*] What shall Cordelia speak? Love and be silent.

 Lear. Of all these bounds, even from this line to this,
With shadowy forests and with champains rich'd,
With plenteous rivers and wide-skirted meads,
We make thee lady. To thine and Albany's issues
Be this perpetual. What says our second daughter,
Our dearest Regan, wife of Cornwall? Speak.

 Reg. I am made of that self metal as my sister,
And prize me at her worth. In my true heart
I find she names my very deed of love;
Only she comes too short, that I profess
Myself an enemy to all other joys
Which the most precious square of sense possesses;
And find I am alone felicitate
In your dear Highness' love.

 Cor.   [*Aside.*] Then poor Cordelia!
And yet not so; since, I am sure, my love 's
More ponderous than my tongue.

 Lear. To thee and thine hereditary ever
Remain this ample third of our fair kingdom;
No less in space, validity, and pleasure,
Than that conferr'd on Goneril. Now, our joy,

Although our last and least, to whose young love
The vines of France and milk of Burgundy
Strive to be interess'd, what can you say to draw
A third more opulent than your sisters? Speak.
    Cor. Nothing, my lord.
    Lear. Nothing!
    Cor. Nothing.
    Lear. Nothing will come of nothing. Speak again.
    Cor. Unhappy that I am, I cannot heave
My heart into my mouth. I love your Majesty
According to my bond; no more nor less.
    Lear. How, how, Cordelia! Mend your speech a little,
Lest you may mar your fortunes.
    Cor.   Good my lord,
You have begot me, bred me, lov'd me: I
Return those duties back as are right fit;
Obey you, love you, and most honour you.
Why have my sisters husbands, if they say
They love you all? Haply, when I shall wed,
That lord whose hand must take my plight shall carry
Half my love with him, half my care and duty.
Sure, I shall never marry like my sisters
[To love my father all].
    Lear. But goes thy heart with this?
    Cor.   Ay, my good lord.
    Lear. So young, and so untender?
    Cor. So young, my lord, and true.
    Lear. Let it be so; thy truth, then, be thy dower!
For, by the sacred radiance of the sun,
The mysteries of Hecate, and the night;
By all the operation of the orbs
From whom we do exist, and cease to be;
Here I disclaim all my paternal care,
Propinquity and property of blood,
And as a stranger to my heart and me

Hold thee, from this, for ever. The barbarous Scythian,
Or he that makes his generation messes
To gorge his appetite, shall to my bosom
Be as well neighbour'd, piti'd, and reliev'd,
As thou my sometime daughter.

    Kent.   Good my liege,—
    Lear. Peace, Kent!
Come not between the dragon and his wrath.
I lov'd her most, and thought to set my rest
On her kind nursery. [*To* Cor.] Hence, and avoid my sight!—
So be my grave my peace, as here I give
Her father's heart from her! Call France.—Who stirs?
Call Burgundy. Cornwall and Albany,
With my two daughters' dowers digest the third;
Let pride, which she calls plainness, marry her.
I do invest you jointly with my power,
Pre-eminence, and all the large effects
That troop with majesty. Ourself, by monthly course,
With reservation of an hundred knights,
By you to be sustain'd, shall our abode
Make with you by due turn. Only we shall retain
The name, and all the addition to a king;
The sway, revenue, execution of the rest,
Beloved sons, be yours; which to confirm,
This coronet part between you.

    Kent.   Royal Lear,
Whom I have ever honour'd as my king,
Lov'd as my father, as my master follow'd,
As my great patron thought on in my prayers,—
    Lear. The bow is bent and drawn; make from the shaft.
    Kent. Let it fall rather, though the fork invade
The region of my heart: be Kent unmannerly
When Lear is mad. What wouldst thou do, old man?
Thinkst thou that duty shall have dread to speak,
When power to flattery bows? To plainness honour's bound,
When majesty falls to folly. Reserve thy state;

171

And, in thy best consideration, check
This hideous rashness. Answer my life my judgement,
Thy youngest daughter does not love thee least;
Nor are those empty-hearted whose low sounds
Reverb no hollowness.

Lear.   Kent, on thy life, no more.

Kent. My life I never held but as a pawn
To wage against thy enemies, ne'er fear to lose it.
Thy safety being motive.

Lear.   Out of my sight!

Kent. See better, Lear; and let me still remain
The true blank of thine eye.

Lear. Now, by Apollo,—

Kent.   Now, by Apollo, king,
Thou swear'st thy gods in vain.

Lear.   O, vassal! miscreant!
                                  [*Laying his hand on his sword.*]

Alb. }
Corn. } Dear sir, forbear.

Kent. Kill thy physician, and thy fee bestow
Upon the foul disease. Revoke thy gift;
Or, whilst I can vent clamour from my throat,
I'll tell thee thou dost evil.

Lear.   Hear me, recreant!
On thine allegiance, hear me!
That thou hast sought to make us break our vows,
Which we durst never yet, and with strain'd pride
To come betwixt our sentences and our power,
Which nor our nature nor our place can bear,
Our potency made good, take thy reward.
Five days we do allot thee, for provision
To shield thee from disasters of the world;
And on the sixth to turn thy hated back
Upon our kingdom. If, on the tenth day following,
Thy banish'd trunk be found in our dominions,

KING LEAR

The moment is thy death. Away! By Jupiter,
This shall not be revok'd.
   Kent. Fare thee well, king! Sith thus thou wilt appear,
Freedom lives hence, and banishment is here.
[*To* CORDELIA.] The gods to their dear shelter take thee, maid,
That justly think'st, and hast most rightly said!
[*To* REGAN *and* GONERIL.] And your large speeches may your deeds
    approve,
That good effects may spring from words of love.
Thus Kent, O princes, bids you all adieu;
He'll shape his old course in a country new.   *Exit.*

   Flourish. Re-enter GLOUCESTER, *with* FRANCE, BURGUNDY, *and*
                   Attendants

   Glou. Here's France and Burgundy, my noble lord.
   Lear. My Lord of Burgundy,
We first address toward you, who with this king
Hath rivall'd for our daughter. What, in the least,
Will you require in present dower with her,
Or cease your quest of love?
   Bur.   Most royal Majesty,
I crave no more than what your Highness offer'd,
Nor will you tender less.
   Lear.   Right noble Burgundy,
When she was dear to us, we did hold her so;
But now her price is fallen. Sir, there she stands:
If aught within that little-seeming substance,
Or all of it, with our displeasure piec'd,
And nothing more, may fitly like your Grace,
She's there, and she is yours.
   Bur.   I know no answer.
   Lear. Will you, with those infirmities she owes,
Unfriended, new-adopted to our hate,
Dower'd with our curse, and stranger'd with our oath,
Take her, or leave her?

173

 Bur.   Pardon me, royal sir:
Election makes not up in such conditions.
 Lear. Then leave her, sir; for, by the power that made me
I tell you all her wealth. [*To* FRANCE.] For you, great king,
I would not from your love make such a stray,
To match you where I hate; therefore beseech you
To avert your liking a more worthier way
Than on a wretch whom Nature is asham'd
Almost to acknowledge hers.
 France.   This is most strange,
That she, whom even but now was your best object,
The argument of your praise, balm of your age,
The best, the dearest, should in this trice of time
Commit a thing so monstrous, to dismantle
So many folds of favour. Sure, her offence
Must be of such unnatural degree,
That monsters it, or your fore-vouch'd affection
Fallen into taint; which to believe of her,
Must be a faith that reason without miracle
Should never plant in me.
 Cor.   I yet beseech your Majesty,—
If for I want that glib and oily art,
To speak and purpose not; since what I well intend,
I'll do 't before I speak,— that you make known
It is no vicious blot, murder, or foulness,
No unchaste action, or dishonoured step,
That hath depriv'd me of your grace and favour:
But even for want of that for which I am richer,
A still-soliciting eye, and such a tongue
That I am glad I have not, though not to have it
Hath lost me in your liking.
 Lear.   Better thou
Hadst not been born than not to have pleas'd me better.
 France. Is it but this,—a tardiness in nature
Which often leaves the history unspoke
That it intends to do? My Lord of Burgundy.

What say you to the lady? Love's not love
When it is mingled with regards that stand
Aloof from the entire point. Will you have her?
She is herself a dowry.

    Bur.   Royal king,
Give but that portion which yourself propos'd,
And here I take Cordelia by the hand,
Duchess of Burgundy.

    Lear. Nothing. I have sworn; I am firm.

    Bur. I am sorry, then, you have so lost a father
That you must lose a husband.

    Cor.   Peace be with Burgundy!
Since that respect and fortunes are his love,
I shall not be his wife.

    France. Fairest Cordelia, that art most rich being poor,
Most choice forsaken, and most lov'd despis'd!
Thee and thy virtues here I seize upon,
Be it lawful I take up what's cast away.
Gods, gods! 'tis strange that from their cold'st neglect
My love should kindle to inflam'd respect.
Thy dowerless daughter, king, thrown to my chance,
Is queen of us, of ours, and our fair France.
Not all the dukes of waterish Burgundy
Can buy this unpriz'd precious maid of me.
Bid them farewell, Cordelia, though unkind;
Thou losest here, a better where to find.

    Lear. Thou hast her, France. Let her be thine; for we
Have no such daughter, nor shall ever see
That face of hers again.—[*To* Cor.] Therefore be gone
Without our grace, our love, our benison. —
Come, noble Burgundy.

                  Flourish. Exeunt [*all but* FRANCE, GONERIL,
                              REGAN, *and* CORDELIA].

    France. Bid farewell to your sisters.

    Cor. The jewels of our father, with wash'd eyes
Cordelia leaves you. I know you what you are;

175

And like a sister am most loath to call
Your faults as they are named. Love well our father,
To your professed bosoms I commit him;
But yet, alas, stood I within his grace,
I would prefer him to a better place.
So, farewell to you both.
   Reg. Prescribe not us our duty.
   Gon.   Let your study
Be to content your lord, who hath receiv'd you
At fortune's alms. You have obedience scanted,
And well are worth the want that you have wanted.
   Cor. Time shall unfold what plighted cunning hides;
Who covers faults, at last shame them derides.
Well may you prosper!
   France.   Come, my fair Cordelia.
                 Exeunt [FRANCE *and* CORDELIA].
   Gon. Sister, it is not little I have to say of what most nearly appertains to us both. I think our father will hence to-night.
   Reg. That's most certain, and with you; next month with us.
   Gon. You see how full of changes his age is; the observation we have made of it hath not been little. He always lov'd our sister most; and with what poor judgement he hath now cast her off appears too grossly.
   Reg. 'Tis the infirmity of his age; yet he hath ever but slenderly known himself.
   Gon. The best and soundest of his time hath been but rash; then must we look from his age to receive not alone the imperfections of long-engraffed condition, but therewithal the unruly waywardness that infirm and choleric years bring with them.
   Reg. Such unconstant starts are we like to have from him as this of Kent's banishment.
   Gon. There is further compliment of leave-taking between France and him. Pray you, let us hit together; if our father carry authority with such disposition as he bears, this last surrender of his will but offend us.

Reg. We shall further think of it.

Gon. We must do something, and i' the heat.   [*Exeunt.*

SCENE II. [*The Earl of Gloucester's castle*]

Enter Bastard [EDMUND *with a letter*]

Edm. Thou, Nature, art my goddess; to thy law
My services are bound. Wherefore should I
Stand in the plague of custom, and permit
The curiosity of nations to deprive me,
For that I am some twelve or fourteen moonshines
Lag of a brother? Why bastard? Wherefore base?
When my dimensions are as well compact,
My mind as generous, and my shape as true,
As honest madam's issue? Why brand they us
With base? with baseness? bastardy? base, base?
Who, in the lusty stealth of nature, take
More composition and fierce quality
Than doth, within a dull, stale, tired bed,
Go to the creating a whole tribe of fops,
Got 'tween asleep and wake? Well, then,
Legitimate Edgar, I must have your land.
Our father's love is to the bastard Edmund
As to the legitimate. Fine word, "legitimate"!
Well, my legitimate, if this letter speed
And my invention thrive, Edmund the base
Shall top the legitimate. I grow; I prosper.
Now, gods, stand up for bastards!

Enter GLOUCESTER

Glou. Kent banish'd thus! and France in choler parted!
And the King gone to-night! subscrib'd his power!
Confin'd to exhibition! All this done
Upon the gad! Edmund, how now! what news?

177

Edm. So please your lordship, none.   [*Putting up the letter.*]

Glou. Why so earnestly seek you to put up that letter?

Edm. I know no news, my lord.

Glou. What paper were you reading?

Edm. Nothing, my lord.

Glou. No? What needed, then, that terrible dispatch of it into your pocket? The quality of nothing hath not such need to hide itself. Let's see. Come, if it be nothing, I shall not need spectacles.

Edm. I beseech you, sir, pardon me. It is a letter from my brother, that I have not all o'er-read; and for so much as I have perus'd, I find it not fit for your o'er-looking.

Glou. Give me the letter, sir.

Edm. I shall offend, either to detain or give it. The contents, as in part I understand them, are to blame.

Glou. Let's see, let's see.

Edm. I hope, for my brother's justification, he wrote this but as an essay or taste of my virtue.

Glou. (*Reads.*) "This policy and reverence of age makes the world bitter to the best of our times; keeps our fortunes from us till our oldness cannot relish them. I begin to find an idle and fond bondage in the oppression of aged tyranny; who sways, not as it hath power, but as it is suffer'd. Come to me, that of this I may speak more. If our father would sleep till I wak'd him, you should enjoy half his revenue for ever, and live the beloved of your brother,

EDGAR."

Hum—conspiracy!—"Sleep till I wake him, you should enjoy half his revenue!"—My son Edgar! Had he a hand to write this? a heart and brain to breed it in?—When came this to you? Who brought it?

Edm. It was not brought me, my lord; there's the cunning of it. I found it thrown in at the casement of my closet.

Glou. You know the character to be your brother's?

Edm. If the matter were good, my lord, I durst swear it were his; but, in respect of that, I would fain think it were not.

Glou. It is his.

Edm. It is his hand, my lord; but I hope his heart is not in the contents.

Glou. Has he never before sounded you in this business?

Edm. Never, my lord; but I have heard him oft maintain it to be fit that, sons at perfect age, and fathers declin'd, the father should be as ward to the son, and the son manage his revenue.

Glou. O villain, villain! His very opinion in the letter! Abhorred villain! Unnatural, detested, brutish villain! worse than brutish! Go, sirrah, seek him; I'll apprehend him. Abominable villain! Where is he?

Edm. I do not well know, my lord. If it shall please you to suspend your indignation against my brother till you can derive from him better testimony of his intent, you should run a certain course; where, if you violently proceed against him, mistaking his purpose, it would make a great gap in your own honour, and shake in pieces the heart of his obedience. I dare pawn down my life for him, that he hath writ this to feel my affection to your honour, and to no other pretence of danger.

Glou. Think you so?

Edm. If your honour judge it meet, I will place you where you shall hear us confer of this, and by an auricular assurance have your satisfaction; and that without any further delay than this very evening.

Glou. He cannot be such a monster—

[*Edm.* Nor is not, sure.

Glou. To his father, that so tenderly and entirely loves him. Heaven and earth!] Edmund, seek him out; wind me into him, I pray you. Frame the business after your own wisdom. I would unstate myself, to be in a due resolution.

Edm. I will seek him, sir, presently; convey the business as I shall find means, and acquaint you withal.

Glou. These late eclipses in the sun and moon portend no good to us. Though the wisdom of nature can reason it thus and thus, yet nature finds itself scourg'd by the sequent effects. Love cools, friendship falls off, brothers divide: in cities, mutinies; in countries, discord; in palaces, treason; and the bond crack'd 'twixt son and father. This villain of mine comes under the prediction; there's son against father; the King falls from bias of nature; there's father against child. We have seen the best of our time; machinations, hollowness, treachery, and all ruinous disorders, follow us disquietly to our graves. Find out this villain, Edmund; it shall lose thee nothing; do it carefully. And the noble and true-hearted Kent banish'd! his offence, honesty! 'Tis strange.

Exit.

Edm. This is the excellent foppery of the world, that, when we are sick in fortune,—often the surfeits of our own behaviour,—we make guilty of our disasters the sun, the moon, and the stars; as if we were villains on necessity, fools by heavenly compulsion, knaves, thieves, and treachers by spherical predominance, drunkards, liars, and adulterers by an enforc'd obedience of planetary influence, and all that we are evil in, by a divine thrusting on. An admirable evasion of whoremaster man, to lay his goatish disposition on the charge of a star! My father compounded with my mother under the dragon's tail; and my nativity was under *Ursa Major;* so that it follows, I am rough and lecherous. Fut, I should have been that I am, had the maidenliest star in the firmament twinkled on my bastardizing. Edgar—

Enter EDGAR

and pat he comes like the catastrophe of the old comedy. My cue is villanous melancholy, with a sigh like Tom o' Bedlam —O, these eclipses do portend these divisions! *fa, sol, la, mi.*

Edg. How now, brother Edmund! what serious contemplation are you in?

Edm. I am thinking, brother, of a prediction I read this other day, what should follow these eclipses.

Edg. Do you busy yourself with that?

Edm. I promise you, the effects he writes of succeed unhappily; [as of unnaturalness between the child and the parent; death, dearth, dissolutions of ancient amities; divisions in state, menaces and maledictions against king and nobles; needless diffidences, banishment of friends, dissipation of cohorts, nuptial breaches and I know not what.

Edg. How long have you been a sectary astronomical?·
Edm. Come, come;] when saw you my father last?
Edg. [Why,] the night gone by.
Edm. Spake you with him?
Edg. Ay, two hours together.
Edm. Parted you in good terms? Found you no displeasure in him by word nor countenance?
Edg. None at all.
Edm. Bethink yourself wherein you may have offended him; and at my entreaty forbear his presence until some little time hath qualified the heat of his displeasure, which at this instant so rageth in him, that with the mischief of your person it would scarcely allay.
Edg. Some villain hath done me wrong.
Edm. That's my fear. I pray you, have a continent forbearance till the speed of his rage goes slower; and, as I say, retire with me to my lodging, from whence I will fitly bring you to hear my lord speak. Pray ye, go; there's my key. If you do stir abroad, go arm'd.
Edg. Arm'd, brother!
Edm. Brother, I advise you to the best; go armed; I am no honest man if there be any good meaning toward you. I have told you what I have seen and heard; but faintly, nothing like the image and horror of it. Pray you, away.
Edg. Shall I hear from you anon?
Edm. I do serve you in this business.   *Exit* EDGAR.
A credulous father, and a brother noble,
Whose nature is so far from doing harms
That he suspects none; on whose foolish honesty
My practices ride easy. I see the business.
Let me, if not by birth, have lands by wit:
All with me's meet that I can fashion fit.   *Exit.*

SCENE III. [*The Duke of Albany's palace*]

Enter GONERIL, *and* [OSWALD, *her*] Steward

Gon. Did my father strike my gentleman for chiding of his Fool?
Osw. Ay, madam.

181

Gon. By day and night he wrongs me; every hour
He flashes into one gross crime or other
That sets us all at odds. I'll not endure it.
His knights grow riotous, and himself upbraids us
On every trifle. When he returns from hunting,
I will not speak with him; say I am sick.
If you come slack of former services,
You shall do well; the fault of it, I'll answer.
   Osw. He's coming, madam; I hear him.   [*Horns within.*]
   Gon. Put on what weary negligence you please,
You and your fellows; I'd have it come to question.
If he distaste it, let him to my sister,
Whose mind and mine, I know, in that are one,
[Not to be over-rul'd. Idle old man,
That still would manage those authorities
That he hath given away! Now, by my life,
Old fools are babes again, and must be us'd
With checks as flatteries, when they are seen abus'd.]
Remember what I have said.
   Osw.   Well, madam.
   Gon. And let his knights have colder looks among you;
What grows of it, no matter. Advise your fellows so.
[I would breed from hence occasions, and I shall,
That I may speak.] I'll write straight to my sister,
To hold my [very] course. Prepare for dinner.   *Exeunt.*

SCENE IV. [*A hall in the same*]

Enter KENT [*disguised*]

   Kent. If but as well I other accents borrow,
That can my speech defuse, my good intent
May carry through itself to that full issue
For which I raz'd my likeness. Now, banish'd Kent,
If thou canst serve where thou dost stand condemn'd,
So may it come, thy master, whom thou lov'st,
Shall find thee full of labours.

182

Horns within. Enter LEAR, [Knights] *and* Attendants

Lear. Let me not stay a jot for dinner; go get it ready. [*Exit an attendant.*] How now! what art thou?

Kent. A man, sir.

Lear. What dost thou profess? What wouldst thou with us?

Kent. I do profess to be no less than I-seem; to serve him truly that will put me in trust; to love him that is honest; to converse with him that is wise and says little; to fear judgement; to fight when I cannot choose; and to eat no fish.

Lear. What art thou?

Kent. A very honest-hearted fellow, and as poor as the King.

Lear. If thou be'st as poor for a subject as he's for a king, thou art poor enough. What wouldst thou?

Kent. Service.

Lear. Who wouldst thou serve?

Kent. You.

Lear. Dost thou know me, fellow?

Kent. No, sir; but you have that in your countenance which I would fain call master.

Lear. What's that?

Kent. Authority.

Lear. What services canst thou do?

Kent. I can keep honest counsel, ride, run, mar a curious tale in telling it, and deliver a plain message bluntly. That which ordinary men are fit for, I am qualified in; and the best of me is diligence.

Lear. How old art thou?

Kent. Not so young, sir, to love a woman for singing, nor so old to dote on her for anything. I have years on my back forty-eight.

Lear. Follow me; thou shalt serve me. If I like thee no worse after dinner, I will not part from thee yet. Dinner, ho, dinner! Where's my knave, my Fool? Go you, and call my Fool hither.

Exit an Attendant.

Enter Steward [OSWALD]

You, you, sirrah, where's my daughter?

Osw. So please you,—   *Exit.*

Lear. What says the fellow there? Call the clotpoll back. [*Exit a* knight.] Where's my Fool, ho? I think the world's asleep.

[*Re-enter* Knight]

How now! where's that mongrel?

Knight. He says, my lord, your daughter is not well.

Lear. Why came not the slave back to me when I call'd him?

Knight. Sir, he answered me in the roundest˙ manner, he would not.

Lear. He would not!

Knight. My lord, I know not what the matter is; but, to my judgement, your Highness is not entertain'd with that ceremonious affection as you were wont. There's a great abatement of kindness appears as well in the general dependants as in the Duke himself also and your daughter.

Lear. Ha! say'st thou so?

Knight. I beseech you, pardon me, my lord, if I be mistaken; for my duty cannot be silent when I think your Highness wrong'd.

Lear. Thou but rememb'rest me of mine own conception. I have perceived a most faint neglect of late, which I have rather blamed as mine own jealous curiosity than as a very pretence and purpose of unkindness. I will look further into 't. But where's my Fool? I have not seen him this two days.

Knight. Since my young lady's going into France, sir, the Fool hath much pined away.

Lear. No more of that; I have noted it well. Go you, and tell my daughter I would speak with her. [*Exit an* Attendant.] Go you, call hither my Fool. [*Exit an* Attendant.]

Re-enter Steward [OSWALD]

O, you sir, you, come you hither, sir. Who am I, sir?

Osw. My lady's father.

Lear. "My lady's father"! My lord's knave! You whoreson dog! you slave! you cur!

Osw. I am none of these, my lord; I beseech your pardon.

Lear. Do you bandy looks with me, you rascal? [*Striking him.*]

Osw. I'll not be struck, my lord.

Kent. Nor tripp'd neither, you base foot-ball player.

[*Tripping up his heels.*]

Lear. I thank thee, fellow. Thou serv'st me, and I'll love thee.

Kent. Come, sir, arise, away! I'll teach you differences. Away, away! If you will measure your lubber's length again, tarry; but away! go to. Have you wisdom? So. [*Pushes* Oswald *out.*]

Lear. Now, my friendly knave, I thank thee. There's earnest of thy service. [*Giving* Kent *money.*]

Enter Fool

Fool. Let me hire him too; here's my coxcomb.

[*Offering* Kent *his cap.*]

Lear. How now, my pretty knave! how dost thou?

Fool. Sirrah, you were best take my coxcomb.

[*Kent.* Why, Fool?]

Fool. Why? For taking one's part that's out of favour. Nay, an thou canst not smile as the wind sits, thou'lt catch cold shortly. There, take my coxcomb. Why, this fellow has banish'd two on 's daughters, and did the third a blessing against his will; if thou follow him, thou must needs wear my coxcomb.—How now, nuncle! Would I had two coxcombs and two daughters!

Lear. Why, my boy?

Fool. If I gave them all my living, I'd keep my coxcombs myself. There's mine; beg another of thy daughters.

Lear. Take heed, sirrah; the whip.

Fool. Truth's a dog must to kennel; he must be whipp'd out, when Lady the brach may stand by the fire and stink.

Lear. A pestilent gall to me!

Fool. Sirrah, I'll teach thee a speech.

Lear. Do.

Fool. Mark it, nuncle:

"Have more than thou showest,
Speak less than thou knowest,
Lend less than thou owest,
Ride more than thou goest,

Learn more than thou trowest,
Set less than thou throwest;
Leave thy drink and thy whore,
And keep in-a-door,
And thou shalt have more
Than two tens to a score."

Kent. This is nothing, Fool.

Fool. Then 'tis like the breath of an unfee'd lawyer; you gave me nothing for 't. Can you make no use of nothing, nuncle?

Lear. Why, no, boy; nothing can be made out of nothing.

Fool. [*To* KENT.] Prithee, tell him so much the rent of his land comes to. He will not believe a fool.

Lear. A bitter fool!

Fool. Dost thou know the difference, my boy, between a bitter fool and a sweet one?

Lear. No, lad; teach me.

[*Fool.*   "That lord that counsell'd thee
              To give away thy land,
          Come place him here by me,
              Do thou for him stand:
          The sweet and bitter fool
              Will presently appear;
          The one in motley here,
              The other found out there."

Lear. Dost thou call me fool, boy?

Fool. All thy other titles thou hast given away; that thou wast born with.

Kent. This is not altogether fool, my lord.

Fool. No, faith, lords and great men will not let me; if I had a monopoly out, they would have part on 't. And ladies, too, they will not let me have all the fool to myself; they'll be snatching.] Nuncle, give me an egg, and I'll give thee two crowns.

Lear. What two crowns shall they be?

Fool. Why, after I have cut the egg i' the middle, and eat up the meat, the two crowns of the egg. When thou clovest thy crown i' the middle, and gav'st away both parts, thou bor'st thine ass on thy back o'er the dirt. Thou hadst little wit in thy bald crown, when thou gav'st thy golden one away. If I speak like myself in this, let him be whipp'd that first finds it so.

> "Fools had ne'er less grace in a year;
> For wise men are grown foppish,
> And know not how their wits to wear,
> Their manners are so apish."

Lear. When were you wont to be so full of songs, sirrah?

Fool. I have used it, nuncle, e'er since thou mad'st thy daughters thy mothers; for when thou gav'st them the rod, and puttest down thine own breeches,

> "Then they for sudden joy did weep,
> And I for sorrow sung,
> That such a king should play bo-peep,
> And go the fools among."

Prithee, nuncle, keep a schoolmaster that can teach thy Fool to lie. I would fain learn to lie.

Lear. An you lie, sirrah, we'll have you whipp'd.

Fool. I marvel what kin thou and thy daughters are. They'll have me whipp'd for speaking true, thou'lt have me whipp'd for lying; and sometimes I am whipp'd for holding my peace. I had rather be any kind o' thing than a Fool; and yet I would not be thee, nuncle; thou hast pared thy wit o' both sides, and left nothing i' the middle. Here comes one o' the parings.

Enter GONERIL

Lear. How now, daughter! what makes that frontlet on? [Methinks] you are too much of late i' the frown.

Fool. Thou wast a pretty fellow when thou hadst no need to care for her frowning; now thou art an O without a figure. I am better than thou art now; I am a Fool, thou art nothing. [*To Gon.*] Yes, forsooth, I will hold my tongue; so your face bids me, though you say nothing. Mum, mum,

> "He that keeps nor crust nor crumb,
> Weary of all, shall want some."

[*Pointing to* Lear.] That's a sheal'd peascod.

Gon. Not only, sir, this your all-licens'd Fool,
But other of your insolent retinue
Do hourly carp and quarrel, breaking forth
In rank and not-to-be-endured riots. Sir,
I had thought, by making this well known unto you,
To have found a safe redress; but now grow fearful,
By what yourself, too, late have spoke and done,
That you protect this course, and put it on
By your allowance; which if you should, the fault
Would not scape censure, nor the redresses sleep,
Which, in the tender of a wholesome weal,
Might in their working do you that offence,
Which else were shame, that then necessity
Will call discreet proceeding.
    Fool. For, you know, nuncle,
        "The hedge-sparrow fed the cuckoo so long,
        That it had it head bit off by it young."
So, out went the candle, and we were left darkling.
    Lear. Are you our daughter?
    Gon. [Come, sir,]
I would you would make use of your good wisdom,
Whereof I know you are fraught, and put away
These dispositions, which of late transport you
From what you rightly are.
    Fool. May not an ass know when the cart draws the horse?
"Whoop, Jug! I love thee."
    Lear. Doth any here know me? This is not Lear.
Doth Lear walk thus? speak thus? Where are his eyes?
Either his notion weakens, his discernings
Are lethargied—Ha! waking? 'Tis not so.
Who is it that can tell me who I am?
    Fool. Lear's shadow.
    [*Lear.* I would learn that; for, by the marks of sovereignty, knowledge, and reason, I should be false persuaded I had daughters.
    Fool. Which they will make an obedient father.]
    Lear. Your name, fair gentlewoman?

188

Gon. This admiration, sir, is much o' the savour
Of other your new pranks. I do beseech you
To understand my purposes aright.
As you are old and reverend, you should be wise.
Here do you keep a hundred knights and squires;
Men so disorder'd, so debosh'd and bold,
That this our court, infected with their manners,
Shows like a riotous inn. Epicurism and lust
Makes it more like a tavern or a brothel
Than a grac'd palace. The shame itself doth speak
For instant remedy. Be then desir'd
By her, that else will take the thing she begs,
A little to disquantity your train;
And the remainders, that shall still depend,
To be such men as may besort your age,
Which know themselves and you.
   Lear.   Darkness and devils!
Saddle my horses; call my train together!
Degenerate bastard! I'll not trouble thee;
Yet have I left a daughter.
   Gon. You strike my people; and your disorder'd rabble
Make servants of their betters.

Enter ALBANY

   Lear. Woe, that too late repents!—[O, sir, are you come?]
Is it your will? Speak, sir.—Prepare my horses.—
Ingratitude, thou marble-hearted fiend,
More hideous when thou show'st thee in a child
Than the sea-monster!
   Alb.   Pray, sir, be patient.
   Lear. [*To* GON.] Detested kite! thou liest.
My train are men of choice and rarest parts,
That all particulars of duty know,
And in the most exact regard support
The worships of their name. O most small fault,

How ugly didst thou in Cordelia show!
Which, like an engine, wrench'd my frame of nature
From the fix'd place; drew from my heart all love,
And added to the gall. O Lear, Lear, Lear!
Beat at this gate, that let thy folly in,   [*Striking his head.*]
And thy dear judgement out! Go, go, my people.
   Alb. My lord, I am guiltless as I am ignorant
Of what hath moved you.
   Lear.   It may be so, my lord.
Hear, Nature! hear, dear goddess, hear!
Suspend thy purpose, if thou didst intend
To make this creature fruitful!
Into her womb convey sterility!
Dry up in her the organs of increase,
And from her derogate body never spring
A babe to honour her! If she must teem,
Create her child of spleen, that it may live
And be a thwart disnatur'd torment to her!
Let it stamp wrinkles in her brow of youth,
With cadent tears fret channels in her cheeks,
Turn all her mother's pains and benefits
To laughter and contempt, that she may feel
How sharper than a serpent's tooth it is
To have a thankless child!—Away, away!   *Exit.*
   Alb. Now, gods that we adore, whereof comes this?
   Gon. Never afflict yourself to know more of it;
But let his disposition have that scope
As dotage gives it.

Re-enter LEAR

   Lear. What, fifty of my followers at a clap!
Within a fortnight!
   Alb.   What's the matter, sir?
   Lear. I'll tell thee. [*To* GON.] Life and death! I am asham'd
That thou hast power to shake my manhood thus;
That these hot tears, which break from me perforce,

Should make thee worth them. Blasts and fogs upon thee!
The untented woundings of a father's curse
Pierce every sense about thee! Old fond eyes,
Beweep this cause again, I'll pluck ye out,
And cast you, with the waters that you loose,
To temper clay. Ha! [is it come to this?]
Let it be so: I have another daughter,
Who, I am sure, is kind and comfortable.
When she shall hear this of thee, with her nails
She'll flay thy wolvish visage. Thou shalt find
That I'll resume the shape which thou dost think
I have cast off for ever. [Thou shalt, I warrant thee.]

[*Exeunt* LEAR, KENT, *and* Attendants.]

Gon. Do you mark that?
Alb. I cannot be so partial, Goneril,
To the great love I bear you,—
Gon. Pray you, content.—What, Oswald, ho!
[*To the Fool.*] You, sir, more knave than fool, after your master.

Fool. Nuncle Lear, nuncle Lear, tarry! Take the Fool with thee.
A fox, when one has caught her,
And such a daughter,
Should sure to the slaughter,
If my cap would buy a halter.
So the Fool follows after. *Exit.*

Gon. This man hath had good counsel,—a hundred knights!
'Tis politic and safe to let him keep
At point a hundred knights; yes, that, on every dream,
Each buzz, each fancy, each complaint, dislike,
He may enguard his dotage with their powers,
And hold our lives in mercy. Oswald, I say!
Alb. Well, you may fear too far.
Gon.   Safer than trust too far.
Let me still take away the harms I fear,
Not fear still to be taken. I know his heart.
What he hath utter'd I have writ my sister.

191

If she sustain him and his hundred knights,
When I have show'd the unfitness,—

Re-enter Steward [OSWALD]

How now, Oswald!

What, have you writ that letter to my sister?
Osw. Ay, madam.
Gon. Take you some company, and away to horse.
Inform her full of my particular fear;
And thereto add such reasons of your own
As may compact it more. Get you gone;
And hasten your return. [*Exit* OSWALD.] No, no, my lord,
This milky gentleness and course of yours
Though I condemn not, yet, under pardon,
You are much more at task for want of wisdom
Than prais'd for harmful mildness.
Alb. How far your eyes may pierce I cannot tell.
Striving to better, oft we mar what's well.
Gon. Nay, then—
Alb. Well, well; the event. *Exeunt.*

SCENE V. [*Court before the same*]

Enter LEAR, KENT, *and* Fool

Lear. Go you before to Gloucester with these letters. Acquaint my daughter no further with anything you know than comes from her demand out of the letter. If your diligence be not speedy, I shall be there afore you.
Kent. I will not sleep, my lord, till I have delivered your letter.
Exit.
Fool. If a man's brains were in 's heels, were 't not in danger of kibes?
Lear. Ay, boy.
Fool. Then, I prithee, be merry; thy wit shall not go slip-shod.
Lear. Ha, ha, ha!

Fool. Shalt see thy other daughter will use thee kindly; for though she's as like this as a crab's like an apple, yet I can tell what I can tell.

Lear. What canst tell, boy?

Fool. She will taste as like this as a crab does to a crab. Thou canst tell why one's nose stands i' the middle on 's face?

Lear. No.

Fool. Why, to keep one's eyes of either side 's nose, that what a man cannot smell out, he may spy into.

Lear. I did her wrong—

Fool. Canst tell how an oyster makes his shell?

Lear. No.

Fool. Nor I neither; but I can tell why a snail has a house.

Lear. Why?

Fool. Why, to put 's head in; not to give it away to his daughters, and leave his horns without a case.

Lear. I will forget my nature. So kind a father! Be my horses ready?

Fool. Thy asses are gone about 'em. The reason why the seven stars are no more than seven is a pretty reason.

Lear. Because they are not eight?

Fool. Yes, indeed. Thou wouldst make a good Fool.

Lear. To take 't again perforce! Monster ingratitude!

Fool. If thou wert my Fool, nuncle, I'd have thee beaten for being old before thy time.

Lear. How's that?

Fool. Thou shouldst not have been old till thou hadst been wise.

Lear. O, let me not be mad, not mad, sweet heaven! Keep me in temper; I would not be mad!

[*Enter* Gentleman]

How now! are the horses ready?

Gent. Ready, my lord.

Lear. Come, boy.

Fool. She that's a maid now, and laughs at my departure, Shall not be a maid long, unless things be cut shorter.   *Exeunt.*

ACT II

Scene I. [*The Earl of Gloucester's castle*]

Enter Bastard [Edmund] *and* Curan, *severally*

Edm. Save thee, Curan.

Cur. And you, sir. I have been with your father, and given him notice that the Duke of Cornwall and Regan his duchess will be here with him this night.

Edm. How comes that?

Cur. Nay, I know not. You have heard of the news abroad; I mean the whisper'd ones, for they are yet but ear-kissing arguments?

Edm. Not I. Pray you, what are they?

Cur. Have you heard of no likely wars toward, 'twixt the Dukes of Cornwall and Albany?

Edm. Not a word.

Cur. You may do, then, in time. Fare you well, sir.   *Exit.*

Edm. The Duke be here to-night? The better! best!
This weaves itself perforce into my business.
My father hath set guard to take my brother;
And I have one thing, of a queasy question,
Which I must act. Briefness and fortune, work!

Enter Edgar

Brother, a word; descend. Brother, I say!
My father watches; O sir, fly this place;
Intelligence is given where you are hid;
You have now the good advantage of the night.
Have you not spoken 'gainst the Duke of Cornwall?
He's coming hither, now, i' the night, i' the haste,
And Regan with him. Have you nothing said
Upon his party 'gainst the Duke of Albany?
Advise yourself.

Edg.   I am sure on 't, not a word.

Edm. I hear my father coming. Pardon me,

In cunning I must draw my sword upon you.
Draw; seem to defend yourself; now quit you well.
Yield! Come before my father. Light, ho, here!—
Fly, brother.—Torches, torches!—So, farewell.   *Exit* EDGAR.
Some blood drawn on me would beget opinion   [*Wounds his arm.*]
Of my more fierce endeavour. I have seen drunkards
Do more than this in sport.—Father, father!—
Stop, stop!—No help?

Enter GLOUCESTER, *and* Servants *with torches*

Glou. Now, Edmund, where's the villain?
Edm. Here stood he in the dark, his sharp sword out,
Mumbling of wicked charms, conjuring the moon
To stand auspicious mistress,—
    Glou.   But where is he?
Edm. Look, sir, I bleed.
    Glou.   Where is the villain, Edmund?
Edm. Fled this way, sir. When by no means he could—
    Glou. Pursue him, ho! Go after. [*Exeunt some* Servants.] By no
means what?
Edm. Persuade me to the murder of your lordship;
But that I told him, the revenging gods
'Gainst parricides did all the thunder bend;
Spoke, with how manifold and strong a bond
The child was bound to the father; sir, in fine,
Seeing how loathly opposite I stood
To his unnatural purpose, in fell motion,
With his prepared sword, he charges home
My unprovided body, latch'd mine arm;
And when he saw my best alarum'd spirits,
Bold in the quarrel's right, rous'd to the encounter,
Or whether gasted by the noise I made,
Full suddenly he fled.
    Glou.   Let him fly far.
Not in this land shall he remain uncaught;
And found,—dispatch. The noble Duke my master.

My worthy arch and patron, comes to-night.
By his authority I will proclaim it,
That he which finds him shall deserve our thanks,
Bringing the murderous coward to the stake;
He that conceals him, death.

    Edm. When I dissuaded him from his intent,
And found him pight to do it, with curst speech
I threaten'd to discover him; he replied,
"Thou unpossessing bastard! dost thou think,
If I would stand against thee, would the reposal
Of any trust, virtue, or worth in thee
Make thy words faith'd? No! what I should deny,—
As this I would; ay, though thou didst produce
My very character, —I'd turn it all
To thy suggestion, plot, and damned practice;
And thou must make a dullard of the world
If they not thought the profits of my death
Were very pregnant and potential spurs‾
To make thee seek it."

    Glou.   O strange and fast'ned villain!
Would he deny his letter? [I never got him.]   *Tucket within.*
Hark, the Duke's trumpets! I know not why he comes.
All ports I'll bar, the villain shall not scape;
The Duke must grant me that. Besides, his picture
I will send far and near, that all the kingdom
May have due note of him; and of my land,
Loyal and natural boy, I'll work the means
To make thee capable.

        Enter CORNWALL, REGAN, *and* Attendants

    Corn. How now, my noble friend! since I came nither,
Which I can call but now, I have heard strange news.
    Reg. If it be true, all vengeance comes too short
Which can pursue the offender. How dost, my lord?
    Glou. O, madam, my old heart is crack'd, it's crack'd!

196

Reg. What, did my father's godson seek your life?
He whom my father nam'd? your Edgar?
   Glou. O, lady, lady, shame would have it hid!
   Reg. Was he not companion with the riotous knights
That tended upon my father?
   Glou. I know not, madam. 'Tis too bad, too bad.
   Edm. Yes, madam, he was of that consort.
   Reg. No marvel, then, though he were ill affected:
'Tis they have put him on the old man's death,
To have the expense and waste of his revenues.
I have this present evening from my sister
Been well inform'd of them; and with such cautions,
That if they come to sojourn at my house,
I'll not be there.
   Corn.   Nor I, assure thee, Regan.
Edmund, I hear that you have shown your father
A child-like office.
   Edm.   'Twas my duty, sir.
   Glou. He did bewray his practice, and receiv'd
This hurt you see, striving to apprehend him.
   Corn. Is he pursued?
   Glou.   Ay, my good lord.
   Corn. If he be taken, he shall never more
Be fear'd of doing harm. Make your own purpose,
How in my strength you please. For you, Edmund,
Whose virtue and obedience doth this instant
So much commend itself, you shall be ours.
Natures of such deep trust we shall much need;
You we first seize on.
   Edm.   I shall serve you, sir,
Truly, however else.
   Glou.   For him I thank your Grace.
   Corn. You know not why we came to visit you,—
   Reg. Thus out of season, threading dark-ey'd night?
Occasions, noble Gloucester, of some poise,
Wherein we must have use of your advice.

197

Our father he hath writ, so hath our sister,
Of differences, which I best thought it fit
To answer from our home; the several messengers
From hence attend dispatch. Our good old friend,
Lay comforts to your bosom; and bestow
Your needful counsel to our businesses,
Which craves the instant use.
  Glou.   I serve you, madam.
Your Graces are right welcome.   ***Exeunt. Flourish.***

SCENE II. [*Before Gloucester's castle*]

Enter KENT *and* Steward [OSWALD], *severally*

Osw. Good dawning to thee, friend. Art of this house?

Kent. Ay.

Osw. Where may we set our horses?

Kent. I' the mire.

Osw. Prithee, if thou lov'st me, tell me.

Kent. I love thee not.

Osw. Why, then, I care not for thee.

Kent. If I had thee in Lipsbury pinfold, I would make thee care
for me.

Osw. Why dost thou use me thus? I know thee not.

Kent. Fellow, I know thee.

Osw. What dost thou know me for?

Kent. A knave; a rascal; an eater of broken meats; a base, proud,
shallow, beggarly, three-suited, hundred-pound, filthy, worsted-
stocking knave; a lily-livered, action-taking, whoreson, glass-gazing,
superserviceable, finical rogue; one-trunk-inheriting slave; one that
wouldst be a bawd, in way of good service, and art nothing but the
composition of a knave, beggar, coward, pandar, and the son and
heir of a mongrel bitch; one whom I will beat into clamorous whining, if thou deni'st the least syllable of thy addition.

Osw. Why, what a monstrous fellow art thou, thus to rail on one
that is neither known of thee nor knows thee!

Kent. What a brazen-fac'd varlet art thou, to deny thou knowest me! Is it two days since I tripp'd up thy heels, and beat thee before the King? Draw, you rogue; for, though it be night, yet the moon shines. I'll make a sop o' the moonshine of you, you whoreson cullionly barber-monger! Draw! [*Drawing his sword.*]

Osw. Away! I have nothing to do with thee.

Kent. Draw, you rascal! You come with letters against the King; and take Vanity the puppet's part against the royalty of her father. Draw, you rogue, or I'll so carbonado your shanks,—draw, you rascal! Come your ways.

Osw. Help, ho! murder! help!

Kent. Strike, you slave! Stand, rogue, stand!
You neat slave, strike. [*Beating him.*]

Osw. Help, ho! murder! murder!

Enter Bastard [EDMUND] *with his rapier drawn*, CORNWALL, REGAN, GLOUCESTER, *and* Servants

Edm. How now! What's the matter? Part.

Kent. With you, goodman boy, if you please.
Come, I'll flesh ye; come on, young master.

Glou. Weapons! arms! What's the matter here?

Corn. Keep peace, upon your lives!
He dies that strikes again. What is the matter?

Reg. The messengers from our sister and the King.

Corn. What is your difference? Speak.

Osw. I am scarce in breath, my lord.

Kent. No marvel, you have so bestirr'd your valour. You cowardly rascal, Nature disclaims in thee. A tailor made thee.

Corn. Thou art a strange fellow. A tailor make a man?

Kent. A tailor, sir. A stone-cutter or a painter could not have made him so ill, though they had been but two years o' the trade.

Corn. Speak yet, how grew your quarrel?

Osw. This ancient ruffian, sir, whose life I have spar'd at suit of his grey beard,—

Kent. Thou whoreson zed! thou unnecessary letter! My lord,

199

if you will give me leave, I will tread this unbolted   villain into
mortar, and daub the wall of a jakes with him. Spare my grey beard,
you wagtail?

    Corn. Peace, sirrah!
You beastly knave, know you no reverence?

    Kent. Yes, sir; but anger hath a privilege.

    Corn. Why art thou angry?

    Kent. That such a slave as this should wear a sword,
Who wears no honesty. Such smiling rogues as these,
Like rats, oft bite the holy cords a-twain
Which are too intrinse   to unloose; smooth every passion
That in the natures of their lords rebel;
Bring oil to fire, snow to their colder moods;
Renege,   affirm, and turn their halcyon beaks
With every gale and vary of their masters,
Knowing nought, like dogs, but following.
A plague upon your epileptic visage!
Smile you my speeches, as I were a fool?
Goose, if I had you upon Sarum Plain,
I'd drive ye cackling home to Camelot.

    Corn. What, art thou mad, old fellow?

    Glou. How fell you out? Say that.

    Kent. No contraries hold more antipathy
Than I and such a knave.

    Corn. Why dost thou call him knave? What is his fault?

    Kent. His countenance likes   me not.

    Corn. No more, perchance, does mine, nor his, nor hers.

    Kent. Sir, 'tis my occupation to be plain;
I have seen better faces in my time
Than stands on any shoulder that I see
Before me at this instant.

    Corn.   This is some fellow
Who, having been prais'd for bluntness, doth affect
A saucy roughness, and constrains the garb
Quite from his nature. He cannot flatter, he;

An honest mind and plain, he must speak truth!
An they will take it, so; if not, he's plain.
These kind of knaves I know, which in this plainness
Harbour more craft and more corrupter ends
Than twenty silly ducking observants
That stretch their duties nicely.

    Kent. Sir, in good sooth, in sincere verity,
Under the allowance of your great aspect,
Whose influence, like the wreath of radiant fire
On flickering Phœbus' front,—

    Corn.   What mean'st by this?

    Kent. To go out of my dialect, which you discommend so much.
I know, sir, I am no flatterer. He that beguil'd you in a plain accent
was a plain knave; which for my part I will not be, though I should
win your displeasure to entreat me to 't.

    Corn. What was the offence you gave him?

    Osw. I never gave him any.
It pleas'd the King his master very late
To strike at me, upon his misconstruction;
When he, compact, and flattering his displeasure,
Tripp'd me behind; being down, insulted, rail'd,
And put upon him such a deal of man
That 't worthied him, got praises of the King
For him attempting who was self-subdued;
And, in the fleshment of this dread exploit,
Drew on me here again.

    Kent.   None of these rogues and cowards
But Ajax is their fool.

    Corn.   Fetch forth the stocks!
You stubborn ancient knave, you reverend braggart,
We'll teach you—

    Kent.   Sir, I am too old to learn.
Call not your stocks for me; I serve the King,
On whose employment I was sent to you.
You shall do small respects, show too bold malice

Against the grace and person of my master,
Stocking his messenger.

    Corn. Fetch forth the stocks! As I have life and honour,
There shall he sit till noon.

    Reg. Till noon! Till night, my lord; and all night too.

    Kent. Why, madam, if I were your father's dog,
You should not use me so.

    Reg.   Sir, being his knave, I will.

                                         Stocks brought out.

    Corn. This is a fellow of the self-same colour
Our sister speaks of. Come, bring away the stocks!

    Glou. Let me beseech your Grace not to do so.
[His fault is much, and the good King his master
Will check him for 't. Your purpos'd low correction
Is such as basest and contemned'st wretches
For pilferings and most common trespasses
Are punish'd with.] The King must take it ill
That he's so slightly valued in his messenger,
Should have him thus restrained.

    Corn.   I'll answer that.

    Reg. My sister may receive it much more worse
To have her gentleman abus'd, assaulted,
[For following her affairs. Put in his legs.]

                        [KENT *is put in the stocks.*]
Come, my good lord, away.

                 Exeunt [*all but* GLOUCESTER *and* KENT].

    Glou. I am sorry for thee, friend; 'tis the Duke's pleasure,
Whose disposition, all the world well knows,
Will not be rubb'd nor stopp'd. I'll entreat for thee.

    Kent. Pray, do not, sir. I have watch'd and travell'd hard;
Some time I shall sleep out, the rest I'll whistle.
A good man's fortune may grow out at heels.
Give you good morrow!

    Glou. The Duke's to blame in this; 'twill be ill taken.   *Exit.*

    Kent. Good King, that must approve the common saw,
Thou out of heaven's benediction com'st

To the warm sun!
Approach, thou beacon to this under globe,
That by thy comfortable beams I may
Peruse this letter! Nothing, almost, sees miracles
But misery. I know 'tis from Cordelia,
Who hath most fortunately been inform'd
Of my obscured course; [*reads*] "—and shall find time
From this enormous state—seeking to give
Losses their remedies."—All weary and o'erwatch'd,
Take vantage, heavy eyes, not to behold
This shameful lodging.
Fortune, good-night! Smile once more; turn thy wheel! [*Sleeps.*]

[SCENE III. *The same*]

Enter EDGAR

Edg. I heard myself proclaim'd;
And by the happy hollow of a tree
Escap'd the hunt. No port is free; no place
That guard and most unusual vigilance
Does not attend my taking. Whiles I may scape
I will preserve myself, and am bethought
To take the basest and most poorest shape
That ever penury, in contempt of man,
Brought near to beast. My face I'll grime with filth,
Blanket my loins, elf all my hairs in knots,
And with presented nakedness out-face
The winds and persecutions of the sky.
The country gives me proof and precedent
Of Bedlam beggars, who, with roaring voices,
Strike in their numb'd and mortified arms
Pins, wooden pricks, nails, sprigs of rosemary;
And with this horrible object, from low farms,
Poor pelting villages, sheep-cotes, and mills,

Sometimes with lunatic bans, sometimes with prayers,
Enforce their charity. Poor Turlygod! poor Tom!
That's something yet. Edgar I nothing am.   *Exit.*

[SCENE IV. *The same*]

Enter LEAR, Fool, *and* Gentleman. [KENT *in the stocks*]

Lear. 'Tis strange that they should so depart from home,
And not send back my messengers.
     Gent.   As I learn'd,
The night before there was no purpose in them
Of this remove.
     Kent.   Hail to thee, noble master!
     Lear. Ha!
Mak'st thou this shame thy pastime?
     Kent.   No, my lord.
Fool. Ha, ha! he wears cruel garters. Horses are tied by the heads,
dogs and bears by the neck, monkeys by the loins, and men by the
legs. When a man's over-lusty at legs, then he wears wooden nether-
stocks.
     Lear. What's he that hath so much thy place mistook
To set thee here?
     Kent.   It is both he and she;
Your son and daughter.
     Lear. No.
     Kent. Yes.
     Lear. No, I say.
     Kent. I say, yea.
     [*Lear.* No, no, they would not.
     Kent. Yes, they have.]
     Lear. By Jupiter, I swear, no.
     Kent. By Juno, I swear, ay.
     Lear.   They durst not do 't;
They could not, would not do 't. 'Tis worse than murder,
To do upon respect such violent outrage.

Resolve me, with all modest haste, which way
Thou mightst deserve, or they impose, this usage,
Coming from us.
    Kent.   My lord, when at their home
I did commend your Highness' letters to them,
Ere I was risen from the place that show'd
My duty kneeling, came there a reeking post,
Stew'd in his haste, half breathless, panting forth
From Goneril, his mistress, salutations;
Deliver'd letters, spite of intermission,
Which presently they read. On those contents,
They summon'd up their meiny, straight took horse;
Commanded me to follow, and attend
The leisure of their answer; gave me cold looks:
And meeting here the other messenger,
Whose welcome, I perceiv'd, had poison'd mine,—
Being the very fellow which of late
Display'd so saucily against your Highness,—
Having more man than wit about me, drew.
He rais'd the house with loud and coward cries.
Your son and daughter found this trespass worth
The shame which here it suffers.
    Fool. Winter's not gone yet, if the wild geese fly that way.

            "Fathers that wear rags
                Do make their children blind;
            But fathers that bear bags
                Shall see their children kind.
            Fortune, that arrant whore,
            Ne'er turns the key to the poor."

But, for all this, thou shalt have as many dolours for thy daughters
as thou canst tell in a year.
    Lear. O, how this mother swells up toward my heart!
Hysterica passio, down, thou climbing sorrow,
Thy element's below!—Where is this daughter?
    Kent. With the Earl, sir, here within.

Lear. Follow me not;
Stay here. *Exit.*

Gent. Made you no more offence but what you speak of?

Kent. None.
How chance the King comes with so small a number?

Fool. An thou hadst been set i' the stocks for that question, thou'dst well deserv'd it.

Kent. Why, Fool?

Fool. We'll set thee to school to an ant, to teach thee there's no labouring i' the winter. All that follow their noses are led by their eyes but blind men; and there's not a nose among twenty but can smell him that's stinking. Let go thy hold when a great wheel runs down a hill, lest it break thy neck with following; but the great one that goes upward, let him draw thee after. When a wise man gives thee better counsel, give me mine again; I would have none but knaves follow it, since a fool gives it.

> "That sir which serves and seeks for gain,
>   And follows but for form,
> Will pack when it begins to rain,
>   And leave thee in the storm.
> But I will tarry; the Fool will stay,
>   And let the wise man fly.
> The knave turns fool that runs away;
>   The Fool no knave, perdy."

Re-enter LEAR *and* GLOUCESTER

Kent. Where learn'd you this, Fool?

Fool. Not i' the stocks, fool.

Lear. Deny to speak with me? They are sick? They are weary!
They have travell'd all the night? Mere fetches;
The images of revolt and flying off.
Fetch me a better answer.

Glou. My dear lord,
You know the fiery quality of the Duke;
How unremovable and fix'd he is
In his own course.

Lear. Vengeance! plague! death! confusion!
"Fiery"? What "quality"? Why, Gloucester, Gloucester,
I'd speak with the Duke of Cornwall and his wife.
 Glou. Well, my good lord, I have inform'd them so.
 Lear. "Inform'd" them! Dost thou understand me, man?
 Glou. Ay, my good lord.
 Lear. The King would speak with Cornwall; the dear father
Would with his daughter speak, commands her service.
Are they "inform'd" of this? My breath and blood!
"Fiery"? The fiery duke? Tell the hot duke that—
No, but not yet; may be he is not well.
Infirmity doth still neglect all office
Whereto our health is bound; we are not ourselves
When nature, being oppress'd, commands the mind
To suffer with the body. I'll forbear;
And am fallen out with my more headier will,
To take the indispos'd and sickly fit
For the sound man.—Death on my state! wherefore
          [*Looking on* KENT.]
Should he sit here? This act persuades me
That this remotion of the Duke and her
Is practice only. Give me my servant forth.
Go tell the Duke and 's wife I'd speak with them,
Now, presently. Bid them come forth and hear me,
Or at their chamber-door I'll beat the drum
Till it cry sleep to death.
 Glou. I would have all well betwixt you.   *Exit.*
 Lear. O me, my heart, my rising heart! But, down!
 Fool. Cry to it, nuncle, as the cockney did to the eels when she
put 'em i' the paste alive; she knapp'd 'em o' the coxcombs with a
stick, and cried, "Down, wantons, down!" 'Twas her brother that,
in pure kindness to his horse, buttered his hay.

 Enter CORNWALL, REGAN, GLOUCESTER, *and* Servants

 Lear. Good morrow to you both.
 Corn.   Hail to your Grace!

KENT *is set at liberty.*

Reg. I am glad to see your Highness.

Lear. Regan, I think you are; I know what reason
I have to think so. If thou shouldst not be glad,
I would divorce me from thy mother's tomb,
Sepulchring an adulteress. [*To* KENT.] O, are you free?
Some other time for that. Beloved Regan,
Thy sister's naught. O Regan, she hath tied
Sharp-tooth'd unkindness, like a vulture, here.

[*Points to his heart.*]

I can scarce speak to thee; thou'lt not believe
With how deprav'd a quality—O Regan!

Reg. I pray you, sir, take patience. I have hope
You less know how to value her desert
Than she to scant her duty.

Lear.   Say, how is that?

Reg. I cannot think my sister in the least
Would fail her obligation. If, sir, perchance
She have restrain'd the riots of your followers,
'Tis on such ground, and to such wholesome end,
As clears her from all blame.

Lear. My curses on her!

Reg.   O, sir, you are old;
Nature in you stands on the very verge
Of her confine. You should be rul'd and led
By some discretion that discerns your state
Better than you yourself. Therefore, I pray you,
That to our sister you do make return;
Say you have wrong'd her, sir.

Lear.   Ask her forgiveness?
Do you but mark how this becomes the house:
"Dear daughter, I confess that I am old;   [*Kneeling.*]
Age is unnecessary. On my knees I beg
That you'll vouchsafe me raiment, bed, and food."

Reg. Good sir, no more; these are unsightly tricks.
Return you to my sister.

Lear.   [*Rising.*] Never, Regan:
She hath abated   me of half my train;
Look'd black upon me; struck me with her tongue,
Most serpent-like, upon the very heart.
All the stor'd vengeances of heaven fall
On her ingrateful top! Strike her young bones,
You taking airs, with lameness!
   Corn.   Fie, sir, fie!
   Lear. You nimble lightnings, dart your blinding flames
Into her scornful eyes! Infect her beauty,
You fen-suck'd fogs, drawn by the powerful sun,
To fall   and blast her pride!
   Reg. O the blest gods! so will you wish on me,
When the rash mood is on.
   Lear. No, Regan, thou shalt never have my curse.
Thy tender-hefted   nature shall not give
Thee o'er to harshness. Her eyes are fierce; but thine
Do comfort and not burn. 'Tis not in thee
To grudge my pleasures, to cut off my train,
To bandy hasty words, to scant my sizes,
And, in conclusion, to oppose the bolt
Against my coming in. Thou better know'
The offices of nature, bond of childhood,
Effects of courtesy, dues of gratitude.
Thy half o' the kingdom hast thou not forgot,
Wherein I thee endow'd.
   Reg.   Good sir, to the purpose.

                                         Tucket within

   Lear. Who put my man i' the stocks?

              Enter Steward [OSWALD]

   Corn.   What trumpet's that?
   Reg. I know 't; my sister's. This approves her letter,
That she would soon be here. [*To* OSWALD.] Is your lady come?

Lear. This is a slave whose easy-borrowed pride
Dwells in the fickle grace of her he follows.
Out, varlet, from my sight!
Corn.   What means your Grace?

Enter GONERIL

Lear. Who stock'd my servant? Regan, I have good hope
Thou didst not know on 't. Who comes here? O heavens,
If you do love old men, if your sweet sway
Allow obedience, if you yourselves are old,
Make it your cause; send down, and take my part!
[*To* GON.] Art not asham'd to look upon this beard?
O Regan, will you take her by the hand?
Gon. Why not by the hand, sir? How have I offended?
All's not offence that indiscretion finds
And dotage terms so.
Lear.   O sides, you are too tough;
Will you yet hold? How came my man i' the stocks?
Corn. I set him there, sir; but his own disorders
Deserv'd much less advancement.
Lear.   You! did you?
Reg. I pray you, father, being weak, seem so
If, till the expiration of your month,
You will return and sojourn with my sister,
Dismissing half your train, come then to me.
I am now from home, and out of that provision
Which shall be needful for your entertainment.
Lear. Return to her, and fifty men dismiss'd!
No, rather I abjure all roofs, and choose
To wage against the enmity o' the air;
To be a comrade with the wolf and owl,—
Necessity's sharp pinch. Return with her?
Why, the hot-blooded France, that dowerless took
Our youngest born, I could as well be brought
To knee his throne, and, squire-like, pension beg

To keep base life afoot. Return with her?
Persuade me rather to be slave and sumpter
To this detested groom.   *[Pointing at* OSWALD.]

Gon.   At your choice, sir.

Lear. I prithee, daughter, do not make me mad;
I will not trouble thee, my child; farewell!
We'll no more meet, no more see one another.
But yet thou art my flesh, my blood, my daughter;
Or rather a disease that's in my flesh,
Which I must needs call mine; thou art a boil,
A plague-sore, an embossed carbuncle,
In my corrupted blood. But I'll not chide thee;
Let shame come when it will, I do not call it.
I do not bid the thunder-bearer shoot,
Nor tell tales of thee to high-judging Jove.
Mend when thou canst; be better at thy leisure.
I can be patient; I can stay with Regan,
I and my hundred knights.

Reg.   Not altogether so;
I look'd not for you yet, nor am provided
For your fit welcome. Give ear, sir, to my sister;
For those that mingle reason with your passion
Must be content to think you old, and so—
But she knows what she does.

Lear.   Is this well spoken?

Reg. I dare avouch it, sir. What, fifty followers!
Is it not well? What should you need of more?
Yea, or so many, sith that both charge and danger
Speak 'gainst so great a number? How, in one house,
Should many people, under two commands,
Hold amity? 'Tis hard; almost impossible.

Gon. Why might not you, my lord, receive attendance
From those that she calls servants or from mine?

Reg. Why not, my lord? If then they chanc'd to slack ye,
We could control them. If you will come to me,—

211

For now I spy a danger—I entreat you
To bring but five and twenty; to no more
Will I give place or notice.

   Lear. I gave you all.

   Reg.   And in good time you gave it.

   Lear. Made you my guardians, my depositaries,
But kept a reservation to be followed
With such a number. What, must I come to you
With five and twenty, Regan? Said you so?

   Reg. And speak 't again, my lord; no more with me.

   Lear. Those wicked creatures yet do look well-favour'd
When others are more wicked; not being the worst
Stands in some rank of praise. [*To* GON.] I'll go with thee.
Thy fifty yet doth double five and twenty,
And thou art twice her love.

   Gon.   Hear me, my lord:
What need you five and twenty, ten, or five,
To follow in a house where twice so many
Have a command to tend you?

   Reg.   What need one?

   Lear. O, reason not the need! Our basest beggars
Are in the poorest thing superfluous.
Allow not nature more than nature needs,
Man's life is cheap as beast's. Thou art a lady;
If only to go warm were gorgeous,
Why, nature needs not what thou gorgeous wear'st,
Which scarcely keeps thee warm. But, for true need,—
You heavens, give me that patience, patience I need!
You see me here, you gods, a poor old man,
As full of grief as age; wretched in both!
If it be you that stirs these daughters' hearts
Against their father, fool me not so much
To bear it tamely; touch me with noble anger,
And let not women's weapons, water-drops,
Stain my man's cheeks! No, you unnatural hags,
I will have such revenges on you both

That all the world shall—I will do such things,—
What they are, yet I know not; but they shall be
The terrors of the earth. You think I'll weep:
No, I'll not weep.
I have full cause of weeping; but this heart   *Storm and tempest.*
Shall break into a hundred thousand flaws,
Or ere I'll weep. O, Fool! I shall go mad!

Exeunt LEAR, GLOUCESTER, KENT,
and Fool.

Corn. Let us withdraw; 'twill be a storm.
Reg. This house is little; the old man and 's people
Cannot be well bestow'd.
Gon. 'Tis his own blame; hath put himself from rest,
And must needs taste his folly.
Reg. For his particular, I'll receive him gladly,
But not one follower.
Gon.   So am I purpos'd.
Where is my Lord of Gloucester?

Re-enter GLOUCESTER

Corn. Followed the old man forth. He is return'd.
Glou. The King is in high rage.
Corn.   Whither is he going?
Glou. He calls to horse; but will I know not whither.
Corn. 'Tis best to give him way; he leads himself.
Gon. My lord, entreat him by no means to stay.
Glou. Alack, the night comes on, and the high winds
Do sorely ruffle; for many miles about
There's scarce a bush.
Reg.   O, sir, to wilful men,
The injuries that they themselves procure
Must be their schoolmasters. Shut up your doors.
He is attended with a desperate train;
And what they may incense him to, being apt
To have his ear abus'd, wisdom bids fear.

Corn. Shut up your doors, my lord; 'tis a wild night:
My Regan counsels well. Come out o' the storm.   [*Exeunt.*

ACT III

Scene I. [*The open country near Gloucester's castle*]

Storm still. Enter Kent *and a* Gentleman, *severally*

Kent. Who's there, besides foul weather?
Gent. One minded like the weather, most unquietly.
Kent. I know you. Where's the King?
Gent. Contending with the fretful elements;
Bids the wind blow the earth into the sea,
Or swell the curled waters 'bove the main,
That things might change or cease; [tears his white hair,
Which the impetuous blasts, with eyeless rage,
Catch in their fury, and make nothing of;
Strives in his little world of man to out-scorn
The to-and-fro-conflicting wind and rain.
This night, wherein the cub-drawn bear would couch,
The lion and the belly-pinched wolf
Keep their fur dry, unbonneted he runs,
And bids what will take all.]
   Kent.   But who is with him?
   Gent. None but the Fool; who labours to outjest
His heart-struck injuries.
   Kent.   Sir, I do know you;
And dare, upon the warrant of my note,
Commend a dear thing to you. There is division,
Although as yet the face of it is cover'd
With mutual cunning, 'twixt Albany and Cornwall;
Who have—as who have not, that their great stars'
Thron'd and set high?—servants, who seem no less,
Which are to France the spies and speculations
Intelligent of our state; what hath been seen,

214

Either in snuffs and packings of the Dukes,
Or the hard rein which both of them have borne
Against the old kind king, or something deeper,
Whereof perchance these are but furnishings;
[But, true it is, from France there comes a power
Into this scattered kingdom; who already,
Wise in our negligence, have secret feet
In some of our best ports, and are at point
To show their open banner. Now to you:
If on my credit you dare build so far
To make your speed to Dover, you shall find
Some that will thank you, making just report
Of how unnatural and bemadding sorrow
The King hath cause to plain.
I am a gentleman of blood and breeding;
And, from some knowledge and assurance, offer
This office to you.]
 Gent. I will talk further with you.
 Kent.   No, do not.
For confirmation that I am much more
Than my out-wall, open this purse, and take
What it contains. If you shall see Cordelia,—
As fear not but you shall,—show her this ring;
And she will tell you who that fellow is
That yet you do not know. Fie on this storm!
I will go seek the King.
 Gent. Give me your hand. Have you no more to say?
 Kent. Few words, but, to effect, more than all yet;
That, when we have found the King,—in which your pain
That way, I'll this,—he that first lights on him
Holla the other.   *Exeunt* [*severally*].

SCENE II. [*The same.*] *Storm still*

Enter LEAR *and* Fool

Lear. Blow, winds, and crack your cheeks! Rage! Blow!
You cataracts and hurricanoes, spout
Till you have drench'd our steeples, drown'd the cocks!
You sulphurous and thought-executing fires,
Vaunt-couriers of oak-cleaving thunderbolts,
Singe my white head! And thou, all-shaking thunder,
Strike flat the thick rotundity o' the world!
Crack nature's moulds, all germens¨ spill at once,
That makes ingrateful man!
    Fool. O nuncle, court holy-water in a dry house is better than this
rain-water out o' door. Good nuncle, in; ask thy daughters' blessing.
Here's a night pities neither wise men nor fools.
    Lear. Rumble thy bellyful! Spit, fire! Spout, rain!
Nor rain, wind, thunder, fire, are my daughters.
I tax not you, you elements, with unkindness;
I never gave you kingdom, call'd you children;
You owe me no subscription.   Then let fall
Your horrible pleasure. Here I stand, your slave,
A poor, infirm, weak, and despis'd old man;
But yet I call you servile ministers,
That will with two pernicious daughters join
Your high engender'd battles 'gainst a head
So old and white as this. Oh! Oh! 'tis foul!
    Fool. He that has a house to put 's head in has a good head-piece
        "The cod-piece that will house
            Before the head has any,
        The head and he shall louse;
            So beggars marry many.
        The man that makes his toe
            What he his heart should make

> Shall of a corn cry woe,
>   And turn his sleep to wake."
> For there was never yet fair woman but she made mouths in a glass.

Enter KENT

Lear. No, I will be the pattern of all patience; I will say nothing.

Kent. Who's there?

Fool. Marry, here's grace and a cod-piece; that's a wise man and a fool.

Kent. Alas, sir, are you here? Things that love night
Love not such nights as these; the wrathful skies
Gallow the very wanderers of the dark,
And make them keep their caves. Since I was man,
Such sheets of fire, such bursts of horrid thunder,
Such groans of roaring wind and rain, I never
Remember to have heard. Man's nature cannot carry
The affliction nor the fear.

Lear.   Let the great gods,
That keep this dreadful pudder o'er our heads,
Find out their enemies now. Tremble, thou wretch,
That hast within thee undivulged crimes,
Unwhipp'd of justice! Hide thee, thou bloody hand;
Thou perjur'd, and thou simular of virtue
That art incestuous! Caitiff, to pieces shake,
That under covert and convenient seeming
Has practis'd on man's life! Close pent-up guilts,
Rive your concealing continents, and cry
These dreadful summoners grace. I am a man
More sinn'd against than sinning.

Kent.   Alack, bare-headed!
Gracious my lord, hard by here is a hovel;
Some friendship will it lend you 'gainst the tempest.
Repose you there; while I to this hard house—
More harder than the stones whereof 'tis rais'd;

Which even but now, demanding after you,
Deni'd me to come in—return, and force
Their scanted courtesy.
    Lear.   My wits begin to turn.
Come on, my boy. How dost, my boy? Art cold?
I am cold myself. Where is this straw, my fellow?
The art of our necessities is strange,
And can make vile things precious. Come, your hovel.
Poor Fool and knave, I have one part in my heart
That's sorry yet for thee.
    Fool. [*Singing.*]
        "He that has and a little tiny wit,—
           With heigh-ho, the wind and the rain,—
        Must make content with his fortunes fit,
           For the rain it raineth every day."
Lear. True, boy. Come, bring us to this hovel.
                      Exeunt [LEAR *and* KENT].
    Fool. This is a brave night to cool a courtezan.
I'll speak a prophecy ere I go:
        When priests are more in word than matter;
        When brewers mar their malt with water;
        When nobles are their tailors' tutors;
        No heretics burn'd, but wenches' suitors;
        When every case in law is right;
        No squire in debt, nor no poor knight;
        When slanders do not live in tongues;
        Nor cutpurses come not to throngs;
        When usurers tell their gold i' the field;
        And bawds and whores do churches build:
        Then shall the realm of Albion
        Come to great confusion.
        Then comes the time, who lives to see 't,
        That going shall be us'd with feet.
This prophecy Merlin shall make; for I live before his time.   *Exit.*

SCENE III. [*Gloucester's castle*]

Enter GLOUCESTER *and* EDMUND

Glou. Alack, alack, Edmund, I like not this unnatural dealing. When I desired their leave that I might pity him, they took from me the use of mine own house; charg'd me, on pain of perpetual displeasure, neither to speak of him, entreat for him, or any way sustain him.

Edm. Most savage and unnatural!

Glou. Go to; say you nothing. There is division between the Dukes, and a worse matter than that. I have received a letter this night; 'tis dangerous to be spoken; I have lock'd the letter in my closet. These injuries the King now bears will be revenged home; there is part of a power already footed.` We must incline to the King. I will look him, and privily relieve him. Go you and maintain talk with the Duke, that my charity be not of him perceived. If he ask for me, I am ill, and gone to bed. If I die for it, as no less is threat'ned me, the King my old master must be relieved. There is strange things toward, Edmund; pray you, be careful.   *Exit.*

Edm. This courtesy, forbid thee, shall the Duke
Instantly know; and of that letter too.
This seems a fair deserving, and must draw me
That which my father loses; no less than all.
The younger rises when the old doth fall.   *Exit.*

SCENE IV. [*The open country. Before a hovel*]

Enter LEAR, KENT, *and* Fool

Kent. Here is the place, my lord; good my lord, enter.
The tyranny of the open night's too rough
For nature to endure.   *Storm still.*

Lear.   Let me alone.

Kent. Good my lord, enter here.

Lear.   Wilt break my heart?

Kent. I had rather break mine own. Good my lord, enter.

Lear. Thou think'st 'tis much that this contentious storm
Invades us to the skin; so 'tis to thee;
But where the greater malady is fix'd,
The lesser is scarce felt. Thou 'dst shun a bear;
But if thy flight lay toward the roaring sea,
Thou 'dst meet the bear i' the mouth. When the mind's free,
The body's delicate; the tempest in my mind
Doth from my senses take all feeling else
Save what beats there. Filial ingratitude!
Is it not as this mouth should tear this hand
For lifting food to 't? But I will punish home.
No, I will weep no more. In such a night
To shut me out! Pour on! I will endure.
In such a night as this! O Regan, Goneril!
Your old kind father, whose frank heart gave all,—
O, that way madness lies; let me shun that;
No more of that.

    Kent.   Good my lord, enter here.

    Lear. Prithee, go in thyself; seek thine own ease.
This tempest will not give me leave to ponder
On things would hurt me more. But I'll go in.
[*To the* Fool.] In, boy; go first. You houseless poverty,—
Nay, get thee in. I'll pray, and then I'll sleep.   *Exit* [**Fool**]
Poor naked wretches, wheresoe'er you are,
That bide the pelting of this pitiless storm,
How shall your houseless heads and unfed sides,
Your loop'd and window'd raggedness, defend you
From seasons such as these? O, I have ta'en
Too little care of this! Take physic, pomp;
Expose thyself to feel what wretches feel,
That thou mayst shake the superflux to them,
And show the heavens more just.

    Edg. [*Within.*] Fathom and half, fathom and half! Poor Tom.
                [*The* Fool *runs out from the hovel.*
    Fool. Come not in here, nuncle, here's a spirit. Help me, help me!

Kent. Give me thy hand. Who's there?

Fool. A spirit, a spirit! He says his name 's poor Tom.

Kent. What art thou that dost grumble there i' the straw? Come
forth.

[*Enter* EDGAR, *disguised as a madman*]

Edg. Away! the foul fiend follows me!
   "Through the sharp hawthorn blow-the winds."
Hum! go to thy bed, and warm thee.

Lear. Did'st thou give all to thy daughters, and art thou come to
this?

Edg. Who gives anything to poor Tom? whom the foul fiend
hath led through fire and through flame, and through ford and
whirlpool, o'er bog and quagmire; that hath laid knives under his
pillow, and halters in his pew; set ratsbane by his porridge; made
him proud of heart, to ride on a bay trotting-horse over four-inch'd
bridges, to course his own shadow for a traitor. Bless thy five wits!
Tom's a-cold,—O, do de, do de, do de. Bless thee from whirlwinds,
starblasting, and taking! Do poor Tom some charity, whom the
foul fiend vexes. There could I have him now,—and there,—and
there again, and there.   *Storm still.*

Lear. Has his daughters brought him to this pass?
Couldst thou save nothing? Wouldst thou give 'em all?

Fool. Nay, he reserv'd a blanket, else we had been all sham'd.

Lear. Now, all the plagues that in the pendulous air
Hang fated o'er men's faults light on thy daughters!

Kent. He hath no daughters, sir.

Lear. Death, traitor! nothing could have subdu'd nature
To such a lowness but his unkind daughters.
Is it the fashion, that discarded fathers
Should have thus little mercy on their flesh?
Judicious punishment! 'Twas this flesh begot
Those pelican daughters.

Edg.   "Pillicock sat on Pillicock-hill."
Alow, alow, loo, loo!

Fool. This cold night will turn us all to fools and madmen.

Edg. Take heed o' the foul fiend. Obey thy parents; keep thy word justly; swear not; commit not with man's sworn spouse; set not thy sweet heart on proud array. Tom 's a-cold.

Lear. What hast thou been?

Edg. A serving-man, proud in heart and mind; that curl'd my hair; wore gloves in my cap; serv'd the lust of my mistress' heart, and did the act of darkness with her; swore as many oaths as I spake words, and broke them in the sweet face of heaven: one that slept in the contriving of lust, and wak'd to do it. Wine lov'd I dearly, dice dearly; and in woman out-paramour'd the Turk. false of heart, light of ear, bloody of hand; hog in sloth, fox in stealth, wolf in greediness, dog in madness, lion in prey. Let not the creaking of shoes nor the rustling of silks betray thy poor heart to woman. Keep thy foot out of brothels, thy hand out of plackets, thy pen from lenders' books, and defy the foul fiend.

"Still through the hawthorn blows the cold wind."
Says suum, mun, nonny. Dolphin my boy, boy, sessa! let him trot by.
Storm still.

Lear. Thou wert better in a grave than to answer with thy uncover'd body this extremity of the skies. Is man no more than this? Consider him well. Thou ow'st the worm no silk, the beast no hide, the sheep no wool, the cat no perfume. Ha! here's three on 's are sophisticated! Thou art the thing itself; unaccommodated man is no more but such a poor, bare, forked animal as thou art. Off, off, you lendings! come, unbutton here. [*Tearing off his clothes.*]

Enter GLOUCESTER, *with a torch*

Fool. Prithee, nuncle, be contented; 'tis a naughty night to swim in. Now a little fire in a wild field were like an old lecher's heart; a small spark, all the rest on 's body cold. Look, here comes a walking fire.

Edg. This is the foul [fiend] Flibbertigibbet; he begins at curfew, and walks till the first cock; he gives the web and the pin, squints

the eye, and makes the hare-lip; mildews the white wheat, and hurts
the poor creature of earth.

> "St. Withold footed thrice the 'old;
> He met the night-mare, and her ninefold;
> Bid her alight,
> And her troth plight,
> And, aroint thee, witch, aroint thee!"

Kent. How fares your Grace?

Lear. What's he?

Kent. Who's there? What is 't you seek?

Glou. What are you there? Your names?

Edg. Poor Tom, that eats the swimming frog, the toad, the tad-
pole, the wall-newt, and the water; that in the fury of his heart, when
the foul fiend rages, eats cow-dung for salads; swallows the old rat
and the ditch-dog; drinks the green mantle of the standing pool;
who is whipp'd from tithing to tithing, and stock'd punish'd, and
imprison'd; who hath three suits to his back, six shirts to his body,

> Horse to ride, and weapon to wear;
> But mice and rats, and such small deer,
> Have been Tom's food for seven long year.

Beware my follower. Peace, Smulkin; peace, thou fiend!

Glou. What, hath your Grace no better company?

Edg. The prince of darkness is a gentleman.
Modo he's call'd, and Mahu.

Glou. Our flesh and blood, my lord, is grown so vile
That it doth hate what gets it.

Edg. Poor Tom's a-cold.

Glou. Go in with me; my duty cannot suffer
To obey in all your daughters' hard commands.
Though their injunction be to bar my doors
And let this tyrannous night take hold upon you,
Yet have I ventur'd to come seek you out,
And bring you where both fire and food is ready.

Lear. First let me talk with this philosopher.
What is the cause of thunder?

Kent. Good my lord, take his offer; go into the house.
Lear. I'll talk a word with this same learned Theban.
What is your study?
   Edg. How to prevent the fiend, and to kill vermin.
   Lear. Let me ask you one word in private.
   Kent. Importune him once more to go, my lord;
His wits begin to unsettle.
   Glou.   Canst thou blame him?   *Storm still.*
His daughters seek his death. Ah, that good Kent!
He said it would be thus, poor banish'd man!
Thou say'st the King grows mad; I'll tell thee, friend,
I am almost mad myself. I had a son,
Now outlaw'd from my blood; he sought my life,
But lately, very late. I lov'd him, friend,
No father his son dearer; true to tell thee,
The grief hath craz'd my wits. What a night's this!
I do beseech your Grace,—
   Lear.   O, cry you mercy, sir.
Noble philosopher, your company.
   Edg. Tom's a-cold.
   Glou. In, fellow, there, into the hovel; keep thee warm.
   Lear. Come, let's in all.
   Kent.   This way, my lord.
   Lear.   With him;
I will keep still with my philosopher.
   Kent. Good my lord, soothe him; let him take the fellow.
   Glou. Take him you on.
   Kent. Sirrah, come on; go along with us.
   Lear. Come, good Athenian.
   Glou. No words, no words: hush.
   Edg. "Child Rowland to the dark tower came;
      His word was still,—'Fie, foh, and fum,
        I smell the blood of a British man.'"   [*Exeunt.*

SCENE V. [*Gloucester's castle*]

Enter CORNWALL *and* EDMUND

Corn. I will have my revenge ere I depart his house.

Edm. How, my lord, I may be censured that nature thus gives way to loyalty, something fears me to think of.

Corn. I now perceive, it was not altogether your brother's evil disposition made him seek his death; but a provoking merit, set a-work by a reproveable badness in himself.

Edm. How malicious is my fortune, that I must repent to be just! This is the letter which he spoke of, which approves him an intelligent party to the advantages of France. O heavens! that this treason were not, or not I the detector!

Corn. Go with me to the Duchess.

Edm. If the matter of this paper be certain, you have mighty business in hand.

Corn. True or false, it hath made thee Earl of Gloucester. Seek out where thy father is, that he may be ready for our apprehension.

Edm. [*Aside.*] If I find him comforting the King, it will stuff his suspicion more fully.—I will persevere in my course of loyalty, though the conflict be sore between that and my blood.

Corn. I will lay trust upon thee; and thou shalt find a dearer father in my love.   *Exeunt.*

SCENE VI. [*A building attached to Gloucester's castle*]

Enter KENT *and* GLOUCESTER

Glou. Here is better than the open air; take it thankfully. I will piece out the comfort with what addition I can. I will not be long from you.   *Exit.*

Kent. All the power of his wits have given way to his impatience. The gods reward your kindness!

Enter LEAR, EDGAR, *and* Fool

Edg. Fraretto calls me; and tells me Nero is an angler in the lake of darkness. Pray, innocent, and beware the foul fiend.

Fool. Prithee, nuncle, tell me whether a madman be a gentleman or a yeoman?

Lear. A king, a king!

Fool. No, he's a yeoman that has a gentleman to his son; for he's a mad yeoman that sees his son a gentleman before him.

Lear. To have a thousand with red burning spits
Come hissing in upon 'em,—

[*Edg.* The foul fiend bites my back.

Fool. He's mad that trusts in the tameness of a wolf, a horse's health, a boy's love, or a whore's oath.

Lear. It shall be done; I will arraign them straight.
[*To* EDGAR.] Come, sit thou here, most learned justicer;
[*To the* Fool.] Thou, sapient sir, sit here. Now, you she-foxes!

Edg. Look, where he stands and glares!
Wantest thou eyes at trial, madam?
           "Come o'er the bourn, Bessy, to me,"—

Fool.   "Her boat hath a leak,
           And she must not speak
           Why she dares not come over to thee."

Edg. The foul fiend haunts poor Tom in the voice of a nightingale. Hopdance cries in Tom's belly for two white herring. Croak not, black angel; I have no food for thee.

Kent. How do you, sir? Stand you not so amaz'd:
Will you lie down and rest upon the cushions?

Lear. I'll see their trial first. Bring in their evidence.
[*To* EDGAR.] Thou robed man of justice, take thy place;
[*To the* Fool.] And thou, his yoke-fellow of equity,
Bench by his side. [*To* KENT.] You are o' the commission,
Sit you too.

Edg. Let us deal justly.
        "Sleepest or wakest thou, jolly shepherd?
         Thy sheep be in the corn;
        And for one blast of thy minikin mouth,
         Thy sheep shall take no harm."
Purr! the cat is grey.

Lear. Arraign her first; 'tis Goneril. I here take my oath before this honourable assembly, she kick'd the poor king her father.

Fool. Come hither, mistress. Is your name Goneril?

Lear. She cannot deny it.

Fool. Cry you mercy, I took you for a joint-stool.

Lear. And here's another, whose warp'd looks proclaim
What store her heart is made on. Stop her there!
Arms, arms, sword, fire! Corruption in the place!
False justicer, why hast thou let her scape?

Edg. Bless thy five wits!

Kent. O pity! Sir, where is the patience now
That you so oft have boasted to retain?

Edg. [*Aside.*] My tears begin to take his part so much,
They mar my counterfeiting.

Lear. The little dogs and all,
Tray, Blanch, and Sweetheart, see, they bark at me.

Edg. Tom will throw his head at them.
Avaunt, you curs!
    Be thy mouth or black or white,
    Tooth that poisons if it bite;
    Mastiff, greyhound, mongrel grim,
    Hound or spaniel, brach or lym,
    Or bobtail tike or trundle-tail,
    Tom will make him weep and wail;
    For, with throwing thus my head,
    Dogs leapt the hatch, and all are fled.
Do de, de, de. Sessa! Come, march to wakes and fairs and market-towns. Poor Tom, thy horn is dry.

Lear. Then let them anatomize Regan; see what breeds about her heart. Is there any cause in nature that make these hard hearts? [*To* Edg.] You, sir, I entertain for one of my hundred; only I do not like the fashion of your garments. You will say they are Persian, but let them be chang'd.

Re-enter GLOUCESTER

Kent. Now, good my lord, lie here and rest a while.

Lear. Make no noise, make no noise; draw the curtains; so, so, so.
We'll go to supper i' the morning.

Fool. And I'll go to bed at noon.

Glou. Come hither, friend; where is the King my master?

Kent. Here, sir; but trouble him not, his wits are gone.

Glou. Good friend, I prithee, take him in thy arms;
I have o'erheard a plot of death upon him.
There is a litter ready; lay him in 't,
And drive toward Dover, friend, where thou shalt meet
Both welcome and protection. Take up thy master.
If thou shouldst dally half an hour, his life,
With thine, and all that offer to defend him,
Stand in assured loss. Take up, take up;
And follow me, that will to some provision
Give thee quick conduct.

    Kent.   [Oppressed nature sleeps.
This rest might yet have balm'd thy broken sinews,
Which, if convenience will not allow,
Stand in hard cure. [*To the* Fool.] Come, help to bear thy master;
Thou must not stay behind.]

    Glou.   Come, come, away.

                    Exeunt [*all but* EDGAR]

[*Edg.* When we our betters see bearing our woes,
We scarcely think our miseries our foes.
Who alone suffers, suffers most i' the mind,
Leaving free things and happy shows behind;
But then the mind much sufferance doth o'erskip,
When grief hath mates, and bearing fellowship.
How light and portable my pain seems now,
When that which makes me bend makes the King bow,
He childed as I fathered! Tom, away!
Mark the high noises; and thyself bewray,

When false opinion, whose wrong thoughts defile thee,
In thy just proof repeals and reconciles thee.
What will hap more to-night, safe scape the King!
Lurk, lurk.]   [*Exit.*]

SCENE VII. [*Gloucester's castle*]

Enter CORNWALL, REGAN, GONERIL, Bastard [EDMUND], *and* Servants

Corn. [*To* GON.] Post speedily to my lord your husband; show
him this letter. The army of France is landed.—Seek out the traitor
Gloucester.   [*Exeunt some of the* Servants.]
   Reg. Hang him instantly.
   Gon. Pluck out his eyes.
   Corn. Leave him to my displeasure.—Edmund, keep you our sister
company; the revenges we are bound to take upon your traitorous
father are not fit for your beholding. Advise the Duke, where you
are going, to a most festinate preparation; we are bound to the like.
Our posts shall be swift and intelligent betwixt us. Farewell, dear
sister; farewell, my lord of Gloucester.

Enter Steward [OSWALD]

How now! where's the King?
   Osw. My Lord of Gloucester hath convey'd him hence.
Some five or six and thirty of his knights,
Hot questrists after him, met him at gate,
Who, with some other of the lords dependants,
Are gone with him toward Dover, where they boast
To have well-armed friends.
   Corn.   Get horses for your mistress.
   Gon. Farewell, sweet lord, and sister.
   Corn. Edmund, farewell.
                        Exeunt [GONERIL, EDMUND, *and* OSWALD].
                        Go seek the traitor Gloucester,
Pinion him like a thief, bring him before us. [*Exeunt other* Servants.]
Though well we may not pass upon his life
Without the form of justice, yet our power

Shall do a courtesy to our wrath, which men
May blame, but not control.

Enter GLOUCESTER *and* Servants

                   Who's there? The traitor?

Reg. Ingrateful fox! 'tis he.

Corn. Bind fast his corky arms.

Glou. What means your Graces? Good my friends, consider
You are my guests. Do me no foul play, friends.

Corn. Bind him, I say.   [Servants *bind him.*]

Reg.   Hard, hard. O filthy traitor!

Glou. Unmerciful lady as you are, I'm none.

Corn. To this chair bind him. Villain, thou shalt find—

                  [REGAN *plucks his beard.*]

  Glou. By the kind gods, 'tis most ignobly done
To pluck me by the beard.

Reg. So white, and such a traitor!

Glou.   Naughty lady,
These hairs, which thou dost ravish from my chin,
Will quicken, and accuse thee. I am your host:
With robber's hands my hospitable favours
You should not ruffle thus. What will you do?

Corn. Come, sir, what letters had you late from France?

Reg. Be simple-answer'd, for we know the truth.

Corn. And what confederacy have you with the traitors
Late footed in the kingdom?

Reg. To whose hands you have sent the lunatic king,
Speak.

Glou. I have a letter guessingly set down,
Which came from one that's of a neutral heart,
And not from one oppos'd.

Corn.   Cunning.

Reg.   And false.

Corn. Where hast thou sent the King?

Glou. To Dover.

230

Reg. Wherefore to Dover? Wast thou not charg'd at peril—
Corn. Wherefore to Dover? Let him answer that.
Glou. I am tied to the stake, and I must stand the course.
Reg. Wherefore to Dover?
Glou. Because I would not see thy cruel nails
Pluck out his poor old eyes; nor thy fierce sister
In his anointed flesh stick boarish fangs.
The sea, with such a storm as his bare head
In hell-black night endur'd, would have buoy'd up
And quench'd the stelled fires;
Yet, poor old heart, he holp the heavens to rain.
If wolves had at thy gate howl'd that stern time,
Thou shouldst have said, "Good porter, turn the key."
All cruels else subscribe; but I shall see
The winged vengeance overtake such children.
Corn. See 't shalt thou never. Fellows, hold the chair.
Upon these eyes of thine I'll set my foot.
Glou. He that will think to live till he be old,
Give me some help!—O cruel! O you gods!
Reg. One side will mock another; the other too.
Corn. If you see vengeance,—
[1.] *Serv.*   Hold your hand, my lord!
I have serv'd you ever since I was a child;
But better service have I never done you
Than now to bid you hold.
Reg.   How now, you dog!
[1.] *Serv.* If you did wear a beard upon your chin,
I'd shake it on this quarrel. What do you mean?
Corn. My villain!   [*They draw and fight.*]
[1.] *Serv.* Nay, then, come on, and take the chance of anger.
Reg. Give me thy sword. A peasant stand up thus?
                    Takes a sword, and runs at him behind.
[1.] *Serv.* Oh, I am slain! My lord, you have one eye left
To see some mischief on him. Oh!   [*Dies.*]
Corn. Lest it see more, prevent it. Out, vile jelly!

231

Where is thy lustre now?

Glou. All dark and comfortless. Where's my son Edmund?
Edmund, enkindle all the sparks of nature,
To quit this horrid act.

Reg.   Out, treacherous villain!
Thou call'st on him that hates thee. It was he
That made the overture   of thy treasons to us,
Who is too good to pity thee.

Glou. O my follies! then Edgar was abus'd.
Kind gods, forgive me that, and prosper him!

Reg. Go thrust him out at gates, and let him smell
His way to Dover. *Exit [one] with* GLOUCESTER. How is 't, my lord?
     How look you?

Corn. I have received a hurt; follow me, lady.
Turn out that eyeless villain; throw this slave
Upon the dunghill. Regan, I bleed apace;
Untimely comes this hurt. Give me your arm.

                              [*Exit* CORNWALL, *led by* REGAN.]

     [2. *Serv.* I'll never care what wickedness I do,
If this man come to good.

     3. *Serv.*   If she live long,
And in the end meet the old course of death,
Women will all turn monsters.

     2. *Serv.* Let's follow the old earl, and get the Bedlam
To lead him where he would: his roguish madness
Allows itself to anything.

     3. *Serv.* Go thou: I'll fetch some flax and whites of eggs
To apply to his bleeding face. Now, Heaven help him!]

                              Exeunt [severally].

ACT IV

SCENE I. [*The open country near Gloucester's castle*]

Enter EDGAR

Edg. Yet better thus, and known to be contemn'd,
Than, still contemn'd and flatter'd, to be worst,

The lowest and most dejected thing of fortune
Stands still in esperance, lives not in fear.
The lamentable change is from the best;
The worst returns to laughter. Welcome, then,
Thou unsubstantial air that I embrace!
The wretch that thou hast blown unto the worst
Owes nothing to thy blasts.

Enter GLOUCESTER, *led by an* Old Man

                          But who comes here?
My father, poorly led? World, world, O world!
But that thy strange mutations make us hate thee,
Life would not yield to age.

    Old Man. O, my good lord, I have been your tenant, and your
father's tenant, these fourscore years.

    Glou. Away, get thee away! Good friend, be gone;
Thy comforts can do me no good at all;
Thee they may hurt.

    Old Man. [Alack, sir,] you cannot see your way.

    Glou. I have no way, and therefore want no eyes;
I stumbled when I saw. Full oft 'tis seen,
Our means secure us, and our mere defects
Prove our commodities. O dear son Edgar,
The food of thy abused father's wrath!
Might I but live to see thee in my touch,
I'd say I had eyes again!

    Old Man.   How now! Who's there?

    Edg. [*Aside.*] O gods! Who is 't can say, "I am at the worst"?
I am worse than e'er I was.

    Old Man.   'Tis poor mad Tom.

    Edg. [*Aside.*] And worse I may be yet; the worst is not
So long as we can say, "This is the worst."

    Old Man. Fellow, where goest?

    Glou.   Is it a beggar-man?

    Old Man. Madman and beggar

Glou. He has some reason, else he could not beg.
I' the last night's storm I such a fellow saw,
Which made me think a man a worm. My son
Came then into my mind, and yet my mind
Was then scarce friends with him. I have heard more since.
As flies to wanton boys, are we to the gods,
They kill us for their sport.
    Edg.   [*Aside.*] How should this be?
Bad is the trade that must play fool to sorrow,
Ang'ring itself and others.—Bless thee, master!
    Glou. Is that the naked fellow?
    Old Man.   Ay, my lord.
    Glou. [Then, prithee,] get thee away. If, for my sake,
Thou wilt o'ertake us, hence a mile or twain
I' the way toward Dover, do it for ancient love;
And bring some covering for this naked soul,
Which I'll entreat to lead me.
    Old Man.   Alack, sir, he is mad.
    Glou. 'Tis the time's plague, when madmen lead the blind.
Do as I bid thee, or rather do thy pleasure;
Above the rest, be gone
    Old Man. I'll bring him the best 'parel that I have,
Come on 't what will.   *Exit.*
    Glou. Sirrah, naked fellow,—
    Edg. Poor Tom's a-cold. [*Aside.*] I cannot daub it further.
    Glou. Come hither, fellow.
    Edg. [*Aside.*] And yet I must.—Bless thy sweet eyes, they bleed.
    Glou. Know'st thou the way to Dover?
    Edg. Both stile and gate, horse-way and foot-path. Poor Tom hath
been scar'd out of his good wits. Bless thee, good man's son, from
the foul fiend! [Five fiends have been in poor Tom at once; of lust,
as Obidicut; Hobbididence, prince of dumbness; Mahu, of stealing;
Modo, of murder; Flibbertigibbet, of mopping and mowing, who
since possesses chambermaids and waiting-women. So, bless thee,
master!]
    Glou. Here, take this purse, thou whom the heavens' plagues

Have humbled to all strokes. That I am wretched
Makes thee the happier; heavens, deal so still!
Let the superfluous and lust-dieted man,
That slaves your ordinance, that will not see
Because he does not feel, feel your power quickly;
So distribution should undo excess,
And each man have enough. Dost thou know Dover?
   Edg. Ay, master.
   Glou. There is a cliff, whose high and bending head
Looks fearfully in the confined deep.
Bring me but to the very brim of it,
And I'll repair the misery thou dost bear
With something rich about me. From that place
I shall no leading need.
   Edg.   Give me thy arm;
Poor Tom shall lead thee.   *Exeunt.*

SCENE II. [*Before the Duke of Albany's palace*]

Enter GONERIL, Bastard [EDMUND], *and* Steward [OSWALD]

   Gon. Welcome, my lord! I marvel our mild husband
Not met us on the way.—Now, where's your master?
   Osw. Madam, within; but never man so chang'd.
I told him of the army that was landed;
He smil'd at it. I told him you were coming;
His answer was, "The worse." Of Gloucester's treachery,
And of the loyal service of his son,
When I inform'd him, then he call'd me sot,
And told me I had turn'd the wrong side out.
What most he should dislike seems pleasant to him;
What like, offensive.
   Gon. [*To* EDM.] Then shall you go no further.
It is the cowish terror of his spirit,
That dares not undertake; he'll not feel wrongs
Which tie him to an answer. Our wishes on the way

May prove effects. Back, Edmund, to my brother;
Hasten his musters and conduct his powers.
I must change names at home, and give the distaff
Into my husband's hands. This trusty servant
Shall pass between us. Ere long you are like to hear,
If you dare venture in your own behalf,
A mistress's command. Wear this; spare speech;
Decline your head. This kiss, if it durst speak,
Would stretch thy spirits up into the air.
Conceive, and fare thee well.

 Edm. Yours in the ranks of death.   *Exit.*
 Gon.   My most dear Gloucester!
O, the difference of man and man!
To thee a woman's services are due;
My Fool usurps my body.
 Osw.   Madam, here comes my lord. *Exit.*

    Enter the DUKE OF ALBANY

 Gon. I have been worth the whistle.
 Alb.   O Goneril!
You are not worth the dust which the rude wind
Blows in your face. [I fear your disposition.
That nature which contemns its origin
Cannot be bordered certain in itself.
She that herself will sliver and disbranch
From her material sap, perforce must wither
And come to deadly use.
 Gon. No more; the text is foolish.
 Alb. Wisdom and goodness to the vile seem vile;
Filths savour but themselves. What have you done?
Tigers, not daughters, what have you perform'd?
A father, and a gracious aged man,
Whose reverence even the head-lugg'd bear would lick,
Most barbarous, most degenerate! have you madded.

Could my good brother suffer you to do it?
A man, a prince, by him so benefited!
If that the heavens do not their visible spirits
Send quickly down to tame these vile offences,
It will come,
Humanity must perforce prey on itself,
Like monsters of the deep.]
   Gon.   Milk-liver'd man!
That bear'st a cheek for blows, a head for wrongs,
Who hast not in thy brows an eye discerning
Thine honour from thy suffering, [that not know'st
Fools do those villains pity who are punish'd
Ere they have done their mischief, where's thy drum?
France spreads his banners in our noiseless land,
With plumed helm thy state begins to threat;
Whiles thou, a moral fool, sits still, and cries,
"Alack, why does he so?"]
   Alb.   See thyself, devil!
Proper deformity seems not in the fiend
So horrid as in woman.
   Gon.   O vain fool!
   [*Alb.* Thou changed and self-cover'd thing, for shame!
Be-monster not thy feature. Were 't my fitness
To let these hands obey my blood,
They are apt enough to dislocate and tear
Thy flesh and bones. Howe'er thou art a fiend
A woman's shape doth shield thee.
   Gon. Marry, your manhood—Mew!

Enter a Messenger

   Alb. What news?]
   Mess. O, my good lord, the Duke of Cornwall's dead;
Slain by his servant, going to put out
The other eye of Gloucester.
   Alb.   Gloucester's eyes!

Mess. A servant that he bred, thrill'd with remorse,
Oppos'd against the act, bending   his sword
To his great master; who, thereat enrag'd,
Flew on him, and amongst them fell'd him dead;
But not without that harmful stroke, which since
Hath pluck'd him after.
    Alb.   This shows you are **above,**
You justicers, that these our nether crimes.
So speedily can venge! But, O poor Gloucester!
Lost he his other eye?
    Mess.   Both, both, my lord.
This letter, madam, craves a speedy answer.
'Tis from your sister.
    Gon. [*Aside.*] One way I like this well;
But being widow, and my Gloucester with her,
May all the building in my fancy pluck
Upon my hateful life.   Another way,
The news is not so tart.—I'll read, and answer.   *Exit.*
    Alb. Where was his son when they did take his eyes?
    Mess. Come with my lady hither.
    Alb.   He is not here.
    Mess. No, my good lord; I met him back again.
    Alb. Knows he the wickedness?
    Mess. Ay, my good lord; 'twas he inform'd against him;
And quit the house on purpose, that their punishment
Might have the freer course.
    Alb.   Gloucester, I live
To thank thee for the love thou show'dst the King,
And to revenge thine eyes. Come hither, friend;
Tell me what more thou know'st.   *Exeunt.*

[SCENE III. *The French camp near Dover*

Enter KENT *and a* Gentleman

    Kent. Why the King of France is so suddenly gone back, know
you no reason?

238

Gent. Something he left imperfect in the state, which since his coming forth is thought of; which imports to the kingdom so much fear and danger that his personal return was most required and necessary.

Kent. Who hath he left behind him General?

Gent. The Marshal of France, Monsieur La Far.

Kent. Did your letters pierce the Queen to any demonstration of grief?

Gent. Ay, sir; she took them, read them in my presence;
And now and then an ample tear trill'd down
Her delicate cheek. It seem'd she was a queen
Over her passion, who, most rebel-like,
Sought to be king o'er her.

Kent.   O, then it mov'd her.

Gent. Not to a rage; patience and sorrow strove
Who should express her goodliest. You have seen
Sunshine and rain at once: her smiles and tears
Were like a better way; those happy smilets
That play'd on her ripe lip seem'd not to know
What guests were in her eyes, which, parted thence,
As pearls from diamonds dropp'd. In brief,
Sorrow would be a rarity most beloved,
If all could so become it.

Kent.   Made she no verbal question?

Gent. Faith, once or twice she heav'd the name of "father"
Pantingly forth, as if it press'd her heart;
Cried, "Sisters! sisters! Shame of ladies! sisters!
Kent! father! sisters! What, i' the storm? i' the night?
Let pity not be believ'd!" There she shook
The holy water from her heavenly eyes;
And, clamour-moistened, then away she started
To deal with grief alone.

Kent.   It is the stars,
The stars above us, govern our conditions;
Else one self mate and make could not beget
Such different issues. You spoke not with her since?

Gent. No.

Kent. Was this before the King return'd?

Gent.   No, since.

Kent. Well, sir, the poor distressed Lear's i' the town;
Who sometime, in his better tune, remembers
What we are come about, and by no means
Will yield to see his daughter.

Gent.   Why, good sir?

Kent. A sovereign shame so elbows him. His own unkind-
ness,
That stripp'd her from his benediction, turn'd her
To foreign casualties, gave her dear rights
To his dog-hearted daughters,—these things sting
His mind so venomously, that burning shame
Detains him from Cordelia.

Gent.   Alack, poor gentleman!

Kent. Of Albany's and Cornwall's powers you heard not?

Gent. 'Tis so, they are afoot.

Kent. Well, sir, I'll bring you to our master Lear,
And leave you to attend him. Some dear cause
Will in concealment wrap me up a while;
When I am known aright, you shall not grieve
Lending me this acquaintance. I pray you, go
Along with me.]   *Exeunt.*

SCENE [IV. *The same. A tent*]

Enter, with drum and colours, CORDELIA, Doctor, *and* Soldiers

Cor. Alack, 'tis he! Why, he was met even now
As mad as the vex'd sea, singing aloud,
Crown'd with rank fumiter and furrow-weeds,
With hardocks, hemlock, nettles, cuckoo-flowers,
Darnel, and all the idle weeds that grow
In our sustaining corn. A sentry send forth;
Search every acre in the high-grown field,
And bring him to our eye. [*Exit an* Officer.] What can man's
wisdom

In the restoring his bereaved sense?
He that helps him take all my outward worth.
   Doct. There is means, madam.
Our foster-nurse of nature is repose,
The which he lacks; that to provoke in him,
Are many simples operative, whose power
Will close the eye of anguish.
   Cor.   All blest secrets,
All you unpublish'd virtues of the earth,
Spring with my tears! be aidant and remediate
In the good man's distress! Seek, seek for him,
Lest his ungovern'd rage dissolve the life
That wants the means to lead it.

Enter a Messenger

   Mess.   News, madam!
The British powers are marching hitherward.
   Cor. 'Tis known before; our preparation stands
In expectation of them. O dear father,
It is thy business that I go about;
Therefore great France
My mourning and importune tears hath pitied.
No blown ambition doth our arms incite,
But love, dear love, and our ag'd father's right.
Soon may I hear and see him!   *Exeunt.*

SCENE [V. *Gloucester's castle*]

Enter REGAN *and* Steward [OSWALD]

   Reg. But are my brother's powers set forth?
   Osw.   Ay, madam.
   Reg. Himself in person there?
   Osw.   Madam, with much ado.
Your sister is the better soldier.
   Reg. Lord Edmund spake not with your lord at home?
   Osw. No, madam.

Reg. What might import my sister's letter to him?

Osw. I know not, lady.

Reg. Faith, he is posted hence on serious matter.
It was great ignorance, Gloucester's eyes being out,
To let him live; where he arrives he moves
All hearts against us. Edmund, I think, is gone,
In pity of his misery, to dispatch
His nighted life; moreover, to descry
The strength o' the enemy.

Osw. I must needs after him, madam, with my letter.

Reg. Our troops set forth to-morrow, stay with us;
The ways are dangerous.

Osw.   I may not, madam:
My lady charg'd my duty in this business.

Reg. Why should she write to Edmund? Might not you
Transport her purposes by word? Belike
Some things—I know not what. I'll love thee much,
Let me unseal the letter.

Osw.   Madam, I had rather—

Reg. I know your lady does not love her husband;
I am sure of that; and at her late being here
She gave strange œillades and most speaking looks
To noble Edmund. I know you are of her bosom.

Osw. I, madam?

Reg. I speak in understanding; y' are, I know 't.
Therefore I do advise you, take this note:
My lord is dead; Edmund and I have talk'd;
And more convenient is he for my hand
Than for your lady's. You may gather more.
If you do find him, pray you, give him this;
And when your mistress hears thus much from you,
I pray, desire her call her wisdom to her.
So, fare you well.
If you do chance to hear of that blind traitor,
Preferment falls on him that cuts him off.

KING LEAR

Osw. Would I could meet him, madam! I should show
What party I do follow.
   Reg.   Fare thee well.   [*Exeunt.*

SCENE [VI. *Fields near Dover*]

Enter GLOUCESTER, *and* EDGAR [*dressed like a peasant*]

Glou. When shall I come to the top of that same hill?
Edg. You do climb up it now; look, how we labour.
Glou. Methinks the ground is even.
   Edg.   Horrible steep.
Hark, do you hear the sea?
   Glou.   No, truly.
Edg. Why, then, your other senses grow imperfect
By your eyes' anguish.
   Glou.   So may it be, indeed.
Methinks thy voice is alter'd, and thou speak'st
In better phrase and matter than thou didst.
   Edg. You're much deceiv'd. In nothing am I chang'd
But in my garments.
   Glou.   Methinks you're better spoken.
   Edg. Come on, sir, here's the place; stand still. How fearful
And dizzy 'tis, to cast one's eyes so low!
The crows and choughs that wing the midway air
Show scarce so gross as beetles. Half way down
Hangs one that gathers samphire, dreadful trade!
Methinks he seems no bigger than his head.
The fishermen, that walk upon the beach,
Appear like mice; and yond tall anchoring bark,
Diminish'd to her cock; her cock, a buoy
Almost too small for sight. The murmuring surge,
That on the unnumb'red idle pebbles chafes,
Cannot be heard so high. I'll look no more,
Lest my brain turn, and the deficient sight
Topple down headlong.

Glou.   Set me where you stand.

Edg. Give me your hand; you are now within a foot
Of the extreme verge. For all beneath the moon
Would I not leap upright.

Glou.   Let go my hand.
Here, friend, 's another purse; in it a jewel
Well worth a poor man's taking. Fairies and gods
Prosper it with thee! Go thou further off;
Bid me farewell, and let me hear thee going.

Edg. Now fare ye well, good sir.

Glou.   With all my heart.

Edg. Why I do trifle thus with his despair
Is done to cure it.

Glou. [*Kneeling.*] O you mighty gods!
This world I do renounce, and in your sights
Shake patiently my great affliction off.
If I could bear it longer, and not fall
To quarrel with your great opposeless wills,
My snuff and loathed part of nature should
Burn itself out. If Edgar live, O bless him!
Now, fellow, fare thee well.

Edg.   Gone, sir; farewell!
—And yet I know not how conceit may rob
The treasury of life, when life itself
Yields to the theft. [GLOU. *throws himself forward.*] Had he been
        where he thought,
By this had thought been past. Alive or dead?—
Ho, you sir! friend! Hear you, sir! speak!—
Thus might he pass indeed; yet he revives.—
What are you, sir?

Glou.   Away, and let me die.

Edg. Hadst thou been aught but gossamer, feathers, air,
So many fathom down precipitating,
Thou 'dst shiver'd like an egg: but thou dost breathe;
Hast heavy substance; bleed'st not; speak'st; art sound.
Ten masts at each make not the altitude

Which thou hast perpendicularly fell.
Thy life's a miracle. Speak yet again.
   Glou. But have I fallen, or no?
   Edg. From the dread summit of this chalky bourn.
Look up a-height; the shrill-gorg'd lark so far
Cannot be seen or heard. Do but look up.
   Glou. Alack, I have no eyes.
Is wretchedness depriv'd that benefit,
To end itself by death? 'Twas yet some comfort,
When misery could beguile the tyrant's rage,
And frustrate his proud will.
   Edg.   Give me your arm.
Up: so. How is 't? Feel you your legs? You stand.
   Glou. Too well, too well.
   Edg.   This is above all strangeness.
Upon the crown o' the cliff, what thing was that
Which parted from you?
   Glou.   A poor unfortunate beggar.
   Edg. As I stood here below, methought his eyes
Were two full moons; he had a thousand noses,
Horns whelk'd and waved like the enridged sea.
It was some fiend; therefore, thou happy father,
Think that the clearest gods, who make them honours
Of men's impossibilities, have preserv'd thee.
   Glou. I do remember now. Henceforth I'll bear
Affliction till it do cry out itself,
"Enough, enough," and die. That thing you speak of,
I took it for a man; often 'twould say,
"The fiend, the fiend!" He led me to that place.
   Edg. Bear free and patient thoughts.

     Enter LEAR [*fantastically dressed with wild flowers*]

                         But who comes here?

The safer sense will ne'er accommodate
His master thus.

Lear. No, they cannot touch me for coining;
I am the King himself.

Edg. O thou side-piercing sight!

Lear. Nature's above art in that respect. There's your press-money.
That fellow handles his bow like a crow-keeper; draw me a clothier's
yard. Look, look, a mouse! Peace, peace; this piece of toasted cheese
will do 't. There's my gauntlet; I'll prove it on a giant. Bring up the
brown bills. O, well flown, bird! I' the clout, i' the clout! Hewgh!
Give the word.

Edg. Sweet marjoram.

Lear. Pass.

Glou. I know that voice.

Lear. Ha! Goneril, with a white beard! They flatter'd me like a
dog, and told me I had the white hairs in my beard ere the black ones
were there. To say "ay" and "no" to everything that I said! "Ay"
and "no" too was no good divinity. When the rain came to wet me
once, and the wind to make me chatter; when the thunder would not
peace at my bidding; there I found 'em, there I smelt 'em out. Go to,
they are not men o' their words: they told me I was everything; 'tis
a lie, I am not ague-proof.

Glou. The trick of that voice I do well remember.
Is 't not the King?

Lear.   Ay, every inch a king!
When I do stare, see how the subject quakes.
I pardon that man's life. What was thy cause?
Adultery?
Thou shalt not die. Die for adultery! No:
The wren goes to 't, and the small gilded fly
Does lecher in my sight.
Let copulation thrive; for Gloucester's bastard son
Was kinder to his father than my daughters
Got 'tween the lawful sheets.
To 't, luxury, pell-mell! for I lack soldiers.
Behold yond simp'ring dame,
Whose face between her forks presages snow,
That minces virtue, and does shake the head

To hear of pleasure's name,—
The fitchew, nor the soiled horse, goes to 't
With a more riotous appetite.
Down from the waist they are Centaurs,
Though women all above;
But to the girdle do the gods inherit,
Beneath is all the fiends';
There's hell, there's darkness, there's the sulphurous pit,
Burning, scalding, stench, consumption; fie, fie, fie! pah, pah!
Give me an ounce of civet; good apothecary, sweeten my imagination.
There's money for thee.

Glou. O, let me kiss that hand!

Lear. Let me wipe it first; it smells of mortality.

Glou. O ruin'd piece of nature! This great world
Shall so wear out to nought. Dost thou know me?

Lear. I remember thine eyes well enough. Dost thou squiny at me? No, do thy worst, blind Cupid; I'll not love. Read thou this challenge; mark but the penning of it.

Glou. Were all thy letters suns, I could not see.

Edg. [*Aside.*] I would not take this from report. It is; and my heart breaks at it.

Lear. Read.

Glou. What, with the case of eyes?

Lear. O, ho, are you there with me? No eyes in your head, nor no money in your purse? Your eyes are in a heavy case, your purse in a light; yet you see how this world goes.

Glou. I see it feelingly.

Lear. What, art mad? A man may see how this world goes with no eyes. Look with thine ears; see how yond justice rails upon yond simple thief. Hark, in thine ear: change places, and, handy-dandy, which is the justice, which is the thief? Thou has seen a farmer's dog bark at a beggar?

Glou. Ay, sir.

Lear. And the creature run from the cur? There thou mightst behold the great image of authority: a dog's obey'd in office.
Thou rascal beadle, hold thy bloody hand!

Why dost thou lash that whore? Strip thy own back;
Thou hotly lusts to use her in that kind
For which thou whip'st her. The usurer hangs the cozener
Through tatter'd clothes great vices do appear;
Robes and furr'd gowns hide all. Plate sins with gold,
And the strong lance of justice hurtless breaks;
Arm it in rags, a pigmy's straw does pierce it.
None does offend, none, I say, none; I'll able 'em.
Take that of me, my friend, who have the power
To seal the accuser's lips. Get thee glass eyes,
And, like a scurvy politician, seem
To see the things thou dost not. Now, now, now, now.
Pull off my boots; harder, harder: so.
    Edg. O, matter and impertinency mix'd!
Reason in madness!
    Lear. If thou wilt weep my fortunes, take my eyes.
I know thee well enough; thy name is Gloucester.
Thou must be patient; we came crying hither.
Thou know'st, the first time that we smell the air,
We wawl and cry. I will preach to thee; mark.
    Glou. Alack, alack the day!
    Lear. When we are born, we cry that we are come
To this great stage of fools.—This a good block.
It were a delicate stratagem, to shoe
A troop of horse with felt. I'll put 't in proof;
And when I have stol'n upon these son-in-laws,
Then, kill, kill, kill, kill, kill, kill!

        Enter a Gentleman [*with* Attendants]

    Gent. O, here he is! Lay hand upon him. Sir,
Your most dear daughter—
    Lear. No rescue? What, a prisoner? I am even
The natural fool of fortune. Use me well;
You shall have ransom. Let me have surgeons;
I am cut to the brains.

Gent.   You shall have anything.

Lear. No seconds? All myself?
Why, this would make a man a man of salt,
To use his eyes for garden water-pots,
[Ay, and laying autumn's dust.

Gent.   Good sir,—]

Lear. I will die bravely, like a smug bridegroom. What! I will
    be jovial. Come, come; I am a king,
My masters, know you that?

Gent. You are a royal one, and we obey you.

Lear. Then there's life in 't. Come, an you get it, you shall get it
by running. Sa, sa, sa, sa.   *Exit [running;* Attendants *follow].*

Gent. A sight most pitiful in the meanest wretch,
Past speaking of in a king! Thou hast one daughter
Who redeems Nature from the general curse
Which twain have brought her to.

Edg. Hail, gentle sir.

Gent.   Sir, speed you: what's your will?

Edg. Do you hear aught, sir, of a battle toward?

Gent. Most sure and vulgar; every one hears that,
Which can distinguish sound.

Edg.   But, by your favour,
How near's the other army?

Gent. Near and on speedy foot; the main descry
Stands on the hourly thought.

Edg.   I thank you, sir; that's all.

Gent. Though that the Queen on special cause is here,
Her army is mov'd on.   *Exit.*

Edg.   I thank you, sir.

Glou. You ever-gentle gods, take my breath from me;
Let not my worser spirit tempt me again
To die before you please!

Edg.   Well pray you, father.

Glou. Now, good sir, what are you?

Edg. A most poor man, made tame to fortune's blows;

Who, by the art of known and feeling sorrows,
Am pregnant to good pity. Give me your hand,
I'll lead you to some biding.

Glou.   Hearty thanks;
The bounty and the benison of Heaven
To boot, and boot!

Enter Steward [Oswald]

Osw.   A proclaim'd prize! Most happy!
That eyeless head of thine was first fram'd flesh
To raise my fortunes. Thou old unhappy traitor,
Briefly thyself remember; the sword is out
That must destroy thee.

Glou.   Now let thy friendly hand
Put strength enough to 't.   [EDGAR *interposes.*]

Osw.   Wherefore, bold peasant,
Dar'st thou support a publish'd traitor? Hence;
Lest that the infection of his fortune take
Like hold on thee. Let go his arm.

Edg. 'Chill not let go, zir, without vurther 'casion.

Osw. Let go, slave, or thou diest!

Edg. Good gentleman, go your gait, and let poor volk pass. An
'chud ha' bin zwagger'd out of my life, 't would not ha' bin zo long
as 'tis by a vortnight. Nay, come not near th' old man; keep out,
'che vor ye, or Ise try whether your costard or my ballow be the
harder. 'Chill be plain with you.

Osw. Out, dunghill!

Edg. 'Chill pick your teeth, zir. Come, no matter vor your foins.
                    [*They fight, and* EDGAR *knocks him down.*]

Osw. Slave, thou hast slain me. Villain, take my purse.
If ever thou wilt thrive, bury my body;
And give the letters which thou find'st about me
To Edmund, Earl of Gloucester; seek him out
Upon the English party. O, untimely death!
Death!   *Dies.*

Edg. I know thee well; a serviceable villain,
As duteous to the vices of thy mistress
As badness would desire.
 Glou.   What, is he dead?
 Edg. Sit you down, father; rest you.
Let's see these pockets; the letters that he speaks of
May be my friends. He's dead; I am only sorry
He had no other death's-man. Let us see.
Leave, gentle wax; and, manners, blame us not.
To know our enemies' minds, we rip their hearts;
Their papers, is more lawful.
 (*Reads the letter.*) "Let our reciprocal vows be rememb'red. You
have many opportunities to cut him off; if your will want not, time
and place will be fruitfully offer'd. There is nothing done, if he
return the conqueror; then am I the prisoner, and his bed my gaol;
from the loathed warmth whereof deliver me, and supply the place
for your labour.
      "Your—wife, so I would say—
       "Affectionate servant,
          "GONERIL."

O indistinguish'd space of woman's will!
A plot upon her virtuous husband's life;
And the exchange my brother! Here, in the sands,
Thee I'll rake up, the post unsanctified
Of murderous lechers; and in the mature time
With this ungracious paper strike the sight
Of the death-practis'd duke. For him 'tis well
That of thy death and business I can tell.
 Glou. The King is mad; how stiff is my vile sense
That I stand up and have ingenious feeling
Of my huge sorrows! Better I were distract;
So should my thoughts be sever'd from my griefs,
           Drum afar off.

And woes by wrong imaginations lose
The knowledge of themselves.

Edg.   Give me your hand.
Far off, methinks, I hear the beaten drum.
Come, father, I'll bestow you with a friend.   *Exeunt.*

SCENE VII. [*A tent in the French camp*]

Enter CORDELIA, KENT, *and* Doctor

Cor. O thou good Kent, how shall I live and work
To match thy goodness? My life will be too short,
And every measure fail me.
    Kent. To be acknowledg'd, madam, is o'er-paid.
All my reports go with the modest truth;
Nor more nor clipp'd, but so.
    Cor.   Be better suited;
These weeds are memories of those worser hours.
I prithee, put them off.
    Kent.   Pardon, dear madam;
Yet to be known shortens my made intent.
My boon I make it, that you know me not
Till time and I think meet.
    Cor. Then be 't so, my good lord. [*To the* Doctor.]
        How does the King?
    Doct. Madam, sleeps still.
    Cor. O you kind gods,
Cure this great breach in his abused nature!
The untun'd and jarring senses, O, wind up
Of this child-changed father!
    Doct.   So please your Majesty
That we may wake the King? He hath slept long.
    Cor. Be govern'd by your knowledge, and proceed
I' the sway of your own will.

Enter LEAR *in a chair carried by* Servants. [Gentleman *in attendance*]
                          Is he array'd?
    Gent. Ay, madam; in the heaviness of sleep
We put fresh garments on him.

Doct. Be by, good madam, when we do awake him;
I doubt not of his temperance.
  [*Cor.*   Very well.
  Doct. Please you, draw near.—Louder the music there!]
  Cor. O my dear father! Restoration hang
Thy medicine on my lips; and let this kiss
Repair those violent harms that my two sisters
Have in thy reverence made!
  Kent.   Kind and dear princess!
  Cor. Had you not been their father, these white flakes
Did challenge pity of them. Was this a face
To be oppos'd against the warring winds?
[To stand against the deep dread-bolted thunder?
In the most terrible and nimble stroke
Of quick, cross lightning? to watch—poor perdu!—
With this thin helm?] Mine enemy's dog,
Though he had bit me, should have stood that night
Against my fire; and wast thou fain, poor father,
To hovel thee with swine and rogues forlorn
In short and musty straw? Alack, alack!
'Tis wonder that thy life and wits at once
Had not concluded all. He wakes; speak to him.
  Doct. Madam, do you; 'tis fittest.
  Cor. How does my royal lord? How fares your Majesty?
  Lear. You do me wrong to take me out o' the grave.
Thou art a soul in bliss; but I am bound
Upon a wheel of fire, that mine own tears
Do scald like molten lead.
  Cor.   Sir, do you know me?
  Lear. You are a spirit, I know; when did you die?
  Cor. Still, still, far wide!
  Doct. He's scarce awake; let him alone a while.
  Lear. Where have I been? Where am I? Fair daylight?
I am mightily abus'd. I should even die with pity,
To see another thus. I know not what to say.
I will not swear these are my hands. Let's see;

I feel this pin prick. Would I were assur'd
Of my condition!
    Cor.   O, look upon me, sir,
And hold your hand in benediction o'er me.
[No, sir,] you must not kneel.
    Lear.   Pray, do not mock me.
I am a very foolish fond old man,
Fourscore and upward, not an hour more nor less;
And, to deal plainly,
I fear I am not in my perfect mind.
Methinks I should know you, and know this man;
Yet I am doubtful; for I am mainly ignorant
What place this is, and all the skill I have
Remembers not these garments; nor I know not
Where I did lodge last night. Do not laugh at me;
For, as I am a man, I think this lady
To be my child Cordelia.
    Cor.   And so I am, I am.
    Lear. Be your tears wet? Yes, faith. I pray, weep not.
If you have poison for me, I will drink it.
I know you do not love me; for your sisters
Have, as I do remember, done me wrong;
You have some cause, they have not.
    Cor.   No cause, no cause.
    Lear. Am I in France?
    Kent.   In your own kingdom, sir.
    Lear. Do not abuse me.
    Doct. Be comforted, good madam; the great rage,
You see, is kill'd in him: [and yet it is danger
To make him even o'er the time he has lost.]
Desire him to go in; trouble him no more
Till further settling.
    Cor. Will 't please your Highness walk?
    Lear.   You must bear with me.
Pray you now, forget and forgive; I am old and foolish.
                Exeunt [*all but* KENT *and* Gentleman].

254

[*Gent.* Holds it true, sir, that the Duke of Cornwall was so slain?

Kent. Most certain, sir.

Gent. Who is conductor of his people?

Kent. As 'tis said, the bastard son of Gloucester.

Gent. They say Edgar, his banish'd son, is with the Earl of Kent
in Germany.

Kent. Report is changeable. 'Tis time to look about; the powers of
the kingdom approach apace.

Gent. The arbitrement   is like to be bloody.
Fare you well, sir.   [*Exit.*]

Kent. My point and period will be throughly wrought,
Or well or ill, as this day's battle's fought.]   *Exit.*

ACT V

Scene I. [*The British camp, near Dover*]

Enter, with drum and colours, EDMUND, REGAN, *Gentlemen,*
and Soldiers

Edm. Know of the Duke if his last purpose hold,
Or whether since he is advis'd by aught
To change the course. He's full of alteration
And self-reproving; bring his constant pleasure.
                                    [*To a* Gentleman, *who goes out.*]

Reg. Our sister's man is certainly miscarried.

Edm. 'Tis to be doubted, madam.

Reg.   Now, sweet lord,
You know the goodness I intend upon you.
Tell me—but truly—but then speak the truth,
Do you not love my sister?

Edm.   In honour'd love.

Reg. But have you never found my brother's way
To the forfended place?

[*Edm.*   That thought abuses you.

Reg. I am doubtful that you have been conjunct
And bosom'd with her,—as far as we call hers.]

Edm. No, by mine honour, madam.

Reg. I never shall endure her. Dear my lord,
Be not familiar with her.

Edm.   Fear me not.
She and the Duke her husband!

   Enter, with drum and colours, ALBANY, GONERIL, *and* Soldiers

   [*Gon.* [*Aside.*] I had rather lose the battle than that sister
Should loosen him and me.]

   Alb. Our very loving sister, well be-met.
Sir, this I heard: the King is come to his daughter,
With others whom the rigour of our state
Forc'd to cry out. [Where I could not be honest,
I never yet was valiant. For this business,
It toucheth us, as France invades our land,
Not bolds the King, with others, whom, I fear,
Most just and heavy causes make oppose.

   Edm. Sir, you speak nobly.]

   Reg.   Why is this reason'd?

   Gon. Combine together 'gainst the enemy;
For these domestic and particular broils
Are not the question here.

   Alb.   Let's then determine.
With the ancient of war on our proceeding.

   [*Edm.* I shall attend you presently at your tent.]

   Reg. Sister, you'll go with us?

   Gon. No.

   Reg. 'Tis most convenient; pray you, go with us.

   Gon. [*Aside.*] O, ho, I know the riddle.—I will go.

                         Exeunt both the armies.

   [*As they are going out,*] *enter* EDGAR [*disguised.* ALBANY *remains*]

   Edg. If e'er your Grace had speech with man so poor,
Hear me one word.

   Alb.   I'll overtake you.—Speak.

   Edg. Before you fight the battle, ope this letter.

If you have victory, let the trumpet sound
For him that brought it. Wretched though I seem,
I can produce a champion that will prove
What is 'avouched there. If you miscarry,
Your business of the world hath so an end,
And machination ceases. Fortune love you!

   Alb. Stay till I have read the letter.

   Edg.   I was forbid it.
When time shall serve, let but the herald cry,
And I'll appear again.   *Exit.*

   Alb. Why, fare thee well; I will o'erlook thy paper.

Re-enter EDMUND

   Edm. The enemy's in view; draw up your powers.
Here is the guess of their true strength and forces
By diligent discovery; but your haste
Is now urg'd on you.

   Alb.   We will greet the time.   *Exit.*

   Edm. To both these sisters have I sworn my love;
Each jealous of the other, as the stung
Are of the adder. Which of them shall I take?
Both? one? or neither? Neither can be enjoy'd,
If both remain alive. To take the widow
Exasperates, makes mad her sister Goneril;
And hardly shall I carry out my side,
Her husband being alive. Now then we'll use
His countenance for the battle; which being done,
Let her who would be rid of him devise
His speedy taking off. As for the mercy
Which he intends to Lear and to Cordelia,
The battle done, and they within our power,
Shall never see his pardon; for my state
Stands on me to defend, not to debate.   *Exit.*

SCENE II. [*A field between the two camps*]

Alarum within. Enter with drum and colours, LEAR, CORDELIA, *and* Soldiers, *over the stage; and exeunt*

Enter EDGAR *and* GLOUCESTER

Edg. Here, father, take the shadow of this tree
For your good host; pray that the right may thrive.
If ever I return to you again,
I'll bring you comfort.
   Glou.   Grace go with you, sir!   *Exit* [EDGAR].

Alarum and retreat within. Re-enter EDGAR

Edg. Away, old man; give me thy hand; away!
King Lear hath lost, he and his daughter ta'en.
Give me thy hand; come on.
   Glou. No further, sir; a man may rot even here.
   Edg. What, in ill thoughts again? Men must endure
Their going hence, even as their coming hither;
Ripeness is all. Come on.
   Glou.   And that's true too.   *Exeunt.*

SCENE III. [*The British camp near Dover*]

Enter, in conquest, with drum and colours, EDMUND; LEAR *and* COR-
DELIA *as prisoners:* Captain, Soldiers, *etc.*

   Edm. Some officers take them away. Good guard,
Until their greater pleasures first be known
That are to censure them.
   Cor.   We are not the first
Who, with best meaning, have incurr'd the worst.
For thee, oppressed king, I am cast down;
Myself could else out-frown false Fortune's frown.
Shall we not see these daughters and these sisters?
   Lear. No, no, no, no! Come, let's away to prison;
We two alone will sing like birds i' the cage.

When thou dost ask me blessing, I'll kneel down
And ask of thee forgiveness. So we'll live,
And pray, and sing, and tell old tales, and laugh
At gilded butterflies, and hear poor rogues
Talk of court news; and we'll talk with them too,
Who loses and who wins; who's in, who's out;
And take upon 's the mystery of things
As if we were God's spies; and we'll wear out,
In a wall'd prison, packs and sects of great ones,
That ebb and flow by the moon.
 Edm.   Take them away.
 Lear. Upon such sacrifices, my Cordelia,
The gods themselves throw incense. Have I caught thee?
He that parts us shall bring a brand from heaven,
And fire us hence like foxes. Wipe thine eyes;
The good-years shall devour them, flesh and fell,
Ere they shall make us weep. We'll see 'em starv'd first.
Come.   *Exeunt* [LEAR *and* CORDELIA, *guarded*].
 Edm. Come hither, captain; hark.
Take thou this note [*giving a paper*]; go follow them to prison.
One step I have advanc'd thee; if thou dost
As this instructs thee, thou dost make thy way
To noble fortunes. Know thou this, that men
Are as the time is; to be tender-minded
Does not become a sword. Thy great employment
Will not bear question, either say thou'lt do 't,
Or thrive by other means.
 Capt.   I'll do 't, my lord.
 Edm. About it; and write happy when thou hast done.
Mark, I say, instantly; and carry it so
As I have set it down.
 [*Capt.* I cannot draw a cart, nor eat dried oats;
If it be man's work, I'll do 't.]   *Exit.*

Flourish. Enter ALBANY, GONERIL, REGAN, [*another* Captain] *and*
Soldiers

    Alb. Sir, you have show'd to-day your valiant strain,
And fortune led you well. You have the captives
Who were the opposites of this day's strife;
I do require them of you, so to use them
As we shall find their merits and our safety
May equally determine.
    Edm.   Sir, I thought it fit
To send the old and miserable king
To some retention [and appointed guard];
Whose age had charms in it, whose title more,
To pluck the common bosom on his side,
And turn our impress'd lances in our eyes
Which do command them. With him I sent the Queen,
My reason all the same; and they are ready
To-morrow, or at further space, to appear
Where you shall hold your session. [At this time
We sweat and bleed: the friend hath lost his friend;
And the best quarrels, in the heat, are curs'd
By those that feel their sharpness:
The question of Cordelia and her father
Requires a fitter place.]
    Alb.   Sir, by your patience,
I hold you but a subject of this war,
Not as a brother.
    Reg.   That's as we list to grace him.
Methinks our pleasure might have been demanded,
Ere you had spoke so far. He led our powers,
Bore the commission of my place and person;
The which immediacy may well stand up,
And call itself your brother.
    Gon.   Not so hot.
In his own grace he doth exalt himself,
More than in your addition

Reg.   In my rights,
By me invested, he compeers the best.
  Gon. That were the most, if he should husband you.
  Reg. Jesters do oft prove prophets.
  Gon.   Holla, holla!
That eye that told you so look'd but a-squint.
  Reg. Lady, I am not well; else I should answer
From a full-flowing stomach. General,
Take thou my soldiers, prisoners, patrimony;
Dispose of them, of me; the walls are thine.
Witness the world, that I create thee here
My lord and master.
  Gon.   Mean you to enjoy him?
  Alb. The let-alone lies not in your good will.
  Edm. Nor in thine, lord.
  Alb.   Half-blooded fellow, yes.
  Reg. [*To* EDMUND.] Let the drum strike, and prove my title thine.
  Alb. Stay yet; hear reason. Edmund, I arrest thee
On capital treason; and, in thy arrest,
This gilded serpent. [*Pointing to* GON.] For your claim, fair
        sister,
I bar it in the interest of my wife.
'Tis she is sub-contracted to this lord,
And I, her husband, contradict your bans.
If you will marry, make your loves to me,
My lady is bespoke.
  Gon.   An interlude !
  Alb. Thou art armed, Gloucester; let the trumpet sound.
If none appear to prove upon thy person
Thy heinous, manifest, and many treasons,
There is my pledge [*throwing down a glove*]. I'll prove it on thy
        heart,
Ere I taste bread, thou art in nothing less
Than I have here proclaim'd thee.
  Reg.   Sick, O sick!
  Gon. [*Aside.*] If not, I'll ne'er trust medicine.

Edm. There's my exchange [*throwing down a glove*].
    What in the world he is
That names me traitor, villain-like he lies.
Call by the trumpet;—he that dares approach,
On him, on you, who not? I will maintain
My truth and honour firmly.
    Alb. A herald, ho!
    [*Edm.*   A herald, ho, a herald!]
    Alb. Trust to thy single virtue, for thy soldiers,
All levied in my name, have in my name
Took their discharge.
    Reg.   My sickness grows upon me.
    Alb. She is not well; convey her to my tent.   [*Exit* REGAN, *led.*]

Enter *a* Herald

Come hither, herald,—Let the trumpet sound—
And read out this.
    [*Capt.* Sound, trumpet!]   *A trumpet sounds.*
    Her. (*Reads.*) "If any man of quality or decree within the lists
of the army will maintain upon Edmund, supposed Earl of Gloucester, that he is a manifold traitor, let him appear by the third
sound of the trumpet. He is bold in his defence."
    [*Edm.* Sound!]   *First trumpet.*
    Her. Again!   *Second trumpet.*
    Her. Again!   *Third trumpet.*
                         Trumpet answers within.

Enter EDGAR, *at the third sound, armed, with a trumpet before him.*

    Alb. Ask him his purposes, why he appears
Upon this call o' the trumpet.
    Her.   What are you?
Your name, your quality? and why you answer
This present summons?
    Edg.   Know, my name is lost,
By treason's tooth bare-gnawn and canker-bit;

Yet am I noble as the adversary
I come to cope.
    Alb.   Which is that adversary?
    Edg. What's he that speaks for Edmund Earl of Gloucester?
    Edm. Himself; what say'st thou to him?
    Edg.   Draw thy sword,
That, if my speech offend a noble heart,
Thy arm may do thee justice; here is mine.
Behold, it is the privilege of mine honours,
My oath, and my profession. I protest,
Maugre thy strength, place, youth, and eminence,
Despite thy victor-sword and fire-hewn fortune,
Thy valour, and thy heart, thou art a traitor;
False to thy gods, thy brother, and thy father;
Conspirant 'gainst this high illustrious prince;
And, from the extremest upward of thy head
To the descent and dust below thy foot,
A most toad-spotted traitor. Say thou "No,"
This sword, this arm, and my best spirits are bent
To prove upon thy heart, whereto I speak,
Thou liest.
    Edm.   In wisdom I should ask thy name;
But, since thy outside looks so fair and warlike,
And that thy tongue some 'say of breeding breathes,
What safe and nicely I might well delay,
By rule of knighthood, I disdain and spurn.
Back do I toss these treasons to thy head;
With the hell-hated lie o'erwhelm thy heart;
Which, for they yet glance by and scarcely bruise,
This sword of mine shall give them instant way,
Where they shall rest for ever. Trumpets, speak!
                  Alarums. They fight. [EDMUND *falls.*]
    Alb. Save him, save him!
    Gon.   This is [mere] practice, Gloucester.
By the law of war thou wast not bound to answer

An unknown opposite. Thou art not vanquish'd,
But cozen'd and beguil'd.

 Alb.   Shut your mouth, dame,
Or with this paper shall I stop it. Hold, sir.—
Thou worse than any name, read thine own evil.
No tearing, lady; I perceive you know it.

 Gon. Say, if I do, the laws are mine, not thine.
Who can arraign me for 't?   [*Exit.*]

 Alb.   Most monstrous! oh!—
Know'st thou this paper?

 Edm.   Ask me not what I know.

 Alb. Go after her; she's desperate; govern her.

 Edm. What you have charg'd me with, that have I done;
And more, much more; the time will bring it out.
'Tis past, and so am I. But what art thou
That hast this fortune on me? If thou 'rt noble,
I do forgive thee.

 Edg.   Let's exchange charity.
I am no less in blood than thou art, Edmund;
If more, the more thou 'st wrong'd me.
My name is Edgar, and thy father's son.
The gods are just, and of our pleasant vices
Make instruments to plague us.
The dark and vicious place where thee he got
Cost him his eyes.

 Edm.   Thou 'st spoken right, 'tis true.
The wheel is come full circle; I am here.

 Alb. Methought thy very gait did prophesy
A royal nobleness. I must embrace thee.
Let sorrow split my heart, if ever I
Did hate thee or thy father!

 Edg.   Worthy prince, I know 't.

 Alb. Where have you hid yourself?
How have you known the miseries of your father?

 Edg. By nursing them, my lord. List a brief tale;
And when 'tis told, oh, that my heart would burst!

The bloody proclamation to escape,
That follow'd me so near,—oh, our lives' sweetness!
That we the pain of death would hourly die
Rather than die at once!—taught me to shift
Into a madman's rags, to assume a semblance
That very dogs disdain'd; and in this habit
Met I my father with his bleeding rings,
Their precious stones new lost; became his guide,
Led him, begg'd for him, sav'd him from despair;
Never,—O fault!—reveal'd myself unto him,
Until some half-hour past, when I was arm'd.
Not sure, though hoping, of this good success,
I ask'd his blessing, and from first to last
Told him our pilgrimage; but his flaw'd heart,
Alack, too weak the conflict to support!
'Twixt two extremes of passion, joy and grief,
Burst smilingly.

 Edm.   This speech of yours hath mov'd me,
And shall perchance do good. But speak you on;
You look as you had something more to say.

 Alb. If there be more, more woeful, hold it in;
For I am almost ready to dissolve,
Hearing of this.

 [*Edg.*   This would have seem'd a period
To such as love not sorrow; but another,
To amplify too much, would make much more,
And top extremity.
Whilst I was big in clamour came there in a man,
Who, having seen me in my worst estate,
Shunn'd my abhorr'd society; but then, finding
Who 'twas that so endur'd, with his strong arms
He fastened on my neck, and bellowed out
As he'd burst heaven; threw him on my father;
Told the most piteous tale of Lear and him
That ever ear received; which in recounting,
His grief grew puissant, and the strings of life

265

Began to crack. Twice then the trumpets sounded,
And there I left him tranc'd.

 Alb.   But who was this?

 Edg. Kent, sir, the banish'd Kent; who in disguise
Follow'd his enemy king, and did him service
Improper for a slave.]

    Enter a Gentleman *with a bloody knife*

 Gent. Help, help, O, help?

 Edg.   What kind of help?

 Alb.   Speak, man.

 Edg. What means this bloody knife?

 Gent.   'Tis hot, it smokes;
It came even from the heart of—O, she's dead!

 Alb. Who dead? Speak, man.

 Gent. Your lady, sir, your lady; and her sister
By her is poison'd; she confesses it.

 Edm. I was contracted to them both. All three
Now marry in an instant.

 Edg.   Here comes Kent.

      Enter KENT

 Alb. Produce the bodies, be they alive or dead.
This judgement of the heavens, that makes us tremble,
Touches us not with pity.   [*Exit* Gentleman.]

    —O, is this he?
The time will not allow the compliment
Which very manners urges.

 Kent.   I am come
To bid my king and master aye good-night.
Is he not here?

 Alb.   Great thing of us forgot!
Speak, Edmund, where's the King? and where's Cordelia?

    The bodies of GONERIL *and* REGAN *are brought in.*
See'st thou this object, Kent?

 Kent. Alack, why thus?

Edm.   Yet Edmund was belov'd!
The one the other poison'd for my sake,
And after slew herself.
    Alb. Even so. Cover their faces.
    Edm. I pant for life. Some good I mean to do,
Despite of mine own nature. Quickly send,
Be brief in it, to the castle; for my writ
Is on the life of Lear and on Cordelia.
Nay, send in time.
    Alb.   Run, run, O, run!
    Edg. To who, my lord? Who has the office? Send
Thy token of reprieve.
    Edm. Well thought on. Take my sword,
Give it the captain.
    Edg.   Haste thee, for thy life. [*Exit* Gentleman.]
    Edm. He hath commission from thy wife and me
To hang Cordelia in the prison, and
To lay the blame upon her own despair,
That she fordid herself.
    Alb. The gods defend her! Bear him hence a while.
                                    [EDMUND *is borne off.*]

Re-enter LEAR, *with* CORDELIA *in his arms;* [Gentleman *following*]

    Lear. Howl, howl, howl! O, you are men of stones!
Had I your tongues and eyes, I'd use them so
That heaven's vault should crack. She's gone for ever!
I know when one is dead, and when one lives;
She's dead as earth. Lend me a looking-glass;
If that her breath will mist or stain the stone,
Why, then she lives.
    Kent.   Is this the promis'd end?
    Edg. Or image of that horror?
    Alb.   Fall, and cease!
    Lear. This feather stirs; she lives! If it be so,
It is a chance which does redeem all sorrows

That ever I have felt.

Kent. [*Kneeling.*] O my good master!

Lear. Prithee, away.

Edg. 'Tis noble Kent, your friend.

Lear. A plague upon you, murderers, traitors all!
I might have sav'd her; now she's gone for ever!
Cordelia, Cordelia! stay a little. Ha!
What is 't thou say'st? Her voice was ever soft,
Gentle, and low; an excellent thing in woman.
I kill'd the slave that was a-hanging thee.

Gent. 'Tis true, my lords, he did.

Lear. Did I not, fellow?
I have seen the day, with my good biting falchion
I would have made him skip. I am old now,
And these same crosses spoil me. Who are you?
Mine eyes are not o' the best. I'll tell you straight.

Kent. If Fortune brag of two she lov'd and hated,
One of them we behold.

Lear. This is a dull sight. Are you not Kent?

Kent. The same,
Your servant Kent. Where is your servant Caius?

Lear. He's a good fellow, I can tell you that;
He'll strike, and quickly too. He's dead and rotten.

Kent. No, my good lord; I am the very man,—

Lear. I'll see that straight.

Kent. That, from your first of difference and decay,
Have follow'd your sad steps.

Lear. You are welcome hither.

Kent. Nor no man else; all's cheerless, dark, and deadly.
Your eldest daughters have fordone themselves,
And desperately are dead.

Lear. Ay, so I think.

Alb. He knows not what he says; and vain is it
That we present us to him.

Enter a Messenger

Edg. Very bootless.

Mess. Edmund is dead, my lord.

Alb.   That's but a trifle here.
You lords and noble friends, know our intent.
What comfort to this great decay may come
Shall be appli'd. For us, we will resign,
During the life of this old majesty,
To him our absolute power; [*to* EDGAR *and* KENT] you, to your rights,
With boot, and such addition as your honours
Have more than merited. All friends shall taste
The wages of their virtue, and all foes
The cup of their deservings. O, see, see!

Lear. And my poor fool is hang'd! No, no, no life!
Why should a dog, a horse, a rat, have life,
And thou no breath at all? Thou'lt come no more,
Never, never, never, never, never!
Pray you, undo this button. Thank you, sir.
Do you see this? Look on her, look, her lips,
Look there, look there!   *Dies.*

Edg.   He faints! My lord, my lord!

Kent. Break, heart; I prithee, break!

Edg.   Look up, my lord.

Kent. Vex not his ghost; O, let him pass! He hates him
That would upon the rack of this tough world
Stretch him out longer.

Edg.   He is gone, indeed.

Kent. The wonder is he hath endur'd so long;
He but usurp'd his life.

Alb. Bear them from hence. Our present business
Is general woe. [*To* KENT *and* EDGAR.] Friends of my soul, you twain
Rule in this realm, and the gor'd state sustain.

Kent. I have a journey, sir, shortly to go.
My master calls me; I must not say no.

Edg. The weight of this sad time we must obey;
Speak what we feel, not what we ought to say.
The oldest hath borne most; we that are young
Shall never see so much, nor live so long.

                    Exeunt, with a dead march.

269

Miguel de Cervantes,   DON QUIXOTE
(Trans. by Thomas Shelton)

1. What is the importance of Don Quixote's character and his socio-economic status as he prepares for his adventures?

2. How was Sancho persuaded to accompany Don Quixote?

3. How does Don Quixote explain reality when he discovers that his giants are actually windmills?

4. What are the standards of behavior Don Quixote applies to himself and his squire?

5. Contrast the shepherdesses of Don Quixote's fantasy with the girl in Anthony's Ditty.

6. At what is Cervantes really laughing?

7. Give some examples of ambiguity in Don Quixote's character.

Miguel de Cervantes Saavedra (1547-1616) was a Spanish writer of poems, plays, and romances whose most famous work, *The Ingenious Gentleman Don Quixote de la Mancha* is considered by some to be the first and greatest modern novel. It was published in two parts in 1605 and 1615, and is a satire on chivalry. It was popular at once because of its humor and adventures, and passed through many printings and pirated editions. *Don Quixote* set the stylistic standards for modern Spanish and is a seminal work which continued to enrich literature, art, music, and dance.

THE FIRST BOOK

CHAPTER I

Wherein Is Rehearsed the Calling and Exercise of the Renowned Gentleman, Don Quixote of the Mancha

THERE lived not long since, in a certain village of the Mancha, the name whereof I purposely omit, a gentleman of their calling that use to pile up in their halls old lances, halberds, morions, and such other armours and weapons. He was, besides, master of an ancient target, a lean stallion, and a swift greyhound. His pot consisted daily of somewhat more beef than mutton: a gallimaufry each night, collops and eggs on Saturdays, lentils on Fridays, and now and then a lean pigeon on Sundays, did consume three parts of his rents; the rest and remnant thereof was spent on a jerkin of fine puce, a pair of velvet hose, with pantofles of the same for the holy-days, and one suit of the finest vesture; for therewithal he honoured and set out his person on the workdays. He had in his house a woman-servant of about forty years old, and a niece not yet twenty, and a man that served him both in field and at home, and could saddle his horse, and likewise manage a pruning-hook. The master himself was about fifty years old, of a strong complexion, dry flesh, and a withered face. He was an early riser, and a great friend of hunting. Some affirm that his surname was Quixada, or Quesada (for in this there is some variance among the authors that write his life), although it may be gathered, by very probable conjectures, that he was called Quixana. Yet all this concerns our historical relation but little: let it then suffice, that in the narration thereof we will not vary a jot from the truth.

You shall therefore wit, that this gentleman above named, the spurts that he was idle (which was the longer part of the year), did apply himself wholly to the reading of books of knighthood, and that with such gusts and delights, as he almost wholly neglected the exercise of hunting; yea, and the very administration of his household affairs. And his curiosity and folly came to that pass, that he made away many acres of arable land to buy him books of that kind, and therefore he brought to his house as many as ever he could get of that subject. And among them all, none pleased him better than those which famous Felician of Silva composed. For the smoothness of his prose, with now and then some intricate sentence meddled, seemed to him peerless; and principally when he did read the courtings, or letters of challenge, that knights sent to ladies, or one to another; where, in many places, he found written: 'The reason of the unreasonableness which against my reason is wrought, doth so weaken my reason, as with all reason I do justly complain on your beauty.' And also when he read: 'The high heavens, which with your divinity do fortify you divinely with the stars, and make you deserveress of the deserts which your greatness deserves,' etc. With these and other such passages the poor gentleman grew distracted, and was breaking his brains day and night, to understand and unbowel their sense, an endless labour; for even Aristotle himself would not understand them, though he were again resuscitated only for that purpose. He did not like so much the unproportionate blows that Don Belianis gave and took in fight; for, as he imagined, were the surgeons never so cunning that cured them, yet was it impossible but that the patient his face and all his body must remain full of scars and tokens. Yet did he praise, notwithstanding, in the author of that history, the conclusion of his book, with the promise of the Endless Adventure; and many times he himself had a desire to take pen and finish it exactly, as it is there promised; and would doubtless have performed it, and that certes with happy success, if other more urgent and continual thoughts had not disturbed him.

Many times did he fall at variance with the curate of his village (who was a learned man, graduated in Ciguenca) touching who was the better knight, Palmerin of England, or Amadis de Gaul. But Master Nicholas, the barber of the same town, would affirm that none of both arrived in worth to the Knight of the Sun; and if any one knight might paragon with him, it was infallibly Don Galaor, Amadis de Gaul's brother, whose nature might fitly be accommodated to anything; for he was not so coy and whining a knight as his brother, and that in matters of valour he did not bate him an ace.

In resolution, he plunged himself so deeply in his reading of these books, as he spent many times in the lecture of them whole days and nights; and in the end, through his little sleep and much reading, he dried up his brains in such sort as he lost wholly his judgment. His fantasy was filled with those things that he read, of enchantments, quarrels, battles, challenges, wounds, wooings, loves, tempests, and other impossible follies. And these toys did so firmly possess his imagination with an infallible opinion that all that *machina* of dreamed inventions which he read was true, as he accounted no history in the world to be so certain and sincere as they were. He was wont to say, that the Cid Ruy Diaz was a very good knight, but not to be compared to the Knight of the Burning Sword, which, with one thwart blow, cut asunder two fierce and mighty giants. He agreed better with Bernardo del Carpio, because he slew the enchanted Roland in Roncesvalles. He likewise liked of the shift Hercules used when he smothered Anteon, the son of the earth, between his arms. He praised the giant Morgant marvellously, because, though he was of that monstrous progeny, who are commonly all of them proud and rude, yet he was affable and courteous. But he agreed best of all with Reinauld of Mount Alban; and most of all then, when he saw him sally out of his castle to rob as many as ever he could meet; and when, moreover, he robbed the idol of Mahomet, made all of gold, as his history recounts, and would be content to give his old woman, yea, and his niece also, for a good opportunity on the traitor Galalon, that he might lamb-skin and trample him into powder.

Finally, his wit being wholly extinguished, he fell into one of the strangest conceits that ever madman stumbled on in this world; to wit, it seemed unto him very requisite and behooveful, as well for the augmentation of his honour as also for the benefit of the commonwealth, that he himself should become a knight-errant, and go throughout the world, with his horse and armour, to seek adventures, and practise in person all that he had read was used by knights of yore; revenging of all kinds of injuries, and offering himself to occasions and dangers, which, being once happily achieved, might gain him eternal renown. The poor soul did already figure himself crowned, through the valour of his arm, at least Emperor of Trapisonda; and led thus by these soothing thoughts, and borne away with the exceeding delight he found in them, he hastened all that he might, to effect his urging desires.

And first of all he caused certain old rusty arms to be scoured, that belonged to his great-grandfather, and lay many ages neglected and forgotten in a by-corner of his house; he trimmed and dressed them the best he might, and then perceived a great defect they had; for they wanted a helmet, and had only a plain morion; but he by his industry supplied that want, and framed, with certain papers pasted together, a beaver for his morion. True it is, that to make trial whether his pasted beaver was strong enough, and might abide the adventure of a blow, he out with his sword and gave it a blow or two, and with the very first did quite undo his whole week's labour. The facility wherewithal it was dissolved liked him nothing; wherefore, to assure himself better the next time from the like danger, he made it anew, placing certain iron bars within it, in so artificial a manner, as he rested at once satisfied, both with his invention, and also the solidity of the work; and without making a second trial, he deputed and held it in estimation of a most excellent beaver. Then did he presently visit his horse, who (though he had more quarters than pence in a sixpence, through leanness, and more faults than Gonella's), having nothing on him but skin and bone; yet he thought that neither Alexander's Bucephalus, nor the Cid his horse Balieca, were in any respect equal to him. He spent four days devising him a name; for (as he reasoned to himself) it was not fit that so famous a knight's horse, and chiefly being so good a beast, should want a known name; and therefore he endeavoured to give him such a one as should both declare what sometime he had been, before he pertained to a knight-errant, and also what at present he was; for it stood greatly with reason, seeing his lord and master changed his estate and vocation, that he should alter likewise his denomination, and get a new one, that were famous and altisonant, as became the new order and exercise which he now professed; and therefore, after many other names which he framed, blotted out, rejected, added, undid, and turned again to frame in his memory and imagination, he finally concluded to name him Rozinante, a name in his opinion lofty, full, and significant of what he had been when he was a plain jade, before he was exalted to his new dignity; being, as he thought, the best carriage beast of the world. The name being thus given to his horse, and so to his mind, he resolved to give himself a name also; and in that thought he laboured other eight days; and, in conclusion, called himself Don Quixote; whence (as is said) the authors of this most true history deduce, that he was undoubtedly named Quixada, and not Quesada, as others would have it. And remembering that the valorous Amadis was not satisfied only with the dry name of Amadis, but added thereunto the name of his kingdom and country, to render his own more redoubted, terming himself Amadis de Gaul; so he, like a good knight, would add to his own that also of his province, and call himself Don Quixote of the Mancha, wherewith it appeared that he very lively declared his lineage and country, which he did honour, by taking it for his surname.

His armour being scoured, his morion transformed into a helmet, his horse named, and himself confirmed with a new name also, he forthwith bethought himself, that now he wanted nothing but a lady on whom he might bestow his service and affection; for the knight-errant that is loveless resembles a tree that wants leaves and fruit, or a body without a soul: and therefore he was wont to say, 'If I should for my sins, or by good hap, encounter there abroad with some giant (as knights-errant do ordinarily), and that I should overthrow him with one blow to the ground, or cut him with a stroke in two halves, or finally overcome, and make him yield to me, would it not be very expedient to have some lady to whom I might present him? And that he, entering in her presence, do kneel before my sweet lady, and say unto her, with an humble and submissive voice, "Madam, I am the giant Caraculiambro, lord of the island called Malindrania, whom the never-too-much-praised knight, Don Quixote de la Mancha, hath overcome in single combat; and hath commanded to present myself to your greatness, that it may please your highness to dispose of me according unto your liking!" ' Oh, how glad was our knight when he had made this discourse to himself, but chiefly when he had found out one whom he might call his lady! For, as it is imagined, there dwelt in the next village unto his manor, a young handsome wench, with whom he was sometime in love, although, as is understood, she never knew or took notice thereof. She was called Aldonsa Lorenzo, and her he thought fittest to entitle with the name of Lady of his thoughts, and searching a name for her that should not vary much from her own, and yet should draw and aveer somewhat to that of a princess or great lady, he called her Dulcinea del Toboso (for there she was born), a name in his conceit harmonious, strange, and significant, like to all the others that he had given to his things.

CHAPTER VII

OF THE SECOND DEPARTURE WHICH OUR GOOD KNIGHT, DON QUIXOTE, MADE FROM HIS HOUSE TO SEEK ADVENTURES

WHILE they were thus busied, Don Quixote began to cry aloud, saying, 'Here, here, valorous knights! Here it is needful that you show the force of your valiant arms; for the courtiers begin to bear away the best of the tourney.' The folk repairing to this rumour and noise, was an occasion that any further speech and visitation of the books was omitted; and therefore it is to be suspected, that the *Carolea* and *Lion of Spain,* with the *Acts of the Emperor Charles the Fifth,* written by Don Louis de Avila, were burned, without being ever seen or heard; and perhaps if the curate had seen them, they should not have passed under so rigorous a sentence. When they all arrived to Don Quixote his chamber, he was risen already out of his bed, and continued still his outcries, cutting and slashing on every side, being so broadly awake as if he never had slept. Wherefore, taking him in their arms, they returned him by main force into his bed, and, after he was somewhat quiet and settled, he said, turning himself to the curate, 'In good sooth, Lord Archbishop Turpin, it is a great dishonour to us that are called the twelve Peers, to permit the knights of the court to bear thus away the glory of the tourney without more ado, seeing that we the adventurers have gained the prize thereof the three foremost days.' 'Hold your peace, good gossip,' quoth the curate, 'for fortune may be pleased to change the success, and what is lost to-day may be won again to-morrow. Look you to your health for the present; for you seem at least to be very much tired, if besides you be not sore wounded.' 'Wounded! no,' quoth Don Quixote; 'but doubtless I am somewhat bruised, for that bastard, Don Rowland, hath beaten me to powder with the stock of an oak-tree; and all for envy, because he sees that I only dare oppose myself to his valour. But let me be never again called Raynold of Montealban if he pay not dearly for

277

it, as soon as I rise from this bed, in despite of all his enchantment. But, I pray you, call for my breakfast, for I know it will do me much good, and leave the revenge of this wrong to my charge.' Presently meat was brought; and after he had eaten he fell asleep, and they remained astonished at his wonderful madness. That night the old woman burned all the books that she found in the house and yard; and some there were burnt that deserved, for their worthiness, to be kept up in everlasting treasuries, if their fortunes and the laziness of the searchers had permitted it. And so the proverb was verified in them, 'that the just pays sometimes for the sinners.' One of the remedies which the curate and the barber prescribed for that present, to help their friend's disease, was that they should change his chamber, and dam up his study, to the end that, when he arose, he might not find them; for, perhaps, by removing the cause, they might also take away the effects: and, moreover, they bade them to say that a certain enchanter had carried them away, study and all; which device was presently put in practice. And, within two days after, Don Quixote got up, and the first thing he did was to go and visit his books; and seeing he could not find the chamber in the same place where he had left it, he went up and down to find it. Sometimes he came to the place where the door stood, and felt it with his hands, and then would turn his eyes up and down here and there to seek it, without speaking a word. But at last, after deliberation, he asked of the old woman the way to his books. She, as one well schooled before what she should answer, said, 'What study, or what nothing, is this you look for? There is now no more study nor books in this house; for the very devil himself carried all away with him.' 'It was not the devil,' said his niece, 'but an enchanter, that came here one night upon a cloud, the day after you departed from hence; and, alighting down from a serpent upon which he rode, he entered into the study, and what he did therein I know not; and within a while after he fled out at the roof of the house, and left all the house full of smoke; and when we accorded to see what he had done, we could neither see book nor study: only this much the old woman and I do remember very well, that the naughty old man, at his departure, said, with a loud voice, that he, for hidden enmity that he bore to the lord of those books, had done all the harm to the house that they might perceive when he were departed, and added that he was named the wise Muniaton. 'Frestron, you would have said,' quoth Don Quixote. 'I know not,' quoth the old woman, 'whether he hight Frestron or Friton, but well I wot that his name ended with "ton."' 'That is true,' quoth Don Quixote; 'and he is a very wise enchanter, and my great adversary, and looks on me with a sinister eye; for he knows, by his art and science, that I shall in time fight a single combat with a knight, his very great friend, and overcome him in battle, without being able to be by him assisted, and therefore he labours to do me all the hurt he may; and I have sent him word, that he strives in vain to divert or shun that which is by Heaven already decreed.' 'Who doubts of that?' quoth his niece. 'But I pray you, good uncle, say, what need have you to thrust yourself into these difficulties and brabbles? Were it not better to rest you quietly in your own house, than to wander through the world, searching bread of blasted corn, without once considering how many there go to seek for wool that return again shorn themselves?' 'Oh, niece,' quoth Don Quixote, 'how ill dost thou understand the matter! Before I permit myself to be shorn, I will pill and pluck away the beards of as many as shall dare or imagine to touch but a hair only of me.' To these words the women would make no reply, because they saw his choler increase.

Fifteen days he remained quietly at home, without giving any argument of seconding his former vanities; in which time passed many pleasant encounters between him and his two gossips, the curate and barber, upon that point which he defended, to wit, that the world needed nothing so much as knights-errant, and that the erratical knighthood ought to be again renewed therein. Master parson would contradict him sometimes, and other times yield unto that he urged; for had they not observed that manner of proceeding, it were impossible to bring him to any conformity. In this space Don Quixote dealt with a certain labourer, his neighbour, an honest man (if the title of honesty may be given to the poor), but one of a very shallow wit; in resolution, he said so much to him, and persuaded him so earnestly, and made him so large promises, as the poor fellow determined to go away with him, and serve him as his squire. Don Quixote, among many other things, bade him to

279

dispose himself willingly to depart with him; for now and then such an adventure might present itself, that, in as short space as one would take up a couple of straws, an island might be won, and he be left as governor thereof. With these and such like promises, Sancho Panza (for so he was called) left his wife and children, and agreed to be his squire. Afterward, Don Quixote began to cast plots how to come by some money; which he achieved by selling one thing, pawning another, and turning all upside down. At last he got a pretty sum, and, accommodating himself with a buckler which he had borrowed of a friend, and patching up his broken beaver again as well as he could, he advertised his squire Sancho of the day and hour wherein he meant to depart, that he might likewise furnish himself with that which he thought needful; but above all things he charged him to provide himself of a wallet; which he promised to perform, and said that he meant also to carry a very good ass, which he had of his own, because he was not wont to travel much a-foot. In that of the ass Don Quixote stood a while pensive, calling to mind whether ever he had read that any knight-errant carried his squire assishly mounted; but he could not remember any authority for it; yet, notwithstanding, he resolved that he might bring his beast, with intention to accommodate him more honourably, when occasion were offered, by dismounting the first discourteous knight they met, from his horse, and giving it to his squire; he also furnished himself with shirts, and as many other things as he might, according unto the innkeeper's advice. All which being finished, Sancho Panza, without bidding his wife and children farewell, or Don Quixote his niece and old servant, they both departed one night out of the village, unknown to any person living; and they travelled so far that night, as they were sure in the morning not to be found, although they were pursued. Sancho Panza rode on his beast like a patriarch, with his wallet and bottle, and a marvellous longing to see himself governor of the island which his master had promised unto him.

Don Quixote took by chance the very same course and way that he had done in his first voyage through the field of Montiel, wherein he travelled then with less vexation than the first; for, by reason it was early, and the sunbeams striking not directly down, but athwart, the heat did not trouble them much. And Sancho Panza, seeing the opportunity good, said to his master, 'I pray you, have care, good sir knight, that you forget not that government of the island which you have promised me, for I shall be able to govern it were it never so great.' To which Don Quixote replied: 'You must understand, friend Sancho Panza, that it was a custom very much used by ancient knights-errant, to make their squires governors of the islands and kingdoms that they conquered; and I am resolved that so good a custom shall never be abolished by me, but rather I will pass and exceed them therein; for they sometimes, and as I take it, did, for the greater part, expect until their squires waxed aged; and after they were cloyed with service, and had suffered many bad days and worse nights, then did they bestow upon them some title of an earl, or at least of a marquis, of some valley or province, of more or less account. But if thou livest, and I withal, it may happen that I may conquer such a kingdom within six days, that hath other kingdoms adherent to it, which would fall out as just as it were cast in a mould for thy purpose, whom I would crown presently king of one of them. And do not account this to be any great matter; for things and chances do happen to such knights-adventurers as I am, by so unexpected and wonderful ways and means, as I might give thee very easily a great deal more than I have promised.' 'After that manner,' said Sancho Panza, 'if I were a king, through some miracle of those which you say, then should Joan Gutierez, my wife, become a queen, and my children princes!' 'Who doubts of that?' said Don Quixote. 'That do I,' replied Sancho Panza; 'for I am fully persuaded, that although God would rain kingdoms down upon the earth, none of them would sit well on Mary Gutierez her head; for, sir, you must understand that she's not worth a dodkin for a queen. To be a countess would agree with her better; and yet, I pray God that she be able to discharge that calling.' 'Commend thou the matter to God,' quoth Don Quixote, 'that He may give her that which is most convenient for her. But do not thou abase thy mind so much as to content thyself with less than at the least to be a viceroy.' 'I will not, good sir,' quoth Sancho, 'especially seeing I have so worthy a lord and master as yourself, who knows how to give me all that may turn to my benefit, and that I shall be able to discharge in good sort.'

CHAPTER VIII

Of the Good Success Don Quixote Had, in the Dreadful and Never-imagined Adventure of the Windmills, with Other Accidents Worthy to Be Recorded

AS they discoursed, they discovered some thirty or forty windmills, that are in that field; and as soon as Don Quixote espied them, he said to his squire, 'Fortune doth address our affairs better than we ourselves could desire; for behold there, friend Sancho Panza, how there appears thirty or forty monstrous giants, with whom I mean to fight, and deprive them all of their lives, with whose spoils we will begin to be rich; for this is a good war, and a great service unto God, to take away so bad a seed from the face of the earth.' 'What giants?' quoth Sancho Panza. 'Those that thou seest there,' quoth his lord, 'with the long arms; and some there are of that race whose arms are almost two leagues long.' 'I pray you understand,' quoth Sancho Panza, 'that those which appear there are no giants, but windmills; and that which seems in them to be arms, are their sails, that, swung about by the wind, do also make the mill go.' 'It seems well,' quoth Don Quixote, 'that thou art not yet acquainted with matter of adventures. They are giants; and, if thou beest afraid, go aside and pray, whilst I enter into cruel and unequal battle with them.' And, saying so, he spurred his horse Rozinante, without taking heed to his squire Sancho's cries, advertising him how they were doubtless windmills that he did assault, and no giants; but he went so fully persuaded that they were giants as he neither heard his squire's outcries, nor did discern what they were, although he drew very near to them, but rather said, as loud as he could, 'Fly not, ye cowards and vile creatures! for it is only one knight that assaults you.'

With this the wind increased, and the mill sails began to turn about; which Don Quixote espying, said, 'Although thou movest more arms than the giant Briareus thou shalt stoop to me.' And, after saying this, and commending himself most devoutly to his Lady Dulcinea, desiring her to succor him in that trance, covering himself well with his buckler, and setting his lance on his rest, he spurred on Rozinante, and encountered with the first mill that was before him, and, striking his lance into the sail, the wind swung it about with such fury, that it broke his lance into shivers, carrying him and his horse after it, and finally tumbled him a good way off from it on the field in evil plight. Sancho Panza repaired presently to succor him as fast as his ass could drive; and when he arrived, he found him not able to stir, he had gotten such a crush with Rozinante. 'Good God!' quoth Sancho, 'did I not foretell unto you that you should look well what you did, for they were none other than windmills? nor could any think otherwise, unless he had also windmills in his brains.' 'Peace, Sancho,' quoth Don Quixote; 'for matters of war are more subject than any other thing to continual change; how much more, seeing I do verily persuade myself, that the wise Frestron, who robbed my study and books, hath transformed these giants into mills, to deprive me of the glory of the victory, such is the enmity he bears towards me. But yet, in fine, all his bad arts shall but little prevail against the goodness of my sword.' 'God grant it as he may!' said Sancho Panza, and then helped him to arise; and presently he mounted on Rozinante, who was half shoulder-pitched by rough encounter; and, discoursing upon that adventure, they followed on the way which guided towards the passage or gate of Lapice; for there, as Don Quixote avouched, it was not possible but to find many adventures, because it was a thoroughfare much frequented; and yet he affirmed that he went very much grieved, because he wanted a lance; and, telling it to his squire, he said, 'I remember how I have read that a certain Spanish knight, called Diego Peres of Vargas, having broken his sword in a battle, tore off a great branch or stock from an oak-tree, and did such marvels with it that day, and battered so many Moors, as he remained with the surname of Machuca, which signifies a stump, and as well he as all his progeny were ever after that day called Vargas and Machuca. I tell thee this, because I mean to tear another branch, such, or as good as that at least, from the first oak we shall encounter, and I mean to achieve such adventures therewithal, as thou wilt account thyself fortunate for having merited to behold them, and be a witness of things almost incredible.' 'In God's name!' quoth Sancho, 'I do believe every word you said. But, I pray you, sit right in your saddle; for you ride sideling, which proceeds, as I suppose, of the bruising you got by your fall.' 'Thou sayst true,' quoth Don Quixote; 'and if I do not complain of the grief, the reason is, because knights-errant use not to complain of any wound, although their guts did issue out thereof.' 'If it be so,' quoth Sancho, 'I know not what to say; but God knows that I would be glad to hear you to complain when anything grieves you. Of myself I dare affirm, that I must complain of the least grief that I have, if it be not likewise meant that the squires of knights-errant must not complain of any harm.' Don Quixote could not refrain laughter, hearing the simplicity of his squire; and after showed unto him that he might lawfully complain, both when he pleased, and as much as he listed with desire, or without it; for he had never yet read anything to the contrary in the order of knighthood. Then Sancho said unto him that it was dinner-time. To whom he answered, that he needed no repast; but if he had will to e.., he might begin when he pleased. Sancho, having obtained his license, did accommodate himself on his ass's back the best he might. Taking out of his wallet some belly-munition, he rode after his master, travelling and eating at once, and that with great leisure; and ever and anon he lifted up his bottle with such pleasure as the best-fed victualler of Malaga might envy his state; and whilst he rode, multiplying of quaffs in that manner, he never remembered any of the promises his master had made him, nor did he hold the fetch of adventures to be a labour, but rather a great recreation and ease, were they never so dangerous. In conclusion, they passed over that night under certain trees, from one of which Don Quixote tore a withered branch, which might serve him in some sort for a lance; and therefore he set thereon the iron of his own, which he had reserved when it was broken.

All that night Don Quixote slept not one wink, but thought upon his Lady Dulcinea, that he might conform himself to what he had read in his books of adventures, when knights passed over many nights without sleep in forests and fields, only entertained by the memory of their mistresses. But Sancho spent not his time so vainly;

for, having his stomach well stuffed, and that not with succory water, he carried smoothly away the whole night in one sleep; and if his master had not called him up, neither the sunbeams which struck on his visage, nor the melody of the birds, which were many, and did cheerfully welcome the approach of the new day, could have been able to awake him. At his arising he gave one assay to the bottle, which he found to be somewhat more weak than it was the night before, whereat his heart was somewhat grieved; for he mistrusted that they took not a course to remedy that defect so soon as he wished. Nor could Don Quixote break his fast, who, as we have said, meant only to sustain himself with pleasant remembrances.

Then did they return to their commenced way towards the port of Lapice, which they discovered about three of the clock in the afternoon. 'Here,' said Don Quixote, as soon as he kenned it, 'may we, friend Sancho, thrust our hands up to the very elbows in that which is called adventures. But observe well this caveat which I shall give thee, that, although thou seest me in the greatest dangers of the world, thou must not set hand to thy sword in my defence, if thou dost not see that those which assault me be base and vile vulgar people; for in such a case thou mayst assist me. Marry, if they be knights, thou mayst not do so in anywise, nor is it permitted, by the laws of arms, that thou mayst help me, until thou beest likewise dubbed knight thyself.' 'I do assure you, sir,' quoth Sancho, 'that herein you shall be most punctually obeyed; and therefore chiefly in respect that I am of mine own nature a quiet and peaceable man, and a mortal enemy of thrusting myself into stirs or quarrels; yet it is true that, touching the defence of mine own person, I will not be altogether so observant of those laws, seeing that both divine and human allow every man to defend himself from any one that would wrong him.' 'I say no less,' answered Don Quixote; 'but in this of aiding me against any knight, thou must set bounds to thy natural impulses.' 'I say I will do so,' quoth Sancho; 'and I will observe this commandment as punctually as that of keeping holy the Sabbath day.'

Whilst thus they reasoned, there appeared in the way two monks of St. Benet's order, mounted on two dromedaries; for the mules whereon they rode were but little less. They wore masks with spectacles in them, to keep away the dust from their faces; and each of them besides bore their umbrills. After them came a coach, and four or five a-horseback accompanying it, and two lackeys that ran hard by it. There came therein, as it was after known, a certain Biscaine lady, which travelled towards Seville, where her husband sojourned at the present, and was going to the Indies with an honorable charge. The monks rode not with her, although they travelled the same way. Scarce had Don Quixote perceived them, when he said to his squire, 'Either I am deceived, or else this will prove the most famous adventure that ever hath been seen; for these two great black bulks, which appear there, are, questionless, enchanters, that steal, or carry away perforce, some princess in that coach; and therefore I must, with all my power, undo that wrong.' 'This will be worse than the adventure of the windmills,' quoth Sancho. 'Do not you see, sir, that those are friars of St. Benet's order? and the coach can be none other than of some travellers. Therefore, listen to mine advice, and see well what you do, lest the devil deceive you.' 'I have said already to thee, Sancho, that thou art very ignorant in matter of adventures. What I say is true, as now thou shalt see.' And, saying so, he spurred on his horse, and placed himself just in the midst of the way by which the friars came; and when they approached so near as he supposed they might hear him, he said, with a loud voice, 'Devilish and wicked people! leave presently those high princesses which you violently carry away with you in that coach; or, if you will not, prepare yourselves to receive sudden death, as a just punishment of your bad works.' The friars held their horses, and were amazed both at the shape and words of Don Quixote; to whom they answered: 'Sir knight, we are neither devilish nor wicked, but religious men of St. Benet's order, that travel about our affairs; and we know not whether or no there come any princesses forced in this coach.' 'With me fair words take no effect,' quoth Don Quixote; 'for I know you very well, treacherous knaves!' And then, without expecting their reply, he set spurs to Rozinante, and, laying his lance on the thigh, charged the first friar with such fury and rage, that if he had not suffered himself willingly to fall off his mule, he would not only have overthrown him against his will, but likewise have slain, or at least wounded him very ill with the blow. The second religious man, seeing how ill his companion was used, made no words; but, setting spurs to that castle his mule, did fly away through the field, as swift as the wind itself. Sancho Panza, seeing the monk overthrown, dismounted very speedily off his ass, and ran over to him, and would have ransacked his habits. In this arrived the monks' two lackeys, and demanded of him why he thus despoiled the friar. Sancho replied that it was his due, by the law of arms, as lawful spoils gained in battle by his lord, Don Quixote. The lackeys, which understood not the jest, nor knew not what words of battle or spoils meant, seeing that Don Quixote was now out of the way, speaking with those that came in the coach, set both at once upon Sancho, and left him not a hair in his beard but they plucked, and did so trample him under their feet, as they left him stretched on the ground without either breath or feeling. The monk, cutting off all delays, mounted again on horseback, all affrighted, having scarce any drop of blood left in his face through fear; and, being once up, he spurred after his fellow, who expected him a good way off, staying to see the success of that assault; and, being unwilling to attend the end of that strange adventure, they did prosecute their journey, blessing and crossing themselves as if the devil did pursue them.

Don Quixote, as is rehearsed, was in this season speaking to the lady of the coach, to whom he said: 'Your beauty, dear lady, may dispose from henceforth of your person as best ye liketh; for the pride of your robbers lies now prostrated on the ground, by this my invincible arm. And because you may not be troubled to know your deliverer his name, know that I am called Don Quixote de la Mancha, a knight-errant and adventurer, and captive to the peerless and beautiful Lady Dulcinea of Toboso. And, in reward of the benefit which you have received at my hands, I demand nothing else but that you return to Toboso, and there present yourselves, in my name, before my lady, and recount unto her what I have done to obtain your liberty.' To all these words which Don Quixote said, a certain Biscaine squire, that accompanied the coach, gave ear; who, seeing that Don Quixote suffered not the coach to pass onward, but said that it must presently turn back to Toboso, he drew near to him, and, laying hold on his lance, he said, in his bad Spanish and worse

Basquish: 'Get thee away, knight, in an ill hour. By the God that created me, if thou leave not the coach, I will kill thee, as sure as I am a Biscaine.' Don Quixote, understanding him, did answer, with great staidness: 'If thou were a knight, as thou art not, I would by this have punished thy folly and presumption, caitiff creature!' The Biscaine replied, with great fury: 'Not I a gentleman! I swear God thou liest, as well as I am a Christian. If thou cast away thy lance, and draw thy sword, thou shalt see the water as soon as thou shalt carry away the cat: a Biscaine by land, and a gentleman by sea, a gentleman in spite of the devil; and thou liest, if other things thou sayst!' ' "Straight thou shalt see that," said Agrages,' replied Don Quixote; and, throwing his lance to the ground, he out with his sword, and took his buckler, and set on the Biscaine, with resolution to kill him. The Biscaine, seeing him approach in that manner, although he desired to alight off his mule, which was not to be trusted, being one of those naughty ones which are wont to be hired, yet had he no leisure to do any other thing than to draw out his sword; but it befel him happily to be near to the coach, out of which he snatched a cushion, that served him for a shield; and presently the one made upon the other like mortal enemies. Those that were present laboured all that they might, but in vain, to compound the matter between them; for the Biscaine swore, in his bad language, that if they hindered him from ending the battle, he would put his lady, and all the rest that dared to disturb him, to the sword.

The lady, astonished and fearful of that which she beheld, commanded the coachman to go a little out of the way, and sat aloof, beholding the rigorous conflict; in the progress whereof the Biscaine gave Don Quixote over the target a mighty blow on one of the shoulders, where, if it had not found resistance in his armour, it would doubtlessly have cleft him down to the girdle. Don Quixote, feeling the weight of that unmeasurable blow, cried, with a loud voice, saying, 'O Dulcinea! lady of my soul! the flower of all beauty! succor this thy knight, who to set forth thy worth, finds himself in this dangerous trance!' The saying of these words, the gripping fast of his sword, the covering of himself well with his buckler, and the assailing of the Biscaine, was done all in one instant, resolving to venture all the success of the battle on that one only blow. The

288

Biscaine, who perceived him come in that manner, perceived, by his doughtiness, his intention, and resolved to do the like; and therefore expected him very well, covered with his cushion, not being able to manage his mule as he wished from one part to another, who was not able to go a step, it was so wearied, as a beast never before used to the like toys. Don Quixote, as we have said, came against the wary Biscaine with his sword lifted aloft, with full resolution to part him in two; and all the beholders stood, with great fear suspended, to see the success of those monstrous blows wherewithal they threatened one another. And the lady of the coach, with her gentlewomen, made a thousand vows and offerings to all the devout places of Spain, to the end that God might deliver the squire and themselves out of that great danger wherein they were.

But it is to be deplored how, in this very point and term, the author of this history leaves his battle depending, excusing himself that he could find no more written of the acts of Don Quixote than those which he hath already recounted. True it is, that the second writer of this work would not believe that so curious a history was drowned in the jaws of oblivion, or that the wits of the Mancha were so little curious as not to reserve among their treasures or records some papers treating of this famous knight; and therefore, encouraged by this presumption, he did not despair to find the end of this pleasant history; which, Heaven being propitious to him, he got at last, after the manner that shall be recounted in the Second Part.

THE SECOND BOOK

CHAPTER I

WHEREIN IS RELATED THE EVENTS OF THE FEARFUL BATTLE WHICH THE GALLANT BISCAINE FOUGHT WITH DON QUIXOTE

WE left the valorous Biscaine and the famous Don Quixote, in the First Part, with their swords lifted up and naked, in terms to discharge one upon another two furious cleavers, and such, as if they had lighted rightly, would cut and divide them both from the top to the toe, and open them like a pomegranate; and in that so doubtful a taking the delightful history stopped and remained dismembered, the author thereof leaving us no notice where we might find the rest of the narration. This grieved me not a little, but wholly turned the pleasure I took in reading the beginning thereof into disgust, thinking how small commodity was offered to find out so much as in my opinion wanted of this so delectable a tale. It seemed unto me almost impossible, and contrary to all good order, that so good a knight should want some wise man that would undertake his wonderful prowess and feats of chivalry: a thing that none of those knights-errant ever wanted, of whom people speak; for each of them had one or two wise men, of purpose, that did not only write their acts, but also depainted their very least thoughts and toys, were they never so hidden. And surely so good a knight could not be so unfortunate as to want that wherewith Platyr and others his like abounded; and therefore could not induce myself to believe that so gallant a history might remain maimed and lame, and did rather cast the fault upon the malice of the time, who is a consumer and devourer of all things, which had either hidden or consumed it. Methought, on the other side, seeing that among his books were found some modern works, such as the *Undeceiving of Jealousy,* and the *Nymphs and Shepherds of Henares,* that also his own history must have been new; and if that it were not written, yet was the memory of him fresh among the dwellers of his own village and the other villages adjoining. This imagination held me suspended, and desirous to learn really and truly all the life and miracles of our famous Spaniard, Don Quixote of the Mancha, the light and mirror of all Manchical chivalry, being the first who, in this our age and time, so full of calamities, did undergo the travels and exercise of arms-errant; and undid wrongs, succored widows, protected damsels that rode up and down with their whips and palfreys, and with all their virginity on their backs, from hill to hill and dale to dale; for, if it happened not that some lewd miscreant, or some clown with a hatchet and long hair, or some monstrous giant, did force them, damsels there were in times past that at the end of fourscore years old, all which time they never slept one day under a roof, went as entire and pure maidens to their graves as the very mother that bore them. Therefore I say, that as well for this as for many other good respects, our gallant Don Quixote is worthy of continual and memorable praises; nor can the like be justly denied to myself, for the labour and diligence which I used to find out the end of this grateful history, although I know very well that, if Heaven, chance, and fortune had not assisted me, the world had been deprived of the delight and pastime that they may take for almost two hours together, who shall with attention read it. The manner, therefore, of finding it was this:

Being one day walking in the exchange of Toledo, a certain boy by chance would have sold divers old quires and scrolls of books to a squire that walked up and down in that place, and I, being addicted to read such scrolls, though I found them torn in the streets, borne away by this my natural inclination, took one of the quires in my hand, and perceived it to be written in Arabical characters, and seeing that, although I knew the letters, yet could I not read the substance, I looked about to view whether I could perceive any Moor turned Spaniard thereabouts, that could read them; nor was it very difficult to find there such an interpreter; for, if I had searched one of another better and more ancient language, that place would easily afford him. In fine, my good fortune presented one to me; to whom telling my desire, and setting the book in his hand, he opened it, and, having read a little therein, began to laugh.

I demanded of him why he laughed; and he answered, at that marginal note which the book had. I bade him to expound it to me, and with that took him a little aside; and he, continuing still his laughter, said: 'There is written there, on this margin, these words: "This Dulcinea of Toboso, so many times spoken of in this history, had the best hand for powdering of porks of any woman in all the Mancha."' When I heard it make mention of Dulcinea of Toboso, I rested amazed and suspended, and imagined forthwith that those quires contained the history of Don Quixote. With this conceit I hastened him to read the beginning, which he did, and, translating the Arabical into Spanish in a trice, he said that it begun thus: *'The History of Don Quixote of the Mancha, written by Cid Hamete Benengeli, an Arabical historiographer.'* Much discretion was requisite to dissemble the content of mind I conceived when I heard the title of the book, and preventing the squire, I bought all the boy's scrolls and papers for a real; and were he of discretion, or knew my desire, he might have promised himself easily, and also have borne away with him, more than six reals for his merchandise. I departed after with the Moor to the cloister of the great church, and I requested him to turn me all the Arabical sheets that treated of Don Quixote into Spanish, without adding or taking away anything from them, and I would pay him what he listed for his pains. He demanded fifty pounds of raisins and three bushels of wheat, and promised to translate them speedily, well, and faithfully. But I, to hasten the matter more, lest I should lose such an unexpected and welcome treasure, brought him to my house, where he translated all the work in less than a month and a half, even in the manner that it is here recounted.

There was painted, in the first quire, very naturally, the battle betwixt Don Quixote and the Biscaine; even in the same manner that the history relateth it, with their swords lifted aloft, the one covered with his buckler, the other with the cushion; and the Biscaine's mule was delivered so naturally as a man might perceive it was hired, although he stood farther off than the shot of a cross-bow. The Biscaine had a title written under his feet that said, 'Don Sancho de Azpetia,' for so belike he was called; and at Rozinante his feet there was another, that said 'Don Quixote.' Rozinante was marvellous well portraited; so long and lank, so thin and lean, so like one labouring with an incurable consumption, as he did show very clearly with what consideration and propriety he had given unto him the name Rozinante. By him stood Sancho Panza, holding his ass by the halter; at whose feet was another scroll, saying, 'Sancho Zancas,' and I think the reason thereof was, that, as his picture showed, he had a great belly, a short stature, and thick legs; and therefore, I judge, he was called Panza, or Zanca; for both these names were written of him indifferently in the history. There were other little things in it worthy noting; but all of them are of no great importance, nor anything necessary for the true relation of the history; for none is ill, if it be true. And if any objection be made against the truth of this, it can be none other than that the author was a Moor; and it is a known propriety of that nation to be lying: yet, in respect that they hate us so mortally, it is to be conjectured that in this history there is rather want and concealment of our knight's worthy acts than any superfluity; which I imagine the rather, because I find in the progress thereof, many times, that when he might and ought to have advanced his pen in our knight's praises, he doth, as it were of purpose, pass them over in silence; which was very ill done, seeing that historiographers ought and should be very precise, true, and unpassionate; and that neither profit nor fear, rancour nor affection, should make them to tread awry from the truth, whose mother is history, the emulatress of time, the treasury of actions, the witness of things past, the advertiser of things to come. In this history I know a man may find all that he can desire in the most pleasing manner; and if they want anything to be desired, I am of opinion that it is through the fault of that ungracious knave that translated it, rather than through any defect in the subject. Finally, the Second Part thereof (according to the translation) began in this manner:

The trenchant swords of the two valorous and enraged combatants being lifted aloft, it seemed that they threatened heaven, the earth, and the depths, such was their hardiness and courage. And the first that discharged his blow was the Biscaine, which fell with such force and fury, as if the sword had not turned a little in the way, that only blow had been sufficient to set an end to the rigorous contention, and all other the adventures of our knight. But his good fortune, which reserved him for greater affairs, did wrest his adversary's sword awry in such sort, as though he struck him on the left shoulder, yet did it no more harm than disarm all that side, carrying away with it a great part of his beaver, with the half of his ear; all which fell to the ground with a dreadful ruin, leaving him in very ill case for a good time. Good God! who is he that can well describe, at this present, the fury that entered in the heart of our Manchegan, seeing himself used in that manner. Let us say no more, but that it was such that, stretching himself again in the stirrups, and gripping his sword fast in both his hands, he discharged such a terrible blow on the Biscaine, hitting him right upon the cushion, and by it on the head, that the strength and thickness thereof so little availed him, that, as if a whole mountain had fallen upon him, the blood gushed out of his mouth, nose, and ears, all at once, and he tottered so on his mule, that every step he took he was ready to fall off, as he would indeed if he had not taken him by the neck; yet, nevertheless, he lost the stirrups, and, losing his grip of the mule, it being likewise frighted by that terrible blow, ran away as fast as it could about the fields, and within two or three winches overthrew him to the ground. All which Don Quixote stood beholding with great quietness; and as soon as he saw him fall, he leaped off his horse, and ran over to him very speedily; and, setting the point of his sword on his eyes, he bade him yield himself, or else he would cut off his head. The Biscaine was so amazed as he could not speak a word; and it had succeeded very ill with him, considering Don Quixote's fury, if the ladies of the coach, which until then had beheld the conflict with great anguish, had not come where he was, and earnestly besought him to do them the favour to pardon their squire's life. Don Quixote answered, with a great loftiness and gravity: 'Truly, fair ladies, I am well apaid to grant you your request, but it must be with this agreement and condition, that this knight shall promise me to go to Toboso, and present himself, in my name, to the peerless Lady Dulcinea, to the end she may dispose of him as she pleaseth.' The timorous and comfortless lady, without considering what Don Quixote demanded, or asking what Dulcinea was, promised that her squire should accomplish all that he pleased to command. 'Why, then,' quoth Don Quixote, 'trusting to your promise, I'll do him no more harm, although he hath well deserved it at my hands."

CHAPTER II

Of That Which after Befel Don Quixote When He Had Left the Ladies

BY this Sancho Panza had gotten up, though somewhat abused by the friars' lackeys, and stood attentively beholding his lord's combat, and prayed to God with all his heart, that it would please Him to give him the victory; and that he might therein win some island, whereof he might make him governor, as he had promised. And, seeing the controversy ended at last, and that his lord remounted upon Rozinante, he came to hold him the stirrup, and cast himself on his knees before him ere he got up, and, taking him by the hand, he kissed it, saying, 'I desire that it will please you, good my lord Don Quixote, to bestow upon me the government of that island which in this terrible battle you have won; for though it were never so great, yet do I find myself able enough to govern it, as well as any other whatsoever that ever governed island in this world.' To this demand Don Quixote answered: 'Thou must note, friend Sancho, that this adventure, and others of this kind, are not adventures of islands, but of thwartings and highways, wherein nothing else is gained but a broken pate, or the loss of an ear. Have patience a while; for adventures will be offered whereby thou shalt not only be made a governor, but also a greater man.' Sancho rendered him many thanks, and, kissing his hand again, and the skirt of his habergeon, he did help him to get up on Rozinante, and he leapt on his ass, and followed his lord, who, with a swift pace, without taking leave or speaking to those of the coach, entered into a wood that was hard at hand. Sancho followed him as fast as his beast could trot; but Rozinante went off so swiftly, as he, perceiving he was like to be left behind, was forced to call aloud to his master that he would stay for him, which Don Quixote did, by checking Rozinante with the bridle, until his wearied squire did arrive; who,

295

as soon as he came, said unto him, 'Methinks, sir, that it will not be amiss to retire ourselves to some church; for, according as that man is ill dight with whom you fought, I certainly persuade myself that they will give notice of the fact to the holy brotherhood, and they will seek to apprehend us, which if they do, in good faith, before we can get out of their claws, I fear me we shall sweat for it.' 'Peace!' quoth Don Quixote; 'where hast thou ever read or seen that knight-errant that hath been brought before the judge, though he committed never so many homicides and slaughters?' 'I know nothing of omicills,' quoth Sancho, 'nor have I cared in my life for any; but well I wot that it concerns the Holy Brotherhood to deal with such as fight in the fields, and in that other I will not intermeddle.' 'Then be not afraid, friend,' quoth Don Quixote; 'for I will deliver thee out of the hands of the Chaldeans, how much more out of those of the brotherhood. But tell me, in very good earnest, whether thou didst ever see a more valorous knight than I am throughout the face of the earth? Didst thou ever read in histories of any other that hath, or ever had, more courage in assailing, more breath in persevering, more dexterity in offending, or more art in overthrowing, than I?' 'The truth is,' quoth Sancho, 'that I have never read any history; for I can neither read nor write: but that which I dare wager is, that I never in my life served a bolder master than you are; and I pray God that we pay not for this boldness there where I have said. That which I request you is, that you will cure yourself; for you lose much blood by that ear, and here I have lint and a little *unguentum album* in my wallet.' 'All this might be excused,' quoth Don Quixote, 'if I had remembered to make a vialful of the Balsam of Fierebras; for, with one drop of it, we might spare both time, and want well all those other medicines.' 'What vial, and what balsam, is that?' said Sancho Panza. 'It is,' answered Don Quixote, 'a balsam whereof I have the recipe in memory, which one possessing he needs not fear death, nor ought he to think that he may be killed by any wound; and therefore, after I have made it, and given it unto thee, thou hast nothing else to do, but when thou shalt see that in any battle I be cloven in twain (as many times it happens), thou shalt take fair and softly that part of my body that is fallen to the ground, and put it up again, with great subtlety, on the part that rests in the saddle, before the blood congeal, having

296

evermore great care that thou place it just and equally; then presently after thou shalt give me two draughts of that balsam of which I have spoken, and thou shalt see me straight become sounder than an apple.' 'If that be true,' quoth Sancho, 'I do presently here renounce the government of the island you promised, and will demand nothing else in recompense of my services of you, but only the recipe of this precious liquor; for I am certain that an ounce thereof will be worth two reals in any place, and when I have it I should need nothing else to gain my living easily and honestly. But let me know, is it costly in making?' 'With less than three reals,' quoth Don Quixote, 'a man may make three gallons of it. But I mean to teach thee greater secrets than this, and do thee greater favours also. And now, let me cure myself; for mine ear grieves me more than I would wish.' Sancho then took out of his wallet his lint and ointment to cure his master. But when Don Quixote saw that the visor of his helmet was broken, he was ready to run mad; and, setting his hand to his sword, and lifting up his eyes to heaven, he said: 'I vow to the Creator of all things, and to the four gospels where they are largest written, to lead such another life as the great Marquis of Mantua did, when he swore to revenge the death of his nephew Valdovinos: which was, not to eat on table-cloth, nor sport with his wife, and other things, which, although I do not now remember, I give them here for expressed, until I take complete revenge on him that hath done me this outrage.'

Sancho, hearing this, said: 'You must note, Sir Don Quixote, that if the knight had accomplished that which you ordained, to go and present himself before my Lady Dulcinea of Toboso, then hath he fully satisfied his debt, and deserves no new punishment, except he commit a new fault.' 'Thou hast spoken well, and hit the mark right,' said Don Quixote; 'and therefore I disannul the oath, in that of taking any new revenge on him; but I make it, and confirm it again, that I will lead the life I have said until I take another helmet like, or as good as this, perforce from some knight. And do not think, Sancho, that I make this resolution lightly, or, as they say, with the smoke of straws, for I have an author whom I may very well imitate herein; for the very like, in every respect, passed about Mambrino's helmet, which cost Sacriphante so dearly.' 'I would have you resign those kind of oaths to the devil,' quoth Sancho; 'for they will hurt your health, and prejudice your conscience. If not, tell me now, I beseech you, if we shall not these many days encounter with any that wears a helmet, what shall we do? Will you accomplish the oath in despite of all the inconveniences and discommodities that ensue thereof? to wit, to sleep in your clothes, nor to sleep in any dwelling, and a thousand other penitences, which the oath of the mad old man, the Marquis of Mantua, contained, which you mean to ratify now? Do not you consider that armed men travel not in any of these ways, but carriers and waggoners, who not only carry no helmets, but also, for the most part, never heard speak of them in their lives?' 'Thou dost deceive thyself saying so,' replied Don Quixote; 'for we shall not haunt these ways two hours before we shall see more armed knights than were at the siege of Albraca, to conquer Angelica the fair.'

'Well, then, let it be so,' quoth Sancho; 'and I pray God it befall us well, whom I devoutly beseech that the time may come of gaining that island which costs me so dear, and after let me die presently, and I care not.' 'I have already said to thee, Sancho,' quoth his lord, 'that thou shouldst not trouble thyself in any wise about this affair; for if an island were wanting, we have then the kingdom of Denmark, or that of Sobradisa, which will come as fit for thy purpose as a ring to thy finger; and principally thou art to rejoice because they are on the continent. But, omitting this till his own time, see whether thou hast anything in thy wallet, and let us eat it, that afterward we may go search out some castle wherein we may lodge this night, and make the balsam which I have told thee; for I vow to God that this ear grieves me marvellously.' 'I have here an onion,' replied the squire, 'a piece of cheese, and a few crusts of bread; but such gross meats are not befitting so noble a knight as you are.' 'How ill dost thou understand it!' answered Don Quixote. 'I let thee to understand, Sancho, that it is an honour for knights-errant not to eat once in a month's space; and if by chance they should eat, to eat only of that which is next at hand; and this thou mightest certainly conceive, hadst thou read so many books as I have done; for though I passed over many, yet did I never find recorded in any that knights-errant did ever eat, but by mere chance and adventure, or in some costly banquets that were made for them, and all the other days they passed over with herbs and roots: and though it is to be understood that they could not live without meat, and supplying the other needs of nature, because they were in effect men as we are, it is likewise to be understood, that spending the greater part of their lives in forests and deserts, and that, too, without a cook, that their most ordinary meats were but coarse and rustical, such as thou dost now offer unto me. So that, friend Sancho, let not that trouble thee which is my pleasure, nor go not thou about to make a new world, or to hoist knight-errantry off her hinges.' 'Pardon me, good sir,' quoth Sancho; 'for, by reason I can neither read nor write, as I have said once before, I have not fallen rightly in the rules and laws of knighthood; and from henceforth my wallet shall be well furnished with all kinds of dry fruits for you, because you are a knight; and for myself, seeing I am none, I will provide fowls and other things, that are of more substance.' 'I say not, Sancho,' quoth Don Quixote, 'that it is a forcible law to knights-errant not to eat any other things than such fruits, but that their most ordinary sustenance could be none other than those, and some herbs they found up and down the fields, which they knew very well, and so do I also.' 'It is a virtue,' quoth Sancho, 'to know those herbs; for, as I imagine, that knowledge will some day stand us in stead.' And, saying so, he took out the provision he had, which they both ate together with good conformity. But, being desirous to search out a place where they might lodge that night, they did much shorten their poor dinner, and, mounting anon a-horseback, they made as much haste as they could to find out some dwellings before the night did fall; but the sun and their hopes did fail them at once, they being near the cabins of certain goatherds; and therefore they concluded to take up their lodging there for that night: for, though Sancho's grief was great to lie out of a village, yet Don Quixote's joy exceeded it far, considering he must sleep under open heaven; because he made account, as oft as this befel him, that he did a worthy act, which did facilitate and ratify the practice of his chivalry.

CHAPTER III

Of That Which Passed Between Don Quixote and Certain Goatherds

HE was entertained very cheerfully by the goatherds; and Sancho, having set up Rozinante and his ass as well as he could, he presently repaired to the smell of certain pieces of goat-flesh, that stood boiling in a kettle over the fire; and although he thought, in that very moment, to try whether they were in season to be translated out of the kettle into the stomach, he did omit it, because he saw the herds take them off the fire, and, spreading certain sheepskins, which they had for that purpose, on the ground, lay in a trice their rustical table, and invited the master and man, with very cheerful mind, to come and take part of that which they had. There sat down round about the skins six of them, which were all that dwelt in that fold; having first (using some coarse compliments) placed Don Quixote upon a trough, turning the bottom up. Don Quixote sat down, and Sancho stood to serve the cup, which was made of horn. His master, seeing him afoot, said, 'Sancho, to the end thou mayst perceive the good included in wandering knighthood, and also in what possibility they are which exercised themselves in any ministry thereof, to arrive briefly to honour and reputation in the world, my will is, that thou dost sit here by my side, and in company with this good people, and that thou beest one and the very selfsame thing with me, who am thy master and natural lord; that thou eat in my dish and drink in the same cup wherein I drink; for the same may be said of chivalry that is of love, to wit, that it makes all things equal.' 'I yield you great thanks,' quoth Sancho; 'yet dare I avouch unto you, that so I had therewithal to eat well, I could eat it as well, or better, standing and alone, than if I sat by an emperor. And besides, if I must say the truth, methinks that which I eat in a corner, without ceremonies, curiosity, or respect of any, though it were but bread and an onion, smacks a great deal better than turkey-cocks at other tables, where I must chew my meat leisurely, drink but little, wipe my hands often, must not neese nor cough though I have a desire, or be like to choke, nor do other things that solitude and liberty bring with them. So that, good sir, I would have you convert these honours that you would bestow upon me, in respect that I am an adherent to chivalry (as I am, being your squire), into things more essential and profitable for me than these; and though I remain as thankful for them as if they were received, yet do I here renounce, from this time until the world's end.' 'For all that, thou shalt sit; for the humble shall be exalted.' And so, taking him by the arm, he forced him to sit down near himself.

The goatherds did not understand that gibberish of squires and knights-errant, and therefore did nothing else but eat and hold their peace, and look on their guests, that tossed in with their fists whole slices, with good grace and stomachs. The course of flesh being ended, they served in on the rugs a great quantity of shelled acorns, and half a cheese, harder than if it were made of rough-casting. The horn stood not the while idle; for it went round about so often, now full, now empty, much like a conduit of Noria; and in a trice it emptied one of the two wine-bags that lay there in the public view. After that Don Quixote had satisfied his appetite well, he took up a handful of acorns, and, beholding them earnestly, he began to discourse in this manner: 'Happy time, and fortunate ages were those, whereon our ancestors bestowed the title of golden! not because gold (so much prized in this our iron age) was gotten in that happy time without any labours, but because those which lived in that time knew not these two words, 'thine' and 'mine'; in that holy age all things were in common. No man needed, for his ordinary sustenance, to do ought else than lift up his hand, and take it from the strong oak, which did liberally invite them to gather his sweet and savoury fruit. The clear fountains and running rivers did offer them these savoury and transparent waters in magnificent abundance. In the clefts of rocks and hollow trees did the careful and discreet bees erect their commonwealth, offering to every hand, without interest, the fertile crop of their sweetest travails. The lofty cork-trees did dismiss of themselves, without any other art than

301

that of their native liberality, their broad and light rinds; wherewithal houses were at first covered, being sustained by rustical stakes,
to none other end but for to keep back the inclemencies of the air.
All then was peace, all amity, and all concord. As yet the plough-
share presumed not, with rude encounter, to open and search the
compassionate bowels of our first mother; for she, without compulsion, offered up, through all the parts of her fertile and spacious
bosom, all that which might satisfy, sustain, and delight those children which it then had. Yea, it was then that the simple and beautiful young shepherdesses went from valley to valley and hill to
hill, with their hair sometimes plaited, sometimes dishevelled, without other apparel than that which was requisite to cover comely
that which modesty wills, and ever would have, concealed. Then
were of no request the attires and ornaments which are now used
by those that esteem the purple of Tyre and the so-many-ways-mar-
tyrised silk so much, but only certain green leaves of burdocks and
ivy intertexed and woven together; wherewithal, perhaps, they went
as gorgeously and comely decked as now our court dames, with all
their rare and outlandish inventions that idleness and curiosity hath
found out. Then were the amorous conceits of the mind simply and
sincerely delivered, and embellished in the very form and manner
that she had conceived them, without any artificial contexture of
words to endear them. Fraud, deceit, or malice had not then meddled themselves with plainness and truth. Justice was then in her
proper terms, favour daring not to trouble or confound her, or the
respect of profit, which do now persecute, blemish, and disturb her
so much. The law of corruption, or taking bribes, had not yet possessed the understanding of the judge; for then was neither judge,
nor person to be judged. Maidens and honesty wandered then, I
say, where they listed, alone, signiorising, secure that no stranger
liberty, or lascivious intent could prejudice it, or their own native
desire or will any way endamage it. But now, in these our detest-
able times, no damsel is safe, although she be hid and shut up in
another new labyrinth, like that of Crete; for even there itself the
amorous plague would enter, either by some cranny, or by the air,
or by the continual urgings of cursed care, to infect her; for whose

protection and security was first instituted, by success of times, the order of knighthood, to defend damsels, protect widows, and assist orphans and distressed wights. Of this order am I, friends goatherds, whom I do heartily thank for the good entertainment which you do give unto me and my squire; for although that every one living is obliged, by the law of nature, to favour knights-errant, yet notwithstanding, knowing that you knew not this obligation, and yet did receive and make much of me, it stands with all reason that I do render you thanks with all my heart!'

Our knight made this long oration (which might have been well excused), because the acorns that were given unto him called to his mind the golden world, and therefore the humour took him to make the goatherds that unprofitable discourse; who heard him, all amazed and suspended, with very great attention all the while. Sancho likewise held his peace, eating acorns, and in the meanwhile visited very often the second wine-bag, which, because it might be fresh, was hanged upon a cork-tree. Don Quixote had spent more time in his speech than in his supper; at the end whereof one of the goatherds said, 'To the end that you may more assuredly know, sir knight-errant, that we do entertain you with prompt and ready will, we will likewise make you some pastime by hearing one of our companions sing, who is a herd of good understanding, and very amorous withal, and can besides read and write, and play so well on a rebec, that there is nothing to be desired.' Scarce had the goatherd ended his speech, when the sound of the rebec touched his ear; and within a while after he arrived that played on it, being a youth of some twenty years old, and one of a very good grace and countenance. His fellows demanded if he had supped; and, answering that he had, he which did offer the courtesy, said, 'Then, Anthony, thou mayst do us a pleasure by singing a little, that this gentleman our guest may see that we enjoy, amidst these groves and woods, those that know what music is. We have told him already thy good qualities, and therefore we desire that thou show them, to verify our words; and therefore I desire thee, by thy life, that thou wilt sit and sing the ditty which thy uncle the prebendary made of thy love, and was so well liked of in our village.' 'I am content,' quoth

the youth; and, without further entreaty, sitting down on the trunk
of a lopped oak, he tuned his rebec, and after a while began, with a
singular good grace, to sing in this manner:

'I know, Olalia, thou dost me adore!
    Though yet to me the same thou hast not said;
Nor shown it once by one poor glance or more,
    Since love is soonest by such tongues bewray'd.

'Yet, 'cause I ever held thee to be wise,
    It me assures thou bearest me good will;
And he is not unfortunate that sees
    How his affections are not taken ill.

'Yet for all this, Olalia, 'tis true!
    I, by observance, gather to my woe;
Thy mind is framed of brass, by art undue,
    And flint thy bosom is, though it seem snow.

'And yet, amidst thy rigour's winter-face,
    And other shifts, thou usest to delay me,
Sometimes hope, peeping out, doth promise grace;
    But, woe is me! I fear 'tis to betray me.

'Sweetest! once in the balance of thy mind,
    Poise with just weights my faith, which never yet
Diminish'd, though disfavour it did find;
    Nor can increase more, though thou favoured'st it.

'If love be courteous (as some men say),
    By thy humanity, I must collect
My hopes, hows'ever thou dost use delay,
    Shall reap, at last, the good I do expect.

'If many services be of esteem
    Or power to render a hard heart benign,
Such things I did for thee, as made me deem
    I have the match gain'd, and thou shalt be mine.

'For, if at any time thou hast ta'en heed,
    Thou more than once might'st view how I was clad,
To honour thee on Mondays, with the weed
    Which, worn on Sundays, got me credit had.

ANTHONY'S DITTY

'For love and brav'ry still themselves consort,
  Because they both shoot ever at one end;
Which made me, when I did to thee resort,
  Still to be neat and fine I did contend.

'Here I omit the dances I have done,
  And musics I have at thy window given;
When thou didst at cock-crow listen alone,
  And seem'dst, hearing my voice, to be in heaven.

'I do not, eke, the praises here recount
  Which of thy beauty I so oft have said;
Which, though they all were true, were likewise wont
  To make thee envious me for spite upbraid.

'When to Teresa, she of Berrocal,
  I, of thy worth, discourse did sometime shape:
"Good God!" quoth she, "you seem an angel's thrall,
  And yet, for idol, you adore an ape.

' "She to her bugles thanks may give, and chains,
  False hair, and other shifts that she doth use
To mend her beauty, with a thousand pains
  And guiles, which might love's very self abuse."

'Wroth at her words, I gave her straight the lie,
  Which did her and her cousin so offend,
As me to fight he challenged presently,
  And well thou know'st of our debate the end.

'I mean not thee to purchase at a clap,
  Nor to that end do I thy favour sue;
Thereby thine honour either to entrap,
  Or thee persuade to take courses undue.

'The Church hath bands which do so surely hold,
  As no silk string for strength comes to them near;
To thrust thy neck once in the yoke be bold,
  And see if I, to follow thee, will fear.

'If thou wilt not, here solemnly I vow,
  By holiest saint, enwrapt in precious shrine,
Never to leave those hills where I dwell now,
  If 't be not to become a Capucine.'

305

Here the goatherd ended his ditty, and although Don Quixote entreated him to sing somewhat else, yet would not Sancho Panza consent to it; who was at that time better disposed to sleep than to hear music; and therefore said to his master, 'You had better provide yourself of a place wherein to sleep this night than to hear music; for the labour that these good men endure all the day long doth not permit that they likewise spend the night in singing.' 'I understand thee well enough, Sancho,' answered Don Quixote; 'nor did I think less, but that thy manifold visitations of the wine-bottle would rather desire to be recompensed with sleep than with music.' 'The wine liked us all well,' quoth Sancho. 'I do not deny it,' replied Don Quixote; 'but go thou and lay thee down where thou pleasest, for it becomes much more men of my profession to watch than to sleep. Yet, notwithstanding, it will not be amiss to lay somewhat again to mine ear, for it grieves me very much.' One of the goatherds, beholding the hurt, bade him be of good cheer, for he would apply a remedy that should cure it easily. And, taking some rosemary-leaves of many that grew thereabouts, he hewed them, and after mixed a little salt among them; and, applying this medicine to the ear, he bound it up well with a cloth, assuring him that he needed to use no other medicine; as it proved after, in effect.

CHAPTER IV

Of That Which One of the Goatherds Recounted to Those That Were with Don Quixote

ABOUT this time arrived another youth, one of those that brought them provision from the village, who said, 'Companions, do not you know what passeth in the village?' 'How can we know it, being absent?' says another of them. 'Then, wit,' quoth the youth, 'that the famous shepherd and student, Chrysostom, died this morning, and they murmur that he died for love of that devilish lass Marcela, William the Rich his daughter, she that goes up and down these plains and hills among us, in the habit of a shepherdess.' 'Dost thou mean Marcela?' quoth one of them. 'Even her, I say,' answered the other; 'and the jest is, that he hath commanded, in his testament, that he be buried in the fields, as if he were a Moor; and that it be at the foot of the rock, where the fountain stands off the cork-tree; for that, according to fame, and as they say he himself affirmed, was the place wherein he viewed her first. And he hath likewise commanded such other things to be done, as the ancienter sort of the village do not allow, nor think fit to be performed; for they seem to be ceremonies of the Gentiles. To all which objections, his great friend, Ambrosio the student, who likewise apparelled himself like a shepherd at once with him, answers, that all shall be accomplished, without omission of anything, as Chrysostom hath ordained; and all the village is in an aproar about this affair; and yet it is said that what Ambrosio and all the other shepherds his friends do pretend, shall in fine be done; and to-morrow morning they will come to the place I have named, to bury him with great pomp. And as I suppose it will be a thing worthy the seeing, at leastwise I will not omit to go and behold it although I were sure that I could not return the same day to the village.' 'We will all do the same,' quoth the goatherds, 'and will draw lots who shall tarry here to keep all our herds.' 'Thou sayst well, Peter,' quoth one of them, 'although that labour may be excused; for I mean to stay behind for you all, which you must not attribute to any virtue, or little curiosity in me, but rather to the fork that pricked my foot the other day, and makes me unable to travel from hence.' 'We do thank thee, notwithstanding,' quoth Peter, 'for thy good-will.' And Don Quixote, who heard all their discourse, entreated Peter to tell him who that dead man was, and what the shepherdess of whom they spoke.

Peter made answer, that what he knew of the affair was, 'that the dead person was a rich gentleman of a certain village seated among those mountains, who had studied many years in Salamanca, and after returned home to his house, with the opinion to be a very wise and learned man; but principally it was reported of him, that he was skilful in astronomy, and all that which passed above in heaven, in the sun and the moon, for he would tell us most punctually the clipse of the sun and the moon.' 'Friend,' quoth Don Quixote, 'the darkening of these two great luminaries is called an eclipse, not a clipse.' But Peter, stopping not at those trifles, did prosecute his history, saying, 'He did also prognosticate when the year would be abundant or estile.' 'Thou wouldst say sterile,' quoth Don Quixote. 'Sterile or estile,' said Peter, 'all is one for my purpose. And I say that, by his words, his father and his other friends, that gave credit to him, became very rich; for they did all that he counselled them: who would say unto them, Sow barley this year, and no wheat; in this, you may sow peas, and no barley; the next year will be good for oil; the three ensuing, you shall not gather a drop.' 'That science is called astrology,' quoth Don Quixote. 'I know not how it is called,' replied Peter; 'but I know well he knew all this, and much more.

'Finally, a few months after he came from Salamanca, he appeared one day apparelled like a shepherd, with his flock, and leather coat, having laid aside the long habits that he wore, being a scholar; and jointly with him came also a great friend of his and fellow-student, called Ambrosio, apparelled like a shepherd. I did almost forget to tell how Chrysostom, the dead man, was a great maker of verses; insomuch that he made the carols of Christmas Day at night, and the plays for Corpus Christi Day, which the youths of our village did represent, and all of them affirmed that they were most excellent. When those of the village saw the two scholars so suddenly clad like shepherds, they were amazed, and could not guess the cause that moved them to make so wonderful a change. And about this time Chrysostom's father died, and he remained possessed of a great deal of goods, as well moveable as immoveable; and no little quantity of cattle, great and small, and also a great sum of money; of all which the young man remained a dissolute lord. And truly he deserved it all; for he was a good fellow, charitable, and a friend of good folk, and he had a face like a blessing. It came at last to be understood, that the cause of changing his habit was none other than for to go up and down through these deserts after the shepherdess Marcela, whom our herd named before; of whom the poor dead Chrysostom was become enamoured. And I will tell you now, because it is fit you should know it, what this wanton lass is; perhaps, and I think without perhaps, you have not heard the like thing in all the days of your life, although you had lived more years than Sarna.' 'Say Sarra,' quoth Don Quixote, being not able any longer to hear him to change one word for another.

'The Sarna, or Scab,' quoth Peter, 'lives long enough too. And if you go thus, sir, interrupting my tale at every pace, we shall not be able to end it in a year.' 'Pardon me, friend,' quoth Don Quixote; 'for I speak to thee by reason there was such difference between Sarna and Sarra. But thou dost answer well; for the Sarna or Scab lives longer than Sarra. And therefore prosecute thy history; for I will not interrupt thee any more.' 'I say, then, dear sir of my soul,' quoth the goatherd, 'that there was, in our village, a farmer that was yet richer than Chrysostom's father, who was called William, to whom fortune gave, in the end of his great riches, a daughter called Marcela, of whose birth her mother died, who was the best woman that dwelt in all this circuit. Methinks I do now see her quick before me, with that face which had on the one side the sun and on the other side the moon; and above all, she was a thrifty housewife, and a great friend to the poor; for which I believe that her soul is this very hour enjoying of the gods in the other world. For grief of the loss of so good a wife, her husband William likewise died, leaving his daughter Marcela, young and rich, in the custody

of his uncle, who was a priest, and curate of our village. The child
grew with such beauty as it made us remember that of her mother,
which was very great; and yet, notwithstanding, they judged that
the daughter's would surpass hers, as indeed it did; for when she
arrived to the age of fourteen or fifteen years old, no man beheld
her that did not bless God for making her so fair, and most men
remained enamoured and cast away for her love. Her uncle kept
her with very great care and closeness; and yet, nevertheless, the
fame of her great beauty did spread itself in such sort that, as well
for it as for her great riches, her uncle was not only requested by
those of our village, but also was prayed, solicited, and importuned
by all those that dwelt many leagues about, and that by the very
best of them, to give her to them in marriage. But he (who is a
good Christian, every inch of him), although he desired to marry
her presently, as soon as she was of age, yet would he not do it
without her goodwill, without ever respecting the gain and profit
he might make by the possession of her goods whilst he desired her
marriage. And, in good sooth, this was spoken of, to the good priest
his commendation, in more than one meeting of the people of our
village; for I would have you to wit, sir errant, that in these little
villages they talk of all things, and make account, as I do, that the
priest must have been too good who could oblige his parishioners
to speak so well of him, and especially in the villages.' 'Thou hast
reason,' quoth Don Quixote; 'and therefore follow on, for the history is very pleasant, and thou, good Peter, dost recount it with a
very good grace.' 'I pray God,' said Peter, 'that I never want our
Herd's; for it is that which makes to the purpose. And in the rest
you shall understand, that although her uncle propounded, and told
to his niece the quality of every wooer of the many that desired her
for wife, and entreated her to marry and choose at her pleasure, yet
would she never answer other but that she would not marry as then,
and that, in respect of her over green years, she did not find herself
able enough yet to bear the burden of marriage. With these just
excuses which she seemed to give, her uncle left off importuning of
her, and did expect until she were further entered into years, and
that she might know how to choose one that might like her; for he
was wont to say, and that very well, that parents were not to place

or bestow their children where they bore no liking. But, see here! when we least imagined it, the coy Marcela appeared one morning to become a shepherdess; and neither her uncle, nor all those of the village which dissuaded her from it, could work any effect, but she would needs go to the fields, and keep her own sheep with the other young lasses of the town. And she coming thus in public, when her beauty was seen without hindrance, I cannot possibly tell unto you how many rich youths, as well gentlemen as farmers, have taken on them the habit of Chrysostom, and follow, wooing of her, up and down those fields; one of which, as is said already, was our dead man, of whom it is said, that learning to love her, he had at last made her his idol. Nor is it to be thought that because Marcela set herself in that liberty, and so loose a life, and of so little or no keeping, that therefore she hath given the least token or shadow of dishonesty or negligence. Nay, rather, such is the watchfulness wherewithal she looks to her honour, that among so many as serve and solicit her, not one hath praised or can justly vaunt himself to have received, at her hands, the least hope that may be to obtain his desires; for, although she did not fly or shun the company and conversation of shepherds, and doth use them courteously and friendly, whensoever any one of them begin to discover their intention, be it ever so just and holy, as that of matrimony, she casts them away from her, as with a sling.

'And with this manner of proceeding she does more harm in this country than if the plague had entered into it by her means; for her affability and beauty doth draw to it the hearts of those which do serve and love her, but her disdain and resolution do conduct them to terms of desperation. And so they know not what to say unto her, but to call her with a loud voice cruel and ungrateful, with other titles like unto this, which do clearly manifest the nature of her condition; and, sir, if you stayed here but a few days, you should hear these mountains resound with the lamentations of those wretches that follow her. There is a certain place not far off, wherein are about two dozen of beech-trees, and there is not any one of them in whose rind is not engraven Marcela's name, and over some names graven also a crown in the same tree, as if her lover would plainly denote that Marcela bears it away, and deserves the garland of all human beauty. Here sighs one shepherd, there another complains; in another place are heard amorous ditties; here, in another, doleful and despairing laments. Some one there is that passeth over all the whole hours of the night at the foot of an oak or rock, and, without folding once his weeping eyes, swallowed and transported by his thoughts, the sun finds him there in the morning; and some other there is, who, without giving way or truce to his sighs, doth, amidst the fervour of the most fastidious heat of the summer, stretched upon the burning sand, breathe his pitiful complaints to heaven. And of this, and of him, and of those, and these, the beautiful Marcela doth indifferently and quietly triumph. All we that know her do wait to see wherein this her loftiness will finish, or who shall be so happy as to gain dominion over so terrible a condition, and enjoy so peerless a beauty. And because all that I have recounted is so notorious a truth, it makes me more easily believe that our companion hath told, that is said of the occasion of Chrysostom's death; and therefore I do counsel you, sir, that you do not omit to be present to-morrow at his burial, which will be worthy the seeing; for Chrysostom hath many friends, and the place wherein he commanded himself to be buried is not half a league from hence.' 'I do mean to be there,' said Don Quixote; 'and do render thee many thanks for the delight thou hast given me by the relation of so pleasant a history.' 'Oh,' quoth the goatherd, 'I do not yet know the half of the adventures succeeded to Marcela's lovers; but peradventure we may meet some shepherd on the way to-morrow that will tell them unto us. And for the present you will do well to go take your rest under some roof, for the air might hurt your wound, although the medicine be such that I have applied to it that any contrary accidents need not much to be feared.' Sancho Panza, being wholly out of patience with the goatherd's long discourse, did solicit, for his part, his master so effectually as he brought him at last into Peter's cabin, to take his rest for that night; whereinto, after he had entered, he bestowed the remnant of the night in remembrances of his Lady Dulcinea, in imitation of Marcela's lovers. Sancho Panza did lay himself down between Rozinante and his ass, and slept it out, not like a disfavoured lover, but like a man stamped and bruised with tramplings.

CHAPTER V

BUT scarce had the day begun to discover itself by the oriental windows, when five of the six goatherds arising, went to awake Don Quixote, and demanded of him whether he yet intended to go to Chrysostom's burial, and that they would accompany him. Don Quixote, that desired nothing more, got up, and commanded Sancho to saddle and empannel in a trice; which he did with great expedition, and with the like they all presently began their journey. And they had not yet gone a quarter of a league, when, at the crossing of a pathway, they saw six shepherds coming towards them, apparelled with black skins, and crowned with garlands of cypress and bitter *enula campana*. Every one of them carried in his hand a thick truncheon of elm. There came likewise with them two gentlemen a-horseback, very well furnished for the way, with other three lackeys that attended on them. And, as soon as they encountered, they saluted one another courteously, and demanded whither they travelled; and knowing that they all went towards the place of the burial, they began their journey together. One of the horsemen, speaking to his companion, said, 'I think, Mr. Vivaldo, we shall account the time well employed that we shall stay to see this so famous an entertainment; for it cannot choose but be famous, according to the wonderful things these shepherds have recounted unto us, as well of the dead shepherd as also of the murdering shepherdess.' 'It seems so to me likewise,' quoth Vivaldo; 'and I say, I would not only stay one day, but a whole week, rather than miss to behold it.' Don Quixote demanded of them what they had heard of Marcela and Chrysostom. The traveller answered that they had encountered that morning with those shepherds, and that, by reason they had seen them apparelled in that mournful attire, they demanded of them the occasion thereof, and one of them

313

rehearsed it, recounting the strangeness and beauty of a certain shepherdess called Marcela, and the amorous pursuits of her by many, with the death of that Chrysostom to whose burial they rode. Finally, he told all that again to him that Peter had told the night before.

This discourse thus ended, another began, and was, that he who was called Vivaldo demanded of Don Quixote the occasion that moved him to travel thus armed through so peaceable a country. To whom Don Quixote answered: 'The profession of my exercise doth not license or permit me to do other. Good days, cockering, and ease were invented for soft courtiers; but travels, unrest, and arms were only invented and made for those which the world terms knights-errant, of which number I myself (although unworthy) am one, and the least of all.' Scarce had they heard him say this, when they all held him to be wood. And, to find out the truth better, Vivaldo did ask him again what meant the word knights-errant. 'Have you not read, then,' quoth Don Quixote, 'the histories and annals of England, wherein are treated the famous acts of King Arthur, whom we continually call, in our Castilian romance, King Artus? of whom it is an ancient and common tradition, in the kingdom of Great Britain, that he never died, but that he was turned, by art of enchantment, into a crow; and that, in process of time, he shall return again to reign, and recover his sceptre and kingdom; for which reason it cannot be proved that, ever since that time until this, any Englishman hath killed a crow. In this good king's time was first instituted the famous order of knighthood of the Knights of the Round Table, and the love that is there recounted did in every respect pass as it is laid down between Sir Launcelot du Lake and Queen Genever, the honourable Lady Quintaniona being a dealer, and privy thereto; whence sprung that so famous a ditty, and so celebrated here in Spain, of, "Never was knight of ladies so well served as Launcelot when that he in Britain arrived," etc., with that progress so sweet and delightful of his amorous and valiant acts; and from that time forward, the order of knight went from hand to hand, dilating and spreading itself through many and sundry parts of the world; and in it were, famous and renowned for their feats of arms, the valiant Amadis of Gaul, with all his progeny until the fifth generation; and the valorous Felixmarte of Hircania, and the never-duly-praised Tirante the White, together with Sir Bevis of Hampton, Sir Guy of Warwick, Sir Eglemore, with divers others of that nation and age; and almost in our days we saw, and communed, and heard of the invincible and valiant knight, Don Belianis of Greece. This, then, good sirs, is to be a knight-errant; and that which I have said is the order of chivalry: wherein, as I have already said, I, although a sinner, have made profession, and the same do I profess that those knights professed whom I have above mentioned; and therefore I travel through these solitudes and deserts, seeking adventures, with full resolution to offer mine own arm and person to the most dangerous that fortune shall present, in the aid of weak and needy persons.'

By these reasons of Don Quixote's the travellers perfectly perceived that he was none of the wisest; and knew the kind of folly wherewithal he was crossed, whereat those remained wonderfully admired, that by the relation of the others came to understand it.

And Vivaldo, who was very discreet, and likewise of a pleasant disposition, to the end they might pass over the rest of the way without heaviness unto the rock of the burial, which the shepherds said was near at hand, he resolved to give him further occasion to pass onward with his follies, and therefore said unto him, 'Methinks, sir knight, that you have professed one of the most austere professions in the world; and I do constantly hold that even that of the Charterhouse monks is not near so strait.' 'It may be as strait as our profession,' quoth Don Quixote, 'but that it should be so necessary for the world, I am within the breadth of two fingers to call it in doubt; for, if we would speak a truth, the soldier that puts in execution his captain's command doth no less than the very captain that commands him. Hence I infer, that religious men do with all peace and quietness seek of Heaven the good of the earth; but soldiers and we knights do put in execution that which they demand, defending it with the valour of our arms and files of our swords; not under any roof, but under the wide heavens, made, as it were, in summer a mark to the insupportable sunbeams, and in winter to the rage of withering frosts. So that we are the ministers of God on earth, and the armies wherewith He executeth His justice; and as the affairs of war, and things thereunto pertaining, cannot be put in execution without sweat, labour, and travail, it follows that those which profess warfare take, questionless, greater pain than those which, in quiet, peace, and rest, do pray unto God that He will favour and assist those that need it. I mean not therefore to affirm, nor doth it once pass through my thought, that the state of a knight-errant is as perfect as that of a retired religious man, but only would infer, through that which I myself suffer, that it is doubtlessly more laborious, more battered, hungry, thirsty, miserable, torn, and lousy. For the knights-errant of times past did, without all doubt, suffer much woe and misery in the discourse of their life; and if some of them ascended at last to empires, won by the force of their arms, in good faith, it cost them a great part of their sweat and blood; and if those which mounted to so high a degree had wanted those enchanters and wise men that assisted them, they would have remained much defrauded of their desires, and greatly deceived of their hopes.' 'I am of the same opinion,' replied the traveller; 'but one thing among many others hath seemed to me very ill in knights-errant, which is, when they perceive themselves in any occasion to begin any great and dangerous adventure, in which appears manifest peril of losing their lives, they never, in the instant of attempting it, remember to commend themselves to God, as every Christian is bound to do in like dangers, but rather do it to their ladies, with so great desire and devotion as if they were their gods—a thing which, in my opinion, smells of Gentilism.' 'Sir,' quoth Don Quixote, 'they can do no less in any wise, and the knight-errant which did any other would digress much from his duty; for now it is a received use and custom of errant chivalry, that the knight adventurous who, attempting of any great feat of arms, shall have his lady in place, do mildly and amorously turn his eyes towards her, as it were by them demanding that she do favour and protect him in that ambiguous trance which he undertakes; and, moreover, if none do hear him, he is bound to say certain words between his teeth, by which he shall, with all his heart, commend himself to her: and of this we have innumerable examples in histories. Nor is it therefore to be understood that they do omit to commend themselves to God; for they have time and leisure enough to do it in the progress of the work.'

'For all that,' replied the traveller, 'there remains in me yet one scruple which is, that oftentimes, as I have read, some speech begins between two knights-errant, and from one word to another their choler begins to be inflamed, and they to turn their horses, and to take up a good piece of the field, and, without any more ado, to run as fast as ever they can drive to encounter again, and, in the midst of their race, do commend themselves to their dames; and that which commonly ensues of this encountering is, that one of them falls down, thrown over the crupper of his horse, passed through and through by his enemy's lance; and it befalls the other that, if he had not caught fast of his horse's mane, he had likewise fallen; and I here cannot perceive how he that is slain had any leisure to commend himself unto God in the discourse of this so accelerate and hasty a work. Methinks it were better that those words which he spent in his race on his lady were bestowed as they ought, and as every Christian is bound to bestow them; and the rather, because I conjecture that all knights-errant have not ladies to whom they may commend themselves, for all of them are not amorous.'

'That cannot be,' answered Don Quixote; 'I say it cannot be that there's any knight-errant without a lady; for it is as proper and essential to such to be enamoured as to heaven to have stars: and I dare warrant that no history hath yet been seen wherein is found a knight-errant without love; for, by the very reason that he were found without them, he would be convinced to be no legitimate knight, but a bastard; and that he entered into the fortress of chivalry, not by the gate, but by leaping over the staccado like a robber and a thief.'

'Yet, notwithstanding,' replied the other, 'I have read (if I do not forget myself) that Don Galaor, brother to the valorous Amadis de Gaul, had never any certain mistress to whom he might commend himself; and yet, for all that, he was nothing less accounted of, and was a most valiant and famous knight.' To that objection our Don Quixote answered: 'One swallow makes not a summer. How much more that I know, that the knight whom you allege was secretly very much enamoured; besides that, that his inclination of loving all ladies well, which he thought were fair, was a natural inclination, which he could not govern so well; but it is, in conclusion, sufficiently verified, that yet he had one lady whom he crowned queen of his will, to whom he did also commend himself very often and secretly; for he did not a little glory to be so secret in his loves.'

'Then, sir, if it be of the essence of all knights-errant to be in love,' quoth the traveller, 'then may it likewise be presumed that you are also enamoured, seeing that it is annexed to the profession? And if you do not prize yourself to be as secret as Don Galaor, I do entreat you, as earnestly as I may, in all this company's name and mine own, that it will please you to tell us the name, country, quality, and beauty of your lady; for I am sure she would account herself happy to think that all the world doth know she is beloved and served by so worthy a knight as is yourself.' Here Don Quixote, breathing forth a deep sigh, said: 'I cannot affirm whether my sweet enemy delight or no that the world know how much she is beloved, or that I serve her. Only I dare avouch (answering to that which you so courteously demanded) that her name is Dulcinea, her country Toboso, a village of Mancha. Her calling must be at least of a princess, seeing she is my queen and lady; her beauty sovereign, for in her are verified and give glorious lustre to all those impossible and chimerical attributes of beauty that poets give to their mistresses, that her hairs are gold, her forehead the Elysian fields, her brows the arcs of heaven, her eyes suns, her cheeks roses, her lips coral, her teeth pearls, her neck alabaster, her bosom marble, ivory her hands, and her whiteness snow; and the parts which modesty conceals from human sight, such as I think and understand that the discreet consideration may prize, but never be able to equalize them.' 'Her lineage, progeny, we desire to know likewise,' quoth Vivaldo. To which Don Quixote answered: 'She is not of the ancient Roman Curcios, Cayos, or Scipios; nor of the modern Colonnas, or Ursinos; nor of the Moncadas or Requesenes of Catalonia; and much less of the Rebelias and Villanovas of Valencia; Palafoxes, Nucas, Rocabertis, Corelias, Alagones, Urreas, Fozes, and Gurreas of Aragon; Cerdas, Manriquez, Mendoças, and Guzmanes of Castile; Lancasters, Palias, and Meneses of Portugal; but she is of those of Toboso of the Mancha; a lineage which, though it be

318

modern, is such as may give a generous beginning to the most noble
families of ensuing ages. And let none contradict me in this, if it
be not with those conditions that Cerbino put at the foot of Orlando's
armour, to wit:

> "Let none from hence presume these arms to move,
> But he that with Orlando dares his force to prove." '

'Although my lineage be of the Cachopines of Laredo,' replied
the traveller, 'yet dare I not to compare it with that of Toboso in
the Mancha; although, to speak sincerely, I never heard any mention of that lineage you say until now.' 'What!' quoth Don Quixote,
'is it possible that you never heard of it till now?'

All the company travelled, giving marvellous attention to the
reasons of those two; and even the very goatherds and shepherds
began to perceive the great want of judgment that was in Don
Quixote: only Sancho Panza did verily believe that all his master's
words were most true, as one that knew what he was from the very
time of his birth; but that wherein his belief staggered somewhat,
was of the beautiful Dulcinea of Toboso; for he had never heard
speak in his life before of such a name or princess, although he had
dwelt so many years hard by Toboso.

And as they travelled in these discourses, they beheld descending,
betwixt the cleft of two lofty mountains, to the number of twenty
shepherds, all apparelled in skins of black wool and crowned with
garlands, which, as they perceived afterward, were all of yew and
cypress. Six of them carried a bier, covered with many sorts of
flowers and boughs; which one of the goatherds espying, he said,
'Those that come there are they which bring Chrysostom's body,
and the foot of that mountain is the place where he hath commanded
them to bury him.' These words were occasion to make them haste
to arrive in time, which they did just about the instant that the
others had laid down the corpse on the ground. And four of them,
with sharp pickaxes, did dig the grave at the side of a hard rock.
The one and the others saluted themselves very courteously; and
then Don Quixote, and such as came with him, began to behold
the bier, wherein they saw laid a dead body, all covered with flowers, and apparelled like a shepherd of some thirty years old; and

his dead countenance showed that he was very beautiful, and an able-bodied man. He had, placed round about him in the bier, certain books and many papers, some open and some shut, and altogether, as well those that beheld this as they which made the grave, and all the others that were present, kept a marvellous silence, until one of them which carried the dead man said to another: 'See well, Ambrosio, whether this be the place that Chrysostom meant, seeing that thou wouldst have all so punctually observed which he commanded in his testament.' 'This is it,' answered Ambrosio; 'for many times my unfortunate friend recounted to me in it the history of his mishaps. Even there he told me that he had seen that cruel enemy of mankind first; and there it was where he first broke his affections too, as honest as they were amorous; and there was the last time wherein Marcela did end to resolve, and began to disdain him, in such sort as she set end to the tragedy of his miserable life; and here, in memory of so many misfortunes, he commanded himself to be committed to the bowels of eternal oblivion.' And, turning himself to Don Quixote and to the other travellers, he said, 'This body, sirs, which you do now behold with pitiful eyes, was the treasury of a soul wherein heaven had hoarded up an infinite part of his treasures. This is the body of Chrysostom, who was peerless in wit, without fellow for courtesy, rare for comeliness, a phoenix for friendship, magnificent without measure, grave without presumption, pleasant without offence; and finally, the first in all that which is good, and second to none in all unfortunate mischances. He loved well, and was hated; he adored, and was disdained; he prayed to one no less savage than a beast; he importuned a heart as hard as marble, he pursued the wind, he cried to deserts, he served ingratitude, and he obtained for reward the spoils of death in the midst of the career of his life: to which a shepherdess hath given end whom he laboured to eternize, to the end she might ever live in the memories of men, as those papers which you see there might very well prove, had he not commanded me to sacrifice them to the fire as soon as his body was rendered to the earth.'

'If you did so,' quoth Vivaldo, 'you would use greater rigour and cruelty towards them than their very lord, nor is it discreet or justly done that his will be accomplished who commands anything repugnant to reason; nor should Augustus Caesar himself have gained the reputation of wisdom, if he had permitted that to be put in execution which the divine Mantuan had by his will ordained. So that, Senor Ambrosio, now that you commit your friend's body to the earth, do not therefore commit his labour to oblivion; for though he ordained it as one injured, yet are not you to accomplish it as one void of discretion; but rather cause, by giving life to these papers, that the cruelty of Marcela may live eternally, that it may serve as a document to those that shall breathe in ensuing ages how they may avoid and shun the like downfalls; for both myself, and all those that come here in my company, do already know the history of your enamoured and despairing friend, the occasion of his death, and what he commanded ere he deceased: out of which lamentable relation may be collected how great hath been the cruelty of Marcela, the love of Chrysostom, the faith of your affection, and the conclusion which those make which do rashly run through that way which indiscreet love doth present to their view. We understood yesternight of Chrysostom's death, and that he should be interred in this place, and therefore we omitted our intended journeys, both for curiosity and pity, and resolved to come and behold with our eyes that the relation whereof did so much grieve us in the hearing; and therefore we desire thee, discreet Ambrosio, both in reward of this our compassion, and also of the desire which springs in our breasts, to remedy this disaster, if it were possible; but chiefly I, for my part, request thee, that, omitting to burn these papers, thou wilt license me to take away some of them. And, saying so, without expecting the shepherd's answer, he stretched out his hand and took some of them that were next to him; which Ambrosio perceiving, said, 'I will consent, sir, for courtesy's sake, that you remain lord of those which you have seized upon; but to imagine that I would omit to burn these that rest were a very vain thought.' Vivaldo, who did long to see what the papers contained which he had gotten, did unfold presently one of them, which had this title, 'A Ditty of Despair.' Ambrosio overheard him, and said: 'That is the last paper which this unfortunate shepherd wrote; and because, sir, that you may see the terms to which his mishaps conducted him, I pray you to read it, but in such manner as you may be heard; for you shall have leisure enough to do it whilst the grave is a-digging.' 'I will do it with all my heart,' replied Vivaldo; and all those that were present having the like desire, they gathered about him, and he, reading it with a clear voice, pronounced it thus.

THE THIRD BOOK

CHAPTER I

WHEREIN IS REHEARSED THE UNFORTUNATE ADVENTURE WHICH HAPPENED TO DON QUIXOTE, BY ENCOUNTERING WITH CERTAIN YANGUESIAN CARRIERS

THE wise Cid Hamet Benengeli recounteth that, as soon as Don Quixote had taken leave of the goatherds, his hosts the night before, and of all those that were present at the burial of the shepherd Chrysostom, he and his squire did presently enter into the same wood into which they had seen the beautiful shepherdess Marcela enter before. And, having travelled in it about the space of two hours without finding of her, they arrived in fine to a pleasant meadow, enriched with abundance of flourishing grass, near unto which runs a delightful and refreshing stream, which did invite, yea, constrain them thereby to pass over the heat of the day, which did then begin to enter with great fervour and vehemency. Don Quixote and Sancho alighted, and, leaving the ass and Rozinante to the spaciousness of these plains to feed on the plenty of grass that was there, they ransacked their wallet, where, without any ceremony, the master and man did eat, with good accord and fellowship, what they found therein. Sancho had neglected to tie Rozinante, sure that he knew him to be so sober and little wanton as all the mares of the pasture of Cordova could not make him to think the least sinister thought. But fortune did ordain, or rather the devil, who sleeps not at all hours, that a troop of Gallician mares, belonging to certain Yanguesian carriers, did feed up and down in the same valley; which carriers are wont, with their beasts, to pass over the heats in places situated near unto grass and water, and that wherein Don Quixote happened to be was very fit for their purpose. It therefore befel that Rozinante took a certain desire to solace himself with the lady mares, and therefore, as soon as he

323

had smelt them, abandoning his natural pace and custom, without taking leave of his master, he began a little swift trot, and went to communicate his necessities to them. But they, who, as it seemed, had more desire to feed than to solace them, entertained him with their heels and teeth in such sort as they broke all his girths, and left him in his naked hair, having overthrown the saddle. But that which surely grieved him most was, that the carriers, perceiving the violence that was offered by him to their mares, repaired presently to their succours, with clubs and truncheons, and did so belabour him as they fairly laid him along. Now, in this season, Don Quixote and Sancho (which beheld the bombasting of Rozinante) approached breathless; and Don Quixote said to Sancho, 'For as much as I can perceive, friend Sancho, these men are no knights, but base, rascally people of vile quality; I say it, because thou mayst help me to take due revenge for the outrage which they have done before our face to Rozinante.' 'What a devil' quoth Sancho, 'what revenge should we take, if these be more than twenty, and we but two, and peradventure but one and a half?' 'I am worth a hundred,' replied Don Quixote; and, without making any longer discourse, he set hand to his sword, and flew upon the Yanguesians; and Sancho Panza, moved by his lord's example, did the like; when, with the first blow, Don Quixote piercing a buff coat that one of them wore, wounded him grievously in the shoulder. The Yanguesians, seeing themselves so rudely handled by two men only, they being so many, ran to the stakes and truncheons of their carriage, and, hemming in their adversaries in the midst of them, they laid on them with admirable speed and vehemency. True it is, that at the second peal they struck Sancho down to the ground; and the like happened to Don Quixote, his dexterity and courage being nothing available in that trance, and, his fate so ordaining, he fell just at his courser's feet, who had not yet gotten up; by which we may ponder the fury wherewithal truncheons batter, being placed in wrathful and rustical fists. The carriers perceiving the evil they had committed, trussing up their loading with all possible speed, followed on their way, leaving both the adventures in a bad fashion, and a worse talent.

The first that came to himself was Sancho Panza, who, seeing his lord near unto him, said, with a weak and pitiful voice, 'Sir

Don Quixote! oh, sir Don Quixote!' 'What wouldst thou have, brother Sancho?' replied the knight, with the like effeminate and doleful tune. 'I would,' quoth Sancho, 'have of your worship a draught or two of the liquor of Feoblas, if you have any of it at hand; perhaps it is good to cure broken bones as well as it helps wounds.' 'What would we want, unhappy that I am!' replied Don Quixote, 'if I had it here; but I swear unto thee, Sancho Panza, by the faith of a knight-errant, that before two days pass (if fortune dispose not otherwise), I will have it in my power, or it shall hardly escape my hands.' 'I pray you,' quoth Sancho, 'within how many days, think you, shall we be able to stir our feet?' 'I can say of myself,' quoth the crushed knight, 'that I cannot set a certain term to the days of our recovery; but I am in the fault of all, for I should not have drawn my sword against men that are not knights as well as I am; and therefore I believe that the god of battles hath permitted that this punishment should be given unto me, in pain of transgressing the laws of knighthood. Wherefore, brother Sancho, it is requisite that thou beest advertised of that which I shall say unto thee now, for it importeth both our goods very much; and is, that when thou beholdest that the like rascally rabble do us any wrong, do not wait till I set hand to my sword against them, for I will not do it in any sort; but draw thou thine, and chastise them at thy pleasure; and if any knights shall come to their assistance and succour, I shall know then how to defend thee, and offend them with all my force; for thou hast by this perceived, by a thousand signs and experiences, how far the valour of this mine invincible arm extendeth itself':—so arrogant remained the poor knight, through the victory he had gotten of the hardy Biscaine. But this advice of his lord seemed not so good to Sancho Panza as that he would omit to answer unto him, saying, 'Sir, I am a peaceable, quiet, and sober man, and can dissemble any injury, for I have wife and children to maintain and bring up; wherefore, let this likewise be an advice to you (seeing it cannot be a commandment), that I will not set hand to my sword in any wise, be it against clown or knight; and that, from this time forward, I do pardon, before God, all the wrongs that they have done, or shall do unto me, whether they were, be, or shall be done by high or low

person, rich or poor, gentleman or churl, without excepting any
state or condition.' Which being heard by his lord, he said: 'I could
wish to have breath enough that I might answer thee with a little
more ease, or that the grief which I feel in this rib were assuaged
ever so little, that I might, Panza, make thee understand the
error wherein thou art. Come here, poor fool! if the gale of fortune,
hitherto so contrary, do turn in our favour, swelling the sails of our
desire in such sort as we may securely and without any hindrance
arrive at the haven of any of those islands which I have promised
unto thee, what would become of thee, if I, conquering it, did
make thee lord thereof, seeing thou wouldst disable thyself, in
respect thou art not a knight, nor desirest to be one, nor wouldst
have valour or will to revenge thine injuries, or to defend thy lordship's? For thou must understand that, in the kingdoms and
provinces newly conquered, the minds of the inhabitants are never
so thoroughly appeased or wedded to the affection of their new lord,
that it is not to be feared that they will work some novelty to alter
things again, and turn, as men say, afresh to try fortune; and it is
therefore requisite that the new possessor have understanding to
govern, and valour to offend, and defend himself in any adventure
whatsoever.' 'In this last that hath befallen us,' quoth Sancho, 'I
would I had had that understanding and valour of which you
speak; but I vow unto you, by the faith of a poor man, that I am
now fitter for plaisters than discourses. I pray you try whether
you can arise, and we will help Rozinante, although he deserves
it not; for he was the principal cause of all these troubles. I would
never have believed the like before of Rozinante, whom I ever held
to be as chaste and peaceable a person as myself. In fine, they say
well, that one must have a long time to come to the knowledge of
bodies, and that there's nothing in this life secure. Who durst
affirm that, after those mighty blows which you gave to that unfortunate knight-errant, would succeed so in post, and as it were
in your pursuit, this so furious a tempest of staves, that hath discharged itself on our shoulders?' 'Thine, Sancho,' replied Don
Quixote, 'are perhaps accustomed to bear the like showers, but
mine, nursed between cottons and hollands, it is most evident that
they must feel the grief of this disgrace. And were it not that I

imagine (but why do I say imagine?) I know certainly that all these incommodities are annexed to the exercise of arms, I would here die for very wrath and displeasure.' To this the squire answered: 'Sir, seeing these disgraces are of the essence of knighthood, I pray you whether they succeed very often, or whether they have certain times limited wherein they befall? For methinks, within two adventures more, we shall wholly remain disenabled for the third, if the gods in mercy do not succour us.'

'Know, friend Sancho,' replied Don Quixote, 'that the life of knights-errant is subject to a thousand dangers and misfortunes; and it is also as well, in the next degree and power, to make them kings and emperors, as experience hath shown in sundry knights, of whose histories I have entire notice. And I could recount unto thee now (did the pain I suffer permit me) of some of them which have mounted to those high degrees which I have said, only by the valour of their arm; and the very same men found them, both before and after, in divers miseries and calamities. For the valorous Amadis of Gaul saw himself in the power of his mortal enemy, Arcalaus the enchanter, of whom the opinion runs infallible, that he gave unto him, being his prisoner, more than two hundred stripes with his horse-bridle, after he had tied him to a pillar in his base-court. And there is, moreover, a secret author of no little credit, who says, that the Cavalier del Febo, being taken in a gin, like unto a snatch, that slipped under his feet in a certain castle, after the fall found himself in a deep dungeon under the earth, bound hands and feet; and there they gave unto him a clyster of snow-water and sand, which brought him almost to the end of his life; and were it not that he was succoured in that great distress by a wise man, his very great friend, it had gone ill with the poor knight. So that I may very well pass among so many worthy persons; for the dangers and disgraces they suffered were greater than those which we do now endure. For, Sancho, I would have thee to understand, that these wounds which are given to one with those instruments that are in one's hand, by chance, do not disgrace a man. And it is written in the laws of single combat, in express terms, that if the shoemaker strike another with the last which he hath in his hand, although it be certainly of wood, yet cannot it be said that he who was striken had the bastinado. I say this, to the end thou mayst not think, al-

327

though we remain bruised in this last conflict, that therefore we be disgraced; for the arms which those men bore, and wherewithal they laboured us, were none other than their pack-staves, and, as far as I can remember, never a one of them had a tuck, sword, or dagger.' 'They gave me no leisure,' answered Sancho, 'to look to them so nearly; for scarce had I laid hand on my truncheon, when they blessed my shoulders with their pins, in such sort as they wholly deprived me of my sight and the force of my feet together, striking me down on the place where I yet lie straught, and where the pain of the disgrace received by our cudgelling doth not so much pinch me as the grief of the blows, which shall remain as deeply imprinted in my memory as they do in my back.'

'For all this, thou shalt understand, brother Panza,' replied Don Quixote, 'that there is no remembrance which time will not end, nor grief which death will not consume.' 'What greater misfortune,' quoth Sancho, 'can there be than that which only expecteth time and death to end and consume it? If this our disgrace were of that kind which might be cured by a pair or two of plaisters, it would not be so evil; but I begin to perceive that all the salves of an hospital will not suffice to bring them to any good terms.' 'Leave off, Sancho, and gather strength out of weakness,' said Don Quixote, 'for so will I likewise do; and let us see how doth Rozinante, for methinks that the least part of this mishap hath not fallen to his lot.' 'You ought not to marvel at that,' quoth Sancho, 'seeing he is likewise a knight-errant; that whereat I wonder is that mine ass remains there without payment, where we are come away without ribs.' 'Fortune leaves always one door open in disasters,' quoth Don Quixote, 'whereby to remedy them. I say it, because that little beast may supply Rozinante's want, by carrying off me from hence unto some castle, wherein I may be cured of my wounds. Nor do I hold this kind of riding dishonourable; for I remember to have read that the good old Silenus, tutor of the merry god of laughter, when he entered into the city of the hundred gates, rode very fairly mounted on a goodly ass.' 'It is like,' quoth Sancho, 'that he rode, as you say, upon an ass; but there is great difference betwixt riding and being cast athwart upon one like a sack of rubbish.' To this Don Quixote answered: 'The wounds that are received in battle do rather give honour than deprive men of it; wherefore, friend Panza, do not reply any more unto me, but, as I have said, arise as well as thou canst, and lay me as thou pleaseth upon thy beast, and let us depart from hence before the night overtake us in these deserts.' 'Yet I have heard you say,' quoth Panza, 'that it was an ordinary custom of knights-errant to sleep in downs and deserts the most of the year, and that so to do they hold for very good hap.' 'That is,' said Don Quixote, 'when they have none other shift, or when they are in love; and this is so true as that there hath been a knight that hath dwelt on a rock, exposed to the sun and the shadow, and other annoyances of heaven, for the space of two years, without his lady's knowledge. And Amadis was one of that kind, when calling himself Beltenebros, he dwelt in the Poor Rock, nor do I know punctually eight years or eight months, for I do not remember the history well; let it suffice that there he dwelt doing of penance, for some disgust which I know not, that his lady, Oriana, did him. But, leaving that apart, Sancho, despatch and away before some other disgrace happen, like that of Rozinante, to the ass.'

'Even there lurks the devil,' quoth Sancho; and so, breathing thirty sobs and threescore sighs, and a hundred and twenty discontents and execrations against him that had brought him there, he arose, remaining bent in the midst of the way, like unto a Turkish bow, without being able to address himself; and, notwithstanding all this difficulty, he harnessed his ass (who had been also somewhat distracted by the overmuch liberty of that day), and after he hoisted up Rozinante, who, were he endowed with a tongue to complain, would certainly have borne his lord and Sancho company. In the end Sancho laid Don Quixote on the ass, and tied Rozinante unto him, and, leading the ass by the halter, travelled that way which he deemed might conduct him soonest toward the highway. And fortune, which guided his affairs from good to better, after he had travelled a little league, discovered it unto him, near unto which he saw an inn, which, in despite of him, and for Don Quixote's pleasure, must needs be a castle. Sancho contended that it was an inn, and his lord that it was not; and their controversy endured so long as they had leisure, before they could decide it, to arrive at the lodging; into which Sancho, without further verifying of the dispute, entered with all his loading.

CHAPTER II

OF THAT WHICH HAPPENED UNTO THE INGENUOUS KNIGHT WITHIN THE INN, WHICH HE SUPPOSED TO BE A CASTLE

THE innkeeper, seeing Don Quixote laid overthwart upon the ass, demanded of Sancho what disease he had. Sancho answered that it was nothing but a fall down from a rock, and that his ribs were thereby somewhat bruised. This innkeeper had a wife, not of the condition that those of that trade are wont to be; for she was of a charitable nature, and would grieve at the calamities of her neighbours, and did therefore presently occur to cure Don Quixote, causing her daughter, a very comely young maiden, to assist her to cure her guest. There likewise served in the inn an Asturian wench, who was broad-faced, flat-pated, saddle-nosed, blind of one eye, and the other almost out; true it is, that the comeliness of her body supplied all the other defects. She was not seven palms long from her feet unto her head; and her shoulders, which did somewhat burden her, made her look oftener to the ground than she would willingly. This beautiful piece did assist the young maiden, and both of them made a very bad bed for Don Quixote in an old wide chamber, which gave manifest tokens of itself that it had sometimes served many years only to keep chopped straw for horses; in which was also lodged a carrier, whose bed was made a little way off from Don Quixote's, which, though it was made of canvas and coverings of his mules, was much better than the knight's, that only contained four boards roughly planed, placed on two unequal tressels; a flock-bed, which in the thinness seemed rather a quilt, full of pellets, and had not they shown that they were wool, through certain breaches made by antiquity on the tick, a man would by the hardness rather take them to be stones; a pair of sheets made of the skins of targets; a coverlet, whose threads if a man would number, he should not lose one only of the account. In this ungracious bed did Don Quixote lie, and presently the hostess and her daughter anointed him all over, and Maritornes (for so the Asturian wench was called) did hold the candle. The hostess at the plaistering of him, perceiving him to be so bruised in sundry places, she said unto him that those signs rather seemed to proceed of blows than of a fall. 'They were not blows,' replied Sancho; 'but the rock had many sharp ends and knobs on it, whereof every one left behind it a token; and I desire you, good mistress,' quoth he, 'to leave some flax behind, and there shall not want one that needeth the use of them; for, I assure you, my back doth likewise ache.' 'If that be so,' quoth the hostess, 'it is likely that thou didst also fall.' 'I did not fall,' quoth Sancho Panza, 'but with the sudden affright that I took at my master's fall, my body doth so grieve me, as methinks I have been handsomely belaboured.' 'It may well happen as thou sayst,' quoth the hostess's daughter; 'for it hath befallen me sundry times to dream that I fell down from some high tower, and could never come to the ground; and when I awoke, I did find myself so troubled and broken, as if I had verily fallen.' 'There is the point, masters,' quoth Sancho Panza, 'that I, without dreaming at all, but being more awake than I am at this hour, found myself to have very few less tokens and marks than my lord Don Quixote hath.' 'How is this gentleman called?' quoth Maritornes the Asturian. 'Don Quixote of the Mancha,' replied Sancho Panza; 'and he is a knight-errant, and one of the best and strongest that have been seen in the world these many ages.' 'What is that, a knight-errant?' quoth the wench. 'Art thou so young in the world that thou knowest it not?' answered Sancho Panza. 'Know then, sister mine, that a knight-errant is a thing which, in two words, you see well cudgelled, and after becomes an emperor. To-day he is the most unfortunate creature of the world, and the most needy; and to-morrow he will have two or three crowns of kingdoms to bestow upon his squire.' 'If it be so,' quoth the hostess, 'why, then, hast not thou gotten at least an earldom, seeing thou art this good knight his squire?' 'It is yet too soon,' replied Sancho; 'for it is but a month since we began first to seek adventures, and we have not yet encountered any worthy of the name. And sometimes it befalls, that searching for one thing we encounter another. True it is that, if my lord Don Quixote recover of this wound or fall, and that I be not changed by it, I would not make an exchange of my hopes for the best title of Spain.' Don Quixote did very attentively listen unto all these discourses, and, sitting up in his bed as well as he could, taking his hostess by the hand, he said unto her: 'Believe me, beautiful lady, that you may count yourself fortunate for having harboured my person in this your castle, which is such, that if I do not praise it, it is because men say that proper praise stinks; but my squire will inform you what I am: only this I will say myself, that I will keep eternally written in my memory the service that you have done unto me, to be grateful unto you for it whilst I live. And I would it might please the highest heavens that love held me not so enthralled and subject to his laws as he doth, and to the eyes of that ungrateful fair whose name I secretly mutter, then should those of this beautiful damsel presently signiorise my liberty.' The hostess, her daughter, and the good Maritornes remained confounded, hearing the speech of our knight-errant, which they understood as well as if he had spoken Greek unto them; but yet they conceived that they were words of compliments and love, and as people unused to hear the like language, they beheld and admired him, and he seemed unto them a man of the other world; and so, returning him thanks, with tavernly phrase, for his large offers, they departed. And the Asturian Maritornes cured Sancho, who needed her help no less than his master.

The carrier and she had agreed to pass the night together, and she had given unto him her word that, when the guests were quiet and her master sleeping, she would come unto him and satisfy his desire, as much as he pleased. And it is said of this good wench, that she never passed the like promise but that she performed it, although it were given in the midst of a wood, and without any witness; for she presumed to be of gentle blood, and yet she held it no disgrace to serve in an inn; for she was wont to affirm that disgraces and misfortunes brought her to that state. The hard, narrow, niggard, and counterfeit bed whereon Don Quixote lay was the first of the four, and next unto it was his squire's, that only contained a mat and a coverlet, and rather seemed to be of shorn canvas than wool. After these two beds followed that of the carrier, made, as we have said, of the pannels and furniture of two of his best mules, although they were twelve all in number, fair, fat, and goodly beasts; for he was one of the richest carriers of Arevalo, as the author of this history affirmeth, who maketh particular mention of him, because he knew him very well, and besides, some men say that he was somewhat akin unto him; omitting that Cid Mahamet Benengeli was a very exact historiographer, and most curious in all things, as may be gathered very well, seeing that those which are related being so minute and trivial, he would not overslip them in silence.

By which those grave historiographers may take example, which recount unto us matters so short and succinctly as they do scarce arrive to our knowledge, leaving the most substantial part of the works drowned in the ink-horn, either through negligence, malice, or ignorance. Many good fortunes betide the author of *Tablante de Ricamonte,* and him that wrote the book wherein are rehearsed the acts of the Count Tomillas: Lord! with what preciseness do they describe every circumstance. To conclude, I say that, after the carrier had visited his mules, and given unto them their second refreshing, he stretched himself in his coverlets, and expected the coming of the most exquisite Maritornes. Sancho was also, by this, plaistered and laid down in his bed, and though he desired to sleep, yet would not the grief of his ribs permit him. And Don Quixote, with the pain of his sides, lay with both his eyes open, like a hare.

All the inn was drowned in silence, and there was no other light in it than that of a lamp, which hung lighting in the midst of the entry. This marvellous quietness, and the thoughts which always represented to our knight the memory of the successes which at every pace are recounted in books of knighthood (the principal authors of this mishap), called to his imagination one of the strangest follies that easily may be conjectured; which was, he imagined that he arrived to a famous castle (for, as we have said, all the inns wherein he lodged seemed unto him to be such), and that the innkeeper's daughter was the lord's daughter of the castle, who, overcome by his comeliness and valour, was enamoured of him, and had promised that she would come to solace with him for a good space, after her father and mother had gone to bed. And holding all this chimera and fiction, which he himself had built in his brain, for most firm and certain, he began to be vexed in mind, and to think on the dangerous trance, wherein his honesty was like to fall, and did firmly purpose in heart not to commit any disloyalty against his lady, Dulcinea of Toboso, although very Queen Genever, with her lady, Queintanonia, should come to solicit him. Whilst thus he lay thinking of these follies, the hour approached (that was unlucky for him) wherein the Asturian wench should come, who entered into the chamber in search of her carrier, in her smock, barefooted, and her hair trussed up in a coif of fustian, with soft and wary steps. But she was scarce come to the door when Don Quixote felt her, and, arising and sitting up in his bed, in despite of his plaisters and with great grief of his ribs, he stretched forth his arms to receive his beautiful damsel, the Asturian, who, crouching and silently, went groping with her hands to find out her sweet heart, and encountered Don Quixote's arms, who presently seized very strongly upon one of her wrists, and, drawing her towards him (she daring not to speak a word,) he caused her to sit upon his bed's side, and presently groped her smock, and although it was of the strongest canvas, he thought it was most subtle and fine holland. She wore on her wrists certain bracelets of glass, which he esteemed to be precious oriental pearls. Her hair which was almost as rough as a horse-tail, he held to be wires of the glisteringest gold of Arabia, whose brightness did obscure that of the sun; and her breath, which certainly smelled like to stale salt-fish reserved from over night, seemed unto him a most redolent, aromatical, and sweet smell. And finally, he painted her in his fantasy of the same very form and manner as he had read in his books of knighthood, of a certain princess which came to visit a knight who was grievously wounded, being overcome by his love, embellished with all the ornaments that here we have recounted; and the blindness of this poor gallant was such, as neither the touching, savour, or other things that accompanied the good damsel, could undeceive him, being such as were able to make any other, save a carrier, vomit up his bowels; but rather he made full account that he held the goddess of love between his arms, and, holding her still very fast, he began to court her, with a low and amorous voice, in this manner: 'I could wish to find myself in terms, most high and beautiful lady, to be able to recompense so great a favour as that which, with the presence of your matchless feature, you have shown unto me; but fortune (who is never weary of persecuting the good) hath pleased to lay me in this bed, wherein I lie so broken and bruised, that although I were desirous to satisfy your will, yet it is impossible; especially seeing to that impossibility may be added a greater, to wit, the promised faith which I have given to the unmatchable Dulcinea of Toboso, the only lady of my most hidden thoughts; for did not this let me, do not hold me to be so senseless and mad a knight as to overslip so fortunate an occasion as this which your bounty hath offered to me.'

Maritornes remained sweating, through anxiety, to see herself held so fast by Don Quixote, and, without either understanding or giving attention to his words, she laboured all that she could to free herself from him without speaking a word. The carrier, whose bad intention kept him still waking, did hear his lady from the time that she first entered into the room, and did attentively give ear to all Don Quixote's discourses; and, jealous that the Asturian should break promise with him for any other, he drew nearer unto Don Quixote's bed, and stood quiet to see whereunto those words which he could not understand tended; but viewing that the wench strove to depart, and Don Quixote laboured to withhold her, the jest seeming evil unto him, he up with his arm, and discharged so terrible a blow on the enamoured knight's jaws as he bathed all his mouth in blood; and, not content herewithal, he mounted upon the knight, and did tread on his ribs, and passed them all over with more than a trot.

The bed, which was somewhat weak, and not very firm of foundation, being unable to suffer the addition of the carrier, fell down to the ground with so great a noise as it waked the innkeeper; who, presently suspecting that it was one of Maritornes' conflicts, because she answered him not, having called her loudly, he forthwith arose, and, lighting of a lamp, he went towards the place where he heard the noise. The wench, perceiving that her master came, and that he was extreme choleric, did, all ashamed and troubled, run into Sancho Panza's bed, who slept all this while very soundly, and there crouched, and made herself as little as an egg.

Her master entered, crying, "Whore, where art thou? I dare warrant that these are some of thy doings?' By this Sancho awaked,

335

and, feeling that bulk lying almost wholly upon him, he thought it was the nightmare, and began to lay with his fists here and there about him very swiftly, and among others wrought Maritornes I know not how many blows; who, grieved for the pain she endured there, casting all honesty aside, gave Sancho the exchange of his blows so trimly as she made him to awake in despite of his sluggishness. And, finding himself to be so abused of an uncouth person, whom he could not behold, he arose and caught hold of Maritornes as well as he could, and they both began the best fight and pleasantest skirmish in the world.

The carrier, perceiving by the light which the innkeeper brought in with him, the lamentable state of his mistress, abandoning Don Quixote, he instantly repaired to give her the succour that was requisite, which likewise the innkeeper did, but with another meaning; for he approached with intention to punish the wench, believing that she was infallibly the cause of all that harmony. And so, as men say, the cat to the rat, the rat to the cord, the cord to the post; so the carrier struck Sancho, Sancho the wench, she returned him again his liberality with interest, and the inn-keeper laid load upon his maid also; and all of them did mince it with such expedition, as there was no leisure at all allowed to any one of them for breathing. And the best of all was, that the innkeeper's lamp went out, and then, finding themselves in darkness, they belaboured one another so without compassion, and at once, as wheresoever the blow fell, it bruised the place pitifully.

There lodged by chance that night in the inn one of the squadron of these which are called of the old Holy Brotherhood of Toledo; he likewise hearing the wonderful noise of the fight, laid hand on his rod of office and the tin box of his titles, and entered into the chamber without light, saying, 'Stand still to the officer of justice and to the holy brotherhood.' And, saying so, the first whom he met was the poor battered Don Quixote, who lay overthrown in his bed, stretched, with his face upward, without any feeling; and taking hold of his beard, he cried out incessantly, 'Help the justice!' But, seeing that he whom he held fast bowed neither hand nor foot, he presently thought that he was dead, and that those battaillants that fought so eagerly in the room had slain him; wherefore he lifted his voice and cried out loudly, saying, 'Shut the inn-door, and see that none escape; for here they have killed a man!' This word astonished all the combatants so much, as every one left the battle in the very terms wherein this voice had overtaken them. The innkeeper retired himself to his chamber, the carrier to his coverlets, the wench to her couch; and only the unfortunate Don Quixote and Sancho were not able to move themselves from the place wherein they lay. The officer of the Holy Brotherhood in this space letting slip poor Don Quixote's beard, went out for light to search and apprehend the delinquents; but he could not find any, for the innkeeper had purposely quenched the lamp as he retired to his bed; wherefore the officer was constrained to repair to the chimney, where, with great difficulty, after he had spent a long while doing of it he at last lighted a candle.

Christopher Marlowe, DR. FAUSTUS

1. Before Faustus decides to become a magician, he rejects various scholarly pursuits. List them and discuss his objections to each one.

2. Modern literary criticism has come to value irony and ambiguity more than other aspects of literature. Enumerate examples of irony and ambiguity present in this play.

3. How does Faustus plan to employ his magical powers? How does he, in fact, use them?

4. In some respects, Faustus resembles the mythological figure, Icarus. Discuss the similarities and comment on the play as a chronicle of the hero's quest.

5. What is the function of the chorus?

6. Act I, scene iv contains a serio-comic exchange between Wagner and Robin in which the former asserts that the clown would "give his soul to the devil for a shoulder of mutton, though it were blood-raw." Robin replies that he would not do so; he continues, "I had need to have it well roasted, and good sauce to it, if I pay so dear..." How does this bit of dialogue reflect on Faustus and his bargain with Lucifer?

7. Analyze the character of Mephistopheles.

8. Does this play contain a repudiation of Christian values or an endorsement of them?

9. Evaluate this play in light of your reading of *The Poetics*.

A contemporary of Shakespeare, Christopher Marlowe (1564-1593) led a violent, productive, and abbreviated life, that included brawls, six plays, and death at knifepoint. Neither real nor fabricated biographical details, though, should overshadow a serious consideration of his literary efforts. Despite artistic inconsistencies, possibly resulting from the hand of a collaborator, and textual corruptions, *The Tragical History of the Life and Death of Doctor Faustus* remains a grand achievement and clearly demonstrates the power of Marlowe's blank verse as well as his dramatic sense.

THE TRAGICAL HISTORY OF
DR. FAUSTUS

DRAMATIS PERSONÆ

[THE POPE.   CARDINAL OF LORRAIN.   EMPEROR OF GERMANY.
DUKE OF VANHOLT.   FAUSTUS.
VALDES and CORNELIUS, Friends to Faustus.
WAGNER, Servant to FAUSTUS.
Clown.   ROBIN.   RALPH.
Vintner, Horse-Courser, Knight, Old Man,
Scholars, Friars, and Attendants.
DUCHESS OF VANHOLT.
LUCIFER.   BELZEBUB.   MEPHISTOPHILIS.
Good Angel, Evil Angel, The Seven Deadly Sins, Devils,
Spirits in the shape of ALEXANDER THE GREAT,
of his Paramour, and of HELEN OF TROY.
Chorus.]

Enter CHORUS

Chorus

NOT marching now in fields of Trasimene,
  Where Mars did mate[1] the Carthaginians;
  Nor sporting in the dalliance of love,
In courts of kings where state is overturn'd;
Nor in the pomp of proud audacious deeds,
Intends our Muse to vaunt his heavenly verse:
Only this, gentlemen,—we must perform
The form of Faustus' fortunes, good or bad.
To patient judgments we appeal our plaud,[2]
And speak for Faustus in his infancy.
Now is he born, his parents base of stock,
In Germany, within a town call'd Rhodes;[3]
Of riper years to Wittenberg he went,
Whereas his kinsmen chiefly brought him up.
So soon he profits in divinity,
The fruitful plot of scholarism grac'd,[4]
That shortly he was grac'd with doctor's name,
Excelling all those sweet delight disputes
In heavenly matters of theology;
Till swollen with cunning,[5] of a self-conceit,
His waxen wings[6] did mount above his reach,
And, melting, Heavens conspir'd his overthrow;
For, falling to a devilish exercise,
And glutted [now] with learning's golden gifts,
He surfeits upon cursed necromancy.
Nothing so sweet as magic is to him,
Which he prefers before his chiefest bliss.
And this the man that in his study sits!   [*Exit.*

Faustus [*discovered*] *in his Study*

Faust. Settle my studies, Faustus, and begin
To sound the depth of that thou wilt profess[7];
Having commenc'd, be a divine in show,
Yet level[8] and at the end of every art,
And live and die in Aristotle's works.
Sweet Analytics,[9] 'tis thou hast ravish'd me,
Bene disserere est finis logices.[10]
Is to dispute well logic's chiefest end?
Affords this art no greater miracle?
Then read no more, thou hast attain'd the end;
A greater subject fitteth Faustus' wit.
Bid ὄν καὶ μὴ ὄν[11] farewell; Galen come,
Seeing *Ubi desinit Philosophus ibi incipit Medicus;*[12]
Be a physician, Faustus, heap up gold,
And be eternis'd for some wondrous cure.
Summum bonum medicinæ sanitas,[13]
"The end of physic is our body's health."
Why, Faustus, hast thou not attain'd that end!
Is not thy common talk sound Aphorisms?[14]
Are not thy bills[15] hung up as monuments,
Whereby whole cities have escap'd the plague,
And thousand desperate maladies been eas'd?
Yet art thou still but Faustus and a man.
Couldst thou make men to live eternally,
Or, being dead, raise them to life again,
Then this profession were to be esteem'd.
Physic, farewell.—Where is Justinian?   [*Reads.*]
Si una eademque res legatur duobus, alter rem, alter valo-
   rem rei, &c.[16]
A pretty case of paltry legacies!   [*Reads.*]
Ex hæreditare filium non potest pater nisi, &c.[17]
Such is the subject of the Institute[18]
And universal Body of the Law.[19]
His[20] study fits a mercenary drudge,
Who aims at nothing but external trash;
Too servile and illiberal for me.
When all is done, divinity is best;
Jerome's Bible,[21] Faustus, view it well.   [*Reads.*]

Stipendium peccati mors est. Ha! *Stipendium, &c.*
"The reward of sin is death." That's hard.   [*Reads.*]
Si peccasse negamus fallimur et nulla est in nobis veritas.
"If we say that we have no sin we deceive ourselves, and there's
no truth in us." Why then, belike we must sin and so con-
sequently die.
Ay, we must die an everlasting death.
What doctrine call you this, *Che sera sera,*
"What will be shall be?" Divinity, adieu
These metaphysics of magicians
And necromantic books are heavenly;
Lines, circles, scenes, letters, and characters,
Ay, these are those that Faustus most desires.
O what a world of profit and delight,
Of power, of honour, of omnipotence
Is promised to the studious artisan!
All things that move between the quiet poles
Shall be at my command. Emperors and kings
Are but obeyed in their several provinces,
Nor can they raise the wind or rend the clouds;
But his dominion that exceeds[22] in this
Stretcheth as far as doth the mind of man.
A sound magician is a mighty god:
Here, Faustus, try thy[23] brains to gain a deity.
Wagner!

Enter WAGNER

Commend me to my dearest friends,
The German Valdes and Cornelius;
Request them earnestly to visit me.
  Wag. I will, sir.   *Exit.*
  Faust. Their conference will be a greater help to me
Than all my labours, plod I ne'er so fast.

Enter GOOD ANGEL *and* EVIL ANGEL

  G. Ang. O Faustus! lay that damned book aside,
And gaze not upon it lest it tempt thy soul,
And heap God's heavy wrath upon thy head.
Read, read the Scriptures: that is blasphemy.
  E. Ang. Go forward, Faustus, in that famous art,
Wherein all Nature's treasure is contain'd:
Be thou on earth as Jove is in the sky,

342

Lord and commander of these elements.   [*Exeunt* Angels.]

Faust. How am I glutted with conceit²⁴ of this!
Shall I make spirits fetch me what I please,
Resolve me of all ambiguities,
Perform what desperate enterprise I will?
I'll have them fly to India for gold,
Ransack the ocean for orient pearl,
And search all corners of the new-found world
For pleasant fruits and princely delicates;
I'll have them read me strange philosophy
And tell the secrets of all foreign kings;
I'll have them wall all Germany with brass,
And make swift Rhine circle fair Wittenberg;
I'll have them fill the public schools with silk,²⁵
Wherewith the students shall be bravely clad;
I'll levy soldiers with the coin they bring,
And chase the Prince of Parma from our land,²⁶
And reign sole king of all the provinces;
Yea, stranger engines for the brunt of war
Than was the fiery keel²⁷ at Antwerp's bridge,
I'll make my servile spirits to invent.

Enter VALDES *and* CORNELIUS²⁸

Come, German Valdes and Cornelius,
And make me blest with your sage conference.
Valdes, sweet Valdes, and Cornelius,
Know that your words have won me at the last
To practise magic and concealed arts:
Yet not your words only, but mine own fantasy
That will receive no object, for my head
But ruminates on necromantic skill.
Philosophy is odious and obscure,
Both law and physic are for petty wits;
Divinity is basest of the three,
Unpleasant, harsh, contemptible, and vile:
'Tis magic, magic, that hath ravish'd me.
Then, gentle friends, aid me in this attempt;
And I that have with concise syllogisms
Gravell'd the pastors of the German church,
And made the flowering pride of Wittenberg
Swarm to my problems, as the infernal spirits
On sweet Musæus,²⁹ when he came to hell,

Will be as cunning as Agrippa was,
Whose shadows made all Europe honour him.
    Vald. Faustus, these books, thy wit, and our experience
Shall make all nations to canònise us.
As Indian Moors[30] obey their Spanish lords,
So shall the subjects [31] of every element
Be always serviceable to us three;
Like lions shall they guard us when we please;
Like Almain rutters[32] with their horsemen's staves
Or Lapland giants, trotting by our sides;
Sometimes like women or unwedded maids,
Shadowing more beauty in their airy brows
Than have the white breasts of the queen of love:
From Venice shall they drag huge argosies,
And from America the golden fleece
That yearly stuffs old Philip's treasury;
If learned Faustus will be resolute.
    Faust. Valdes, as resolute am I in this
As thou to live; therefore object it not.
    Corn. The miracles that magic will perform
Will make thee vow to study nothing else.
He that is grounded in astrology,
Enrich'd with tongues, as well seen[33] in minerals,
Hath all the principles magic doth require.
Then doubt not, Faustus, but to be renown'd,
And more frequented for this mystery
Than heretofore the Delphian Oracle.
The spirits tell me they can dry the sea,
And fetch the treasure of all foreign wrecks,
Ay, all the wealth that our forefathers hid
Within the massy entrails of the earth;
Then tell me, Faustus, what shall we three want?
    Faust. Nothing, Cornelius! O this cheers my soul!
Come show me some demonstrations magical,
That I may conjure in some lusty grove,
And have these joys in full possession.
    Vald. Then haste thee to some solitary grove,
And bear wise Bacon's[34] and Albanus' [35] works,
The Hebrew Psalter and New Testament;
And whatsoever else is requisite
We will inform thee ere our conference cease.
    Corn. Valdes, first let him know the words of art;
And then, all other ceremonies learn'd,
Faustus may try his cunning by himself.

Vald. First I'll instruct thee in the rudiments,
And then wilt thou be perfecter than I.
   Faust. Then come and dine with me, and after meat,
We'll canvass every quiddity thereof;
For ere I sleep I'll try what I can do:
This night I'll conjure though I die therefore.   [*Exeunt.*

[SCENE II.—*Before* FAUSTUS's *House*]

Enter two SCHOLARS

   1st Schol. I wonder what's become of Faustus that was wont to
make our schools ring with *sic probo?*[1]
   2nd Schol. That shall we know, for see here comes his boy.

Enter WAGNER

   1st Schol. How now, sirrah! Where's thy master?
   Wag. God in heaven knows!
   2nd Schol. Why, dost not thou know?
   Wag. Yes, I know. But that follows not.
   1st Schol. Go to, sirrah! Leave your jesting, and tell us where
he is.
   Wag. That follows not necessary by force of argument, that you,
being licentiate, should stand upon't: therefore, acknowledge your
error and be attentive.
   2nd Schol. Why, didst thou not say thou knew'st?
   Wag. Have you any witness on't?
   1st Schol. Yes, sirrah, I heard you.
   Wag. Ask my fellow if I be a thief.
   2nd Schol. Well, you will not tell us?
   Wag. Yes, sir, I will tell you; yet if you were not dunces, you
would never ask me such a question; for is not he *corpus naturale?*[2]
and is not that *mobile?* Then wherefore should you ask me such a
question? But that I am by nature phlegmatic, slow to wrath, and
prone to lechery (to love, I would say), it were not for you to come
within forty feet of the place of execution, although I do not doubt
to see you both hang'd the next sessions. Thus having triumph'd
over you, I will set my countenance like a precisian,[3] and begin to
speak thus:—Truly, my dear brethren, my master is within at dinner, with Valdes and Cornelius, as this wine, if it could speak, would
inform your worships; and so the Lord bless you, preserve you, and
keep you, my dear brethren, my dear brethren.
   1st Schol. Nay, then, I fear he has fallen into that damned Art,
for which they two are infamous through the world.

2nd Schol. Were he a stranger, and not allied to me, yet should I grieve for him. But come, let us go and inform the Rector, and see if he by his grave counsel can reclaim him.

1st Schol. O, but I fear me nothing can reclaim him.

2nd Schol. Yet let us try what we can do.　　　　　*[Exeunt.*

[SCENE III.—*A Grove.*]
Enter FAUSTUS *to conjure*

Faust. Now that the gloomy shadow of the earth
Longing to view Orion's drizzling look,

Leaps from the antarctic world unto the sky,
And dims the welkin with her pitchy breath,
Faustus, begin thine incantations,
And try if devils will obey thy hest,
Seeing thou hast pray'd and sacrific'd to them.
Within this circle is Jehovah's name,
Forward and backward anagrammatis'd,
The breviated names of holy saints,
Figures of every adjunct to the Heavens,
And characters of signs and erring¹ stars,
By which the spirits are enforc'd to rise:
Then fear not, Faustus, but be resolute,
And try the uttermost magic can perform.

　*Sint mihi Dei Acherontis propitii! Valeat numen triplex Jehovæ!
Ignei, aerii, aquatani spiritus, salvete! Orientis princeps Belzebub,
inferni ardentis monarcha, et Demogorgon, propitiamus vos, ut ap-
pareat et surgat Mephistophilis. Quid tu moraris? per Jehovam,
Gehennam, et consecratum aquam quam nunc spargo, signumque
crucis quod nunc facio, et per vota nostra, ipse nunc surgat nobis
dicatus Mephistophilis!²*

Enter [MEPHISTOPHILIS] *a* DEVIL

I charge thee to return and change thy shape;
Thou art too ugly to attend on me.
Go, and return an old Franciscan friar;
That holy shape becomes a devil best.　　　　　*[Exit* DEVIL
I see there's virtue in my heavenly words;
Who would not be proficient in this art?
How pliant is this Mephistophilis,
Full of obedience and humility!
Such is the force of magic and my spells.
[Now,] Faustus, thou art conjuror laureat,

Thou canst command great Mephistophilis:
Quin regis Mephistophilis fratris imagine.[3]

Re-enter MEPHISTOPHILIS [*like a Franciscan* Friar]

Meph. Now, Faustus, what would'st thou have me to do?
Faust. I charge thee wait upon me whilst I live,
To do whatever Faustus shall command,
Be it to make the moon drop from her sphere,
Or the ocean to overwhelm the world.
Meph. I am a servant to great Lucifer,
And may not follow thee without his leave
No more than he commands must we perform.
Faust. Did not he charge thee to appear to me?
Meph. No, I came hither of mine own accord.
Faust. Did not my conjuring speeches raise thee? Speak.
Meph. That was the cause, but yet *per accidens;*
For when we hear one rack[4] the name of God,
Abjure the Scriptures and his Saviour Christ,
We fly in hope to get his glorious soul;
Nor will we come, unless he use such means
Whereby he is in danger to be damn'd:
Therefore the shortest cut for conjuring
Is stoutly to abjure the Trinity,
And pray devoutly to the Prince of Hell.
Faust. So Faustus hath
Already done; and holds this principle.
There is no chief but only Belzebub,
To whom Faustus doth dedicate himself.
This word "damnation" terrifies not him,
For he confounds hell in Elysium;[5]
His ghost be with the old philosophers!
But, leaving these vain trifles of men's souls,
Tell me what is that Lucifer thy lord?
Meph. Arch-regent and commander of all spirits.
Faust. Was not that Lucifer an angel once?
Meph. Yes, Faustus, and most dearly lov'd of God.
Faust. How comes it then that he is Prince of devils?
Meph. O, by aspiring pride and insolence;
For which God threw him from the face of Heaven.
Faust. And what are you that you live with Lucifer?
Meph. Unhappy spirits that fell with Lucifer,
Conspir'd against our God with Lucifer,
And are for ever damn'd with Lucifer.

Faust. Where are you damn'd?

Meph. In hell.

Faust. How comes it then that thou art out of hell?

Meph. Why this is hell, nor am I out of it.
Think'st thou that I who saw the face of God,
And tasted the eternal joys of Heaven,
Am not tormented with ten thousand hells,
In being depriv'd of everlasting bliss?
O Faustus! leave these frivolous demands,
Which strike a terror to my fainting soul.

Faust. What, is great Mephistophilis so passionate
For being depriv'd of the joys of Heaven?
Learn thou of Faustus manly fortitude,
And scorn those joys thou never shalt possess.
Go bear these tidings to great Lucifer:
Seeing Faustus hath incurr'd eternal death
By desperate thoughts against Jove's deity,
Say he surrenders up to him his soul,
So he will spare him four and twenty years,
Letting him live in all voluptuousness;
Having thee ever to attend on me;
To give me whatsoever I shall ask,
To tell me whatsoever I demand,
To slay mine enemies, and aid my friends,
And always be obedient to my will.
Go and return to mighty Lucifer,
And meet me in my study at midnight,
And then resolve[6] me of thy master's mind.

Meph. I will, Faustus.   *Exit.*

Faust. Had I as many souls as there be stars,
I'd give them all for Mephistophilis.
By him I'll be great Emperor of the world,
And make a bridge through the moving air,
To pass the ocean with a band of men:
I'll join the hills that bind the Afric shore,
And make that [country] continent to Spain,
And both contributory to my crown.
The Emperor shall not live but by my leave,
Nor any potentate of Germany.
Now that I have obtain'd what I desire,
I'll live in speculation[7] of this art
Till Mephistophilis return again.   *Exit.*

Enter WAGNER *and* CLOWN

Wag. Sirrah, boy, come hither.

Clown. How, boy! Swowns,[1] boy! I hope you have seen many boys with such pickadevaunts[2] as I have. Boy, quotha!

Wag. Tell me, sirrah, hast thou any comings in?

Clown. Ay, and goings out too. You may see else.

Wag. Alas, poor slave! See how poverty jesteth in his nakedness! The villain is bare and out of service, and so hungry that I know he would give his soul to the devil for a shoulder of mutton, though it were blood-raw.

Clown. How?· My soul to the Devil for a shoulder of mutton, though 'twere blood-raw! Not so, good friend. By'r Lady, I had need have it well roasted and good sauce to it, if I pay so dear.

Wag. Well, wilt thou serve me, and I'll make thee go like *Qui mihi discipulus?*[3]

Clown. How, in verse?

Wag. No, sirrah; in beaten silk and stavesacre.[4]

Clown. How, how, Knave's acre!· Ay, I thought that was all the land his father left him. Do you hear? I would be sorry to rob you of your living.

Wag. Sirrah, I say in stavesacre.

Clown. Oho! Oho! Stavesacre! Why, then, belike if I were your man I should be full of vermin.

Wag. So thou shalt, whether thou beest with me or no. But, sirrah, leave your jesting, and bind yourself presently unto me for seven years, or I'll turn all the lice about thee into familiars, and they shall tear thee in pieces.

Clown. Do you hear, sir? You may save that labour; they are too familiar with me already. Swowns! they are as bold with my flesh as if they had paid for [their] meat and drink.

Wag. Well, do you hear, sirrah? Hold, take these guilders.

[*Gives money.*]

Clown. Gridirons! what be they?

Wag. Why, French crowns.

Clown. Mass, but for the name of French crowns, a man were as good have as many English counters. And what should I do with these?

Wag. Why, now, sirrah, thou art at an hour's warning, whensoever and wheresoever the Devil shall fetch thee.

349

Clown. No, no. Here, take your gridirons again.

Wag. Truly I'll none of them.

Clown. Truly but you shall.

Wag. Bear witness I gave them him.

Clown. Bear witness I gave them you again.

Wag. Well, I will cause two devils presently to fetch thee away—Baliol and Belcher.

Clown. Let your Baliol and your Belcher come here, and I'll knock them, they were never so knock'd since they were devils. Say I should kill one of them, what would folks say? "Do you see yonder tall fellow in the round slop⁶—he has kill'd the devil." So I should be called Kill-devil all the parish over.

Enter two Devils: *the* Clown *runs up and down crying*

Wag. Baliol and Belcher! Spirits, away!　　　*Exeunt* Devils.

Clown. What, are they gone? A vengeance on them, they have vile long nails! There was a he-devil, and a she-devil! I'll tell you how you shall know them: all he-devils has horns, and all she-devils has clifts and cloven feet.

Wag. Well, sirrah, follow me.

Clown. But, do you hear—if I should serve you, would you teach me to raise up Banios and Belcheos?

Wag. I will teach thee to turn thyself to anything; to a dog, or a cat, or a mouse, or a rat, or anything.

Clown. How! a Christian fellow to a dog or a cat, a mouse or a rat! No, no, sir. If you turn me into anything, let it be in the likeness of a little pretty frisky flea, that I may be here and there and everywhere. Oh, I'll tickle the pretty wenches' plackets; I'll be amongst them, i' faith.

Wag. Well, sirrah, come.

Clown. But, do you hear, Wagner?

Wag. How! Baliol and Belcher!

Clown. O Lord! I pray, sir, let Banio and Belcher go sleep.

Wag. Villain—call me Master Wagner, and let thy left eye be diametarily⁷ fixed upon my right heel, with *quasi vestigias nostras insistere*.⁸　　　　　　　　　　　　　　　　　　　　　*Exit.*

Clown. God forgive me, he speaks Dutch fustian. Well, I'll follow him, I'll serve him, that's flat.　　　　　　　　　　　　*Exit.*

FAUSTUS [*discovered*] *in his Study*

Faust. Now, Faustus, must
Thou needs be damn'd, and canst thou not be sav'd:
What boots it then to think of God or Heaven?
Away with such vain fancies, and despair:
Despair in God, and trust in Belzebub.
Now go not backward: no, Faustus, be resolute.
Why waverest thou? O, something soundeth in mine ears
"Abjure this magic, turn to God again!"
Ay, and Faustus will turn to God again.
To God?—He loves thee not—
The God thou serv'st is thine own appetite,
Wherein is fix'd the love of Belzebub;
To him I'll build an altar and a church,
And offer lukewarm blood of new-born babes.

Enter GOOD ANGEL *and* EVIL ANGEL

G. Ang. Sweet Faustus, leave that execrable art.
Faust. Contrition, prayer, repentance! What of them?
G. Ang. O, they are means to bring thee unto Heaven.
E. Ang. Rather, illusions, fruits of lunacy,
That makes men foolish that do trust them most.
G. Ang. Sweet Faustus, think of Heaven, and heavenly things.
E. Ang. No, Faustus, think of honour and of wealth.
[*Exeunt* ANGELS.

Faust. Of wealth!
What the signiory of Embden¹ shall be mine.
When Mephistophilis shall stand by me,
What God can hurt thee, Faustus? Thou art safe;
Cast no more doubts. Come, Mephistophilis,
And bring glad tidings from great Lucifer;—
Is't not midnight? Come, Mephistophilis;
Veni, veni, Mephistophile!

Enter MEPHISTOPHILIS

Now tell me, what says Lucifer thy lord?
Meph. That I shall wait on Faustus whilst he lives,
So he will buy my service with his soul.

Faust. Already Faustus hath hazarded that for thee.

Meph. But, Faustus, thou must bequeath it solemnly,

And write a deed of gift with thine own blood,
For that security craves great Lucifer.
If thou deny it, I will back to hell.

Faust. Stay, Mephistophilis! and tell me what good
Will my soul do thy lord.

Meph. Enlarge his kingdom.

Faust. Is that the reason why he tempts us thus?

Meph. Solamen miseris socios habuisse doloris.[2]

Faust. Why, have you any pain that torture others?

Meph. As great as have the human souls of men.
But tell me, Faustus, shall I have thy soul?
And I will be thy slave, and wait on thee,
And give thee more than thou hast wit to ask.

Faust. Ay, Mephistophilis, I give it thee.

Meph. Then, Faustus, stab thine arm courageously.
And bind thy soul that at some certain day
Great Lucifer may claim it as his own;
And then be thou as great as Lucifer.

Faust. [*stabbing his arm.*] Lo, Mephistophilis, for love of thee,
I cut mine arm, and with my proper blood
Assure my soul to be great Lucifer's,
Chief lord and regent of perpetual night!
View here the blood that trickles from mine arm.
And let it be propitious for my wish.

Meph. But, Faustus, thou must
Write it in manner of a deed of gift.

Faust. Ay, so I .will. [*Writes.*] But, Mephistophilis,
My blood congeals, and I can write no more.

Meph. I'll fetch thee fire to dissolve it straight.   *Exit.*

Faust. What might the staying of my blood portend?
Is it unwilling I should write this bill?
Why streams it not that I may write afresh?
Faustus gives to thee his soul. Ah, there it stay'd.
Why should'st thou not? Is not thy soul thine own?
Then write again, *Faustus gives to thee his soul.*

Re-enter MEPHISTOPHILIS *with a chafer of coals*

Meph. Here's fire. Come, Faustus, set it on.

Faust. So now the blood begins to clear again;
Now will I make an end immediately.   [*Writes.*]

   Meph. O what will not I do to obtain his soul.   [*Aside.*]

   Faust. *Consummatum est:*[3] this bill is ended,
And Faustus hath bequeath'd his soul to Lucifer—
But what is this inscription on mine arm?
Homo, fuge![4] Whither should I fly?
If unto God, he'll throw me down to hell.
My senses are deceiv'd; here's nothing writ:—
I see it plain; here in this place is writ
Homo, fuge! Yet shall not Faustus fly.

   Meph. I'll fetch him somewhat to delight his mind.   [*Exit.*

Re-enter [MEPHISTOPHILIS] *with* Devils, *giving crowns and rich
apparel to* FAUSTUS, *dance, and depart*

Faust. Speak, Mephistophilis, what means this show?

   Meph. Nothing, Faustus, but to delight thy mind withal,
And to show thee what magic can perform.

   Faust. But may I raise up spirits when I please?

   Meph. Ay, Faustus, and do greater things than these.

   Faust. Then there's enough for a thousand souls.
Here, Mephistophilis, receive this scroll,
A deed of gift of body and of soul:
But yet conditionally that thou perform
All articles prescrib'd between us both.

   Meph. Faustus, I swear by hell and Lucifer
To effect all promises between us made.

   Faust. Then hear me read them: *On these conditions following:
First, that Faustus may be a spirit in form and substance. Secondly,
that Mephistophilis shall be his servant, and at his command.
Thirdly, that Mephistophilis shall do for him and bring him whatsoever* [*he desires*]. *Fourthly, that he shall be in his chamber or
house invisible. Lastly, that he shall appear to the said John Faustus,
at all times, and in what form or shape soever he pleases. I, John
Faustus, of Wittenberg, Doctor, by these presents do give both body
and soul to Lucifer, Prince of the East, and his minister, Mephis-*

tophilis; and furthermore grant unto them, that twenty-four years being expired, the articles above written inviolate, full power to fetch or carry the said John Faustus, body and soul, flesh, blood, or goods, into their habitation wheresoever. By me,   *John Faustus.*

Meph. Speak, Faustus, do you deliver this as your deed?

Faust. Ay, take it, and the Devil give thee good on't.

Meph. Now, Faustus, ask what thou wilt.

Faust. First will I question with thee about hell.
Tell me where is the place that men call hell?

Meph. Under the Heaven.

Faust. Ay, but whereabout?

Meph. Within the bowels of these elements,
Where we are tortur'd and remain for ever;
Hell hath no limits, nor is circumscrib'd
In one self place; for where we are is hell,
And where hell is there must we ever be:
And, to conclude, when all the world dissolves,
And every creature shall be purified,
All places shall be hell that is not Heaven.

Faust. Come, I think hell's a fable.

Meph. Ay, think so still, till experience change thy mind.

Faust. Why, think'st thou then that Faustus shall be damn'd?

Meph. Ay, of necessity, for here's the scroll
Wherein thou hast given thy soul to Lucifer.

Faust. Ay, and body too; but what of that?
Think'st thou that Faustus is so fond[5] to imagine
That, after this life, there is any pain?
Tush; these are trifles, and mere old wives' tales.

Meph. But, Faustus, I am an instance to prove the contrary,
For I am damned, and am now in hell.

Faust. How! now in hell!
Nay, an this be hell, I'll willingly be damn'd here;

What? walking, disputing, &c.?
But, leaving off this, let me have a wife,
The fairest maid in Germany;
For I am wanton and lascivious,
And cannot live without a wife.

Meph. How—a wife?
I prithee, Faustus, talk not of a wife.

354

Faust. Nay, sweet Mephistophilis, fetch me one, for I will have one.

Meph. Well—thou wilt have one. Sit there till I come:
I'll fetch thee a wife in the Devil's name.   [*Exit.*]

Re-enter MEPHISTOPHILIS *with a* DEVIL *dressed like a woman, with
fireworks*

Meph. Tell me, Faustus, how dost thou like thy wife?

Faust. A plague on her for a hot whore!

Meph. Tut, Faustus,
Marriage is but a ceremonial toy;
And if thou lovest me, think no more of it.
I'll cull thee out the fairest courtesans,
And bring them every morning to thy bed;
She whom thine eye shall like, thy heart shall have,
Be she as chaste as was Penelope,
As wise as Saba,[6] or as beautiful
As was bright Lucifer before his fall.
Here, take this book, peruse it thoroughly: [*Gives a book.*]
The iterating[7] of these lines brings gold;
The framing of this circle on the ground
Brings whirlwinds, tempests, thunder and lightning;
Pronounce this thrice devoutly to thyself,
And men in armour shall appear to thee,
Ready to execute what thou desir'st.

Faust. Thanks, Mephistophilis; yet fain would I have a book
wherein I might behold all spells and incantations, that I might raise
up spirits when I please.

Meph. Here they are, in this book.   *Turns to them.*

Faust. Now would I have a book where I might see all characters

and planets of the heavens, that I might know their motions and
dispositions.

Meph. Here they are too.   *Turns to them.*

Faust. Nay, let me have one book more,—and then I have done,—
wherein I might see all plants, herbs, and trees that grow upon the
earth.

Meph. Here they be.

Faust. O, thou art deceived.

Meph. Tut, I warrant thee.   *Turns to them. Exeunt.*

[SCENE VI.—*The Same.*]

Enter FAUSTUS *and* MEPHISTOPHILIS

Faust. When I behold the heavens, then I repent,
And curse thee, wicked Mephistophilis,
Because thou hast depriv'd me of those joys.

Meph. Why, Faustus,
Thinkest thou Heaven is such a glorious thing?
I tell thee 'tis not half so fair as thou,
Or any man that breathes on earth.

Faust. How provest thou that?

Meph. 'Twas made for man, therefore is man more excellent.

Faust. If it were made for man, 'twas made for me:
I will renounce this magic and repent.

Enter GOOD ANGEL *and* EVIL ANGEL

G. Ang. Faustus, repent; yet God will pity thee.

E. Ang. Thou art a spirit; God can not pity thee.

Faust. Who buzzeth in mine ears I am a spirit?
Be I a devil, yet God may pity me;
Ay, God will pity me if I repent.

E. Ang. Ay, but Faustus never shall repent.   *Exeunt ANGELS.*

Faust. My heart's so hard'ned I cannot repent.
Scarce can I name salvation, faith, or heaven,
But fearful echoes thunder in mine ears
"Faustus, thou art damn'd!" Then swords and knives,
Poison, gun, halters, and envenom'd steel

Are laid before me to despatch myself,
And long ere this I should have slain myself,
Had not sweet pleasure conquer'd deep despair.
Have I not made blind Homer sing to me
Of Alexander's love and Œnon's death?
And hath not he that built the walls of Thebes
With ravishing sound of his melodious harp,
Made music with my Mephistophilis?
Why should I die then, or basely despair?
I am resolv'd: Faustus shall ne'er repent.
Come, Mephistophilis, let us dispute again,
And argue of divine astrology.
Tell me, are there many heavens above the moon?
Are all celestial bodies but one globe,
As is the substance of this centric earth?

Meph. As are the elements, such are the spheres
Mutually folded in each other's orb,
And, Faustus,
All jointly move upon one axletree
Whose terminine is termed the world's wide pole;
Nor are the names of Saturn, Mars, or Jupiter
Feign'd, but are erring stars.

Faust. But tell me, have they all one motion, both *situ et tempore?*[1]

Meph. All jointly move from east to west in twenty-four hours upon the poles of the world; but differ in their motion upon the poles of the zodiac.

Faust. Tush!
These slender trifles Wagner can decide;
Hath Mephistophilis no greater skill?
Who knows not the double motion of the planets?
The first is finish'd in a natural day;
The second thus: as Saturn in thirty years; Jupiter in twelve; Mars in four; the Sun, Venus, and Mercury in a year; the moon in twenty-eight days. Tush, these are freshmen's suppositions. But tell me, hath every sphere a dominion or *intelligentia?*

Meph. Ay.

Faust. How many heavens, or spheres, are there?

Meph. Nine: the seven planets, the firmament, and the empyreal heaven.

Faust. Well, resolve me in this question: Why have we not conjunctions, oppositions, aspects, eclipses, all at one time, but in some years we have more, in some less?

Meph. Per inæqualem motum respectu totius.[2]

Faust. Well, I am answered. Tell me who made the world.

Meph. I will not.

Faust. Sweet Mephistophilis, tell me.

Meph. Move me not, for I will not tell thee.

Faust. Villain, have I not bound thee to tell me anything?

Meph. Ay, that is not against our kingdom; but this is.
Think thou on hell, Faustus, for thou art damn'd.

Faust. Think, Faustus, upon God that made the world.

Meph. Remember this.

Faust. Ay, go, accursed spirit, to ugly hell.
'Tis thou hast damn'd distressed Faustus' soul.
Is't not too late?

Re-enter GOOD ANGEL *and* EVIL ANGEL.

E. Ang. Too late.

G. Ang. Never too late, if Faustus can repent.

E. Ang. If thou repent, devils shall tear thee in pieces.

G. Ang. Repent, and they shall never raze thy skin.

[*Exeunt* ANGELS.]

Faust. Ah, Christ, my Saviour,
Seek to save distressed Faustus' soul.

Enter LUCIFER, BELZEBUB, *and* MEPHISTOPHILIS.

Luc. Christ cannot save thy soul, for he is just;
There's none but I have interest in the same.

Faust. O, who art thou that look'st so terrible?

Luc. I am Lucifer,
And this is my companion-prince in hell.

Faust. O Faustus! they are come to fetch away thy soul!

Luc. We come to tell thee thou dost injure us;
Thou talk'st of Christ contrary to thy promise;
Thou should'st not think of God: think of the Devil,
And of his dam, too.

Faust. Nor will I henceforth: pardon me in this,
And Faustus vows never to look to Heaven,
Never to name God, or to pray to him,
To burn his Scriptures, slay his ministers,
And make my spirits pull his churches down.

Luc. Do so, and we will highly gratify thee. Faustus, we are come from hell to show thee some pastime. Sit down, and thou shalt see all the Seven Deadly Sins appear in their proper shapes.

Faust. That sight will be as pleasing unto me,
As Paradise was to Adam the first day
Of his creation.

Luc. Talk not of Paradise nor creation, but mark this show: talk of the Devil, and nothing else.—Come away!

Enter the SEVEN DEADLY SINS.

Now, Faustus, examine them of their several names and dispositions.

Faust. What art thou—the first?

Pride. I am Pride. I disdain to have any parents. I am like to Ovid's flea: I can creep into every corner of a wench; sometimes, like a periwig, I sit upon her brow; or like a fan of feathers, I kiss her lips; indeed I do—what do I not? But, fie, what a scent is here! I'll not speak another word, except the ground were perfum'd, and covered with cloth of arras.

Faust. What art thou—the second?

Covet. I am Covetousness, begotten of an old churl in an old leathern bag: and might I have my wish I would desire that this house and all the people in it were turn'd to gold, that I might lock you up in my good chest. O, my sweet gold!

Faust. What art thou—the third?

Wrath. I am Wrath. I had neither father nor mother: I leapt out of a lion's mouth when I was scarce half an hour old; and ever since I have run up and down the world with this case² of rapiers, wounding myself when I had nobody to fight withal. I was born in hell; and look to it, for some of you shall be my father.

Faust. What art thou—the fourth?

Envy. I am Envy, begotten of a chimney sweeper and an oyster-wife. I cannot read, and therefore wish all books were burnt. I am lean with seeing others eat. O that there would come a famine through all the world, that all might die, and I live alone! then thou should'st see how fat I would be. But must thou sit and I stand! Come down with a vengeance!

Faust. Away, envious rascal! What art thou—the fifth?

Glut. Who, I, sir? I am Gluttony. My parents are all dead, and the devil a penny they have left me, but a bare pension, and that is thirty meals a day and ten bevers⁴—a small trifle to suffice nature. O, I come of a royal parentage! My grandfather was a Gammon of Bacon, my grandmother a Hogshead of Claret-wine; my godfathers were these, Peter Pickleherring, and Martin Martlemas-beef.⁵ O, but my godmother, she was a jolly gentlewoman, and well beloved in every good town and city; her name was Mistress Margery March-beer. Now, Faustus, thou hast heard all my progeny, wilt thou bid me to supper?

Faust. No, I'll see thee hanged: thou wilt eat up all my victuals.

Glut. Then the Devil choke thee!

Faust. Choke thyself, glutton! Who art thou—the sixth?

Sloth. I am Sloth. I was begotten on a sunny bank, where I have lain ever since; and you have done me great injury to bring me from thence: let me.be carried thither again by Gluttony and **Lechery**. I'll not speak another word for a king's ransom.

Faust. What are you, Mistress Minx, the seventh and last?

Lech. Who, I, sir? I am one that loves an inch of raw mutton better than an ell of fried stockfish; and the first letter of my name begins with Lechery.

Luc. Away to hell, to hell!—Now, Faustus, how dost thou like this?   [*Exeunt the* SINS.

Faust. O, this feeds my soul!

Luc. Tut, Faustus, in hell is all manner of delight.

Faust. O might I see hell, and return again,
How happy were I then!

Luc. Thou shalt; I will send for thee at midnight.
In meantime take this book; peruse it throughly,
And thou shalt turn thyself into what shape thou wilt.

Faust. Great thanks, mighty Lucifer!
This will I keep as chary as my life.

Luc. Farewell, Faustus, and think on the Devil.

Faust. Farewell, great Lucifer! Come, Mephistophilis.   [*Exeunt.*

Enter CHORUS

Chorus. Learned Faustus,
To know the secrets of astronomy,
Graven in the book of Jove's high firmament,
Did mount himself to scale Olympus' top,
Being seated in a chariot burning bright,
Drawn by the strength of yoky dragons' necks.
He now is gone to prove cosmography,
And, as I guess, will first arrive at Rome,
To see the Pope and manner of his court,
And take some part of holy Peter's feast,
That to this day is highly solemnis'd.   [*Exit.*

[SCENE VII.—*The Pope's Privy-chamber.*]

Enter FAUSTUS *and* MEPHISTOPHILIS

Faust. Having now, my good Mephistophilis,
Passed with delight the stately town of Trier,[1]
Environ'd round with airy mountain-tops,
With walls of flint, and deep entrenched lakes,
Not to be won by any conquering prince;
From Paris next, coasting the realm of France,
We saw the river Maine fall into Rhine,
Whose banks are set with groves of fruitful vines;

Then up to Naples, rich Campania,
Whose buildings fair and gorgeous to the eye,
The streets straight forth, and pav'd with finest brick,
Quarter the town in four equivalents.
There saw we learned Maro's[2] golden tomb,
The way he cut, an English mile in length,
Thorough a rock of stone in one night's space;
From thence to Venice, Padua, and the rest,
In one of which a sumptuous temple stands,
That threats the stars with her aspiring top.
Thus hitherto has Faustus spent his time:
But tell me, now, what resting-place is this?
Hast thou, as erst I did command,
Conducted me within the walls of Rome?
    Meph. Faustus, I have; and because we will not be unprovided, I
have taken up his Holiness' privy-chamber for our use.
    Faust. I hope his Holiness will bid us welcome.
    Meph. Tut, 'tis no matter, man, we'll be bold with his good cheer.
And now, my Faustus, that thou may'st perceive
What Rome containeth to delight thee with,
Know that this city stands upon seven hills
That underprop the groundwork of the same.
[Just through the midst runs flowing Tiber's stream,
With winding banks that cut it in two parts:]
Over the which four stately bridges lean,
That make safe passage to each part of Rome:
Upon the bridge called Ponte-Angelo
Erected is a castle passing strong,
Within whose walls such store of ordnance are,
And double cannons fram'd of carved brass,
As match the days within one còmplete year;
Besides the gates and high pyramides,
Which Julius Cæsar brought from Africa.
    Faust. Now by the kingdoms of infernal rule,
Of Styx, of Acheron, and the fiery lake

Of ever-burning Phlegethon, I swear
That I do long to see the monuments
And situation of bright-splendent Rome:
Come therefore, let's away.

    Meph. Nay, Faustus, stay; I know you'd see the Pope,
And take some part of holy Peter's feast,
Where thou shalt see a troop of bald-pate friars,
Whose *summum bonum* is in belly-cheer.

    Faust. Well, I'm content to compass then some sport,
And by their folly make us merriment.
Then charm me, [Mephistophilis,] that I
May be invisible, to do what I please
Unseen of any whilst I stay in Rome.

                  [MEPHISTOPHILIS *charms him.*]

    Meph. So, Faustus, now
Do what thou wilt, thou shalt not be discern'd.

Sound a sennett.[3] *Enter the* POPE *and the* CARDINAL *of* LORRAIN *to
the banquet, with* FRIARS *attending*

    Pope. My Lord of Lorrain, wilt please you draw near?

    Faust. Fall to, and the devil choke you an[4] you spare!

    Pope. How now! Who's that which spake?—Friars, look about.

    First Friar. Here's nobody, if it like your Holiness.

    Pope. My lord, here is a dainty dish was sent me from the Bishop
of Milan.

    Faust. I thank you, sir.   [*Snatches the dish.*]

    Pope. How now! Who's that which snatched the meat from me?
Will no man look? My lord, this dish was sent me from the Cardinal
of Florence.

    Faust. You say true; I'll ha't.   [*Snatches the dish.*]

    Pope. What, again! My lord, I'll drink to your Grace.

    Faust. I'll pledge your Grace.   [*Snatches the cup.*]

    C. of Lor. My lord, it may be some ghost newly crept out of
purgatory, come to beg a pardon of your Holiness.

Pope. It may be so. Friars, prepare a dirge to lay the fury of this ghost. Once again, my lord, fall to.

> *The* POPE *crosses himself.*

Faust. What, are you crossing of yourself?
Well, use that trick no more I would advise you.

> *The* POPE *crosses himself again.*

Well, there's the second time. Aware the third,
I give you fair warning.

> *The* POPE *crosses himself again, and* FAUSTUS *hits him a box 'f the ear; and they all run away.*

Come on, Mephistophilis, what shall we do?

Meph. Nay, I know not. We shall be curs'd with bell, book, and candle.

Faust. How! bell, book, and candle,—candle, book, and bell,
Forward and backward to curse Faustus to hell!
Anon you shall hear a hog grunt, a calf bleat, and an ass bray,
Because it is Saint Peter's holiday.

> *Re-enter all the* FRIARS *to sing the Dirge*

1st. Friar. Come, brethren, let's about our business with good devotion.

> *They sing:*

Cursed be he that stole away his Holiness' meat from the table! *Maledicat Dominus!*[5]
Cursed be he that struck his Holiness a blow on the face! *Maledicat Dominus!*
Cursed be he that took Friar Sandelo a blow on the pate! *Maledicat Dominus!*
Cursed be he that disturbeth our holy dirge! *Maledicat Dominus!*
Cursed be he that took away his Holiness' wine! *Maledicat Dominus! Et omnes sancti!*[6] *Amen!*

> [MEPHISTOPHILIS *and* FAUSTUS *beat the* FRIARS, *and fling fireworks among them: and so exeunt.*

Enter CHORUS

Chorus. When Faustus had with pleasure ta'en the view
Of rarest things, and royal courts of kings,
He stay'd his course, and so returned home;
Where such as bear his absence but with grief,
I mean his friends, and near'st companions,
Did gratulate his safety with kind words,
And in their conference of what befell,
Touching his journey through the world and air,
They put forth questions of Astrology,
Which Faustus answer'd with such learned skill,
As they admir'd and wond'red at his wit.
Now is his fame spread forth in every land;
Amongst the rest the Emperor is one,
Carolus the Fifth, at whose palace now
Faustus is feasted 'mongst his noblemen.
What there he did in trial of his art,
I leave untold—your eyes shall see perform'd.　　　　　*[Exit.]*

[SCENE VIII.—*An Inn-yard.*]

Enter ROBIN *the Ostler with a book in his hand*

Robin. O, this is admirable! here I ha' stolen one of Dr. Faustus's conjuring books, and i' faith I mean to search some circles for my own use. Now will I make all the maidens in our parish dance at my pleasure, stark naked before me; and so by that means I shall see more than e'er I felt or saw yet.

Enter RALPH *calling* ROBIN

Ralph. Robin, prithee come away; there's a gentleman tarries to have his horse, and he would have his things rubb'd and made clean. He keeps such a chafing with my mistress about it; and she has sent me to look thee out; prithee come away.

Robin. Keep out, keep out, or else you are blown up; you are dismemb'red, Ralph: keep out, for I am about a roaring piece of work.

365

Ralph. Come, what dost thou with that same book? Thou canst not read.

Robin. Yes, my master and mistress shall find that I can read, he for his forehead, she for her private study; she's born to bear with me, or else my art fails.

Ralph. Why, Robin, what book is that?

Robin. What book! Why, the most intolerable book for conjuring that e'er was invented by any brimstone devil.

Ralph. Canst thou conjure with it?

Robin. I can do all these things easily with it: first, I can make thee drunk with ippocras[1] at any tabern[2] in Europe for nothing; that's one of my conjuring works.

Ralph. Our Master Parson says that's nothing.

Robin. True, Ralph; and more, Ralph, if thou hast any mind to Nan Spit, our kitchenmaid, then turn her and wind her to thy own use as often as thou wilt, and at midnight.

Ralph. O brave Robin, shall I have Nan Spit, and to mine own use? On that condition I'll feed thy devil with horsebread as long as he lives, of free cost.

Robin. No more, sweet Ralph: let's go and make clean our boots, which lie foul upon our hands, and then to our conjuring in the Devil's name. *Exeunt.*

[Scene IX.—*An Inn.*]

Enter Robin *and* Ralph *with a silver goblet.*

Robin. Come, Ralph, did not I tell thee we were for ever made by this Doctor .Faustus' book? *Ecce signum,*[3] here's a simple purchase[4] for horsekeepers; our horses shall eat no hay as long as this lasts.

Enter the Vintner

Ralph. But, Robin, here come the vintner.

Robin. Hush! I'll gull him supernaturally. Drawer, I hope all is paid: God be with you. Come, Ralph.

Vint. Soft, sir; a word with you. I must yet have a goblet paid from you, ere you go.

Robin. I, a goblet, Ralph; I, a goblet! I scorn you, and you are but a,⁵ &c. I, a goblet! search me.

Vint. I mean so, sir, with your favour.   [*Searches him.*]

Robin. How say you now?

Vint. I must say somewhat to your fellow. You, sir!

Ralph. Me, sir! me, sir! search your fill. [VINTNER *searches him.*] Now, sir, you may be ashamed to burden honest men with a matter of truth.

Vint. Well, t'one of you hath this goblet about you.

Robin. You lie, drawer, 'tis afore me. [*Aside.*] Sirrah you, I'll teach ye to impeach honest men;—stand by;—I'll scour you for a goblet!—stand aside you had best, I charge you in the name of Belzebub. Look to the goblet, Ralph.   [*Aside to* RALPH.]

Vint. What mean you, sirrah?

Robin. I'll tell you what I mean.   *Reads* [*from a book.*]
Sanctobulorum. Periphrasticon—Nay, I'll tickle you, vintner. Look to the goblet, Ralph.   [*Aside to* RALPH.]
Polypragmos Belseborams framanto pacostiphos tostu, Mephistophilis, &c.   [*Reads.*

Enter MEPHISTOPHILIS, *sets squibs at their backs,* [*and then exit*].
They run about

Vint. O *nomine Domini!*⁶ what meanest thou, Robin? Thou hast no goblet.

*Ralph. Peccatum peccatorum!*⁷ Here's thy goblet, good vintner.
               [*Gives the goblet to* VINTNER, *who exit.*]

*Robin. Misericordia pro nobis!*⁸ What shall I do? Good Devil, forgive me now, and I'll never rob thy library more.

Re-enter MEPHISTOPHILIS

Meph. Monarch of hell, under whose black survey
Great potentates do kneel with awful fear,
Upon whose altars thousand souls do lie,
How am I vexed with these villains' charms?

From Constantinople am I hither come
Only for pleasure of these damned slaves.
    Robin. How from Constantinople? You have had a great journey.
Will you take sixpence in your purse to pay for your supper, and
begone?
    Meph. Well, villains, for your presumption, I transform thee into
an ape, and thee into a dog; and so begone.   [*Exit.*
    Robin. How, into an ape? That's brave! I'll have fine sport with
the boys. I'll get nuts and apples enow.
    Ralph. And I must be a dog.
    Robin. I'faith thy head will never be out of the pottage pot.
                                  Exeunt.

[SCENE X.—*The Court of the Emperor.*]

Enter EMPEROR, FAUSTUS, *and a* KNIGHT *with attendants*

    Emp. Master Doctor Faustus, I have heard strange report of thy
knowledge in the black art, how that none in my empire nor in the
whole world can compare with thee for the rare effects of magic;
they say thou hast a familiar spirit, by whom thou canst accomplish
what thou list. This therefore is my request, that thou let me see
some proof of thy skill, that mine eyes may be witnesses to confirm
what mine ears have heard reported; and here I swear to thee by the
honour of mine imperial crown, that, whatever thou doest, thou
shalt be no ways prejudiced or endamaged.
    Knight. I'faith he looks much like a conjuror.   *Aside.*
    Faust. My gracious sovereign, though I must confess myself far
inferior to the report men have published, and nothing answerable[1]
to the honour of your imperial majesty, yet for that love and duty
binds me thereunto, I am content to do whatsoever your majesty
shall command me.
    Emp. Then, Doctor Faustus, mark what I shall say.
As I was sometime solitary set
Within my closet, sundry thoughts arose
About the honour of mine ancestors,
How they had won by prowess such exploits,

Got such riches, subdued so many kingdoms
As we that do succeed, or they that shall
Hereafter possess our throne, shall
(I fear me) ne'er attain to that degree
Of high renown and great authority;
Amongst which kings is Alexander the Great,
Chief spectacle of the world's pre-eminence,
The bright shining of whose glorious acts
Lightens the world with his² reflecting beams,
As when I heard but motion³ made of him
It grieves my soul I never saw the man.
If therefore thou by cunning of thine art
Canst raise this man from hollow vaults below,
Where lies entomb'd this famous conqueror,
And bring with him his beauteous paramour,
Both in their right shapes, gesture, and attire
They us'd to wear during their time of life,
Thou shalt both satisfy my just desire,
And give me cause to praise thee whilst I live.

Faust. My gracious lord, I am ready to accomplish your request
so far forth as by art, and power of my Spirit, I am able to perform.

Knight. I'faith that's just nothing at all.   *Aside.*

Faust. But, if it like your Grace, it is not in my ability to present
before your eyes the true substantial bodies of those two deceased
princes, which long since are consumed to dust.

Knight. Ay, marry, Master Doctor, now there's a sign of grace
in you, when you will confess the truth.   *Aside.*

Faust. But such spirits as can lively resemble Alexander and his
paramour shall appear before your Grace in that manner that they
[best] lived in, in their most flourishing estate; which I doubt not
shall sufficiently content your imperial majesty.

Emp. Go to, Master Doctor, let me see them presently.

Knight. Do you hear, Master Doctor? You bring Alexander and
his paramour before the Emperor!

Faust. How then, sir?

Knight. I'faith that's as true as Diana turn'd me to a stag!

CHRISTOPHER MARLOWE

Faust. No, sir, but when Actæon died, he left the horns for you. Mephistophilis, begone. **Exit Mephisto.**

Knight. Nay, an you go to conjuring, I'll begone. **Exit.**

Faust. I'll meet with you anon for interrupting me so. Here they are, my gracious lord.

Re-enter Mephistophilis *with* [Spirits *in the shape of*] Alexander *and his* Paramour

Emp. Master Doctor, I heard this lady while she liv'd had a wart or mole in her neck: how shall I know whether it be so or no?

Faust. Your Highness may boldly go and see.

Emp. Sure these are no spirits, but the true substantial bodies of those two deceased princes. [*Exeunt* Spirits.]

Faust. Will't please your Highness now to send for the knight that was so pleasant with me here of late?

Emp. One of you call him forth. [*Exit* Attendant.]

Re-enter the Knight *with a pair of horns on his head*

How now, sir knight! why I had thought thou had'st been a bachelor, but now I see thou hast a wife, that not only gives thee horns, but makes thee wear them. Feel on thy head.

Knight. Thou damned wretch and execrable dog,
Bred in the concave of some monstrous rock,
How darest thou thus abuse a gentleman?
Villain, I say, undo what thou hast done!

Faust. O, not so fast, sir; there's no haste; but, good, are you re-memb'red how you crossed me in my conference with the Emperor? I think I have met with you for it.

Emp. Good Master Doctor, at my entreaty release him; he hath done penance sufficient.

Faust. My gracious lord, not so much for the injury he off'red me here in your presence, as to delight you with some mirth, hath Faustus worthily requited this injurious knight; which, being all I desire, I am content to release him of his horns: and, sir knight, hereafter speak well of scholars. Mephistophilis, transform him straight. [Mephistophilis *removes the horns*.] Now, my good lord, having done my duty I humbly take my leave.

370

Emp. Farewell, Master Doctor; yet, ere you go,
Expect from me a bounteous reward.   [*Exeunt.*

[SCENE XI.—*A Green; afterwards the House of Faustus.*]

[*Enter* FAUSTUS *and* MEPHISTOPHILIS]

Faust. Now, Mephistophilis, the restless course
That Time doth run with calm and silent foot,
Short'ning my days and thread of vital life,
Calls for the payment of my latest years;
Therefore, sweet Mephistophilis, let us
Make haste to Wittenberg.

Meph. What, will you go on horseback or on foot?

Faust. Nay, till I'm past this fair and pleasant green, I'll walk
on foot.

Enter a HORSE-COURSER

Horse-C. I have been all this day seeking one Master Fustian:
mass, see where he is! God save you, Master Doctor!

Faust. What, horse-courser! You are well met.

Horse-C. Do you hear, sir? I have brought you forty dollars for
your horse.

Faust. I cannot sell him so: if thou likest him for fifty take him.

Horse-C. Alas, sir, I have no more.—I pray you speak for me.

Meph. I pray you let him have him: he is an honest fellow, and
he has a great charge, neither wife nor child.

Faust. Well, come, give me your money. [HORSE-COURSER *gives*
FAUSTUS *the money.*] My boy will deliver him to you. But I must
tell you one thing before you have him; ride him not into the water
at any hand.

Horse-C. Why, sir, will he not drink of all waters?

Faust. O yes, he will drink of all waters, but ride him not into the
water: ride him over hedge or ditch, or where thou wilt, but not
into the water.

Horse-C. Well, sir.—Now I am made man for ever. I'll not leave
my horse for forty. If he had but the quality of hey-ding-ding, hey-
ding-ding, I'd made a brave living on him: he has a buttock as slick

as an eel. [*Aside.*] Well, God b' wi' ye, sir, your boy will deliver him me: but hark you, sir; if my horse be sick or ill at ease, if I bring his water to you, you'll tell me what it is.

Faust. Away, you villain; what, dost think I am a horse-doctor?
Exit HORSE-COURSER.

What art thou, Faustus, but a man condemn'd to die?
Thy fatal time doth draw to final end;
Despair doth drive distrust unto my thoughts:
Confound these passions with a quiet sleep:
Tush, Christ did call the thief upon the cross;
Then rest thee, Faustus, quiet in conceit. *Sleeps in his chair.*

Re-enter HORSE-COURSER, *all wet, crying*

Horse-C. Alas, alas! Doctor Fustian quotha? Mass, Doctor Lopus[1] was never such a doctor. Has given me a purgation has purg'd me of forty dollars; I shall never see them more. But yet, like an ass as I was, I would not be ruled by him, for he bade me I should ride him into no water. Now I, thinking my horse had had some rare quality that he would not have had me known of, I, like a venturous youth, rid him into the deep pond at the town's end. I was no sooner in the middle of the pond, but my horse vanished away, and I sat upon a bottle of hay, never so near drowning in my life. But I'll seek out my Doctor, and have my forty dollars again, or I'll make it the dearest horse!—O, yonder is his snipper-snapper.—Do you hear? You hey-pass,[2] where's your master?

Meph. Why, sir, what would you? You cannot speak with him.

Horse-C. But I will speak with him.

Meph. Why, he's fast asleep. Come some other time.

Horse-C. I'll speak with him now, or I'll break his glass windows about his ears.

Meph. I tell thee he has not slept this eight nights.

Horse-C. An he have not slept this eight weeks, I'll speak with him.

Meph. See where he is, fast asleep.

Horse-C. Ay, this is he. God save you, Master Doctor! Master Doctor, Master Doctor Fustian!—Forty dollars, forty dollars for a bottle of hay!

Meph. Why, thou seest he hears thee not.

Horse-C. So ho, ho!—so ho, ho!   (*Hollas in his ear.*) No, will you not wake? I'll make you wake ere I go. (*Pulls* FAUSTUS *by the leg, and pulls it away.*) Alas, I am undone! What shall I do?

Faust. O my leg, my leg! Help, Mephistophilis! call the officers. My leg, my leg!

Meph. Come, villain, to the constable.

Horse-C. O lord, sir, let me go, and I'll give you forty dollars more.

Meph. Where be they?

Horse-C. I have none about me. Come to my ostry³ and I'll give them you.

Meph. Begone quickly.   HORSE-COURSER *runs away.*

Faust. What, is he gone? Farewell he! Faustus has his leg again, and the horse-courser, I take it, a bottle of hay for his labour. Well, this trick shall cost him forty dollars more.

Enter WAGNER

How now, Wagner, what's the news with thee?

Wag. Sir, the Duke of Vanholt doth earnestly entreat your company.

Faust. The Duke of Vanholt! an honourable gentleman, to whom I must be no niggard of my cunning. Come, Mephistophilis, let's away to him.   *Exeunt.*

[SCENE XII.—*The Court of the Duke of Vanholt.*]

Enter the DUKE [*of* VANHOLT], *the* DUCHESS, FAUSTUS, *and* MEPHISTOPHILIS

Duke. Believe me, Master Doctor, this merriment hath much pleased me.

Faust. My gracious lord, I am glad it contents you so well.—But it may be, madam, you take no delight in this. I have heard that great-bellied women do long for some dainties or other. What is it, madam? Tell me, and you shall have it.

Duchess. Thanks, good Master Doctor; and for I see your courteous intent to pleasure me, I will not hide from you the thing my heart desires; and were it now summer, as it is January and the dead time of the winter, I would desire no better meat than a dish of ripe grapes.

Faust. Alas, madam, that's nothing! Mephistophilis, begone. (*Exit* MEPHISTOPHILIS.) Were it a greater thing than this, so it would content you, you should have it.

Re-enter MEPHISTOPHILIS *with the grapes:*

Here they be, madam; wilt please you taste on them?

Duke. Believe me, Master Doctor, this makes me wonder above the rest, that being in the dead time of winter, and in the month of January, how you should come by these grapes.

Faust. If it like your Grace, the year is divided into two circles over the whole world, that, when it is here winter with us, in the contrary circle it is summer with them, as in India, Saba, and farther countries in the East; and by means of a swift spirit that I have I had them brought hither, as ye see.—How do you like them, madam; be they good?

Duchess. Believe me, Master Doctor, they be the best grapes that I e'er tasted in my life before.

Faust. I am glad they content you so, madam.

Duke. Come, madam, let us in, where you must well reward this learned man for the great kindness he hath show'd to you.

Duchess. And so I will, my lord; and, whilst I live, rest beholding for this courtesy.

Faust. I humbly thank your Grace.

Duke. Come, Master Doctor, follow us and receive your reward.

[*Exeunt.*

DR. FAUSTUS

[Scene XIII.—*A room in Faustus's House.*]

Enter WAGNER

Wag. I think my master shortly means to die,
For he hath given to me all his goods;
And yet, methinks, if that death were so near,
He would not banquet and carouse and swill
Amongst the students, as even now he doth,
Who are at supper with such belly-cheer
As Wagner ne'er beheld in all his life.
See where they come! Belike the feast is ended.

Enter FAUSTUS, *with two or three* SCHOLARS [*and*
MEPHISTOPHILIS]

1st Schol. Master Doctor Faustus, since our conference about fair
ladies, which was the beautifullest in all the world, we have determined with ourselves that Helen of Greece was the admirablest
lady that ever lived: therefore, Master Doctor, if you will do us that
favour, as to let us see that peerless dame of Greece, whom all the
world admires for majesty, we should think ourselves much beholding unto you.

Faust. Gentlemen,
For that I know your friendship is unfeigned,
And Faustus' custom is not to deny
The just requests of those that wish him well,
You shall behold that peerless dame of Greece,
No otherways for pomp and majesty
Than when Sir Paris cross'd the seas with her,
And brought the spoils to rich Dardania.
Be silent, then, for danger is in words.

Music sounds, and HELEN *passeth over the stage.*

2nd Schol. Too simple is my wit to tell her praise,
Whom all the world admires for majesty.

3rd Schol. No marvel though the angry Greeks pursued
With ten years' war the rape of such a queen,
Whose heavenly beauty passeth all compare.

1st Schol. Since we have seen the pride of Nature's works,
And only paragon of excellence,
Let us depart; and for this glorious deed
Happy and blest be Faustus evermore.
Faustus. Gentlemen, farewell—the same I wish to you.

Exeunt SCHOLARS [*and* WAGNER].

Enter an OLD MAN

Old Man. Ah, Doctor Faustus, that I might prevail
To guide thy steps unto the way of life,
By which sweet path thou may'st attain the goal
That shall conduct thee to celestial rest!
Break heart, drop blood, and mingle it with tears,
Tears falling from repentant heaviness
Of thy most vile and loathsome filthiness,
The stench whereof corrupts the inward soul
With such flagitious crimes of heinous sins
As no commiseration may expel,
But mercy, Faustus, of thy Saviour sweet,
Whose blood alone must wash away thy guilt.
Faust. Where art thou, Faustus? Wretch, what hast thou done?
Damn'd art thou, Faustus, damn'd; despair and die!
Hell calls for right, and with a roaring voice
Says "Faustus! come! thine hour is [almost] come!"
And Faustus [now] will come to do the right.

MEPHISTOPHILIS *gives him a dagger.*

Old Man. Ah stay, good Faustus, stay thy desperate steps!
I see an angel hovers o'er thy head,
And, with a vial full of precious grace,
Offers to pour the same into thy soul:
Then call for mercy, and avoid despair.
Faust. Ah, my sweet friend, I feel
Thy words do comfort my distressed soul.
Leave me a while to ponder on my sins.
Old Man. I go, sweet Faustus, but with heavy cheer,
Fearing the ruin of thy hopeless soul.   [*Exit.*]

Faust. Accursed Faustus, where is mercy now?
I do repent; and yet I do despair;
Hell strives with grace for conquest in my breast:
What shall I do to shun the snares of death?

Meph. Thou traitor, Faustus, I arrest thy soul
For disobedience to my sovereign lord;
Revolt, or I'll in piecemeal tear thy flesh.

Faust. Sweet Mephistophilis, entreat thy lord
To pardon my unjust presumption.
And with my blood again I will confirm
My former vow I made to Lucifer.

Meph. Do it then quickly, with unfeigned heart,
Lest greater danger do attend thy drift.

[FAUSTUS *stabs his arm and writes on a paper with his blood.*]

Faust. Torment, sweet friend, that base and crooked age,[1]
That durst dissuade me from my Lucifer,
With greatest torments that our hell affords.

Meph. His faith is great, I cannot touch his soul;
But what I may afflict his body with
I will attempt, which is but little worth.

Faust. One thing, good servant, let me crave of thee,
To glut the longing of my heart's desire,—
That I might have unto my paramour
That heavenly Helen, which I saw of late,
Whose sweet embracings may extinguish clean
These thoughts that do dissuade me from my vow,
And keep mine oath I made to Lucifer.

Meph. Faustus, this or what else thou shalt desire
Shall be perform'd in twinkling of an eye.

Re-enter HELEN

Faust. Was this the face that launched a thousand ships
And burnt the topless[2] towers of Ilium?
Sweet Helen, make me immortal with a kiss.   [*Kisses her.*]
Her lips suck forth my soul; see where it flies!—

Come, Helen, come, give me my soul again.
Here will I dwell, for Heaven is in these lips,
And all is dross that is not Helena.   *Enter* OLD MAN.
I will be Paris, and for love of thee,
Instead of Troy, shall Wittenberg be sack'd;
And I will combat with weak Menelaus,
And wear thy colours on my plumed crest;
Yea, I will wound Achilles in the heel,
And then return to Helen for a kiss.
Oh, thou art fairer than the evening air
Clad in the beauty of a thousand stars;
Brighter art thou than flaming Jupiter
When he appear'd to hapless Semele:
More lovely than the monarch of the sky
In wanton Arethusa's azured arms:
And none but thou shalt be my paramour.   *Exeunt.*
    Old Man. Accursed Faustus, miserable man,
That from thy soul exclud'st the grace of Heaven,
And fly'st the throne of his tribunal seat!

Enter DEVILS

Satan begins to sift me with his pride:
As in this furnace God shall try my faith,
My faith, vile hell, shall triumph over thee.
Ambitious fiends! see how the heavens smiles
At your repulse, and laughs your state to scorn!
Hence, hell! for hence I fly unto my God.
        Exeunt [*on one side* DEVILS, *on the other,* OLD MAN].

[SCENE XIV.—*The Same.*]

Enter FAUSTUS *with* SCHOLARS

    Faust. Ah, gentlemen!
    1st Schol. What ails Faustus?
    Faust. Ah, my sweet chamber-fellow, had I lived with thee, then
had I lived still! but now I die eternally. Look, comes he not, comes
he not?

378

2nd Schol. What means Faustus?

3rd Schol. Belike he is grown into some sickness by being over solitary.

1st Schol. If it be so, we'll have physicians to cure him. 'Tis but a surfeit. Never fear, man.

Faust. A surfeit of deadly sin that hath damn'd both body and soul.

2nd Schol. Yet, Faustus, look up to Heaven; remember God's mercies are infinite.

Faust. But Faustus' offenses can never be pardoned: the serpent that tempted Eve may be sav'd, but not Faustus. Ah, gentlemen, hear me with patience, and tremble not at my speeches! Though my heart pants and quivers to remember that I have been a student here these thirty years, oh, would I had never seen Wittenberg, never read book! And what wonders I have done, all Germany can witness, yea, the world; for which Faustus hath lost both Germany and the world, yea Heaven itself, Heaven, the seat of God, the throne of the blessed, the kingdom of joy; and must remain in hell for ever, hell, ah, hell, for ever! Sweet friends! what shall become of Faustus being in hell for ever?

3rd Schol. Yet, Faustus, call on God.

Faust. On God, whom Faustus hath abjur'd! on God, whom Faustus hath blasphemed! Ah, my God, I would weep, but the Devil draws in my tears. Gush forth blood instead of tears! Yea, life and soul! Oh, he stays my tongue! I would lift up my hands, but see, they hold them, they hold them!

All. Who, Faustus?

Faust. Lucifer and Mephistophilis. Ah, gentlemen, I gave them my soul for my cunning!

All. God forbid!

Faust. God forbade it indeed; but Faustus hath done it. For vain pleasure of twenty-four years hath Faustus lost eternal joy and felicity. I writ them a bill with mine own blood: the date is expired; the time will come, and he will fetch me.

1st Schol. Why did not Faustus tell us of this before, that divines might have pray'd for thee?

Faust. Oft have I thought to have done so; but the Devil threat'ned

to tear me in pieces if I nam'd God; to fetch both body and soul if I
once gave ear to divinity: and now 'tis too late. Gentlemen, away!
lest you perish with me.

2nd Schol. Oh, what shall we do to save Faustus?

Faust. Talk not of me, but save yourselves, and depart.

3rd Schol. God will strengthen me. I will stay with Faustus.

1st Schol. Tempt not God, sweet friend; but let us into the next
room, and there pray for him.

Faust. Ay, pray for me, pray for me! and what noise soever ye
hear, come not unto me, for nothing can rescue me.

2nd Schol. Pray thou, and we will pray that God may have mercy
upon thee.

Faust. Gentlemen, farewell! If I live till morning I'll visit you:
if not—Faustus is gone to hell.

All. Faustus, farewell!

                       Exeunt Scholars. *The clock strikes eleven.*

Faust. Ah, Faustus,
Now hast thou but one bare hour to live,
And then thou must be damn'd perpetually!
Stand still, you ever-moving spheres of Heaven,
That time may cease, and midnight never come;
Fair Nature's eye, rise, rise again and make
Perpetual day; or let this hour be but
A year, a month, a week, a natural day,
That Faustus may repent and save his soul!
O lente, lente, currite noctis equi![1]
The stars move still,[2] time runs, the clock will strike,
The Devil will come, and Faustus must be damn'd.
O, I'll leap up to my God! Who pulls me down?
See, see where Christ's blood streams in the firmament!
One drop would save my soul—half a drop: ah, my Christ!
Ah, rend not my heart for naming of my Christ!
Yet will I call on him: O spare me, Lucifer!—
Where is it now? 'Tis gone; and see where God
Stretcheth out his arm, and bends his ireful brows!

Mountain and hills come, come and fall on me,
And hide me from the heavy wrath of God!
No! no!
Then will I headlong run into the earth;
Earth gape! O no, it will not harbour me!
You stars that reign'd at my nativity,
Whose influence hath alloted death and hell,
Now draw up Faustus like a foggy mist
Into the entrails of yon labouring clouds,
That when they vomit forth into the air,
My limbs may issue from their smoky mouths,
So that my soul may but ascend to Heaven.
                    The watch strikes [the half hour].
Ah, half the hour is past! 'Twill all be past anon!
O God!
If thou wilt not have mercy on my soul,
Yet for Christ's sake whose blood hath ransom'd me,
Impose some end to my incessant pain;
Let Faustus live in hell a thousand years—
A hundred thousand, and—at last—be sav'd!
O, no end is limited to damned souls!
Why wert thou not a creature wanting soul?
Or why is this immortal that thou hast?
Ah, Pythagoras' metempsychosis! were that true,
This soul should fly from me, and I be chang'd
Unto some brutish beast! All beasts are happy,
For, when they die,
Their souls are soon dissolv'd in elements;
But mine must live, still to be plagu'd in hell.
Curst be the parents that engend'red me!
No, Faustus: curse thyself: curse Lucifer
That hath depriv'd thee of the joys of Heaven.
                    The clock striketh twelve.

O, it strikes, it strikes! Now, body, turn to air,
Or Lucifer will bear thee quick to hell.
                    Thunder and lightning.

O soul, be chang'd into little water-drops,

381

And fall into the ocean—ne'er be found.
My God! my God! look not so fierce on me!   *Enter* DEVILS.
Adders and serpents, let me breathe awhile!
Ugly hell, gape not! come not, Lucifer!
I'll burn my books!—Ah Mephistophilis!

Exeunt DEVILS *with* FAUSTUS.

Enter CHORUS

Cho. Cut is the branch that might have grown full straight,
And burned is Apollo's laurel bough,
That sometime grew within this learned man.
Faustus is gone; regard his hellish fall,
Whose fiendful fortune may exhort the wise
Only to wonder at unlawful things,
Whose deepness doth entice such forward wits
To practise more than heavenly power permits.   [*Exit.*]

John Keats, ODE ON A GRECIAN URN

Alfred, Lord Tennyson, ULYSSES

William Butler Yeats, LEDA AND THE SWAN
THE SECOND COMING

Robert Browning, ANDREA DEL SARTO

1. Keats' *Ode On A Grecian Urn* addresses the relative values of art and life or, stated another way, permanence and change. What are the advantages of each?

2. In the second stanza of *Ode On A Grecian Urn*, the narrator asserts that "Heard melodies are sweet, but those unheard / Are sweeter..." Explain this thought in the context of the poem and discuss whether or not you agree with it.

3. One of the most famous phrases in all of literature occurs in the final stanza of the *Grecian Urn*: "Beauty is truth, truth beauty, - that is all / Ye know on earth, and all ye need to know." How can we equate beauty and truth? Are these the essential factors of human existence?

4. While we must remember that Tennyson's *Ulysses* is a dramatic monologue and, as such, presents only one speaker's point of view, it contains an interesting contrast between Ulysses, himself, and his son Telemachus, which crystalizes the theme of the poem. Analyze the two characters and decide whom you would prefer as a ruler.

5. The title character of Browning's *Andrea del Sarto* is troubled by his failure to attain the status of such fellow artists as Raphael despite his technical virtuosity, and by his inability to retain the love of his wife. Account for Andrea's lack of success as a painter and as a husband. What trait is missing from his character?

6. Yeats uses the mating of Leda and Zeus, in the form of a swan, as a symbol for the regeneration of mankind. Analyze the metaphor and comment on its effectiveness.

7. What allusions does Yeats employ in *The Second Coming*? How does the image of the "gyre" contribute to the sense of history present in the poem? Is the "Second Coming" something to be desired or feared?

8. All of the poems in this section deal with a response to the past. Compare and contrast the views presented in the assigned works and discuss their implications for the future.

9. Does poetry have any value for you, or is it merely an esoteric art form?

Although scholars still debate the origins of poetry - some, for example, speculating that it first appeared in religious ceremonies, and others arguing that it was originally associated with work - they agree that verse is an integral part of society because it responds to a deep human need. In at least one sense, modern poetry began with the publication in 1798 of the *Lyrical Ballads* - the joint venture of Wordsworth and Coleridge that heralded the Romantic Period in England. This poetry valued the individual, exemplified an organic concept of art, and influenced scores of writers for well over a century and a half. The five poets represented in this section are part of this tradition and are, therefore, speaking directly to us. They include: Keats (1795-1821), Tennyson (1809-1892), Browning (1812-1889), Yeats (1865-1939).

Ode on a Grecian Urn

Thou still unravish'd bride of quietness,
  Thou foster-child of Silence and slow Time,
Sylvan historian, who canst thus express
  A flowery tale more sweetly than our rhyme:
What leaf-fringed legend haunts about thy shape
  Of deities or mortals, or of both,
    In Tempe or the dales of Arcady?
  What men or gods are these? What maidens loth?
What mad pursuit? What struggle to escape?
    What pipes and timbrels? What wild ecstasy?

Heard melodies are sweet, but those unheard
  Are sweeter; therefore, ye soft pipes, play on;
Not to the sensual ear, but, more endear'd,
  Pipe to the spirit ditties of no tone:
Fair youth, beneath the trees, thou canst not leave
  Thy song, nor ever can those trees be bare;
    Bold Lover, never, never canst thou kiss,
Though winning near the goal—yet, do not grieve;
    She cannot fade, though thou hast not thy bliss,
  For ever wilt thou love, and she be fair!

Ah, happy, happy boughs! that cannot shed
  Your leaves, nor ever bid the Spring adieu;
And, happy melodist, unwearièd,
  For ever piping songs for ever new;
More happy love! more happy, happy love!
  For ever warm and still to be enjoy'd,
    For ever panting and for ever young;
All breathing human passion far above,
    That leaves a heart high-sorrowful and cloy'd,
  A burning forehead, and a parching tongue.

Who are these coming to the sacrifice?
  To what green altar, O mysterious priest,
Lead'st thou that heifer lowing at the skies,
  And all her silken flanks with garlands drest?
What little town by river or sea-shore,
  Or mountain-built with peaceful citadel,
    Is emptied of its folk, this pious morn?
And, little town, thy streets for evermore
  Will silent be; and not a soul, to tell
    Why thou art desolate, can e'er return.

O Attic shape! fair attitude! with brede
  Of marble men and maidens overwrought,
With forest branches and the trodden weed;
  Thou, silent form! dost tease us out of thought
As doth eternity. Cold Pastoral!
  When old age shall this generation waste,
    Thou shalt remain, in midst of other woe
  Than ours, a friend to man, to whom thou say'st,
'Beauty is truth, truth beauty,—that is all
    Ye know on earth, and all ye need to know.'

ULYSSES

It little profits that an idle king,
By this still hearth, among these barren crags,
Match'd with an aged wife, I mete and dole
Unequal laws unto a savage race,
That hoard, and sleep, and feed, and know not me.
I cannot rest from travel: I will drink
Life to the lees: all times I have enjoy'd
Greatly, have suffer'd greatly, both with those
That loved me, and alone; on shore, and when
Thro' scudding drifts the rainy Hyades
Vext the dim sea: I am become a name;
For always roaming with a hungry heart
Much have I seen and known: cities of men,
And manners, climates, councils, governments,
Myself not least, but honour'd of them all;
And drunk delight of battle with my peers,
Far on the ringing plains of windy Troy.
I am a part of all that I have met;
Yet all experience is an arch wherethro'
Gleams that untravell'd world, whose margin fades
For ever and for ever when I move.
How dull it is to pause, to make an end,
To rust unburnish'd, not to shine in use!
As tho' to breathe were life. Life piled on life
Were all too little, and of one to me
Little remains: but every hour is saved
From that eternal silence, something more,
A bringer of new things; and vile it were
For some three suns to store and hoard myself,
And this gray spirit yearning in desire

To follow knowledge like a sinking star,
Beyond the utmost bound of human thought.

This is my son, mine own Telemachus,
To whom I leave the sceptre and the isle —
Well-loved of me, discerning to fulfil
This labour, by slow prudence to make mild
A rugged people, and thro' soft degrees
Subdue them to the useful and the good.
Most blameless is he, centred in the sphere

Of common duties, decent not to fail
In offices of tenderness, and pay
Meet adoration to my household gods,
When I am gone. He works his work, I mine.

 There lies the port; the vessel puffs her sail :
There gloom the dark broad seas. My mariners,
Souls that have toil'd, and wrought, and thought with me —
That ever with a frolic welcome took
The thunder and the sunshine, and opposed
Free hearts, free foreheads — you and I are old ;
Old age hath yet his honour and his toil ;
Death closes all : but something ere the end,
Some work of noble note, may yet be done,
Not unbecoming men that strove with Gods.
The lights begin to twinkle from the rocks :
The long day wanes : the slow moon climbs : the deep
Moans round with many voices. Come, my friends,
'T is not too late to seek a newer world.
Push off, and sitting well in order smite
The sounding furrows ; for my purpose holds
To sail beyond the sunset, and the baths
Of all the western stars, until I die.
It may be the gulfs will wash us down :

It may be we shall touch the Happy Isles,
And see the great Achilles, whom we knew.
Tho' much is taken, much abides ; and tho'
We are not now that strength which in old days
Moved earth and heaven ; that which we are, we are ;
One equal temper of heroic hearts,
Made weak by time and fate, but strong in will
To strive, to seek, to find, and not to yield.

LEDA AND THE SWAN

A sudden blow: the great wings beating still
Above the staggering girl, her thighs caressed
By the dark webs, her nape caught in his bill,
He holds her helpless breast upon his breast.

How can those terrified vague fingers push
The feathered glory from her loosening thighs?
And how can body, laid in that white rush,
But feel the strange heart beating where it lies?

A shudder in the loins engenders there
The broken wall, the burning roof and tower
And Agamemnon dead.
                    Being so caught up,
So mastered by the brute blood of the air,
Did she put on his knowledge with his power
Before the indifferent beak could let her drop?

THE SECOND COMING

Turning and turning in the widening gyre
The falcon cannot hear the falconer;
Things fall apart; the centre cannot hold;
Mere anarchy is loosed upon the world,
The blood-dimmed tide is loosed, and everywhere
The ceremony of innocence is drowned;
The best lack all conviction, while the worst
Are full of passionate intensity.

Surely some revelation is at hand;
Surely the Second Coming is at hand.
The Second Coming! Hardly are those words out
When a vast image out of *Spiritus Mundi*
Troubles my sight: somewhere in sands of the desert
A shape with lion body and the head of a man,
A gaze blank and pitiless as the sun,
Is moving its slow thighs, while all about it
Reel shadows of the indignant desert birds.
The darkness drops again; but not I know
That twenty centuries of stony sleep
Were vexed to nightmare by a rocking cradle,
And what rough beast, its hour come round at last,
Slouches towards Bethlehem to be born?

ANDREA DEL SARTO

(*Called " the Faultless Painter "*)

B
UT do not let us quarrel any more,
  No, my Lucrezia! bear with me for once :
Sit down and all shall happen as you wish.
You turn your face, but does it bring your heart?
I 'll work then for your friend's friend, never fear,
Treat his own subject after his own way,
Fix his own time, accept too his own price,
And shut the money into this small hand
When next it takes mine.   Will it? tenderly?
Oh, I 'll content him, — but to-morrow, Love !
I often am much wearier than you think,
This evening more than usual : and it seems
As if — forgive now — should you let me sit
Here by the window, with your hand in mine,
And look a half-hour forth on Fiesole,
Both of one mind, as married people use,
Quietly, quietly the evening through,
I might get up to-morrow to my work
Cheerful and fresh as ever.   Let us try.
To-morrow, how you shall be glad for this !
Your soft hand is a woman of itself,
And mine the man's bared breast she curls inside.
Don't count the time lost, neither ; you must serve
For each of the five pictures we require :
It saves a model.   So ! keep looking so —
My serpentining beauty, rounds on rounds !
— How could you ever prick those perfect ears,
Even to put the pearl there ! oh, so sweet —
My face, my moon, my everybody's moon,
Which everybody looks on and calls his,
And, I suppose, is looked on by in turn,
While she looks — no one 's: very dear, no less.
You smile? why, there 's my picture ready made,
There 's what we painters call our harmony !
A common grayness silvers everything, —
All in a twilight, you and I alike
— You, at the point of your first pride in me
(That 's gone, you know) — but I, at every point ;
My youth, my hope, my art, being all toned down
To yonder sober pleasant Fiesole.
There 's the bell clinking from the chapel-top ;

That length of convent-wall across the way
Holds the trees safer, huddled more inside;
The last monk leaves the garden; days decrease,
And autumn grows, autumn in everything.
Eh? the whole seems to fall into a shape,
As if I saw alike my work and self
And all that I was born to be and do,
A twilight-piece. Love, we are in God's hand.
How strange now, looks the life he makes us lead;
So free we seem, so fettered fast we are!
I feel he laid the fetter: let it lie!
This chamber for example — turn your head —
All that's behind us! You don't understand
Nor care to understand about my art,
But you can hear at least when people speak:
And that cartoon, the second from the door
— It is the thing, Love! so such things should be —
Behold Madonna! — I am bold to say.
I can do with my pencil what I know,
What I see, what at bottom of my heart
I wish for, if I ever wish so deep —
Do easily, too — when I say, perfectly,
I do not boast, perhaps: yourself are judge,
Who listened to the Legate's talk last week;
And just as much they used to say in France.

At any rate 't is easy, all of it!
No sketches first, no studies, that's long past:
I do what many dream of, all their lives,
— Dream? strive to do, and agonize to do,
And fail in doing. I could count twenty such
On twice your fingers, and not leave this town,
Who strive — you don't know how the others strive
To paint a little thing like that you smeared
Carelessly passing with your robes afloat, —
Yet do much less, so much less, Someone says,
(I know his name, no matter) — so much less!
Well, less is more, Lucrezia: I am judged.
There burns a truer light of God in them,
In their vexed beating stuffed and stopped-up brain,
Heart, or whate'er else, than goes on to prompt
This low-pulsed forthright craftsman's hand of mine.
Their works drop groundward, but themselves, I know,
Reach many a time a heaven that's shut to me,
Enter and take their place there sure enough,
Tho' they come back and cannot tell the world.
My works are nearer heaven, but I sit here.
The sudden blood of these men! at a word —
Praise them, it boils, or blame them, it boils too.

I, painting from myself and to myself,
Know what I do, am unmoved by men's blame
Or their praise either. Somebody remarks
Morello's outline there is wrongly traced,
His hue mistaken ; what of that ? or else,
Rightly traced and well ordered ; what of that?
Speak as they please, what does the mountain care?
Ah, but a man's reach should exceed his grasp,
Or what 's a heaven for? All is silver-gray,
Placid and perfect with my art : the worse !
I know both what I want and what might gain,
And yet how profitless to know, to sigh
" Had I been two, another and myself,
Our head would have o'erlooked the world ! " No doubt.
Yonder 's a work now. of that famous youth
The Urbinate who died five years ago.
('T is copied, George Vasari sent it me.)
Well, I can fancy how he did it all,
Pouring his soul, with kings and popes to see,
Reaching, that heaven might so replenish him,
Above and thro' his art — for it gives way;
That arm is wrongly put — and there again —
A fault to pardon in the drawing's lines,
Its body, so to speak ; its soul is right,
He means right — that, a child may understand.
Still, what an arm ! and I could alter it :
But all the play, the insight and the stretch —
Out of me, out of me ! And wherefore out ?
Had you enjoined them on me, given me soul,
We might have risen to Rafael, I and you!
Nay, Love, you did give all I asked, I think —
More than I merit, yes, by many times.
But had you — oh, with the same perfect brow,
And perfect eyes, and more than perfect mouth,
And the low voice my soul hears, as a bird
The fowler's pipe, and follows to the snare —
Had you, with these the same, but brought a mind !
Some women do so. Had the mouth there urged
" God and the glory! never care for gain.
The present by the future, what is that?
Live for fame, side by side with Agnolo !
Rafael is waiting: up to God, all three ! "
I might have done it for you. So it seems :
Perhaps not. All is as God over-rules.
Beside, incentives come from the soul's self;
The rest avail not. Why do I need you ?
What wife had Rafael, or has Agnolo ?

393

In this world, who can do a thing, will not ;
And who would do it, can not, I perceive :
Yet the will 's somewhat — somewhat, too, the power
And thus we half-men struggle. At the end,
God, I conclude, compensates, punishes.
'T is safer for me, if the award be strict,

That I am something underrated here,
Poor this long while, despised, to speak the truth.
I dared not, do you know, leave home all day,
For fear of chancing on the Paris lords.
The best is when they pass and look aside ;
But they speak sometimes ; I must bear it all.
Well may they speak ! That Francis, that first time,
And that long festal year at Fontainebleau !
I surely then could sometimes leave the ground,
Put on the glory, Rafael's daily wear,
In that humane great monarch's golden look, —
One finger in his beard or twisted curl
Over his mouth's good mark that made the smile,
One arm about my shoulder, round my neck,
The jingle of his gold chain in my ear,
I painting proudly with his breath on me,
All his court round him, seeing with his eyes,
Such frank French eyes, and such a fire of souls
Profuse, my hand kept plying by those hearts, —
And, best of all, this, this, this face beyond,
This, in the background, waiting on my work,
To crown the issue with a last reward !
A good time, was it not, my kingly days?
And had you not grown restless . . . but I know —
'T is done and past ; 't was right, my instinct said ;
Too live the life grew, golden and not gray :
And I 'm the weak-eyed bat no sun should tempt
Out of the grange whose four walls make his world.
How could it end in any other way ?
You called me, and I came home to your heart.
The triumph was — to reach and stay there ; since
I reached it ere the triumph, what is lost ?
Let my hands frame your face in your hair's gold,
You beautiful Lucrezia that are mine !
" Rafael did this, Andrea painted that ;
The Roman's is the better when you pray,
But still the other's Virgin was his wife — "
Men will excuse me. I am glad to judge

Both pictures in your presence; clearer grows
My better fortune, I resolve to think.
For, do you know, Lucrezia, as God lives,
Said one day Agnolo, his very self,
To Rafael . . . I have known it all these years . . .
(When the young man was flaming out his thoughts
Upon a palace-wall for Rome to see,
Too lifted up in heart because of it)
" Friend, there 's a certain sorry little scrub
Goes up and down our Florence, none cares how,
Who, were he set to plan and execute
As you are, pricked on by your popes and kings,
Would bring the sweat into that brow of yours ! "
To Rafael's ! — And indeed the arm is wrong.
I hardly dare . . . yet, only you to see,
Give the chalk here — quick, thus the line should go !
Ay, but the soul ! he 's Rafael ! rub it out !
Still, all I care for, if he spoke the truth,
(What he ? why, who but Michel Agnolo ?
Do you forget already words like those ?)
If really there was such a chance so lost, —
Is, whether you 're — not grateful — but more pleased.
Well, let me think so. And you smile indeed!
This hour has been an hour! Another smile ?
If you would sit thus by me every night
I should work better, do you comprehend ?
I mean that I should earn more, give you more.
See, it is settled dusk now ; there 's a star ;
Morello 's gone, the watch-lights show the wall,
The cue-owls speak the name we call them by.
Come from the window, love, — come in, at last,
Inside the melancholy little house
We built to be so gay with. God is just.
King Francis may forgive me : oft at nights
When I look up from painting, eyes tired out,
The walls become illumined, brick from brick
Distinct, instead of mortar, fierce bright gold,
That gold of his I did cement them with !

Let us but love each other. Must you go ?
That Cousin here again ? he waits outside ?
Must see you — you, and not with me ? Those loans ?
More gaming debts to pay ? you smiled for that ?
Well, let smiles buy me ! have you more to spend ?
While hand and eye and something of a heart
Are left me, work 's my ware, and what 's it worth ?
I 'll pay my fancy. Only let me sit
The gray remainder of the evening out,

Idle, you call it, and muse perfectly
How I could paint, were I but back in France,
One picture, just one more — the Virgin's face,
Not yours this time ! I want you at my side
To hear them — that is, Michel Agnolo —
Judge all I do and tell you of its worth.
Will you ? To-morrow, satisfy your friend.
I take the subjects for his corridor.
Finish the portrait out of hand — there, there,
And throw him in another thing or two
If he demurs ; the whole should prove enough
To pay for this same Cousin's freak. Beside,
What 's better and what 's all I care about,
Get you the thirteen scudi for the ruff !
Love, does that please you ? Ah, but what does he,
The Cousin ! what does he to please you more ?

I am grown peaceful as old age to-night.
I regret little, I would change still less.
Since there my past life lies, why alter it ?
The very wrong to Francis ! — it is true
I took his coin, was tempted and complied,
And built this house and sinned, and all is said.
My father and my mother died of want.
Well, had I riches of my own ? you see
How one gets rich ! Let each one bear his lot.
They were born poor, lived poor, and poor they died :
And I have laboured somewhat in my time
And not been paid profusely. Some good son
Paint my two hundred pictures — let him try !
No doubt, there 's something strikes a balance. Yes,
You loved me quite enough, it seems to-night.
This must suffice me here. What would one have ?
In heaven, perhaps, new chances, one more chance —
Four great walls in the New Jerusalem,
Meted on each side by the angel's reed,
For Leonard, Rafael, Agnolo and me
To cover — the three first without a wife,
While I have mine ! So — still they overcome
Because there 's still Lucrezia, — as I choose.

Again the Cousin's whistle ! Go, my Love.

Voltaire,   CANDIDE

1. What does Voltaire think of the proposition that this is the "best of all possible worlds"?

2. What is the point of the episode about the Lisbon earthquake?

3. What does Voltaire think of the "pure state of nature"?

4. What is the point of Candide's adventures in the New World?

5. What is the status of wealth, law, religion, and royalty in Eldorado?

6. Why does Candide leave Eldorado? Is his stated reason a sufficient explanation?

7. Discuss the Dervish's question to Candide: "When his highness sends a ship to Egypt, does he worry about the comfort or discomfort of the rats in the ship?"

8. Compare or contrast Pangloss and Martin as counselors to Candide.

9. Explain the difference between Candide's household and little farm before and after his conversation with the Old Turk.

10. What do you think is the meaning of Candide's final statement, "But we must cultivate our gardens"?

Francois Marie Arouet de Voltaire (1694-1778) was a French philosopher, historian, dramatist, and man of letters whose works so dominated the half century of his productive years that this period sometimes is referred to as "The Age of Voltaire." He wrote *Candide* in 1759, about midway in his career. Here, in an imaginative farce, he attacks the problem of evil, and in doing so attacks also some of the prevailing ideas of his day.

Chapter I

HOW CANDIDE WAS BROUGHT UP IN A NOBLE CASTLE AND HOW HE WAS EXPELLED FROM THE SAME

In the castle of Baron Thunder-ten-tronckh in Westphalia [1] there lived a youth, endowed by Nature with the most gentle character. His face was the expression of his soul. His judgment was quite honest and he was extremely simpleminded; and this was the reason, I think, that he was named Candide. Old servants in the house suspected that he was the son of the Baron's sister and a decent honest gentleman of the neighborhood, whom this young lady would never marry because he could only prove seventy-one quarterings,[2] and the rest of his genealogical tree was lost, owing to the injuries of time.

The Baron was one of the most powerful lords in Westphalia, for his castle possessed a door and windows. His Great Hall was even decorated with a piece of tapestry. The dogs in his stable-yards formed a pack of hounds when necessary; his grooms were his huntsmen; the village curate was his Grand Almoner. They all called him "My Lord," and laughed heartily at his stories.

The Baroness weighed about three hundred and fifty pounds, was therefore greatly respected, and did the honors of the house with a dignity which rendered her still more respectable. Her daughter Cunegonde, aged seventeen, was rosy-cheeked, fresh, plump and tempting. The Baron's son

1. **Westphalia** Section of Germany just east of Holland. In Voltaire's day, it was a poor agricultural province through which he passed in 1750 on his way to the court of Frederick the Great.
2. **quarterings** These divisions on coats of arms are indications of the number of noble ancestors.

appeared in every respect worthy of his father. The tutor Pangloss was the oracle of the house, and little Candide followed his lessons with all the candor of his age and character.

Pangloss taught metaphysico-theologo-cosmolonigology.[3] He proved admirably that there is no effect without a cause and that in this best of all possible worlds, My Lord the Baron's castle was the best of castles and his wife the best of all possible Baronesses.

" 'Tis demonstrated," said he, "that things cannot be otherwise; for, since everything is made for an end, everything is necessarily for the best end. Observe that noses were made to wear spectacles; and so we have spectacles. Legs were visibly instituted to be breeched, and we have breeches.[4] Stones were formed to be quarried and to build castles; and My Lord has a very noble castle; the greatest Baron in the province should have the best house; and as pigs were made to be eaten, we eat pork all the year round; consequently, those who have asserted that all is well [5] talk nonsense; they ought to have said that all is for the best."

Candide listened attentively and believed innocently; for he thought Mademoiselle Cunegonde extremely beautiful, although he was never bold enough to tell her so. He decided that after the happiness of being born Baron of Thunder-ten-tronckh, the second degree of happiness was to be Mademoiselle Cunegonde; the third, to see her every day; and the fourth to listen to Doctor Pangloss, the greatest philosopher of the province and therefore of the whole world.

One day when Cunegonde was walking near the castle, in a little wood which was called The Park, she observed Doctor Pangloss in the bushes, giving a lesson in experi-

3. **cosmolonigology** The suggestion is that Pangloss ("all-tongue") is the teacher of abstract nonsense. Swift used a similar term for similar effect in *Gulliver's Travels.*

4. **breeches** Clear but ludicrous examples of what are called in philosophy "final causes," that is, ends or purposes which serve as causes of created things.

5. **all is well** See Introduction for Pope's phrasing.

mental physics to her mother's waiting maid, a very pretty and docile brunette. Mademoiselle Cunegonde had a great inclination for science and watched breathlessly the reiterated experiments she witnessed; she observed clearly the Doctor's sufficient reason, the effects and the causes, and returned home very much excited, pensive, filled with the desire of learning, reflecting that she might be the sufficient reason of young Candide and that he might be hers.

On her way back to the castle she met Candide and blushed; Candide also blushed. She bade him good-morning in a hesitating voice; Candide replied without knowing what he was saying. Next day, when they left the table after dinner, Cunegonde and Candide found themselves behind a screen; Cunegonde dropped her handkerchief, Candide picked it up; she innocently held his hand; the young man innocently kissed the young lady's hand with remarkable vivacity, tenderness and grace; their lips met, their eyes sparkled, their knees trembled, their hands wandered. Baron Thunder-ten-tronckh passed near the screen, and, observing this cause and effect, expelled Candide from the castle by kicking him in the backside frequently and hard. Cunegonde swooned; when she recovered her senses, the Baroness slapped her in the face; and all was in consternation in the noblest and most agreeable of all possible castles.

Chapter II

WHAT HAPPENED TO CANDIDE
AMONG THE BULGARIANS

Candide, expelled from the earthly paradise, wandered for a long time without knowing where he was going, weeping, turning up his eyes to Heaven, gazing back frequently at the noblest of castles which held the most beautiful of young Baronesses; he lay down to sleep supperless between two furrows in the open fields; it snowed heavily in large flakes. The next morning the shivering Candide, penniless, dying of cold and exhaustion, dragged himself towards the neighboring town, which was called Waldberghoff-trarbk-
10 dikdorff. He halted sadly at the door of an inn. Two men dressed in blue noticed him.

"Comrade," said one, "there's a well-built young man of the right height." They went up to Candide and very civilly invited him to dinner.

"Gentlemen," said Candide with charming modesty, "you do me a great honor, but I have no money to pay my share."

"Ah, sir," said one of the men in blue, "persons of your figure and merit never pay anything; are you not five feet
20 five tall?"

"Yes, gentlemen," said he, bowing, "that is my height."

"Ah, sir, come to table; we will not only pay your expenses, we will never allow a man like you to be short of money; men were only made to help each other."

"You are in the right," said Candide, "that is what Doctor Pangloss was always telling me, and I see that everything is for the best."

They begged him to accept a few crowns, he took them

402

and wished to give them an I O U; they refused to take it
and all sat down to table. "Do you not love tenderly . . ." 30
"Oh, yes," said he. "I love Mademoiselle Cunegonde ten-
derly."
"No," said one of the gentlemen. "We were asking if you
do not tenderly love the King of the Bulgarians." [1]
"Not a bit," said he, "for I have never seen him."
"What! He is the most charming of Kings, and you must
drink his health."
"Oh, gladly, gentlemen." And he drank.
"That is sufficient," he was told. "You are now the support, the aid, the defender, the hero of the Bulgarians; your 40
fortune is made and your glory assured."
They immediately put irons on his legs and took him to
a regiment.[2] He was made to turn to the right and left,
to raise the ramrod and return the ramrod, to take aim, to
fire, to double up,[3] and he was given thirty strokes with a
stick; the next day he drilled not quite so badly, and received only twenty strokes; the day after, he only had ten,
and was looked on as a prodigy by his comrades.
Candide was completely mystified and could not make
out how he was a hero. One fine spring day he thought he 50
would take a walk, going straight ahead, in the belief that
to use his legs as he pleased was a privilege of the human
species as well as of animals. He had not gone two leagues
when four other heroes, each six feet tall, fell upon him,
bound him and dragged him back to a cell. He was asked
by his judges whether he would rather be thrashed thirty-
six times by the whole regiment or receive a dozen lead bul-
lets at once in his brain. Although he protested that men's
wills are free and that he wanted neither one nor the other,
he had to make a choice; by virtue of that gift of God 60
which is called *liberty*, he determined to run the gauntlet

1. **Bulgarians** Voltaire has his reasons to refer to Frederick the
Great, King of Prussia, under this title.
2. **regiment** It was a common practice in England and on the continent to "press" young men into military service.
3. **double up** Double-time.

thirty-six times and actually did so twice. There were two thousand men in the regiment. That made four thousand strokes which laid bare the muscles and nerves from his neck to his backside. As they were about to proceed to a third turn, Candide, utterly exhausted, begged as a favor that they would be so kind as to smash his head; he obtained this favor; they bound his eyes and he was made to kneel down. At that moment the King of the Bulgarians 70 came by and inquired the victim's crime; and as this King was possessed of a vast genius, he perceived from what he learned about Candide that he was a young metaphysician very ignorant in worldly matters, and therefore pardoned him with a clemency which will be praised in all newspapers and all ages. An honest surgeon healed Candide in three weeks with the ointments recommended by Dioscorides.[4] He had already regained a little skin and could walk when the King of the Bulgarians went to war with the King of the Abares.[5]

4. **Dioscorides** Famous Greek doctor.
5. **Abares** The French-Austrian coalition, which fought against Frederick in the Seven Years' War.

Chapter III

HOW CANDIDE ESCAPED FROM THE BULGARIANS AND WHAT BECAME OF HIM

Nothing could be smarter, more splendid, more brilliant, better drawn up than the two armies. Trumpets, fifes, hautboys, drums, cannons, formed a harmony such as has never been heard even in hell. The cannons first of all laid flat about six thousand men on each side; then the musketry removed from the best of worlds some nine or ten thousand blackguards who infested its surface. The bayonet also was the sufficient reason for the death of some thousands of men. The whole might amount to thirty thousand souls. Candide, who trembled like a philosopher, hid himself as well as he could during this heroic butchery. 10

At last, while the two Kings each commanded a *Te Deum* [1] in his camp, Candide decided to go elsewhere to reason about effects and causes. He clambered over heaps of dead and dying men and reached a neighboring village, which was in ashes; it was an Abare village which the Bulgarians had burned in accordance with international law. Here, old men dazed with blows watched the dying agonies of their murdered wives who clutched their children to their bleeding breasts; there, disembowelled girls who had been made to 20 satisfy the natural appetites of heroes gasped their last sighs; others, half-burned, begged to be put to death. Brains were scattered on the ground among dismembered arms and legs.

Candide fled to another village as fast as he could; it belonged to the Bulgarians, and Abarian heroes had treated it in the same way. Candide, stumbling over quivering limbs

1. **Te Deum** A hymn of thanks to God for victory.

405

or across ruins, at last escaped from the theatre of war, carrying a little food in his knapsack, and never forgetting Mademoiselle Cunegonde. His provisions were all gone when
30 he reached Holland; but, having heard that everyone in that country was rich and a Christian, he had no doubt at all but that he would be as well treated as he had been in the Baron's castle before he had been expelled on account of Mademoiselle Cunegonde's pretty eyes.

He asked an alms of several grave persons, who all replied that if he continued in that way he would be shut up in a house of correction to teach him how to live. He then addressed himself to a man who had been discoursing on charity in a large assembly for an hour on end. This orator,
40 glancing at him askance, said: "What are you doing here? Are you for the good cause?"

"There is no effect without a cause," said Candide modestly. "Everything is necessarily linked up and arranged for the best. It was necessary that I should be expelled from the company of Mademoiselle Cunegonde, that I ran the gauntlet, and that I beg my bread until I can earn it; all this could not have happened differently."

"My friend," said the orator, "do you believe that the Pope is Anti-Christ?"
50 "I had never heard so before," said Candide, "but whether he is or isn't, I am starving."

"You don't deserve to eat," said the other. "Hence, rascal; hence, you wretch; and never come near me again."

The orator's wife thrust her head out of the window and seeing a man who did not believe that the Pope was Anti-Christ, she poured on his head a full . . . O Heavens! To what excess religious zeal is carried by ladies!

A man who had not been baptized, an honest Anabaptist [2] named Jacques, saw the cruel and ignominious treat-
60 ment of one of his brothers, a featherless two-legged creature with a soul; he took him home, cleaned him up, gave him bread and beer, presented him with two florins, and even

2. **Anabaptist** Member of a Protestant sect which opposed infant baptism.

offered to teach him to work at the manufacture of Persian stuffs which are made in Holland. Candide threw himself at the man's feet, exclaiming: "Doctor Pangloss was right in telling me that all is for the best in this world, for I am vastly more touched by your extreme generosity than by the harshness of the gentleman in the black cloak and his good lady."

The next day when he walked out he met a beggar cov- 70
ered with sores, dull-eyed, with the end of his nose fallen away, his mouth awry, his teeth black, who talked huskily, was tormented with a violent cough and spat out a tooth at every cough.

Chapter IV

HOW CANDIDE MET HIS OLD MASTER IN PHILOSOPHY, DOCTOR PANGLOSS, AND WHAT HAPPENED

Candide, moved even more by compassion than by horror, gave this horrible beggar the two florins he had received from the honest Anabaptist, Jacques. The phantom gazed fixedly at him, shed tears and threw its arms round his neck. Candide recoiled in terror.

"Alas!" said the wretch to the other wretch, "don't you recognise your dear Pangloss?"

"What do I hear? You, my dear master! You, in this horrible state! What misfortune has happened to you? Why are you no longer in the noblest of castles? What has become of Mademoiselle Cunegonde, the pearl of young ladies, the masterpiece of Nature?"

"I am exhausted," said Pangloss. Candide immediately took him to the Anabaptist's stable where he gave him a little bread to eat; and when Pangloss had recovered: "Well!" said he, "Cunegonde?"

"Dead," replied the other.

At this word Candide swooned; his friend restored him to his senses with a little bad vinegar which happened to be in the stable. Candide opened his eyes. "Cunegonde dead! Ah! best of worlds, where are you? But what illness did she die of? Was it because she saw me kicked out of her father's noble castle?"

"No," said Pangloss. "She was disembowelled by Bulgarian soldiers, after having been raped to the limit of possibility; they broke the Baron's head when he tried to defend her; the Baroness was cut to pieces; my poor pupil was

408

treated exactly like his sister; and as to the castle, there is not one stone standing on another, not a barn, not a sheep, not a duck, not a tree; but we were well avenged, for the 30 Abares did exactly the same to a neighboring barony which belonged to a Bulgarian Lord." At this, Candide swooned again; but, having recovered and having said all that he ought to say, he inquired the cause and effect, the sufficient reason which had reduced Pangloss to so piteous a state.

"Alas!" said Pangloss, " 'tis love; love, the consoler of the human race, the preserver of the universe, the soul of all tender creatures, gentle love."

"Alas!" said Candide, "I am acquainted with this love, this sovereign of hearts, this soul of our soul; it has never 40 brought me anything but one kiss and twenty kicks in the backside. How could this beautiful cause produce in you so abominable an effect?"

Pangloss replied as follows: "My dear Candide! You remember Paquette, the maidservant of our august Baroness; in her arms I enjoyed the delights of Paradise which have produced the tortures of Hell by which you see I am devoured; she was infected and perhaps is dead. Paquette received this present from a most learned monk, who had it from the source; for he received it from an old countess, 50 who had it from a cavalry captain, who owed it to a marchioness, who derived it from a page, who had received it from a Jesuit, who, when a novice, had it in a direct line from one of the companions of Christopher Columbus. For my part, I shall not give it to anyone, for I am dying."

"O Pangloss!" exclaimed Candide, "this is a strange genealogy! Wasn't the devil at the root of it?"

"Not at all," replied that great man. "It was something indispensable in this best of worlds, a necessary ingredient; for, if Columbus in an island of America had not caught 60 this disease, which poisons the source of generation, and often indeed prevents generation, we should not have chocolate and cochineal;[1] it must also be noticed that hitherto in

1. cochineal A scarlet dye, prized in Europe, but an absurdly disproportionate advantage.

our continent this disease is peculiar to us, like theological disputes. The Turks, the Indians, the Persians, the Chinese, the Siamese and the Japanese are not yet familiar with it; but there is a sufficient reason why they in their turn should become familiar with it in a few centuries. Meanwhile, it has made marvellous progress among us, and especially in
70 those large armies composed of honest, well-bred stipendiaries who decide the destiny of States; it may be asserted that when thirty thousand men fight a pitched battle against an equal number of troops, there are about twenty thousand with the pox on either side."

"Admirable!" said Candide. "But you must get cured."

"How can I?" said Pangloss. "I haven't a sou, my friend, and in the whole extent of this globe, you cannot be bled or receive an enema without paying or without someone paying for you."

80 This last speech determined Candide; he went and threw himself at the feet of his charitable Anabaptist, Jacques, and drew so touching a picture of the state to which his friend was reduced that the good easy man did not hesitate to succor Pangloss; he had him cured at his own expense. In this cure Pangloss only lost one eye and one ear. He could write well and knew arithmetic perfectly. The Anabaptist made him his bookkeeper. At the end of two months he was compelled to go to Lisbon on business and took his two philosophers on the boat with him. Pangloss explained to him how
90 everything was for the best. Jacques was not of this opinion.

"Men," said he, "must have corrupted nature a little, for they were not born wolves, and they have become wolves.² God did not give them twenty-four-pounder cannons or bayonets, and they have made bayonets and cannons to destroy each other. I might bring bankruptcies into the account and Justice which seizes the goods of bankrupts in order to deprive the creditors of them."

"It was all indispensable," replied the one-eyed doctor, "and private misfortunes make the public good, so that the

2. **wolves** A favorite contention of Jean-Jacques Rousseau, Voltaire's contemporary.

more private misfortunes there are, the more everything is 100 well." 3

While he was reasoning, the air grew dark, the winds blew from the four quarters of the globe and the ship was attacked by the most horrible tempest in sight of the port of Lisbon.

3. **well** A further step in reducing philosophical optimism to absurdity.

Chapter V

STORM, SHIPWRECK, EARTHQUAKE, AND WHAT HAPPENED TO DR. PANGLOSS, TO CANDIDE AND THE ANABAPTIST JACQUES

Half the enfeebled passengers, suffering from that inconceivable anguish which the rolling of a ship causes in the nerves and in all the humors of bodies shaken in contrary directions, did not retain strength enough even to trouble about the danger. The other half screamed and prayed; the sails were torn, the masts broken, the vessel leaking. Those worked who could, no one cooperated, no one commanded. The Anabaptist tried to help the crew a little; he was on the main deck; a furious sailor struck him violently and stretched him on the deck; but the blow he delivered gave him so violent a shock that he fell head-first out of the ship. He remained hanging and clinging to part of the broken mast. The good Jacques ran to his aid, helped him to climb back, and from the effort he made was flung into the sea in full view of the sailor, who allowed him to drown without condescending even to look at him. Candide came up, saw his benefactor reappear for a moment and then be engulfed for ever. He tried to throw himself after him into the sea; he was prevented by the philosopher Pangloss, who proved to him that the Lisbon roads[1] had been expressly created for the Anabaptist to be drowned in them. While he was proving this *a priori*,[2] the vessel sank, and every one perished except Pangloss, Candide and the brutal sailor who had drowned the virtuous Anabaptist; the blackguard swam

1. **roads** "Where ships may safely ride at anchor."
2. **a priori** The deductive method of argument which proceeds from preestablished principles, rather than from experience.

412

successfully to the shore and Pangloss and Candide were carried there on a plank.

When they had recovered a little, they walked toward Lisbon; they had a little money by the help of which they hoped to be saved from hunger after having escaped the storm. Weeping the death of their benefactor, they had scarcely set foot in the town when they felt the earth tremble under their feet; the sea rose in foaming masses in the port and smashed the ships which rode at anchor. Whirlwinds of flame and ashes covered the streets and squares; the houses collapsed, the roofs were thrown upon the foundations, and the foundations were scattered; thirty thousand inhabitants of every age and both sexes were crushed under the ruins. Whistling and swearing, the sailor said: "There'll be something to pick up here."

"What can be the sufficient reason for this phenomenon?" said Pangloss.

"It is the last day!" [3] cried Candide.

The sailor immediately ran among the debris, dared death to find money, found it, seized it, got drunk, and having slept off his wine, purchased the favors of the first woman of good will he met on the ruins of the houses and among the dead and dying. Pangloss, however, pulled him by the sleeve. "My friend," said he, "this is not well, you are disregarding universal reason, you choose the wrong time."

"Blood and 'ounds!" he retorted, "I am a sailor and I was born in Batavia; four times have I stamped on the crucifix during four voyages to Japan; [4] you have found the right man for your universal reason!"

Candide had been hurt by some falling stones; he lay in the street covered with debris. He said to Pangloss: "Alas! Get me a little wine and oil; I am dying."

"This earthquake is not a new thing," replied Pangloss. "The town of Lima felt the same shocks in America last year; similar causes produce similar effects; there must cer-

3. last day I.e., the Day of Judgment.
4. Japan A regulation imposed on merchants in an attempt to prevent commerce with Christians.

60 tainly be a train of sulphur underground from Lima to Lisbon."

"Nothing is more probable," replied Candide; "but, for God's sake, a little oil and wine."

"What do you mean, probable?" replied the philosopher, "I maintain that it is proved."

Candide lost consciousness, and Pangloss brought him a little water from a neighboring fountain.

Next day they found a little food as they wandered among the ruins and regained a little strength. Afterwards
70 they worked like others to help the inhabitants who had escaped death. Some citizens they had assisted gave them as good a dinner as could be expected in such a disaster; true, it was a dreary meal; the hosts watered their bread with their tears, but Pangloss consoled them by assuring them that things could not be otherwise. "For," said he, "all this is for the best; for, if there is a volcano at Lisbon, it cannot be anywhere else; for it is impossible that things should not be where they are; for all is well."

A little, dark man, a familiar of the Inquisition,[5] who sat
80 beside him, politely took up the conversation, and said: "Apparently, you do not believe in original sin; for, if everything is for the best, there was neither fall nor punishment"[6]

"I most humbly beg your excellency's pardon," replied Pangloss still more politely, "for the fall of man and the curse necessarily entered into the best of all possible worlds."

"Then you do not believe in free will?" said the familiar.

"Your excellency will pardon me," said Pangloss; "free will can exist with absolute necessity; for it was necessary
90 that we should be free; for in short, limited will . . ."

Pangloss was in the middle of his phrase when the familiar nodded to his armed attendant who was pouring out port or Oporto wine for him.

5. **Inquisition** An officer of the Inquisition, or Holy Office, a tribunal which, from the thirteenth century to the eighteenth, attempted to stamp out heresy.

6. **punishment** The fall of man (*Genesis,* iii), with his subsequent redemption, is the orthodox Christian explanation of evil.

Chapter VI

HOW A SPLENDID AUTO-DA-FÉ WAS HELD TO PREVENT EARTHQUAKES, AND HOW CANDIDE WAS FLOGGED

After the earthquake which destroyed three-quarters of Lisbon, the wise men of that country could discover no more efficacious way of preventing a total ruin than by giving the people a splendid *auto-da-fé*.[1] It was decided by the university of Coimbre[2] that the sight of several persons being slowly burned in great ceremony is an infallible secret for preventing earthquakes. Consequently they had arrested a Biscayan convicted of having married his fellow-godmother, and two Portuguese who, when eating a chicken, had thrown away the bacon;[3] after dinner they came and bound Dr. Pangloss and his disciple Candide, one because he had spoken and the other because he had listened with an air of approbation; they were both carried separately to extremely cool apartments,[4] where there was never any discomfort from the sun; a week afterwards each was dressed in a sanbenito[5] and their heads were ornamented with paper mitres; Candide's mitre and sanbenito were painted with flames upside down and with devils who had neither tails nor claws; but Pangloss's devils had claws and tails, and his flames were upright.

Dressed in this manner they marched in procession and

1. **auto-da-fé** "Act of faith"—the ceremony of burning heretics at the stake.
2. **Coimbre** Portuguese city north of Lisbon.
3. **bacon** Thus indicating that they were Jews.
4. **apartments** Ironical for "dank cells."
5. **sanbenito** Ceremonial frocks worn by condemned heretics. Voltaire's description is accurate.

CANDIDE

listened to a most pathetic sermon, followed by lovely plain song music. Candide was flogged in time to the music, while the singing went on; the Biscayan and the two men who had not wanted to eat the bacon were burned, and Pangloss was hanged, although this is not the custom. The very same day, the earth shook again with a terrible clamor.

Candide, terrified, dumbfounded, bewildered, covered with blood, quivering from head to foot, said to himself: "If this is the best of all possible worlds, what are the others? Let it pass that I was flogged, for I was flogged by the Bulgarians, but, O my dear Pangloss! The greatest of philosophers! Must I see you hanged without knowing why! O my dear Anabaptist! The best of men! Was it necessary that you should be drowned in port! O Mademoiselle Cunegonde! The pearl of women! Was it necessary that your belly should be slit!"

He was returning, scarcely able to support himself, preached at, flogged, absolved and blessed, when an old woman accosted him and said: "Courage, my son, follow me."

416

Chapter VII

HOW AN OLD WOMAN TOOK CARE OF CANDIDE AND HOW HE REGAINED THAT WHICH HE LOVED

Candide did not take courage, but he followed the old woman to a hovel; she gave him a pot of ointment to rub on, and left him food and drink; she pointed out a fairly clean bed; near the bed there was a suit of clothes. "Eat, drink, sleep," said she, "and may our Lady of Atocha, my Lord Saint Anthony of Padua and my Lord Saint James of Compostella take care of you; I shall come back tomorrow."

Candide, still amazed by all he had seen, by all he had suffered, and still more by the old woman's charity, tried to kiss her hand. "'Tis not my hand you should kiss," said the old woman, "I shall come back tomorrow. Rub on the ointment, eat and sleep." 10

In spite of all his misfortune, Candide ate and went to sleep. Next day the old woman brought him breakfast, examined his back and smeared him with another ointment; later she brought him dinner, and returned in the evening with supper. The next day she went through the same ceremony.

"Who are you?" Candide kept asking her. "Who has inspired you with so much kindness? How can I thank you?" 20

The good woman never made any reply; she returned in the evening without any supper. "Come with me," said she, "and do not speak a word."

She took him by the arm and walked into the country with him for about a quarter of a mile; they came to an isolated house, surrounded with gardens and canals. The old woman knocked at a little door. It was opened; she led

417

Candide up a back stairway into a gilded apartment, left
him on a brocaded sofa, shut the door and went away. Can-
30 dide thought he was dreaming, and felt that his whole life
was a bad dream and the present moment an agreeable
dream. The old woman soon reappeared; she was supporting with some difficulty a trembling woman of majestic
stature, glittering with precious stones and covered with a
veil.

"Remove the veil," said the old woman to Candide. The
young man advanced and lifted the veil with a timid hand.
What a moment! What a surprise! He thought he saw
Mademoiselle Cunegonde, in fact he was looking at her,
40 it was she herself. His strength failed him, he could not utter a word and fell at her feet. Cunegonde fell on the sofa.[1]
The old woman dosed them with distilled waters; they recovered their senses and began to speak: at first they uttered
only broken words, questions and answers at cross purposes,
sighs, tears, exclamations. The old woman advised them to
make less noise and left them alone.

"What! Is it you?" said Candide. "You are alive, and I
find you here in Portugal! Then you were not raped? Your
belly was not slit, as the philosopher Pangloss assured me?"
50 "Yes, indeed," said the fair Cunegonde; "but those two
accidents are not always fatal."

"But your father and mother were killed?"

" 'Tis only too true," said Cunegonde, weeping.

"And your brother?"

"My brother was killed too."

"And why are you in Portugal? And how did you know
I was here? And by what strange adventure have you
brought me to this house?"

"I will tell you everything," replied the lady, "but first of
60 all you must tell me everything that has happened to you
since the innocent kiss you gave me and the kicks you received."

Candide obeyed with profound respect; and, although he

1. **sofa** Ladylike! Voltaire both uses and parodies the recognition
scenes so frequent in tall tales of adventure.

was bewildered, although his voice was weak and trembling, although his back was still a little painful, he related in the most natural manner all he had endured since the moment of their separation. Cunegonde raised her eyes to heaven; she shed tears at the death of the good Anabaptist and Pangloss, after which she spoke as follows to Candide, who did not miss a word and devoured her with his eyes. 70

Chapter VIII

CUNEGONDE'S STORY

"I was fast asleep in bed when it pleased Heaven to send the Bulgarians to our noble castle of Thunder-ten-tronckh; they murdered my father and brother and cut my mother to pieces. A large Bulgarian six feet tall, seeing that I had swooned at the spectacle, began to rape me; this brought me to, I recovered my senses, I screamed, I struggled, I bit, I scratched, I tried to tear out the big Bulgarian's eyes, not knowing that what was happening in my father's castle was a matter of custom; the brute stabbed me with a knife in the left side where I still have the scar."

"Alas! I hope I shall see it," said the naïf Candide.

"You shall see it," said Cunegonde, "but let me go on."

"Go on," said Candide.

She took up the thread of her story as follows: "A Bulgarian captain came in, saw me covered with blood, and the soldier did not disturb himself. The captain was angry at the brute's lack of respect to him, and killed him on my body. Afterwards, he had me bandaged and took me to his billet as a prisoner of war. I washed the few shirts he had and did the cooking; I must admit he thought me very pretty; and I will not deny that he was very well built and that his skin was white and soft; otherwise he had little wit and little philosophy; it was plain that he had not been brought up by Dr. Pangloss. At the end of three months he lost all his money and got tired of me; he sold me to a Jew named Don Issachar, who traded in Holland and Portugal and had a passion for women. This Jew devoted himself to my person but he could not triumph over it; I resisted him better than the Bulgarian soldier; a lady of honor may be

raped once, but it strengthens her virtue. In order to sub- 30
due me, the Jew brought me to this country house. Up till
then I believed that there was nothing on earth so splendid
as the castle of Thunder-ten-tronckh; I was undeceived.

"One day the Grand Inquisitor noticed me at Mass; he
ogled me continually and sent a message that he wished to
speak to me on secret affairs. I was taken to his palace; I
informed him of my birth; he pointed out how much it was
beneath my rank to belong to an Israelite. A proposition
was made on his behalf to Don Issachar to give me up to
His Lordship. Don Issachar, who is the court banker and 40
a man of influence, would not agree. The Inquisitor threatened him with an *auto-da-fé*. At last the Jew was frightened
and made a bargain whereby the house and I belong to
both in common. The Jew has Mondays, Wednesdays and
the Sabbath day, and the Inquisitor has the other days of
the week. This arrangement has lasted for six months. It
has not been without quarrels; for it has often been debated
whether the night between Saturday and Sunday belonged
to the old law or the new. For my part, I have hitherto resisted them both; and I think that is the reason why they 50
still love me.

"At last My Lord the Inquisitor was pleased to arrange
an *auto-da-fé* to remove the scourge of earthquakes and to
intimidate Don Issachar. He honored me with an invitation.
I had an excellent seat; and refreshments were served to
the ladies between the Mass and the execution. I was indeed
horror stricken when I saw the burning of the two Jews and
the honest Biscayan who had married his fellow-godmother;
but what was my surprise, my terror, my anguish, when I
saw in a sanbenito and under a mitre a face which resem- 60
bled Pangloss's! I rubbed my eyes, I looked carefully, I
saw him hanged; and I fainted. I had scarcely recovered
my senses when I saw you stripped naked; that was the
height of horror, of consternation, of grief and despair. I
will frankly tell you that your skin is even whiter and of a
more perfect tint than that of my Bulgarian captain. This
spectacle redoubled all the feelings which crushed and de-

voured me. I exclaimed, I tried to say: 'Stop, Barbarians!'
but my voice failed and my cries would have been useless.
70 When you had been well flogged, I said to myself: 'How
does it happen that the charming Candide and the wise
Pangloss are in Lisbon, the one to receive a hundred lashes,
and the other to be hanged, by order of My Lord the Inquisitor, whose darling I am? Pangloss deceived me cruelly
when he said that all is for the best in the world.'

"I was agitated, distracted, sometimes beside myself and
sometimes ready to die of faintness, and my head was filled
with the massacre of my father, of my mother, of my
brother, the insolence of my horrid Bulgarian soldier, the
80 gash he gave me, my slavery, my life as a kitchen wench,
my Bulgarian captain, my horrid Don Issachar, my abominable Inquisitor, the hanging of Dr. Pangloss, that long
plain song *miserere*[1] during which you were flogged, and
above all the kiss I gave you behind the screen that day
when I saw you for the last time. I praised God for bringing
you back to me through so many trials, I ordered my old
woman to take care of you and to bring you here as soon
as she could. She has carried out my commission very well;
I have enjoyed the inexpressible pleasure of seeing you
90 again, of listening to you, and of speaking to you. You must
be very hungry; I have a good appetite; let us begin by
having supper."

Both sat down to supper; and after supper they returned
to the handsome sofa we have already mentioned; they were
still there when Signor Don Issachar, one of the masters of
of the house, arrived. It was the day of the Sabbath. He
came to enjoy his rights and to express his tender love.

1. **miserere** The Latin chant: "Have mercy upon me, O God."

Chapter IX

WHAT HAPPENED TO CUNEGONDE, TO CANDIDE, TO THE GRAND INQUISITOR AND TO A JEW

This Issachar was the most choleric Hebrew who had been seen in Israel since the Babylonian captivity.[1] "What!" said he. "Bitch of a Galilean, isn't it enough to have the Inquisitor? Must this scoundrel share with me too?"

So saying, he drew a long dagger which he always carried and, thinking that his adversary was unarmed, threw himself upon Candide; but our good Westphalian had received an excellent sword from the old woman along with his suit of clothes. He drew his sword, and although he had a most gentle character, laid the Israelite stone-dead on the floor at the feet of the fair Cunegonde.

"Holy Virgin!" she exclaimed, "what will become of us? A man killed in my house! If the police come we are lost."

"If Pangloss had not been hanged," said Candide, "he would have given us good advice in this extremity, for he was a great philosopher. In default of him, let us consult the old woman."

She was extremely prudent and was beginning to give her advice when another little door opened. It was an hour after midnight, and Sunday was beginning. This day belonged to My Lord the Inquisitor. He came in and saw the flogged Candide sword in hand, a corpse lying on the ground, Cunegonde in terror, and the old woman giving advice. At this moment, here is what happened in Candide's soul and the manner of his reasoning: "If this holy man

1. captivity The Jews were held in captivity by the Babylonians in the sixth century, B.C.

calls for help, he will infallibly have me burned; he might do as much to Cunegonde; he had me pitilessly lashed; he is my rival; I am in the mood to kill, there is no room for hesitation."

30   His reasoning was clear and swift; and, without giving the Inquisitor time to recover from his surprise, he pierced him through and through and cast him beside the Jew.

"Here's another," said Cunegonde, "there is no chance of mercy; we are excommunicated, our last hour has come. How does it happen that you, who were born so mild, should kill a Jew and a prelate in two minutes?"

"My dear young lady," replied Candide, "when a man is in love, jealous, and has been flogged by the Inquisition, he is beside himself."

40   The old woman than spoke up and said: "In the stable are three Andalusian horses, with their saddles and bridles; let the brave Candide prepare them; mademoiselle has moidores [2] and diamonds; let us mount quickly, although I can only sit on one buttock, and go to Cadiz; the weather is beautifully fine, and it is most pleasant to travel in the coolness of the night."

Candide immediately saddled the three horses. Cunegonde, the old woman and he rode thirty miles without stopping. While they were riding away, the Holy Her-
50   mandad [3] arrived at the house; My Lord was buried in a splendid church and Issachar was thrown into a sewer.

Candide, Cunegonde and the old woman had already reached the little town of Avacena in the midst of the mountains of the Sierra Morena; and they talked in their inn as follows.

2. **moidores** Portuguese coin. As a slight concession to local color and realism, Voltaire invariably used the terms for money and food that were proper to the country concerned.

3. **Hermandad** Holy Brotherhood, an association formed in Spain to track down criminals.

Chapter X

HOW CANDIDE, CUNEGONDE AND THE
OLD WOMAN ARRIVED AT CADIZ
IN GREAT DISTRESS, AND
HOW THEY EMBARKED

"Who can have stolen my pistoles [1] and my diamonds?" said Cunegonde, weeping. "How shall we live? What shall we do? Where shall we find Inquisitors and Jews to give me others?"

"Alas!" said the old woman, "I strongly suspect a reverend Franciscan father who slept in the same inn at Badajoz with us; Heaven forbid that I should judge rashly! But he twice came into our room and left long before we did."

"Alas!" said Candide, "the good Pangloss often proved to me that this world's goods are common to all men and that every one has an equal right to them. According to these principles the monk should have left us enough to continue our journey. Have you nothing left then, my fair Cunegonde?"

"Not a maravedi," [2] said she. "What are we to do?" said Candide.

"Sell one of the horses," said the old woman. "I will ride postillion behind Mademoiselle Cunegonde, although I can only sit on one buttock, and we will get to Cadiz."

In the same hotel there was a Benedictine prior. He bought the horse very cheap.[3] Candide, Cunegonde and the old woman passed through Lucena, Chillas, Lebrixa, and at

1. **pistoles** Spanish gold coin.
2. **maravedi** Copper coin of little value.
3. **cheap** Sudden change in point of view, for ironic effect.

last reached Cadiz.⁴ A fleet was there being equipped and troops were being raised to bring to reason the reverend Jesuit fathers of Paraguay,⁵ who were accused of causing the revolt of one of their tribes against the kings of Spain and Portugal near the town of Sacramento. Candide, having served with the Bulgarians, went through the Bulgarian drill before the general of the little army with so much

30 grace, celerity, skill, pride and agility,⁶ that he was given the command of an infantry company. He was now a captain; he embarked with Mademoiselle Cunegonde, the old woman, two servants, and the two Andalusian horses which had belonged to the Grand Inquisitor of Portugal.

During the voyage they had many discussions about the philosophy of poor Pangloss. "We are going to a new world," said Candide, "and no doubt it is there that everything is for the best; for it must be admitted that one might lament a little over the physical and moral happenings in

40 our own world."

"I love you with all my heart," said Cunegonde, "but my soul is still shocked by what I have seen and undergone."

"All will be well," replied Candide; "the sea in this new world already is better than the seas of our Europe; it is calmer and the winds are more constant. It is certainly the new world which is the best of all possible worlds."

"God grant it!" said Cunegonde, "but I have been so horribly unhappy in mine that my heart is nearly closed to hope."

50 "You complain," said the old woman to them. "Alas! you have not endured such misfortunes as mine."

Cunegonde almost laughed and thought it most amusing of the old woman to assert that she was more unfortunate. "Alas! my dear," said she, "unless you have been raped by two Bulgarians, stabbed twice in the belly, have had two castles destroyed, two fathers and mothers murdered before

4. **Cadiz** Seaport in southern Spain.
5. **Paraguay** This was no imaginary event. Voltaire had a financial interest in one of the ships, the *Pascal*.
6. **agility** The Prussian disciplinary drill was notoriously thorough.

your eyes, and have seen two of your lovers flogged in an *auto-da-fé*, I do not see how you can surpass me; moreover, I was born a Baroness with seventy-two quarterings and I have been a kitchen wench." 60

"You do not know my birth," said the old woman, "and if I showed you my backside you would not talk as you do and you would suspend your judgment."

This speech aroused intense curiosity in the minds of Cunegonde and Candide. And the old woman spoke as follows.

Chapter XVI

WHAT HAPPENED TO THE TWO TRAVELLERS WITH TWO GIRLS, TWO MONKEYS, AND THE SAVAGES CALLED OREILLONS

Candide and his valet were past the barriers before anybody in the camp knew of the death of the German Jesuit. The vigilant Cacambo had taken care to fill his saddlebag with bread, chocolate, ham, fruit, and several bottles of wine. On their Andalusian horses they plunged into an unknown country where they found no road. At last a beautiful plain traversed by streams met their eyes. Our two travellers put their horses to grass. Cacambo suggested to his master that they should eat and set the example.

10   "How can you expect me to eat ham," said Candide, "when I have killed the son of My Lord the Baron and find myself condemned never to see the fair Cunegonde again in my life? What is the use of prolonging my miserable days since I must drag them out far from her in remorse and despair? And what will the Journal de Trévoux [1] say?"

Speaking thus, he began to eat. The sun was setting. The two wanderers heard faint cries which seemed to be uttered by women. They could not tell whether these were cries of pain or of joy; but they rose hastily with that alarm and uneasiness caused by everything in an unknown country.
20 These cries came from two completely naked girls who were running gently along the edge of the plain, while two monkeys pursued them and bit their buttocks. Candide was

1. **Trévoux** The celebrated Journal of the French Jesuits. Voltaire often satirized its editor.

428

CANDIDE

moved to pity; he had learned to shoot among the Bulgarians and could have brought down a nut from a tree without touching the leaves. He raised his double-barrelled Spanish gun, fired, and killed the two monkeys.

"God be praised, my dear Cacambo, I have delivered these two poor creatures from a great danger; if I committed a sin by killing an Inquisitor and a Jesuit, I have atoned for it by saving the lives of these two girls. Perhaps they are young ladies of quality and this adventure may be of great advantage to us in this country."

He was going on, but his tongue clove to the roof of his mouth when he saw the two girls tenderly kissing the two monkeys, shedding tears on their bodies and filling the air with the most piteous cries.

"I did not expect so much human kindliness," he said at last to Cacambo, who replied: "You have performed a wonderful masterpiece; you have killed the two lovers of these young ladies."

"Their lovers! Can it be possible? You are jesting at me, Cacambo; how can I believe you?"

"My dear master," replied Cacambo, "you are always surprised by everything; why should you think it so strange that in some countries there should be monkeys who obtain ladies' favors? They are quarter men, as I am a quarter Spaniard."

"Alas!" replied Candide, "I remember to have heard Dr. Pangloss say that similar accidents occurred in the past and that these mixtures produce Aigypans, fauns and satyrs; that several eminent persons of antiquity have seen them; but I thought they were fables." [2]

"You ought now to be convinced that it is true," said Cacambo, "and you see how people behave when they have not received a proper education; the only thing I fear is that these ladies may get us into difficulty."

These wise reflections persuaded Candide to leave the plain and to plunge into the woods. He ate supper there with

2. fables Voltaire had read these stories in a serious book on mythology by Abbé Banier.

429

60 Cacambo and, after having cursed the Inquisitor of Portugal, the governor of Buenos Ayres and the Baron, they went to sleep on the moss. When they woke up they found they could not move; the reason was that during the night the Oreillons,³ the inhabitants of the country, to whom they had been denounced by the two ladies, had bound them with ropes made of bark. They were surrounded by fifty naked Oreillons, armed with arrows, clubs and stone hatchets. Some were boiling a large cauldron, others were preparing spits and they were all shouting: "Here's a Jesuit,
70 here's a Jesuit! We shall be revenged and have a good dinner; let us eat the Jesuit, let us eat the Jesuit!" ⁴

"I told you so, my dear master," said Cacambo sadly. "I knew those two girls would play us a dirty trick."

Candide perceived the cauldron and the spits and exclaimed: "We are certainly going to be roasted or boiled. Ah! What would Dr. Pangloss say if he saw what the pure state of nature is? All is well, granted; but I confess it is very cruel to have lost Mademoiselle Cunegonde and to be spitted by the Oreillons."

80 Cacambo never lost his head. "Do not despair," he said to the wretched Candide. "I understand a little of their dialect and I will speak to them."

"Do not fail," said Candide, "to point out to them the dreadful inhumanity of cooking men and how very unchristian it is."

"Gentlemen," said Cacambo, "you mean to eat a Jesuit today? 'Tis a good deed; nothing could be more just than to treat one's enemies in this fashion.⁵ Indeed the law of nature teaches us to kill our neighbor and this is how peo-
90 ple behave all over the world. If we do not exert the right of eating our neighbor, it is because we have other means

3. **Oreillons** A tribe of Indians, so called because they distended their ears with ornaments.

4. **Jesuit** The translation should read: "Let us eat Jesuit." The Jesuits were expelled from France five years after *Candide*—but not because of *Candide*.

5. **fashion** It was in fact a common practice among American Indians, a way of acquiring an enemy's valor.

of making good cheer; but you have not the same resources as we, and it is certainly better to eat our enemies than to abandon the fruits of victory to ravens and crows. But, gentlemen, you would not wish to eat your friends. You believe you are about to place a Jesuit on the spit, and 'tis your defender, the enemy of your enemies you are about to roast. I was born in your country; the gentleman you see here is my master and, far from being a Jesuit, he has just killed a Jesuit and is wearing his clothes; which is the cause 100 of your mistake. To verify what I say, take his gown, carry it to the first barrier of the kingdom of *Los Padres* and inquire whether my master has not killed a Jesuit officer. It will not take you long and you will have plenty of time to eat us if you find I have lied. But if I have told the truth, you are too well acquainted with the principles of public law, good morals and discipline, not to pardon us."

The Oreillons thought this a very reasonable speech; they deputed two of their notables to go with all diligence and find out the truth. The two deputies acquitted themselves 110 of their task like intelligent men and soon returned with the good news. The Oreillons unbound their two prisoners, overwhelmed them with civilities, offered them girls, gave them refreshment, and accompanied them to the frontiers of their dominions, shouting joyfully: "He is not a Jesuit, he is not a Jesuit!"

Candide could not cease from wondering at the cause of his deliverance. "What a nation," said he. "What men! What manners! If I had not been so lucky as to stick my sword through the body of Mademoiselle Cunegonde's 120 brother I should infallibly have been eaten. But, after all, there is something good in the pure state of nature, since these people, instead of eating me, offered me a thousand civilities as soon as they knew I was not a Jesuit."

Chapter XVII

ARRIVAL OF CANDIDE AND HIS VALET
IN THE COUNTRY OF ELDORADO [1]
AND WHAT THEY SAW THERE

When they reached the frontiers of the Oreillons, Cacambo said to Candide: "You see this hemisphere is no better than the other; take my advice, let us go back to Europe by the shortest road."

"How can we go back," said Candide, "and where can we go? If I go to my own country, the Bulgarians and the Abares are murdering everybody; if I return to Portugal I shall be burned; if we stay here, we run the risk of being spitted at any moment. But how can I make up my mind to leave that part of the world where Mademoiselle Cunegonde is living?"

"Let us go to Cayenne," [2] said Cacambo, "we shall find Frenchmen there, for they go all over the world; they might help us. Perhaps God will have pity on us."

It was not easy to go to Cayenne. They knew roughly the direction to take, but mountains, rivers, precipices, brigands and savages were everywhere terrible obstacles. Their horses died of fatigue; their provisions were exhausted; for a whole month they lived on wild fruits and at last found themselves near a little river fringed with cocoanut-trees which supported their lives and their hopes.

Cacambo, who always gave advice as prudent as the old woman's, said to Candide: "We can go no farther, we have walked far enough; I can see an empty canoe in the bank,

1. **Eldorado** A fabulous Land of Gold, in which even Sir Walter Raleigh once believed.
2. **Cayenne** Capital of French Guiana.

let us fill it with cocoanuts, get into the little boat and drift with the current; a river always leads to some inhabited place. If we do not find anything pleasant, we shall at least find something new."

"Come on then," said Candide, "and let us trust to Providence." 30

They drifted for some leagues between banks which were sometimes flowery, sometimes bare, sometimes flat, sometimes steep. The river continually became wider; finally it disappeared under an arch of frightful rocks which towered up to the very sky. The two travellers were bold enough to trust themselves to the current under this arch. The stream, narrowed between walls, carried them with horrible rapidity and noise. After twenty-four hours they saw daylight again; but their canoe was wrecked on reefs; they had to crawl from rock to rock for a whole league and at last they 40 discovered an immense horizon, bordered by inaccessible mountains. The country was cultivated for pleasure as well as for necessity; everywhere the useful was agreeable. The roads were covered or rather ornamented with carriages of brilliant material and shape, carrying men and women of singular beauty, who were rapidly drawn along by large red sheep whose swiftness surpassed that of the finest horses of Andalusia, Tetuan, and Mequinez.[3]

"This country," said Candide, "is better than Westphalia." 50

He landed with Cacambo near the first village he came to. Several children of the village, dressed in torn gold brocade, were playing quoits outside the village. Our two men from the other world amused themselves by looking on; their quoits were large round pieces, yellow, red and green which shone with peculiar lustre. The travellers were curious enough to pick up some of them; they were of gold, emeralds and rubies, the least of which would have been the greatest ornament in the Mogul's throne.

3. **Mequinez** Tetuan and Mequinez are Moroccan towns.

60 "No doubt," said Cacambo, "these children are the sons of the King of this country playing at quoits."

At that moment the village schoolmaster appeared to call them into school.

"This," said Candide, "is the tutor of the Royal Family." The little beggars immediately left their game, abandoning their quoits and everything with which they had been playing. Candide picked them up, ran to the tutor, and presented them to him humbly, giving him to understand by signs that their Royal Highnesses had forgotten their gold
70 and their precious stones. The village schoolmaster smiled, threw them on the ground, gazed for a moment at Candide's face with much surprise and continued on his way. The travellers did not fail to pick up the gold, the rubies and the emeralds.

"Where are we?" cried Candide. "The children of the King must be well brought up, since they are taught to despise gold and precious stones."

Cacambo was as much surprised as Candide. At last they reached the first house in the village, which was built like
80 a European palace. There were crowds of people round the door and still more inside; very pleasant music could be heard and there was a delicious smell of cooking. Cacambo went up to the door and heard them speaking Peruvian; it was his maternal tongue, for everyone knows that Cacambo was born in a village of Tucuman where nothing else is spoken.

"I will act as your interpreter," he said to Candide, "this is an inn, let us enter."

Immediately two boys and two girls of the inn, dressed
90 in cloth of gold, whose hair was bound up with ribbons, invited them to sit down to the table d'hôte. They served four soups each garnished with two parrots, a boiled condor which weighed two hundred pounds, two roast monkeys of excellent flavor, three hundred colibris in one dish and six hundred hummingbirds in another, exquisite ragouts and delicious pastries, all in dishes of a sort of rock crystal. The boys and girls brought several sorts of drinks made of sugar-

cane. Most of the guests were merchants and coachmen, all extremely polite, who asked Cacambo a few questions with the most delicate discretion and answered his in a satisfactory manner.   100

When the meal was over, Cacambo, like Candide, thought he could pay the reckoning by throwing on the table two of the large pieces of gold he had picked up; the host and hostess laughed until they had to hold their sides. At last they recovered themselves.

"Gentlemen," said the host, "we perceive you are strangers; we are not accustomed to seeing them. Forgive us if we began to laugh when you offered us in payment the stones from our highways. No doubt you have none of the   110 money of this country, but you do not need any to dine here. All the hotels established for the utility of commerce are paid for by the government. You have been ill entertained here because this is a poor village; but everywhere else you will be received as you deserve to be."

Cacambo explained to Candide all that the host had said, and Candide listened in the same admiration and disorder with which his friend Cacambo interpreted. "What can this country be," they said to each other, "which is unknown to the rest of the world and where all nature is so different   120 from ours? Probably it is the country where everything is for the best; for there must be one country of that sort. And, in spite of what Dr. Pangloss said, I often noticed that everything went very ill in Westphalia."

Chapter XVIII

WHAT THEY SAW IN THE LAND
OF ELDORADO

Cacambo informed the host of his curiosity, and the host said: "I am a very ignorant man and am all the better for it; but we have here an old man who has retired from the court and who is the most learned and most communicative man in the kingdom." And he at once took Cacambo to the old man. Candide now played only the second part and accompanied his valet. They entered a very simple house, for the door was only of silver and the panelling of the apartments in gold, but so tastefully carved that the richest decorations did not surpass it. The antechamber indeed was only encrusted with rubies and emeralds; but the order with which everything was arranged atoned for this extreme simplicity.

The old man received the two strangers on a sofa padded with colibri feathers, and presented them with drinks in diamond cups; after which he satisfied their curiosity in these words: "I am a hundred and seventy-two years old and I heard from my late father, the King's equerry, the astonishing revolutions of Peru of which he had been an eye-witness. The kingdom where we now are is the ancient country of the Incas, who most imprudently left it to conquer part of the world and were at last destroyed by the Spaniards. The princes of their family who remained in their native country had more wisdom; with the consent of the nation, they ordered that no inhabitants should ever leave our little kingdom, and this it is that has preserved our innocence and our felicity. The Spaniards had some vague knowledge of this country, which they called Eldo-

436

rado, and about a hundred years ago an Englishman named Raleigh came very near to it; but, since we are surrounded 30 by inaccessible rocks and precipices, we have hitherto been exempt from the rapacity of the nations of Europe who have an inconceivable lust for the pebbles and mud of our land and would kill us to the last man to get possession of them."

The conversation was long; it touched upon the form of the government, manners, women, public spectacles and the arts. Finally Candide, who was always interested in metaphysics, asked through Cacambo whether the country had a religion. 40

The old man blushed a little. "How can you doubt it?" said he. "Do you think we are ingrates?"

Cacambo humbly asked what was the religion of Eldorado.

The old man blushed again. "Can there be two religions?" said he. "We have, I think, the religion of every one else; we adore God from evening until morning."

"Do you adore only one God?" said Cacambo, who continued to act as the interpreter of Candide's doubts.

"Manifestly," said the old man, "there are not two or 50 three or four. I must confess that the people of your world ask very extraordinary questions."

Candide continued to press the old man with questions; he wished to know how they prayed to God in Eldorado.

"We do not pray," said the good and respectable sage, "we have nothing to ask from him; he has given us everything necessary and we continually give him thanks."

Candide was curious to see the priests; and asked where they were.

The good old man smiled. "My friends," said he, "we 60 are all priests; the King and all the heads of families solemnly sing praises every morning, accompanied by five or six thousand musicians."

"What! Have you no monks to teach, to dispute, to govern, to intrigue and to burn people who do not agree with them?"

"For that, we should have to become fools," said the old man; "here we are all of the same opinion and do not understand what you mean with your monks."

70 At all this Candide was in an ecstasy and said to himself: "This is very different from Westphalia and the castle of His Lordship the Baron; if our friend Pangloss had seen Eldorado, he would not have said that the castle of Thunder-ten-tronckh was the best of all that exists on the earth; certainly, a man should travel."

After this long conversation the good old man ordered a carriage to be harnessed with six sheep and gave the two travellers twelve of his servants to take them to court. "You will excuse me," he said, "if my age deprives me of the 80 honor of accompanying you. The King will receive you in a manner which will not displease you and doubtless you will pardon the customs of the country if any of them disconcert you."

Candide and Cacambo entered the carriage; the six sheep galloped off and in less than four hours they reached the King's palace, which was situated at one end of the capital. The portal was two hundred and twenty feet high and a hundred feet wide; it is impossible to describe its material. Anyone can see the prodigious superiority it must have over 90 the pebbles and sand we call *gold* and *gems*.

Twenty beautiful maidens of the guard received Candide and Cacambo as they alighted from the carriage, conducted them to the baths and dressed them in robes woven from the down of colibris; after which the principal male and female officers of the Crown led them to his Majesty's apartment through two files of a thousand musicians each, according to the usual custom. As they approached the throne-room, Cacambo asked one of the chief officers how they should behave in his Majesty's presence; whether they 100 should fall on their knees or flat on their faces, whether they should put their hands on their heads or on their backsides; whether they should lick the dust of the throneroom; in a word, what was the ceremony?

"The custom," said the chief officer, "is to embrace the King and to kiss him on either cheek."

Candide and Cacambo threw their arms round his Majesty's neck; he received them with all imaginable favor and politely asked them to supper. Meanwhile they were carried to see the town, the public buildings rising to the very skies, the market-places ornamented with thousands of columns, the fountains of rose-water and of liquors distilled from sugarcane, which played continually in the public squares paved with precious stones which emitted a perfume like that of cloves and cinnamon.

Candide asked to see the law courts; he was told there were none, and that nobody ever went to law. He asked if there were prisons and was told there were none. He was still more surprised and pleased by the palace of sciences, where he saw a gallery two thousand feet long, filled with instruments of mathematics and physics.

After they had explored all the afternoon about a thousandth part of the town, they were taken back to the King. Candide sat down to table with his Majesty, his valet Cacambo and several ladies. Never was better cheer, and never was anyone wittier at supper than his Majesty. Cacambo explained the King's witty remarks to Candide and even when translated they still appeared witty. Among all the things which amazed Candide, this did not amaze him the least.

They enjoyed this hospitality for a month. Candide repeatedly said to Cacambo: "Once again, my friend, it is quite true that the castle where I was born cannot be compared with this country; but then Mademoiselle Cunegonde is not here and you probably have a mistress in Europe. If we remain here, we shall only be like everyone else; but if we return to our own world with only twelve sheep laden with Eldorado pebbles, we shall be richer than all the kings put together; we shall have no more Inquisitors to fear and we can easily regain Mademoiselle Cunegonde."

Cacambo agreed with this; it is so pleasant to be on the move, to show off before friends, to make a parade of the things seen on one's travels, that these two happy men resolved to be so no longer and to ask his Majesty's permission to depart.

"You are doing a very silly thing," said the King. "I know my country is small; but when we are comfortable anywhere we should stay there; I certainly have not the right to detain foreigners, that is a tyranny which does not exist either in our manners or our laws; all men are free, 150 leave when you please, but the way out is very difficult. It is impossible to ascend the rapid river by which you miraculously came here and which flows under arches of rock. The mountains which surround the whole of my kingdom are ten thousand feet high and are perpendicular like walls; they are more than ten leagues broad, and you can only get down from them by way of precipices. However, since you must go, I will give orders to the directors of machinery to make a machine which will carry you comfortably. When you have been taken to the other side of the mountains, no-160 body can proceed any farther with you; for my subjects have sworn never to pass this boundary and they are too wise to break their oath. Ask anything else of me you wish."

"We ask nothing of your Majesty," said Cacambo, "except a few sheep laden with provisions, pebbles and the mud of this country."

The King laughed. "I cannot understand," said he, "the taste you people of Europe have for our yellow mud; but take as much as you wish, and much good may it do you."

He immediately ordered his engineers to make a machine 170 to hoist these two extraordinary men out of his kingdom. Three thousand learned scientists worked at it; it was ready in a fortnight and only cost about twenty million pounds sterling in the money of that country. Candide and Cacambo were placed on the machine; there were two large red sheep saddled and bridled for them to ride on when they had passed the mountains, twenty sumpter sheep [1] laden with provisions, thirty carrying presents of the most curious pro-

1. sheep Pack-sheep.

ductions of the country and fifty laden with gold, precious stones and diamonds. The King embraced the two vaga- bonds tenderly. Their departure was a splendid sight and so 180 was the ingenious manner in which they and their sheep were hoisted on to the top of the mountains. The scientists took leave of them after having landed them safely, and Candide's only desire and object was to go and present Mademoiselle Cunegonde with his sheep.

"We have sufficient to pay the governor of Buenos Ayres," said he, "if Mademoiselle Cunegonde can be bought. Let us go to Cayenne, and take ship, and then we will see what kingdom we will buy."

Chapter XIX

WHAT HAPPENED TO THEM AT SURINAM AND HOW CANDIDE MADE THE ACQUAINTANCE OF MARTIN

Our two travellers' first day was quite pleasant. They were encouraged by the idea of possessing more treasures than all Asia, Europe and Africa could collect. Candide in transport carved the name of Cunegonde on the trees. On the second day two of the sheep stuck in a marsh and were swallowed up with their loads; two other sheep died of fatigue a few days later; then seven or eight died of hunger in a desert; several days afterwards others fell off precipices. Finally, after they had travelled for a hundred days, they had only two sheep left.

Candide said to Cacambo: "My friend, you see how perishable are the riches of this world; nothing is steadfast but virtue and the happiness of seeing Mademoiselle Cunegonde again."

"I admit it," said Cacambo, "but we still have two sheep with more treasures than ever the King of Spain will have, and in the distance I see a town I suspect is Surinam,[1] which belongs to the Dutch. We are at the end of our troubles and the beginning of our happiness."

As they drew near the town they came upon a negro lying on the ground wearing only half his clothes, that is to say, a pair of blue cotton drawers; this poor man had no left leg and no right hand. "Good heavens!" said Candide to him in Dutch, "what are you doing there, my friend, in that horrible state?"

1. **Surinam** In Dutch Guiana.

"I am waiting for my master, the famous merchant Monsieur Vanderdendur."

"Was it Monsieur Vanderdendur," said Candide, "who treated you in that way?"

"Yes, sir," said the negro, "it is the custom. We are given 30 a pair of cotton drawers twice a year as clothing. When we work in the sugar mills and the grindstone catches our fingers, they cut off the hand; when we try to run away, they cut off a leg. Both these things happened to me. This is the price paid for the sugar you eat in Europe. But when my mother sold me for ten patagons on the coast of Guinea, she said to me: 'My dear child, give thanks to our fetishes, always worship them, and they will make you happy; you have the honor to be a slave of our lords the white men and thereby you have made the fortune of your father and 40 mother.' Alas! I do not know whether I made their fortune, but they certainly did not make mine. Dogs, monkeys and parrots are a thousand times less miserable than we are; the Dutch fetishes who converted me tell me that we are all of us, whites and blacks, the children of Adam. I am not a genealogist, but if these preachers tell the truth, we are all second cousins. Now, you will admit that no one could treat his relatives in a more horrible way."

"O Pangloss!" cried Candide. "This is an abomination you had not guessed; this is too much, in the end I shall 50 have to renounce optimism."

"What is optimism?" said Cacambo.

"Alas!" said Candide, "it is the mania of maintaining that everything is well when we are wretched." [2] And he shed tears as he looked at his negro; and he entered Surinam weeping.

The first thing they inquired was whether there was any ship in the port which could be sent to Buenos Ayres. The person they addressed happened to be a Spanish captain, who offered to strike an honest bargain with them. 60 He arranged to meet them at an inn. Candide and the faith-

2. **wretched** This is Voltaire's main point. Happiness in the abstract has no meaning for the suffering individual.

443

CANDIDE

ful Cacambo went and waited for him with their two sheep. Candide, who blurted everything out, told the Spaniard all his adventures and confessed that he wanted to elope with Mademoiselle Cunegonde.

"I shall certainly not take you to Buenos Ayres," said the captain. "I should be hanged and you would, too. The fair Cunegonde is his Lordship's favorite mistress."

Candide was thunderstruck; he sobbed for a long time; then he took Cacambo aside. "My dear friend," said he, "this is what you must do. We have each of us in our pockets five or six millions worth of diamonds; you are more skilful than I am; go to Buenos Ayres and get Mademoiselle Cunegonde. If the governor makes any difficulties give him a million; if he is still obstinate give him two; you have not killed an Inquisitor so they will not suspect you. I will fit out another ship, I will go and wait for you at Venice; it is a free country where there is nothing to fear from Bulgarians, Abares, Jews or Inquisitors."

Cacambo applauded this wise resolution; he was in despair at leaving a good master who had become his intimate friend; but the pleasure of being useful to him overcame the grief of leaving him. They embraced with tears. Candide urged him not to forget the good old woman. Cacambo set off that very same day; he was a very good man, this Cacambo.

Candide remained some time longer at Surinam waiting for another captain to take him to Italy with the two sheep he had left. He engaged servants and bought everything necessary for a long voyage. At last Monsieur Vanderdendur, the owner of a large ship, came to see him.

"How much do you want," he asked this man, "to take me straight to Venice with my servants, my baggage and these two sheep?"

The captain asked for ten thousand piastres. Candide did not hesitate. "Oh! Ho!" said the prudent Vanderdendur to himself, "this foreigner gives ten thousand piastres immediately! He must be very rich." He returned a moment aft-

444

erwards and said he could not sail for less than twenty
thousand.   100

"Very well, you shall have them," said Candide.

"Whew!" said the merchant to himself, "this man gives
twenty thousand piastres as easily as ten thousand." He
came back again, and said he could not take him to Venice
for less than thirty thousand piastres.

"Then you shall have thirty thousand," replied Candide.

"Oho!" said the Dutch merchant to himself again, "thirty
thousand piastres is nothing to this man; obviously the two
sheep are laden with immense treasures; I will not insist
any further; first let me make him pay the thirty thousand 110
piastres, and then we will see."

Candide sold two little diamonds, the smaller of which
was worth more than all the money the captain asked. He
paid him in advance. The two sheep were taken on board.
Candide followed in a little boat to join the ship which rode
at anchor; the captain watched his time, set his sails and
weighed anchor; the wind was favorable. Candide, bewildered and stupefied, soon lost sight of him. "Alas!" he cried,
"this is a trick worthy of the old world."

He returned to shore, in grief; for he had lost enough to 120
make the fortunes of twenty kings. He went to the Dutch
judge; and, as he was rather disturbed, he knocked loudly at
the door; he went in, related what had happened and talked
a little louder than he ought to have done. The judge began by fining him ten thousand piastres for the noise he had
made; he then listened patiently to him, promised to look
into his affair as soon as the merchant returned, and charged
him another ten thousand piastres for the expenses of the
audience.

This behavior reduced Candide to despair; he had indeed 130
endured misfortunes a thousand times more painful; but
the calmness of the judge and of the captain who had
robbed him, stirred up his bile and plunged him into a
black melancholy. The malevolence of men revealed itself
to his mind in all its ugliness; he entertained only gloomy
ideas.

At last a French ship was about to leave for Bordeaux and, since he no longer had any sheep laden with diamonds to put on board, he hired a cabin at a reasonable price and
140 announced throughout the town that he would give the passage, food and two thousand piastres to an honest man who would make the journey with him, on condition that this man was the most unfortunate and the most disgusted with his condition in the whole province. Such a crowd of applicants arrived that a fleet would not have contained them. Candide, wishing to choose among the most likely, picked out twenty persons who seemed reasonably sociable and who all claimed to deserve his preference. He collected them in a tavern and gave them supper, on condition that
150 each took an oath to relate truthfully the story of his life, promising that he would choose the man who seemed to him the most deserving of pity and to have the most cause for being discontented with his condition, and that he would give the others a little money. The sitting lasted until four o'clock in the morning. As Candide listened to their adventures he remembered what the old woman had said on the voyage to Buenos Ayres and how she had wagered that there was nobody on the boat who had not experienced very great misfortunes. At each story which was
160 told him, he thought of Pangloss.

"This Pangloss," said he, "would have some difficulty in supporting his system. I wish he were here. Certainly, if everything is well, it is only in Eldorado and not in the rest of the world."

He finally determined in favor of a poor man of letters who had worked ten years for the booksellers at Amsterdam. He judged that there was no occupation in the world which could more disgust a man.[3] This man of letters, who was also a good man, had been robbed by his wife, beaten
170 by his son, and abandoned by his daughter, who had eloped with a Portuguese. He had just been deprived of a small post on which he depended and the preachers of Surinam

3. **man** Voltaire had had unhappy personal dealings with the Dutch publishers.

were persecuting him because they thought he was a Socinian.[4] It must be admitted that the others were at least
as unfortunate as he was; but Candide hoped that this
learned man would help to pass the time during the voyage.
All his other rivals considered that Candide was doing them
a great injustice; but he soothed them down by giving each
of them a hundred piastres.

4. **Socinian** A sect resembling the Unitarians.

Chapter XXVIII

WHAT HAPPENED TO CANDIDE, TO CUNEGONDE, TO PANGLOSS, TO MARTIN, ETC.

"Pardon once more," said Candide to the Baron, "pardon me, reverend father, for having thrust my sword through your body."

"Let us say no more about it," said the Baron. "I admit I was a little too sharp; but since you wish to know how it was you saw me in a galley, I must tell you that after my wound was healed by the brother apothecary of the college, I was attacked and carried off by a Spanish raiding party; I was imprisoned in Buenos Ayres at the time when my sister had just left. I asked to return to the Vicar-General in Rome. I was ordered to Constantinople to act as almoner to the Ambassador of France. A week after I had taken up my office I met towards evening a very handsome young page of the Sultan. It was very hot; the young man wished to bathe; I took the opportunity to bathe also. I did not know that it was a most serious crime for a Christian to be found naked with a young Mahometan. A cadi sentenced me to a hundred strokes on the soles of my feet and condemned me to the galley. I do not think a more horrible injustice has ever been committed. But I should very much like to know why my sister is in the kitchen of a Transylvanian sovereign living in exile among the Turks."

"But, my dear Pangloss," said Candide, "how does it happen that I see you once more?"

"It is true," said Pangloss, "that you saw me hanged; and in the natural course of events I should have been burned.[1]

1. **burned** But burning would not have served Voltaire's purposes.

But you remember, it poured with rain when they were going to roast me; the storm was so violent that they despaired of lighting the fire; I was hanged because they could do nothing better; a surgeon bought my body, carried me home and dissected me. He first made a crucial incision in me from the navel to the collarbone. Nobody could have been worse hanged than I was. The executioner of the holy Inquisition, who was a sub-deacon, was marvellously skilful in burning people, but he was not accustomed to hang them; the rope was wet and did not slide easily and it was knotted; in short, I still breathed. The crucial incision caused me to utter so loud a scream that the surgeon fell over backwards and, thinking he was dissecting the devil, fled away in terror and fell down the staircase in his flight. His wife ran in from another room at the noise; she saw me stretched out on the table with my crucial incision; she was still more frightened than her husband, fled, and fell on top of him. When they had recovered themselves a little, I heard the surgeon's wife say to the surgeon: 'My dear, what were you thinking of, to dissect a heretic? Don't you know the devil always possesses them? I will go and get a priest at once to exorcise him.'

"At this I shuddered and collected the little strength I had left to shout: 'Have pity on me!' At last the Portuguese barber [2] grew bolder; he sewed up my skin; his wife even took care of me, and at the end of a fortnight I was able to walk again. The barber found me a situation and made me lackey to a Knight of Malta who was going to Venice; but, as my master had no money to pay me wages, I entered the service of a Venetian merchant and followed him to Constantinople.

"One day I took it into my head to enter a mosque; there was nobody there except an old Imam and a very pretty young devotee who was reciting her prayers; her breasts were entirely uncovered; between them she wore a bunch of tulips, roses, anemones, ranunculus, hyacinths and auriculas; she dropped her bunch of flowers; I picked it up and

2. **barber** Like the Barber of Seville, he was also the surgeon.

returned it to her with a most respectful alacrity. I was so long putting them back that the Imam grew angry and, seeing I was a Christian, called for help. I was taken to the cadi, who sentenced me to receive a hundred strokes on the soles of my feet and sent me to the galleys. I was chained on the same seat and in the same galley as My Lord the Baron. In this galley there were four young men from Marseilles, five Neapolitan priests and two monks from Corfu, who assured us that similar accidents occurred every day. His Lordship the Baron claimed that he had suffered a greater injustice than I; and I claimed that it was much more permissible to replace a bunch of flowers between a woman's breasts than to be naked with one of the Sultan's pages. We argued continually, and every day received twenty strokes of the bull's pizzle, when the chain of events of this universe led you to our galley and you ransomed us."

"Well! my dear Pangloss," said Candide, "when you were hanged, dissected, stunned with blows and made to row in the galleys, did you always think that everything was for the best in this world?"

"I am still of my first opinion," replied Pangloss, "for after all I am a philosopher; and it would be unbecoming for me to recant, since Leibnitz could not be in the wrong and pre-established harmony is the finest thing imaginable like the plenum and subtle matter." [3]

3. **matter** According to Leibnitz, harmony between the spiritual and material worlds was pre-established by God. The plenum and subtle matter form part of the German philosopher's outmoded physics.

Chapter XXIX

HOW CANDIDE FOUND CUNEGONDE AND
THE OLD WOMAN AGAIN

While Candide, the Baron, Pangloss, Martin and Cacambo were relating their adventures, reasoning upon contingent [1] or non-contingent events of the universe, arguing about effects and causes, moral and physical evil, free will and necessity, and the consolation to be found in the Turkish galleys, they came to the house of the Transylvanian prince on the shores of Propontis.

The first objects which met their sight were Cunegonde and the old woman hanging out towels to dry on the line.

10 At this sight the Baron grew pale. Candide, that tender lover, seeing his fair Cunegonde sunburned, blear-eyed, flat-breasted, with wrinkles round her eyes and red, chapped arms, recoiled three paces in horror, and then advanced from mere politeness. She embraced Candide and her brother. They embraced the old woman; Candide bought them both.

In the neighborhood was a little farm; the old woman suggested that Candide should buy it, until some better fate befell the group. Cunegonde did not know that she had

20 become ugly, for nobody had told her so; she reminded Candide of his promises in so peremptory a tone that the good Candide dared not refuse her. He therefore informed the Baron that he was about to marry his sister.

"Never," said the Baron, "will I endure such baseness on her part and such insolence on yours; nobody shall ever reproach me with this infamy; my sister's children could

1. **contingent** A contingent event is a possible but not inevitable eventuality.

451

never enter the chapters[2] of Germany. No, my sister shall never marry anyone but a Baron of the Empire."

Cunegonde threw herself at his feet and bathed them in tears; but he was inflexible. 30

"Madman," said Candide, "I rescued you from the galleys, I paid your ransom and your sister's; she was washing dishes here, she is ugly, I am so kind as to make her my wife, and you pretend to oppose me! I should re-kill you if I listened to my anger."

"You may kill me again," said the Baron, "but you shall never marry my sister while I am alive."

2. **chapters** Knightly assemblies.

Chapter XXX

CONCLUSION

At the bottom of his heart Candide had not the least wish to marry Cunegonde. But the Baron's extreme impertinence determined him to complete the marriage, and Cunegonde urged it so warmly that he could not retract. He consulted Pangloss, Martin and the faithful Cacambo. Pangloss wrote an excellent memorandum by which he proved that the Baron had no rights over his sister and that by all the laws of the empire she could make a left-handed marriage [1] with Candide. Martin advised that the Baron should be thrown into the sea; Cacambo decided that he should be returned to the Levantine captain and sent back to the galleys, after which he would be returned by the first ship to the Vicar-General at Rome. This was thought to be very good advice; the old woman approved it; they said nothing to the sister; the plan was carried out with the aid of a little money and they had the pleasure of duping a Jesuit and punishing the pride of a German Baron.

It would be natural to suppose that when, after so many disasters, Candide was married to his mistress, and living with the philosopher Pangloss, the philosopher Martin, the prudent Cacambo and the old woman, having brought back so many diamonds from the country of the ancient Incas, he would lead the most pleasant life imaginable.[2] But he was so cheated by the Jews [3] that he had nothing left but his

1. **marriage** A morganatic marriage, which does not give equality to the party of lower rank.

2. **imaginable** If this were an idle tale of adventure, the couple would have been left here, to "live happily ever afterwards."

3. **Jews** Voltaire suffered several severe financial losses through the bankruptcies of Jewish bankers.

453

little farm; his wife, growing uglier every day, became shrewish and unendurable; the old woman was ailing and even more bad tempered than Cunegonde. Cacambo, who worked in the garden and then went to Constantinople to sell vegetables, was overworked and cursed his fate. Pangloss was in despair because he did not shine in some German university.

As for Martin, he was firmly convinced that people are equally uncomfortable everywhere; he accepted things patiently. Candide, Martin and Pangloss sometimes argued about metaphysics and morals. From the windows of the farm they often watched the ships going by, filled with effendis, pashas, and cadis, who were being exiled to Lemnos, to Mitylene and Erzerum. They saw other cadis, other pashas and other effendis coming back to take the place of the exiles and to be exiled in their turn. They saw the neatly impaled heads which were taken to the Sublime Porte.[4] These sights redoubled their discussions; and when they were not arguing, the boredom was so excessive that one day the old woman dared to say to them: "I should like to know which is worse, to be raped a hundred times by negro pirates, to have a buttock cut off, to run the gauntlet among the Bulgarians, to be whipped and flogged in an *auto-da-fé*, to be dissected, to row in a galley, in short, to endure all the miseries through which we have passed, or to remain here doing nothing?"

" 'Tis a great question," said Candide.

These remarks led to new reflections, and Martin especially concluded that man was born to live in the convulsions of distress or in the lethargy of boredom. Candide did not agree, but he asserted nothing. Pangloss confessed that he had always suffered horribly; but, having once maintained that everything was for the best, he had continued to maintain it without believing it.

One thing confirmed Martin in his destestable principles, made Candide hesitate more than ever, and embarrassed

4. **Porte** The Gate of the Turkish Sultan's palace, which was also the Palace of Justice.

Pangloss. And it was this. One day there came to their farm Paquette and Friar Giroflée, who were in the most extreme misery; they had soon wasted their three thousand piastres, had left each other, made it up, quarrelled again, been put in prison, escaped, and finally Friar Giroflée had turned Turk. Paquette continued her occupation everywhere and now earned nothing by it.

"I foresaw," said Martin to Candide, "that your gifts would soon be wasted and would only make them the more 70 miserable. You and Cacambo were once bloated with millions of piastres and you are no happier than Friar Giroflée and Paquette."

"Ah! Ha!" said Pangloss to Paquette, "so Heaven brings you back to us, my dear child? Do you know that you cost me the end of my nose, an eye and an ear! What a plight you are in! Ah! What a world this is!"

This new occurrence caused them to philosophise more than ever. In the neighborhood there lived a very famous Dervish, who was supposed to be the best philosopher in 80 Turkey; they went to consult him; Pangloss was the spokesman and said: "Master, we have come to beg you to tell us why so strange an animal as man was ever created."

"What has it to do with you?" said the Dervish. "Is it your business?"

"But, reverend father," said Candide, "there is a horrible amount of evil in the world."

"What does it matter," said the Dervish, "whether there is evil or good? When his highness sends a ship to Egypt, does he worry about the comfort or discomfort of the rats 90 in the ship?" [5]

"Then what should we do?" said Pangloss.

"Hold your tongue," said the Dervish.

"I flattered myself," said Pangloss, "that I should discuss with you effects and causes, this best of all possible worlds, the origin of evil, the nature of the soul and pre-established harmony."

5. **ship** This pessimistic passage seems to limit severely the extent of Divine Providence. Compare the ending of the Book of Job.

At these words the Dervish slammed the door in their faces.

During this conversation the news went round that at Constantinople two viziers and the mufti had been strangled and several of their friends impaled. This catastrophe made a prodigious noise everywhere for several hours. As Pangloss, Candide and Martin were returning to their little farm, they came upon an old man who was taking the air under a bower of orange trees at his door. Pangloss, who was as curious as he was argumentative, asked him what was the name of the mufti who had just been strangled.

"I do not know," replied the old man. "I have never known the name of any mufti or of any vizier. I am entirely ignorant of the occurrence you mention; I presume that in general those who meddle with public affairs sometimes perish miserably and that they deserve it; but I never inquire what is going on in Constantinople; I content myself with sending there for sale the produce of the garden I cultivate."

Having spoken thus, he took the strangers into his house. His two daughters and his two sons presented them with several kinds of sherbert which they made themselves, caymac flavored with candied citron peel, oranges, lemons, limes, pineapples, dates, pistachios and Mocha coffee which had not been mixed with the bad coffee of Batavia and the Isles. After which this good Mussulman's two daughters perfumed the beards of Candide, Pangloss and Martin.

"You must have a vast and magnificent estate?" said Candide to the Turk.

"I have only twenty acres," replied the Turk. "I cultivate them with my children; and work keeps at bay three great evils: boredom, vice and need." [6]

As Candide returned to his farm he reflected deeply on the Turk's remarks. He said to Pangloss and Martin: "That good old man seems to me to have chosen an existence pref-

6. **need** This is the key to Voltaire's philosophy of life. *Candide* gives abundant examples of all three of these evils.

456

erable by far to that of the six kings with whom we had the honor to sup."

"Exalted rank," said Pangloss, "is very dangerous, according to the testimony of all philosophers; for Eglon, King of the Moabites, was murdered by Ehud; Absalom was hanged by the hair and pierced by three darts; King Nadab, son of Jeroboam, was killed by Baasha; King Elah by Zimri; Ahaziah by Jehu; Athaliah by Jehoiada; the Kings Jehoi-
140 akim, Jeconiah and Zedekiah were made slaves.[7] You know in what manner died Crœsus, Astyages, Darius, Denys of Syracuse, Pyrrhus, Perseus, Hannibal, Jugurtha, Ariovistus, Cæsar, Pompey, Nero, Otho, Vitellius, Domitian, Richard II of England, Edward II, Henry VI, Richard III, Mary Stuart, Charles I, the three Henrys of France, the Emperor Henry IV. You know . . ."

"I also know," said Candide, "that we should cultivate our gardens."

"You are right," said Pangloss, "for, when man was
150 placed in the Garden of Eden, he was placed there *ut operaretur eum,* to dress it and to keep it; which proves that man was not born for idleness."

"Let us work without theorizing," [8] said Martin; " 'tis the only way to make life endurable."

The whole small fraternity entered into this praiseworthy plan, and each started to make use of his talents. The little farm yielded well. Cunegonde was indeed very ugly, but she became an excellent pastry cook; Paquette embroidered; the old woman took care of the linen. Even Friar Giroflée
160 performed some service; he was a very good carpenter and even became a man of honor; and Pangloss sometimes said to Candide: "All events are linked up in this best of all possible worlds; for, if you had not been expelled from the noble castle, by hard kicks in your backside for love of

7. **slaves** To explain these Biblical references would be pedantry—which Voltaire is here satirizing.

8. **theorizing** I.e., since men can never grasp the ultimate ends of life, let us make the best of it without worrying—an "optimistic" acceptance of life as it is.

Mademoiselle Cunegonde, if you had not been clapped into
the Inquisition, if you had not wandered about America on
foot, if you had not stuck your sword in the Baron, if you
had not lost all your sheep from the land of Eldorado, you
would not be eating candied citrons and pistachios here." [9]

" 'Tis well said," replied Candide, "but we must culti- 170
vate our gardens."

9. **here** The final reduction of Pangloss's philosophy to the absurd.